ATHANASIUS AND CONSTANTIUS

ATHANASIUS
AND CONSTANTIUS

THEOLOGY AND POLITICS

IN THE CONSTANTINIAN EMPIRE

TIMOTHY D. BARNES

HARVARD UNIVERSITY PRESS

CAMBRIDGE, MASSACHUSETTS

LONDON, ENGLAND

1993

Library of Congress Cataloging-in-Publication Data

Barnes, Timothy David.
    Athanasius and Constantius : theology and politics in the
Constantinian empire / Timothy D. Barnes.
        p. cm.
    Includes bibliographical references and indexes.
    ISBN 0-674-05067-3 (alk. paper)
    1. Athanasius, Saint, Patriarch of Alexandria, d. 373.
2. Christian saints—Egypt—Alexandria—Biography. 3. Constantius
II, Emperor of Rome, 317–361. 4. Church and state—Rome—History.
5. Rome—History—Empire, 284–476. 6. Church history—Primitive and
early church, ca. 30–600. I. Title.
BR1720.A7B37 1993
270.2'092—dc20
    [B]   92-33050
                                                                CIP

Athanasius was plainly a violent *Party-Man,* and the known *Head of a Party;* and is therefore no more to be depended on in Matters wherein himself and his own Affairs were particularly concern'd than others, the like *Party-Men,* and *Heads of Parties* are to be in parallel Cases. And I need not tell the Honest and Impartial, especially in this Age of Division and Faction, how little Regard is to be given to such Testimonies.

W. WHISTON, *An Historical Preface to Primitive Christianity Reviv'd* (London, 1711), 98

CONTENTS

CONTENTS

PREFACE

THE CENTRAL PURPOSE OF THIS STUDY IS TO USE MODERN TECHNIQUES of historical research to probe behind Athanasius' misrepresentations, many of which have held sway for sixteen centuries, in order to discover the true nature of the ecclesiastical history and the ecclesiastical politics of the fourth century. If some readers feel that too much of what I have written resembles a detective story more than a work of history, that cannot be helped: where important facts have lain concealed for so long, such an investigation as I have undertaken constitutes an essential prerequisite for serious historical analysis. At the end, I have tried to show briefly how my sometimes speculative conclusions about Athanasius himself suggest a coherent and convincing general picture of the role of the Christian church and its bishops in the Roman Empire of Constantine and his imperial successors.

My research would have been impossible without both institutional support and the opportunity to work in a consistently academic environment. In 1983–84 the University of Toronto granted me sabbatical leave, the John S. Guggenheim Foundation a leave fellowship, and Wolfson College, Oxford, a visiting fellowship in order to write what I then envisaged as a straightforward analysis of ecclesiastical politics after the death of Constantine. The task of understanding and interpreting Athanasius' writings on his own behalf proved far more difficult and complex than I had suspected, so that my sabbatical year ended with less than half of a preliminary draft completed and with more problems remaining to be tackled than had seemed even to exist at the outset. Some of my main ideas about the career of Athanasius were presented in a series of seminars in Oxford in 1984, and on several occasions to graduate classes in Toronto between 1985 and 1992: the final form of the work owes much to the comments and penetrating questions of these audiences. The Social Sciences and Humanities Research Council of Canada provided a small research grant which has considerably hastened the completion of the final text, while the University of Toronto not only gave me a year's research leave again in 1990–91, but has over the years deepened my insight into the *modus operandi* of men like Athanasius and Constantius.

That this study has taken so long to complete has enabled me to draw gratefully on some extremely valuable work published since I began—particularly Hanns Christoph Brennecke's dissertation on Hilary of Poitiers and his *Habilitationsschrift* on the homoeans, Rowan Williams' study of the theology of Arius, Alberto Camplani's brilliant elucidation of the problem of Athanasius' *Festal Letters,* and R. P. C. Hanson's large posthumously published investigation of the theological debates of the fourth century. Moreover, during the final revision Dr. Glen Thompson kindly gave me a copy of part of his unpublished Columbia University dissertation on papal correspondence of the third and fourth centuries.

I am most grateful to those who have read and improved the manuscript at various stages. Maurice Wiles read carefully a draft of the first ten chapters in 1988 and made many helpful comments on it. Rowan Williams and Fergus Millar spared precious time during the autumn and winter of 1991–92 to peruse the penultimate version and saved me from some serious errors, while two anonymous referees for Harvard University Press submitted intelligent and perceptive reports which persuaded me to recast the final five chapters. Finally, I owe a deep debt of gratitude to Margaretta Fulton, who waited patiently for many years, selected the helpful referees, and convinced me of the necessity of changes after I thought I had finished. Without such help, this would be a different, even more idiosyncratic book.

CHRONOLOGY OF ATHANASIUS'
CAREER AND WRITINGS

352	*On the Council of Nicaea*
353	*Defense before Constantius* (original version)
356 February	Expelled from his church and leaves Alexandria
356 spring	*Letter to the Bishops of Egypt and Libya*
356–362	In hiding in Alexandria and elsewhere in Egypt
357	*Defense of His Flight*
	History of the Arians
359 autumn	*On the Councils of Ariminum and Seleucia*
362 February 21	Returns to Alexandria
October	Retires to Upper Egypt
363 autumn	Audience with Jovian
	In Antioch
364 February 14	Returns to Alexandria
365 October 5	Retires from Alexandria
366 February	Officially restored as bishop of Alexandria
373 May 2	Dies

ABBREVIATIONS

For the titles and editions of Athanasius' works, see M. Geerard, *Clavis Patrum Graecorum* 2 (Turnhout, 1974), 12–36 Nos. 2090–2170. (Chapter I notes the abbreviations used for those works which are most frequently cited.) The names of other ancient authors are normally given in full: for the abbreviations used for the titles of their works and for the standard collections of inscriptions and papyri, the following works of reference should be consulted:

The Oxford Classical Dictionary, second edition, ed. N. G. L. Hammond and H. H. Scullard (Oxford, 1971), ix–xxii.

H. G. Liddell and R. Scott, *A Greek-English Lexicon,* ninth edition, rev. H. S. Jones (Oxford, 1940), xvi–xlii.

G. W. H. Lampe, *A Patristic Greek Lexicon* (Oxford, 1961), ix–xliii.

The following conventional abbreviations are used for the most frequently cited periodicals, modern series, and works of reference:

AJAH	*American Journal of Ancient History*
BHE	*Bulletin d'histoire ecclésiastique*
*BHG*³	*Bibliotheca Hagiographica Graeca,* third edition in three volumes (*Subsidia Hagiographica* 8a [Brussels, 1957]), with *Auctarium* (*Subsidia Hagiographica* 47 [Brussels, 1969])
BHL	*Bibliotheca Hagiographica Latina antiquae et mediae aetatis,* in two volumes (*Subsidia Hagiographica* 6 [Brussels, 1898–1901]), with *Supplementum* (*Subsidia Hagiographica* 12 [Brussels, 1911]) and *Novum Supplementum* (*Subsidia Hagiographica* 70 [Brussels, 1986])
BHO	*Bibliotheca Hagiographica Orientalis* (*Subsidia Hagiographica* 10 [Brussels, 1910])
BLE	*Bulletin de littérature ecclésiastique*
BZ	*Byzantinische Zeitschrift*
CCL	*Corpus Christianorum,* Series Latina (Turnhout, 1954–)

CP	*Classical Philology*
CPG	*Clavis Patrum Graecorum* (Turnhout, 1974–1987)
CSCO	*Corpus Scriptorum Christianorum Orientalium* (Louvain, 1903–)
CSEL	*Corpus Scriptorum Ecclesiasticorum Latinorum* (Vienna, 1866–)
GCS	*Die griechischen christlichen Schriftsteller der ersten (drei) Jahrhunderte* (Leipzig and Berlin, 1897–)
GRBS	*Greek, Roman, and Byzantine Studies*
HSCP	*Harvard Studies in Classical Philology*
HTR	*Harvard Theological Review*
JEA	*Journal of Egyptian Archaeology*
JEH	*Journal of Ecclesiastical History*
JRS	*Journal of Roman Studies*
JTS	*Journal of Theological Studies*
PG	J.-P. Migne, *Patrologia Graeca* (Paris, 1857–1886)
PL	J.-P. Migne, *Patrologia Latina* (Paris, 1844–1864; second edition 1878–1890)
PLS	*Patrologiae Latinae Supplementum* (Paris, 1958–)
RAC	*Reallexicon für Antike und Christentum* (Stuttgart, 1941–)
RE	G. Pauly, G. Wissowa, and others (eds.), *Real-Encyclopädie der classischen Altertumswissenschaft* (Stuttgart, 1893–1978)
REAug	*Revue des études augustiniennes*
Rech. sci. rel.	*Recherches de science religieuse*
RHE	*Revue d'histoire ecclésiastique*
RIC	*Roman Imperial Coinage* (London, 1923–)
TRE	*Theologische Realenzykolpädie* (Berlin and New York, 1977–)
Vig. Chr.	*Vigiliae Christianae*
ZKG	*Zeitschrift für Kirchengeschichte*
ZNW	*Zeitschrift für die neutestamentliche Wissenschaft und die Kunde der alten Kirche*
ZPE	*Zeitschrift für Papyrologie und Epigraphik*

Otherwise, the titles of both periodicals and modern series are normally given in full. Moreover, since there is no bibliography, the full titles and references of articles and monographs in series are normally given on their first occurrence in each chapter. The following modern works, however, to which frequent reference is made, are always cited with abbreviated titles:

Arianism (1985)

R. C. Gregg (ed.), *Arianism: Historical and Theological Reassessments. Papers from the Ninth International Conference on Patristic Studies. Patristic Monograph Series,* No. 11. Philadelphia, 1985.

Brennecke, *Hilarius* (1984)

H. C. Brennecke, *Hilarius von Poitiers und die Bischofsopposition gegen Konstantius II: Untersuchungen zur dritten Phase des arianischen Streites (337–361). Patristische Texte und Studien* 26. Berlin and New York, 1984.

Brennecke, *Homöer* (1988)

> H. C. Brennecke, *Studien zur Geschichte der Homöer: Der Osten bis zum Ende der homöischen Reichskirche. Beiträge zur historischen Theologie* 73. Tübingen, 1988.

Chastagnol, *Fastes* (1962)

> A. Chastagnol, *Les fastes de la préfecture de Rome au Bas-Empire. Études prosopographiques* 2. Paris, 1962.

Chr. min. 1, 2

> T. Mommsen, *Chronica Minora saec. IV, V, VI, VII* 1, 2. *Monumenta Germaniae Historica,* Auctores Antiquissimi 9, 11. Berlin, 1892, 1894.

Consuls (1987)

> R. S. Bagnall, Alan Cameron, S. R. Schwartz, and K. A. Worp, *Consuls of the Later Roman Empire.* Atlanta, 1987.

Constantine (1981)

> T. D. Barnes, *Constantine and Eusebius.* Cambridge, Mass., 1981.

EOMIA

> C. H. Turner, *Ecclesiae Occidentalis Monumenta Iuris Antiquissima.* Oxford, 1899–1939.

Feder, *Studien* I (1910)

> A. L. Feder, *Studien zu Hilarius von Poitiers* I: *Die sogenannten 'fragmenta historica' und der sogenannte 'Liber I ad Constantium Imperatorem' nach ihrer Überlieferung, inhaltlichen Bedeutung und Entstehung. Sitzungsberichte der kaiserlichen Akademie der Wissenschaften in Wien,* Philosophisch-historische Klasse 162, Abhandlung 4, 1910. (The volume as a whole has the publication date of 1909, but Feder's monograph has the date 1910 on its title page.)

Feder, *Studien* II (1910)

> A. L. Feder, *Studien zu Hilarius von Poitiers* II: *Bischofsnamen und Bischofssitze bei Hilarius, kritische Untersuchungen zur kirchlichen Prosopographie und Topographie des 4. Jahrhunderts. Sitzungsberichte der kaiserlichen Akademie der Wissenschaften in Wien,* Philosophisch-historische Klasse 166, Abhandlung 5, 1910.

Feder, *Studien* III (1912)

> A. L. Feder, *Studien zu Hilarius von Poitiers* III: *Überlieferunsgeschichte und Echtheitskritik des sogenannten Liber II ad Constantium, des Tractatus mysteriorum, der epistula ad Abram filiam, der Hymnen. Kleinere Fragmenta und Spuria. Sitzungsberichte der kaiserlichen Akademie der Wissenschaften in Wien,* Philosophisch-historische Klasse 169, Abhandlung 5, 1912.

Girardet, *Kaisergericht* (1975)

> K. M. Girardet, *Kaisergericht und Bischofsgericht. Studien zu den Anfängen des Donatistenstreites (313–315) und zum Prozess*

Athanasius von Alexandrien (328–346). Antiquitas I.21. Bonn, 1975.

Gwatkin, *Arianism*² (1900)

> H. M. Gwatkin, *Studies of Arianism*. Second edition. Cambridge, 1900.

Hanson, *Search* (1988)

> R. P. C. Hanson, *The Search for the Christian Doctrine of God: The Arian Controversy, 318–381*. Edinburgh, 1988.

Kannengiesser, *Athanase* (1983)

> C. Kannengiesser, *Athanase d'Alexandrie, évêque et écrivain: Une lecture des traités* Contre les Ariens. *Théologie historique* 70. Paris, 1983.

Kelly, *Creeds*³ (1972)

> J. N. D. Kelly, *Early Christian Creeds*. Third edition. London, 1972.

Klein, *Constantius* (1977)

> R. Klein, *Constantius II. und die christliche Kirche. Impulse der Forschung* 26. Darmstadt, 1977.

Kopecek, *Neo-Arianism* (1979)

> T. A. Kopecek, *A History of Neo-Arianism. Patristic Monograph Series*, No. 8. Cambridge, Mass., 1979.

Lorenz, *Osterfestbrief* (1986)

> R. Lorenz, *Der zehnte Osterfestbrief des Athanasius von Alexandrien. Beiheft zür Zeitschrift für die neutestamentliche Wissenschaft* 49. Berlin and New York, 1986.

Matthews, *Ammianus* (1989)

> J. F. Matthews, *The Roman Empire of Ammianus*. London, 1989.

Müller, *Lexicon* (1952)

> G. Müller, *Lexicon Athanasianum*. Berlin, 1952.

New Empire (1982)

> T. D. Barnes, *The New Empire of Diocletian and Constantine*. Cambridge, Mass., 1982.

Opitz

> H.-G. Opitz, *Athanasius Werke* 2. Berlin and Leipzig, 1935–1941. (Seven fascicules comprising pages 1–280 were published in Opitz's lifetime. The rest of the volume, comprising pages 281–336, exists only in page-proof: Opitz was killed in action in 1941 and the plates were destroyed in a bombing raid. I am most grateful to Professor Wilhelm Schneemelcher and Professor Martin Tetz for their generosity in supplying me with a photocopy for my personal use. On principle, I refer to the unpublished portion of Opitz's notes only where earlier scholars have already placed their substance in the public domain. But I have used Opitz's unpublished text for all of the works which he included, noting the fact where it

is relevant. All references to Opitz's notes are keyed to the page and line[s] to which they are appended.)

Piétri, *Roma* (1976)

C. Piétri, *Roma Christiana: Recherches sur l'église de Rome, son organisation, sa politique, son idéologie, de Miltiade à Sixte III (311–440). Bibliothèque des écoles françaises d'Athènes et de Rome* 284. Rome, 1976.

PLRE 1

A. H. M. Jones, J. R. Martindale, and J. Morris, *The Prosopography of the Later Roman Empire* 1: A.D. 260–395. Cambridge, 1971.

PLRE 2

J. R. Martindale, *The Prosopography of the Later Roman Empire* 2: A.D. 395–527. Cambridge, 1980.

Politique et théologie (1974)

C. Kannengiesser (ed.), *Politique et théologie chez Athanase d'Alexandrie: Actes du Colloque de Chantilly, 23–25 Septembre 1973. Théologie historique* 27. Paris, 1974.

Robertson, *Select Writings* (1892)

A. Robertson, *Select Writings and Letters of Athanasius, Bishop of Alexandria. Nicene and Post-Nicene Fathers,* Second Series 4. London, 1892.

Schneemelcher, *Aufsätze* (1974)

W. Schneemelcher, *Gesammelte Aufsätze zum Neuen Testament und zur Patristik.* ΑΝΑΛΕΚΤΑ ΒΛΑΤΑΔΩΝ 22. Thessaloniki, 1974.

Schwartz, *Ges. Schr.* 3 (1959)

E. Schwartz, *Gesammelte Schriften* 3. *Zur Geschichte des Athanasius.* Berlin, 1959. Reprinted from *Nachrichten der königlichen Gesellschaft der Wissenschaften zu Göttingen,* Philologisch-historische Klasse 1904.333–401; 1905.164–187, 257–299; 1908.354–359, 365–374; 1911.367–426, 469–522. (The original publication is cited only where its date is relevant to the point being made.)

Seeck, *Geschichte* 4 (1911)

O. Seeck, *Geschichte des Untergangs der antiken Welt* 4. Berlin, 1911.

Seeck, *Regesten* (1919)

O. Seeck, *Regesten der Kaiser und Päpste für die Jahre 311 bis 476 n.Chr.: Vorarbeit zu einer Prosopographie der christlichen Kaiserzeit.* Stuttgart, 1919.

Simonetti, *Crisi* (1975)

M. Simonetti, *La crisi ariana nel IV secolo. Studia Ephemeridis 'Augustinianum'* 11. Rome, 1975.

Urkunde(n)

> H.-G. Opitz, *Urkunden zur Geschichte des arianischen Streites, 318–328. Athanasius Werke* 3.1. Berlin and Leipzig, 1934. (Documents in this collection are cited by number and paragraph.)

Vogler, *Constance* (1979)

> C. Vogler, *Constance II et l'administration impériale.* Groupe de recherche d'histoire romaine de l'Université de Strasbourg: *Études et travaux* 3. Strasbourg, 1979.

ATHANASIUS AND CONSTANTIUS

I

INTRODUCTION

ATHANASIUS CUTS AN IMPRESSIVE HISTORICAL FIGURE. ALTHOUGH HE
lived in an age whose emperors, thinkers, and ascetics often appear larger than
life, there is something particularly heroic about a man who could face the
threats of Roman emperors totally uncowed and unafraid even when he stood
apparently alone as 'Athanasius contra mundum.' But what precisely was the
nature of Athanasius' greatness? Although he owed his political standing to the
fact that between 328 and 373 he was the bishop of Alexandria and hence the
metropolitan bishop of Egypt in the newly Christian Roman Empire, he could
not have cut such an impressive figure had he not been conspicuously lacking in
the Christian virtues of meekness and humility.

It is no paradox that the most penetrating and most admired portrait of
Athanasius ever delineated in modern times comes from the pen of a man who
detested Christianity. Edward Gibbon discerned in Athanasius 'a superiority of
character and abilities which would have qualified him, far better than the
degenerate sons of Constantine, for the government of a great monarchy.'
Gibbon's hostility toward Christianity and religious fanaticism led him to
emphasise precisely those qualities which most set Athanasius apart from his
more polished and urbane contemporaries—above all, his will-power and determination, that 'force of a single mind, when it is inflexibly applied to the pursuit
of a single object,' which Athanasius combined with an unerring political in-
stinct, an unfailing judgement in knowing when to resist the emperor and when
to yield for future advantage.[1]

Unfortunately, for all its vividness, Gibbon's picture of Athanasius is highly
misleading. For once, Gibbon let his critical guard drop and relaxed his general
scepticism about the motives for human actions. He informs the reader that 'the
diligence of Tillemont and of the Benedictine editors has collected every fact and
examined every difficulty' relevant to Athanasius' career, and that 'we should

enjoy and improve the advantage of drawing our most authentic materials from the rich fund of his own epistles and apologies.' That is mistaken on two quite different levels. Tillemont and the Benedictine editor Montfaucon labored in ignorance of the ancient account of Athanasius' later career which Scipione Maffei gave to the world in 1738:[2] Gibbon inexplicably overlooked this new evidence in his main account of Athanasius and his career, although he refers to it later when he reaches the reigns of Julian and Jovian. Moreover, since Gibbon never owned a text of Athanasius, a suspicion inevitably arises that Tillemont may be the main source of Gibbon's knowledge of Athanasius' career. More serious, Gibbon shirked the task of asking whether Athanasius' pleas on his own behalf can be treated as 'authentic materials.' He presents Athanasius as a model of propriety and honesty, as a high-minded and prudent leader of genius constantly assailed by the false accusations and ignoble machinations of dishonest and mean-spirited adversaries, and he asserts that Athanasius 'never lost the confidence of his friends or the esteem of his enemies.' The last claim is patently false. The synodical letter of the eastern bishops at Serdica in 343 (published as early as 1598) both denounces Athanasius in derogatory and vituperative language and makes several specific charges that he employed violence and intimidation against those who opposed him.

An impartial historian cannot simply pin his faith on the utter veracity of Athanasius or dismiss the testimony of his enemies without due consideration. This study starts from the presumption that Athanasius consistently misrepresented central facts about his ecclesiastical career, in particular about his relationship with the emperor Constantine and his three sons, who ruled the Roman Empire after their father's death in 337, and about his own standing within the Christian church in the eastern half of the empire, which Constantius ruled from 337 to 361. At some levels, therefore, it has a certain logical affinity with two books about modern figures with whom Athanasius has little in common, namely, A. J. A. Symons' biographical study of Frederick Rolfe and Hugh Trevor-Roper's investigation of the colorful career of Sir Edmund Backhouse.[3] Not that Athanasius was a deceiver or forger on the level of a Rolfe or the 'hermit of Peking,' nor alas! that a similar historical or biographical exposé can be built up against Athanasius from original documents. It was with a far nobler motivation, and far more enduring success, that Athanasius imposed his version of events and his verdicts about individuals on contemporaries and on posterity.

The first modern scholar to approach the career of Athanasius critically was Eduard Schwartz, who, in his seven studies 'towards the history of Athanasius,' published between 1904 and 1911 in the proceedings of the Göttingen Society of Sciences, tried to reconstruct the history of the Melitian schism and the Arian controversy primarily from original documents quoted by Athanasius and other ancient writers or preserved in medieval collections.[4] Those studies still remain indispensable for anyone who wishes to understand the nature of the problems posed by our evidence for Athanasius' career. Here as elsewhere, however,

Schwartz pronounced rather than argued: his verdicts are too often both peremptory and arbitrary, and his scholarship is not always impeccable.[5] Schwartz made no real effort to understand Athanasius either as a man or as a writer. Instead, he denounced him as a power-hungry politician concerned with nothing more noble than his own status, and dismissed him as an unscrupulous pamphleteer with no regard for the truth, as 'a politician through and through who could not narrate the facts, only polemicise,' and 'a prince of the church who as a good politician knew the power of propaganda.'[6]

Athanasius may often disregard or pervert the truth, but he is a subtler and more skilful liar than Schwartz realised. Paradoxically, Schwartz built much of his own interpretation of the fourth century upon Athanasius' largest and most successful perversion of the facts—his misrepresentation of how emperors treated the decisions of church councils.[7] Hence the enduring value of Schwartz's studies lies less in the historical reconstruction which he proposed than in his determination to seek out the best evidence, to edit it critically, and to make it the basis for a dispassionate and objective account of ecclesiastical politics in the fourth century.

Schwartz's example inspired the critical edition of Athanasius' works which Hans-Georg Opitz commenced in the 1930s but left incomplete at his death in 1941.[8] Regrettably, historical study of Athanasius has until recently progressed little beyond Schwartz, whose dogmatic and *ex parte* assertions have too often been repeated as if they were fully demonstrated conclusions. In particular, a book which hotly contested the view that Constantius was an 'Arian' emperor tamely and often uncritically accepted what Schwartz laid down as the course of events even where he is demonstrably in error, declaring that it was impossible either to set forth a connected account of the relevant events or properly to investigate the factual basis of the historical judgements made.[9] The brilliance of Schwartz has eclipsed some other modern work which ought to receive due credit—most notably Archibald Robertson's careful and detailed prolegomena to Athanasius' political writings,[10] some characteristically acute observations by Norman Baynes,[11] and Paul Peeters' masterly elucidation of the circumstances of Athanasius' first exile.[12]

The reconstruction of Athanasius' career which this study seeks to establish inevitably owes most to Schwartz's seven classic papers (or at least to the five reprinted in full in his collected scholarly writings),[13] but it seeks to build on whatever valid results have been achieved by earlier scholars who have written about Athanasius and his contemporaries.[14] However, since it proceeds from a particular interpretation of Constantine, it makes certain assumptions which some readers will find controversial.[15] In partial justification, it may be claimed that the reconstruction of the career of Athanasius offered here tends to confirm rather than weaken these controversial theses.

The basic chronological framework for reconstructing the career of Athanasius is provided by two documents originally composed in Alexandria not long after his death and recently edited together in a single volume by A. Martin and M. Albert: they are the so-called *Historia acephala,* which derives its name from the title which Scipione Maffei invented when he published it in 1738 as *Historia acephala ad Athanasium potissimum ac res Alexandrinas pertinens,* and the *Festal Index,* which prefaces the collected edition of Athanasius' *Festal Letters.*[16] Both documents incorporate or draw on archival material from the archiepiscopal records of the see of Alexandria, and both survive only in translation and only in a unique manuscript: neither document is infallible, and each poses distinctive problems of its own.

The *Historia acephala* survives as part of a collection of documents apparently put together by a deacon named Theodosius and now preserved in a Latin manuscript of c. 700 in the cathedral library at Verona (Biblioteca Capitolare LX [58], fols. 37–126, on fols. 105–112).[17] The investigations of several scholars, particularly C. H. Turner, Schwartz himself, W. Telfer, and now A. Martin, have established that the *Historia acephala* in its present form probably represents an original document drawn up in Athanasius' lifetime which has undergone three major alterations.[18] The four main stages in the genesis of the document that survives can be schematised as follows:

(1) In 368, on the occasion of the fortieth anniversary of Athanasius' election as bishop, an account was composed in Greek in Alexandria which summarised the history of the see of Alexandria since the beginning of the Melitian schism in 306, concentrating on the vicissitudes of Athanasius' career.

(2) Each year until 372 someone added to the computation of Athanasius' forty years as bishop on 8 June 368 the consular dates of successive anniversaries and finally in 373 the date of Athanasius' death (5.10).

(3) Shortly after Athanasius' death, probably between 385 and 412, this account was expanded by the inclusion of passages dealing with the churches of Constantinople (1.4–7; 4.5/6) and Antioch (2.7), and by the addition of a chronological postscript (5.14).

(4) C. 420 the existing text was abbreviated, combined with other documents which accompany it in the Verona manuscript, and sent from Alexandria to Carthage, where it was translated into Latin.

Several critical editions of the *Historia acephala* have been published, the most recent by A. Martin with a long introduction, French translation, and copious commentary.[19] Martin's introduction and commentary should be consulted for all historical problems in the *Historia acephala* which are not fully discussed in this book, but there is still much of value in the systematic analysis by G. R. Sievers in a long paper published shortly after his death more than a century and a quarter ago.[20]

The *Festal Index* was composed to serve as the introduction to a collected edition of the *Festal Letters* which Athanasius wrote for each Easter between 329 and 373, presumably by the same man who arranged, numbered, edited, and published the *Letters* as a collection or corpus in Alexandria shortly after Athanasius' death.[21] This editor described the document as

> an index of the months of each year, and of the days, and of the indictions, and of the consulates, and of the governors in Alexandria, and of all the epacts, and of those [days] which are named 'of the gods,' and the reason [a letter] was not sent, and the returns from exile.[22]

But he also appended to the chronological data of many entries other information about Athanasius' activities during the year preceding the relevant Easter.[23] The *Festal Index* survives only as the introduction to the Syriac translation made in the sixth or seventh century of a second, non-Alexandrian corpus of the *Festal Letters*, and this translation itself survives only in a single manuscript which is probably to be dated to the tenth century (British Library, Add. ms. 14569).[24] Fortunately, the historical value of the *Festal Index* is largely independent of the complicated problem of the chronology of the *Festal Letters* themselves.[25]

Apart from the framework provided by the *Historia acephala* and the *Festal Index*, there is no systematic and reliable ancient account of Athanasius' career. It must accordingly be reconstructed from materials which are all partial and unsatisfactory. Least problematical are contemporary documents of which the originals survive. The most important and directly relevant are two letters in which opponents of Athanasius in Alexandria refer to the forthcoming church council of Caesarea in 334 (which never in fact met) and describe events which occurred in the Egyptian metropolis in 335 shortly before the Council of Tyre.[26] More difficult to evaluate are documents preserved in collections (such as two letters of Athanasius in the manuscript which preserves the *Historia acephala*) or quoted by contemporary or later writers. In the late nineteenth and early twentieth centuries there was lively and sometimes acrimonious debate over the genuineness of many of these documents. The controversy has largely subsided in recent decades: hence this study accepts the basic authenticity of all relevant documents preserved in manuscript collections or quoted by authors of the fourth and fifth centuries, confining substantive discussion of the genuineness of a document to those cases where there seems to be real reason to doubt whether what survives accurately represents what was written or said on the relevant occasion.

The next place, in any hierarchy of sources, must be occupied by non-documentary evidence from the middle decades of the fourth century, principally the partisan writings of Athanasius and his contemporaries. Athanasius was a prolific author, and this study makes no attempt to do justice to his doctrinal, homiletic, ascetical, and exegetical writings. The centre of attention will be those works which are sometimes called Athanasius' 'historical writings,' but which show a closer resemblance to political pamphlets.[27] These were collected together after Athanasius' death:[28] the titles which they bear in the manuscripts do not come from Athanasius' own hand, and the date of composition is in some cases disputed. The following list states the English title employed here for each of the most important polemical tracts and treatises which Athanasius wrote during the reign of Constantius, together with its conventional Latin title or titles and an indication of its date:

(1) *Encyclical Letter* (*Epistula encyclica* or *Epistula ad episcopos*), written shortly after 26 March 339;[29]
(2) *Defense against the Arians* (*Apologia contra Arianos* or *Apologia secunda*), probably composed in its present form in 349 and subsequently retouched, though never published or circulated during Athanasius' lifetime;[30]
(3) *On the Council of Nicaea* (*Epistula de decretis Nicaenae synodi* or *De decretis Nicaenae synodi* or, more briefly still, *De decretis*), probably written in 352 in response to a letter from Liberius, the bishop of Rome, and addressed to him;[31]
(4) *Defense before Constantius* (*Apologia ad Constantium*), probably composed in two stages, in early 353 and 357;[32]
(5) *Letter to the Bishops of Egypt and Libya* (*Epistula ad episcopos Aegypti et Libyae*), written in the spring of 356;[33]
(6) *Defense of His Flight* (*Apologia de fuga sua* or *De fuga*), written in 357;[34]
(7) *History of the Arians* (*Historia Arianorum*), probably also written in 357;[35]
(8) *On the Councils of Ariminum and Seleucia* (*Epistula de synodis Arimini et Seleuciae* or *De synodis*), written in late 359, with some later additions.[36]

Among Athanasius' contemporaries, the most important writers for the reconstruction of his career are Lucifer, bishop of Caralis in Sardinia, and Hilary, bishop of Poitiers in Gaul. Unfortunately, the violent and often hysterical diatribes of Lucifer contain distressingly little of real historical value that is not known from other sources, though that little is sometimes highly significant.[37] Hilary, on the other hand, is a crucial and independent figure, whose place in the theological kaleidoscope of the later 350s has been investigated by H. C. Brennecke in a brilliant (even if ultimately mistaken) monograph.[38] The fragments of Hilary's historical-apologetical work directed against the bishops Ursacius of Singidunum and Valens of Mursa preserve many indispensable documents which would otherwise be completely lost, above all the long and revealing letter of the eastern bishops who attended the Council of Serdica in 343.[39] But the panegyric which Gregory of Nazianzus delivered in Constantinople in the year 380 contains regrettably little specific detail about Athanasius' career.[40]

The standard ecclesiastical histories of the fifth century present a picture of the Christian church under Constantine and his sons which not only owes a great deal to Athanasius himself, but appears largely to derive from a tendentious and often inaccurate account composed in the reign of Theodosius. In 402/3

Rufinus of Aquileia published a Latin *Ecclesiastical History* in eleven books. While the first nine books are and profess to be a translation, with certain omissions and some additions, of the edition of his *Ecclesiastical History* which Eusebius of Caesarea published c. 325, the last two books were composed, according to Rufinus, 'partly from the traditions of an earlier generation, partly from what our own memory had committed to mind.'[41] It now seems probable that much of Rufinus' account of the fourth century is more of a translation than he appears to admit and that, at least as far as the reign of Julian, it follows closely the lost *Ecclesiastical History* which Gelasius of Caesarea composed in the reign of Theodosius.[42] Rufinus' originality (it seems) lay not in constructing a basic narrative history of the Christian church under Constantine and his successors, but in incorporating into a framework taken from Gelasius additional material such as the stories of the evangelisation of the kingdoms of Iberia and Axum.[43] Yet it does not matter much whether it was Gelasius or Rufinus (or some other writer) who created the basic picture of the Arian heresy and of Athanasius' struggle against it which reappears in the works of later writers. The important fact is that the narrative framework which the later ecclesiastical historians share with Rufinus is demonstrably flawed.[44] One striking example from the reign of Constantine illustrates how badly this narrative framework can go awry: neither Rufinus nor any of his successors is aware that after his condemnation at Nicaea in 325 Arius was pronounced orthodox by church councils on two separate occasions several years apart—in 327/8 and again in 335/6.[45]

The *scholasticus* Socrates, who continued Eusebius and wrote a history of the church from 306 to 439, which he published in 439 itself or the following year, put out two editions of the first two books of his *Ecclesiastical History*. In the first edition, Socrates confesses, he had too slavishly followed Rufinus, who committed gross errors of fact and chronology: when he discovered the writings of Athanasius himself, he realised the deficiencies of what he had written and composed a second edition quoting documents freely from Eusebius, from Athanasius, and from the collection of documents which Sabinus, the bishop of Heraclea, compiled c. 370.[46] Since the works of Eusebius and Athanasius which Socrates consulted survive, the value of many of his quotations is merely textual. In his youth, however, Socrates had lived in Constantinople and had conversed with one Auxanon, a Novatianist priest, who could remember snippets of information from the days of Constantine, such as what the emperor said to the Novatianist Acesius at the Council of Nicaea.[47] Hence Socrates provides circumstantial accounts of important episodes in the troubled ecclesiastical history of the church of Constantinople in the 330s and 340s, which enable the turbulent career of the bishop Paul, an ally of Athanasius, to be reconstructed in detail.[48] Moreover, Socrates often reproduces a lost source which gave precise and usually accurate dates for imperial events,[49] and he quotes some documents which survive nowhere else, for example, a letter of the emperor Julian to the city of Alexandria.[50]

7

Theodoretus, bishop of Cyrrhus in northern Syria, composed his *Ecclesiastical History* some years later, but, though he appears to have completed the work c. 448, he prudently brought his narrative to a close in the late 420s, so that he avoided any obligation to write about living bishops and theologians. The main value of Theodoretus' *History* for the fourth century is twofold: it provides abundant quotations and includes important documents not preserved elsewhere; and, as a Syrian and native Syriac-speaker, Theodoretus was able to draw on local knowledge and Syrian traditions to give a much fuller account of events concerning the church of Antioch than his predecessors.[51]

Sozomenus, a *scholasticus* like Socrates, was a native of Palestine who traveled, perhaps widely, before settling in Constantinople. He prefaced his *Ecclesiastical History* with a dedication to the emperor Theodosius the younger, which promises a history of the church from 324 to 439—which is precisely the point at which Socrates' work ends. Sozomenus' *History* is unfinished: the ninth and last book, which appears to have been composed in the first half of the year 450, shows obvious signs of incompleteness (it peters out in 425) and lack of stylistic polish. The first eight books, in contrast, are both finished and highly polished: Sozomenus uses Socrates throughout, but he has turned Socrates' simple factual prose into a grandiloquent rhetorical exposition close to the style of traditional historiography, and he supplements Socrates from many other sources, particularly ones of a legal nature.[52] As a result, Sozomenus not infrequently reports the contents of important documents whose actual text has failed to survive: these include the formal verdict of the Council of Tyre which condemned and deposed Athanasius in 335, and the letter of a council held at Antioch which deposed Athanasius again shortly before the death of Constans.[53]

Philostorgius, whose *Ecclesiastical History* closed with events of 425, stands apart from Rufinus, Socrates, Theodoretus, and Sozomenus. For Philostorgius was a Eunomian who defended the good name and orthodoxy of Arius.[54] The original text of Philostorgius' work has perished, but both a brief summary and fuller excerpts from the pen of Photius in the ninth century have permitted the identification of extensive fragments and paraphrases in a variety of Byzantine texts,[55] especially the *Passio Artemii*, long ascribed to one John of Rhodes, but recently attributed to John of Damascus and edited among his works.[56]

One of Philostorgius' lost sources is of the greatest importance—the so-called Arian historiographer of the middle of the fourth century identified by P. Batiffol,[57] whose fragments, derived from authors as diverse as Jerome and Michael the Syrian, Joseph Bidez printed as a separate appendix.[58] The precise vantage-point of this lost historian can be defined quite closely: H. M. Gwatkin noted long ago that he was a homoean and that both Theodoretus and the *Paschal Chronicle* appear to have used him extensively for their accounts of the persecution under Julian, while H. C. Brennecke has recently built on Gwatkin's observations to construct a strong case for dating him to the late 360s and regarding him as the first known continuator of Eusebius' *Ecclesiastical History*.[59]

Such are the principal sources for reconstructing the career of Athanasius. Yet many other writers besides those already named preserve items of reliable information, and all the relevant evidence needs to be assessed on its merits, whatever its date. The political and military narrative of the history of the Roman Empire between 353 and 378 by Ammianus Marcellinus includes notices of the arrest in 355 of Liberius, the bishop of Rome, for supporting Athanasius, and of the death of his rival George in Alexandria in 361.[60] Around 400, Sulpicius Severus found space in his brief chronicle of world history for accounts of both Athanasius and Hilary of Poitiers, which supply the basic narrative of the Council of Ariminum in 359 and many valuable details concerning the ecclesiastical history of the previous decade.[61]

Unfortunately, the hagiography of Athanasius appears to be virtually worthless as historical evidence for his career.[62] On the other hand, two ninth-century sources make explicit statements about the 340s which deserve to be accepted as reliable, even though found in no earlier extant texts—namely, that the sophist Asterius attended the 'Dedication Council' of Antioch in 341, and that Ossius held a council in Corduba to confirm the decisions of the Council of Serdica.[63]

The subject of this investigation is the political career of Athanasius and its historical context. It will be argued that his career is a unique phenomenon which could have taken the course it did only in the Constantinian empire—between the Council of Nicaea and the accession of Theodosius. Of set purpose, no attempt is made to tackle the complex and intricate problems posed by many of the theological, ascetical, and hagiographical writings transmitted under the name of Athanasius except insofar as they are directly relevant to his career or to his standing within the church of his own day. It may be hoped, however, that a new reconstruction of Athanasius' career will lead to a deeper understanding of his personality, thought, and theology.[64]

II

BISHOP ALEXANDER

ATHANASIUS WAS BORN AT THE VERY END OF THE THIRD CENTURY. THE earliest and best evidence for his date of birth stands in the *Festal Index,* which states that his election as bishop of Alexandria on 8 June 328 was challenged on the grounds that he had not yet attained the canonical age (*Index* 3). Since the minimum age for ordination to the priesthood was probably then thirty years (equivalent to twenty-nine, on inclusive reckoning),[1] while Athanasius was only a deacon when his predecessor died, he may well have turned twenty-nine very shortly after his consecration—which would fix the summer of 299 as the probable date of his birth. Whether that precise calculation is correct or not, the reluctant testimony of the *Festal Index* must outweigh a later tradition which puts his birth in 295.[2] For an independent monastic tradition confirms that the new bishop's age was a matter of acute controversy at the time of his election.[3] Athanasius emerges into history as the protégé of Alexander, who became bishop of Alexandria shortly after the emperor Licinius put an end to the 'Great Persecution,' which had begun in spring 303 and which, according to a plausible if unverifiable report, claimed six hundred and sixty lives in Alexandria alone during its first eight years before the 'palinode' of Galerius.[4] A pleasing story current by the end of the fourth century relates that Alexander discovered him as a boy on the beach, playing with his friends at being a bishop. It was the anniversary of the martyrdom of Peter, the predecessor of Alexander, who had been executed in late November 311. Alexander construed the coincidence as an omen and took the boys into his household to give them an education. Athanasius displayed exceptional promise, and as soon as his age permitted, he became a deacon and Alexander's trusted assistant.[5]

The story carries the clear implication that Athanasius came from a humble family in the Egyptian metropolis. The inference is confirmed by the emperor Constantius: in 346 he referred to the city as Athanasius' 'ancestral hearth'

(*Apol. c. Ar.* 51.2) and eleven years later ridiculed his ignoble origin (*Apol. ad Const.* 30.3/4). Hence Athanasius himself can be believed when he protested to Constantine that he was a poor man (*Apol. c. Ar.* 9.4). About his family very little is known. Athanasius mentions an aunt who died not long after his expulsion from the city in 339: he accuses his enemies of trying to prevent her receiving a proper burial, which friends provided by concealing her identity (*Hist. Ar.* 13.2). And Socrates reports that in 365/6 Athanasius spent four months in hiding in his family's ancestral funerary monument.[6]

Athanasius received a thorough grounding in the scriptures and in biblical exegesis, which formed the basis of his thought and writings throughout his life. His education, however, probably did not include close study of the classics of Greek literature. The panegyric on Athanasius delivered in Constantinople in 380 by Gregory of Nazianzus, himself a cultivated and learned man, and at the time bishop of the imperial capital, makes it clear that Athanasius' education was primarily religious. Gregory proclaims that he studied non-Christian matters only enough to avoid seeming either to be totally unacquainted with them or to have decided to despise them out of sheer ignorance.[7]

Large claims have sometimes been made for the culture of Athanasius—that he not only knew Plato well, but also quotes Homer, imitates Aristotle, and models his *Defense before Constantius* on Demosthenes,[8] or that he was in the habit of employing traditional rhetorical techniques wherever they might prove helpful.[9] But Athanasius names Plato only three times in the whole of his considerable *oeuvre*, and the three passages which he adduces are three of the most celebrated and widely known passages in antiquity—the opening scene of the *Republic*, the account of creation in the *Timaeus*, and the comparison of the statesman to a steersman in the *Politicus*.[10] Most of the passages which were supposed to illustrate his wide learning came from the fourth *Oration against the Arians*, which is not by Athanasius at all.[11] Athanasius did not compose and order his works according to contemporary rhetorical theory, not even the *Defense before Constantius*, which is expressly constructed as a forensic speech.[12] Naturally, the structure and method of argument of this work correspond in certain ways with Aristotle's analysis, but that does not suffice to show that Athanasius consciously employed traditional rhetorical methods.[13] The contrast with writers like Tertullian or Basil of Caesarea and Gregory of Nazianzus would in itself be decisive,[14] but an even more telling comparison is available from Egypt itself. Both the *Letter to the Monks* by Serapion of Thmuis and the *Encyclical Letter* of Athanasius' successor Peter use traditional rhetorical devices such as anaphora, parallelism, alliteration, and assonance to a degree never found in any of Athanasius' writings, even the most elaborate.[15]

The general culture of Athanasius reflects the milieu in which he grew up: in Alexandria a Christian education had been available for more than a century.[16] Athanasius regarded himself as the product of a Christian, primarily biblical, education which taught him that what is needful for salvation is 'the study and true knowledge of the scriptures' and 'a good life and pure soul and virtue in Christ.'[17] Virtually everything that he wrote is closely based on scriptural texts.[18] His philosophical culture can be measured from two interconnected treatises, which he wrote early in his career to establish his credentials as a theologian possessing a certain acquaintance with Greek philosophical thought.[19]

The pair of treatises, *Against the Pagans* and *On the Incarnation of the Word*, belong to a literary genre of Christian apologetics already outmoded in the society in which Athanasius grew up. They undertake to show that belief in Christ is not unreasonable. Athanasius assumes and asserts that Christian theology has triumphed over pagan philosophy: the wisdom of the Greeks is disappearing and the demons no longer possess their former power.[20] Athanasius appropriates the language and ideas of Greek philosophy without embarrassment, and he expresses his position easily in the prevailing terminology of Middle Platonism.[21] But the main topic around which the exposition revolves is the Christian's spiritual growth: since Athanasius holds that knowledge of God must come through Christ, he concentrates on the doctrine of redemption and its essential presupposition—that Christ is both truly God and truly man.

The lack of an obvious polemical motive (in contrast to the almost contemporaneous *Preparation for the Gospel* and *Demonstration of the Gospel* by Eusebius of Caesarea, which are directed against Porphyry's *Against the Christians*)[22] inevitably raises two questions about the author's purpose: why did Athanasius write? and for what audience? The two treatises *Against the Pagans* and *On the Incarnation of the Word* continually address a friend who is presented as having already embraced Christianity.[23] This procedure seems to imply that the audience which Athanasius envisaged was primarily Christian. Moreover, Athanasius explicitly asserts that the works of his teachers were not available to him when he wrote.[24] That sounds like an indication that he wrote *Against the Pagans* and *On the Incarnation of the Word* outside Alexandria, and has encouraged the inference that he composed them in exile in the West. But the intellectual, or rather geographical, perspective and horizons of the author of these works appear to be those of someone writing in Alexandria and ignorant of, or at least uninterested in, the West.[25] Hence, if Athanasius wrote the two treatises outside Alexandria, then he might have written them during his journey to the Council of Nicaea in 325, when he spent several weeks in an environment which was less Christian than his native Alexandria. For the two treatises appear to be designed, at least in part, as a *specimen eruditionis* to demonstrate to the world that the young deacon who was clearly being groomed as the next bishop of Alexandria deserved his place at Alexander's side.[26]

The *Against the Pagans* and *On the Incarnation of the Word* conspicuously fail to refer explicitly to the Arian controversy. Hence the problem of dating the double work has almost always been presented as a choice between a date c. 318, before the views of Arius were proscribed, and the period of Athanasius' exile in Trier between the winter of 335/6 and the summer of 337,[27] and powerful statements have recently been made both for a date shortly before the Council of Nicaea and for the traditional date of c. 336.[28] A new proposal will perhaps do justice to the competing arguments for both these dates.

Athanasius' work shows some clear affinities to Eusebius' *Theophany*, which was composed c. 325, and it has been claimed that its author therefore read and copied Eusebius' text.[29] But many of the parallels could be due to independent use of traditional apologetic material.[30] On the other hand, the overall argument of the *Against the Pagans* and *On the Incarnation of the Word* is unusually historical for Athanasius, and some of the individual arguments run closely parallel to Eusebius.[31] Hence the double work creates a strong impression that it was written with Eusebius' *Theophany* in mind to argue a similar general thesis from a different theological viewpoint.[32] It may be, therefore, that Athanasius wrote it between 325 and 328 in order to establish his credentials as a worthy successor of Alexander as bishop of Alexandria—and deliberately avoided polemic against other Christians or any allusion to current controversies within the church.[33]

Athanasius is sometimes regarded as both bilingual and bicultural, equally at home in Coptic and in Greek. Hence his theology can be considered to represent a fusion of Coptic literalism and Hellenic spiritualism.[34] For it seems to be an obvious inference from the time that he spent in exile among the monks of Upper Egypt that he must have been fluent in the native Egyptian language of the majority of the monks,[35] and the preservation of so many of his homiletic and ascetical works in Coptic seems to make it plausible to suppose that he composed at least some of them in that language.[36] Hence Athanasius has been described as a 'Coptic writer' who was also the leader of a bilingual or essentially Coptic church.[37] Such interpretations cannot perhaps be totally excluded on *a priori* grounds, and it must be conceded that a large proportion of Christians in rural Egypt probably could not understand Greek.[38] Yet it is certain that the Coptic versions of all the works of Athanasius which survive are translations from an original Greek text, even where the Greek original has been lost.[39] Athanasius the Coptic patriarch appears to be an anachronistic creation of later hagiography. There is no good evidence that he ever wrote in Coptic—and given the abundance of work that survives from his pen, there can be little probability either. On the other hand, Athanasius may on occasion have written in Latin, since he spent more than eight years in the Latin-speaking parts of the Roman Empire, where he would have needed to use Latin to persuade westerners to support his cause.[40]

Athanasius corresponds in certain particulars to the unflattering stereotype of the quarrelsome Egyptian current in the Greco-Roman world.[41] The educated classes of the Roman Empire would never have recognised in him a fellow member of the cultured élite. The early and reliable evidence consistently indicates that Athanasius was a man of the people. He was not a scion of the local aristocracy of the Greek metropolis of Egypt, born into a leisured and cultivated milieu.

Nor was he by birth a member of the rural peasantry of the Egyptian country-side. Yet there is a sense in which he straddled the Greek and native Egyptian worlds which met in Alexandria.[42] His low-class origin gave him a lack of inhibition which was to serve him well during a long life of conflict.

In 325 the deacon Athanasius accompanied Alexander to the Council of Nicaea, where he attended on his bishop during the debates[43] and presumably made the acquaintance of bishops from outside Egypt who were to be his political allies in later days. The Council of Nicaea tackled a large agenda, from voluntary castration to the jurisdiction of metropolitan bishops and the date of Easter.[44] But the two most serious and most pressing problems which the council attempted to solve concerned Egypt, which was troubled by both schism and doctrinal dispute.

During the 'Great Persecution,' the bishop Peter had withdrawn from Alexandria, perhaps when Maximinus, who began to rule the East in May 305, intensified the persecution of the Christians. Melitius, who appears to have been recently elected bishop of Lycopolis in place of an apostate, stepped in to perform Peter's duties, including the ordination of priests.[45] The bishop of Alexandria objected, then, when he subsequently returned to the city, convened a synod, and excommunicated Melitius (*Apol. c. Ar.* 59.1). As persecution continued, Melitius was deported to the mines of Palestine, where he organised a schismatic 'church of the martyrs.' In 311 the dying Galerius ordered the cessation of persecution, and Melitius returned to Egypt, where he organised a separate network of local churches.[46] Papyri illustrate the extent of his success: by 334 there existed a Melitian monastery at Hathor 'in the eastern desert of the Upper Cynopolite nome' in Middle Egypt, Melitian cells in the Thebaid, and a network of Melitian sympathisers in Alexandria itself who could provide lodging for their confrères.[47]

Arius represented a challenge of a different order. Shortly after Alexander became bishop of Alexandria in 313, the Libyan Arius established a reputation as a popular preacher at the Church of Baucalis, close to the harbor.[48] By custom, and presumably because of the size of the city and its large Christian population, the priests of Alexandria were licensed to preach, each in his own church.[49] Arius, therefore, enjoyed an independence which mere priests in most other cities lacked, and he used the opportunity to advance his own theological views.

Controversy still attaches (and will probably always continue to attach) to the origin and the precise nature of Arius' views, for it is not at all easy to sift authentic reports of his theology from hostile misrepresentation, and Arius himself restated and modified his opinions more than once.[50] Moreover, the historian confronts a problem of terminology and must be sensitive to the risk of anachronism. Can the term 'Arianism' legitimately be used at all for historical analysis, given its demonstrable origin as a derogatory party label? And if the term 'Arianism' is used, should it be defined as the distinctive theology of Arius himself, or does anyone count as an 'Arian' who considered that Arius' views lay within the permissible range of views which the church could tolerate, whether or not he himself shared them? No fourth-century thinker who is normally regarded as an 'Arian' or 'Neo-Arian' would ever have applied the term to himself. The label was a term of abuse: Athanasius and his allies habitually employed a broad definition which turned all their enemies into 'Arians.' In the early middle decades of the fourth century, the crucial political (and perhaps theological) divide lay between those who considered Arius an utter heretic who must be expelled from the church and those who thought that his views, at least when he dropped one or two extreme formulations, fell within the limits allowed by the traditional teaching of the church, within what Eusebius of Caesarea defined as 'ecclesiastical theology.'[51] Those who took the former view had no hesitation in branding all those who took the latter view, including Eusebius of Caesarea, 'Arians' or 'Arian madmen,' but that does not justify the continued use of the term by a modern historian who strives for objectivity.[52]

Whatever their precise nature, Arius' views provoked objection, and a complaint was lodged with Alexander.[53] Arius responded by submitting to his bishop, in his own name and that of a group of other priests and deacons of Alexandria, a statement which claimed that his views reflected both traditional teaching and Alexander's own.[54] Since Arius refused to modify his opinions, the bishop convened a council of about one hundred bishops from Egypt and Libya, which repudiated Arius' novel views and excommunicated all who shared them.[55]

Alexander had miscalculated if he thought that Arius could be cowed or easily suppressed. The Libyan priest possessed powerful friends outside Egypt. Before long Arius had gained the support of important bishops in Palestine and Syria and was able to claim that Alexander had anathematised Eusebius of Caesarea, Theodotus of Laodicea, Paulinus of Tyre, Athanasius of Anazarbus, Gregorius of Berytus, Aetius of Lydda, and almost all the bishops of the East for sharing his view that the Father pre-exists the Son in a non-temporal sense. He wrote to Eusebius, the bishop of Nicomedia and a habitué of the court of the emperor Licinius, whom he saluted as a fellow pupil of the late Lucian of Antioch, urging him to support one who was being persecuted for holding theological views which were perfectly acceptable.[56] The dispute between the bishop of Alexandria and the Alexandrian priest soon engulfed the whole of the eastern church. Councils of bishops weighed in on Arius' side: reports survive of a council in Palestine convened by Paulinus of Tyre, Eusebius of Caesarea, and Patrophilus of Scythopolis, and of one in Bithynia.[57] For his part, Alexander wrote to Alexander, the bishop of Byzantium, and even (it is reported) to Silvester, the bishop of Rome.[58] Moreover, it appears that after Arius had vindicated himself outside Egypt, he returned to Alexandria and organised Arian conventicles in the city, not without violence.[59]

15

The young Athanasius was soon given an opportunity to show his native skill and mettle in polemic. Two circular letters sent from Alexandria in the name of Alexander survive from early in the controversy over Arius. The one is a letter to 'our beloved and most respected fellow workers of the catholic church everywhere,' while the other is addressed to a single fellow bishop Alexander, who is stated by the only ancient writer to quote the letter to be the bishop of Byzantium.[60] The hand of Athanasius has been detected in both letters: the latter, for example, uses the image of the Arians dividing the robe of Christ which his executioners had left whole (John 19.23–24). That was a novel idea at the time when the letter was written, but it became one of Athanasius' favorite images for schism and heresy.[61] The two letters, however, are so different in vocabulary, style, and method of argument that it is hard to suppose them the work of a single writer, and it is the circular letter which reflects the style and thought of Athanasius.[62] The letter to Alexander strives after grandiloquence, but lacks intellectual sharpness and precision, and its writer commits the tactical mistake, which could be disastrous in any controversy, of venturing too many positive statements about the content of his own theology. The author is presumably the bishop of Alexandria himself.[63] The circular letter, in contrast, appears to show the hand of Athanasius: it is a far more effective and tightly argued composition which admirably succeeds in attacking the theology of Arius without setting out a contrary position containing any novelties to provoke disquiet or resistance.[64]

At some stage in the controversy, Licinius prohibited the convening and holding of councils of bishops—possibly on the recommendation of Eusebius of Nicomedia.[65] In 324, when Constantine conquered the East, the suspended quarrel flared up again with even fiercer intensity. Constantine wrote to Alexander and Arius urging them not to quarrel, since they differed only on esoteric points of theology and philosophy, not over the central tenets of the divine law, and he sent his letter to Athanasius with a trusted envoy, apparently Ossius of Corduba, whom he instructed to try to reconcile the parties.[66] Despite a council at Alexandria (*Apol. c. Ar.* 74.3/4, 76.3), Ossius' mission failed, and a great council was called to meet in Ancyra.

As Ossius returned to court, he discovered that the church of Antioch, whose bishop Philogonius had died on 20 December 324,[67] was in disorder. Ossius presided over a council of more than fifty Oriental bishops, which elected Eustathius to succeed Philogonius and attempted to settle the affairs of the Antiochene church. The council also adopted an intricately phrased creed, and provisionally excommunicated three prominent bishops who refused to accept it as the true apostolic teaching necessary for salvation: they were Theodotus of Laodicea, Narcissus of Neronias, and Eusebius of Caesarea. But the decisions of this council of Antioch were merely provisional until ratified by the forthcoming 'great and holy council at Ancyra.'[68]

Constantine transferred the impending council to Nicaea.[69] The excommunicated bishops rehabilitated themselves, and the council began to discuss the theological issues raised in the controversy over Arius. Debate dragged on until a creed was produced which its framers expected to be totally unacceptable not only to Arius but also to his principal supporters. Constantine, however, offered an interpretation of its wording which most of those who sympathised with Arius could accept, and all the bishops present signed the creed except the two Libyan bishops associated with Arius (Secundus of Ptolemais and Theonas of Marmarica), who departed into exile, together with Arius himself and some priests who refused to repudiate his views.[70]

The Melitian schism required less rigorous measures. The Council of Nicaea attempted to reintegrate the Melitian clergy into the catholic church of Egypt. It accepted the status of Melitius himself as bishop of Lycopolis, and it accepted the priests whom Melitius had ordained as validly consecrated. But it forbade Melitius to perform further ordinations, and declared that the Melitian clergy in any locality were to be subordinate in rank to those ordained under Alexander of Alexandria. On the other hand, if a Melitian priest acknowledged Alexander's authority, he should have full clerical privileges. Moreover, if the congregation wished it, and if the bishop of Alexandria agreed, then such a priest might replace a priest of the catholic church who died.[71]

The Council of Nicaea did not bring peace to the church either in Egypt or elsewhere. Eusebius of Nicomedia and Theognis of Nicaea had subscribed to the creed, but not to the anathemas condemning Arius and the specific beliefs attributed to him. The council ordered them to conform, but allowed them time for compliance. Three months later Eusebius and Theognis communicated with certain Alexandrians in conflict with their bishop (either Melitians or followers of the schismatic Colluthus). Constantine declared that, by the decisions made at Nicaea, the two bishops had forfeited their sees, and he invited their congregations to select new bishops.[72] Within two years, however, the allies of Arius gained an ascendancy in the eastern church and prepared for his readmission to communion. Eusebius of Caesarea played a central role. He presided over a council at Antioch in 327 which deposed Eustathius for moral turpitude and replaced him with Paulinus of Tyre. The same council deposed Asclepas of Gaza (*Apol. c. Ar.* 45.2), and probably also another five bishops of Syria and Palestine—Euphration of Balaneae, Cymatius of Paltus, Cymatius of Gabala, Carterius of Antaradus, and Cyrus of Beroea (*Fug.* 3.3; *Hist. Ar.* 5.2).[73] All were replaced by men of whose opinions Eusebius presumably approved, and even though neither Paulinus nor his immediate successor lived long, the metropolitan see of Antioch was by 330 safely in the hands of Flaccillus.[74]

When Eustathius had been removed, it was not long before Arius, Eusebius of Nicomedia, and Theognis expressed their desire to be reunited with the catholic church. Arius and his fellow priest Euzoius submitted a statement of their beliefs: Constantine inspected it and submitted it to the Council of Nicomedia, which he had summoned to put an end to the Melitian schism. The council met in December 327 (or possibly January 328) with the emperor present. It readmitted to communion Arius and Euzoius, Eusebius and Theognis, and it laid down fresh measures for integrating the Melitian clergy into the catholic church of Egypt.[75]

Constantine endorsed the decisions of the Council of Nicomedia. But Alexander of Alexandria had declined to come, and he now refused to readmit Arius to communion with himself or the church in Egypt. He may have been willing to receive Melitian clergy back into the ecclesiastical hierarchy, but he refused any compromise of Arius and sent Athanasius to court with a letter when the emperor persisted in urging his reinstatement.[76] While Athanasius was absent, Alexander died on 17 April 328 (*Index* pr.). Athanasius hurried back to Alexandria to find some fifty-four bishops, supporters of both Alexander and Melitius, deliberating over the choice of a bishop to heal the schism. On 8 June 328, before a common decision was reached, six or seven bishops went to the Church of Dionysius and consecrated him bishop of Alexandria.[77]

III

ATHANASIUS AND CONSTANTINE: HISTORY AND APOLOGIA

ATHANASIUS WAS TO OCCUPY THE METROPOLITAN SEE OF ALEXANDRIA for nearly forty-five years, until his death on 2 May 373. But his tenure was neither unchallenged nor uninterrupted. The Melitians elected a rival bishop of their own, and Athanasius was at once compelled to defend his position. For more than seven years he was successful, but he spent the last eighteen months of the reign of Constantine in exile in Gaul. Although Athanasius was allowed to return in 337, he was soon deposed, and the Cappadocian Gregory replaced him as bishop of Alexandria from the spring of 339 until his death in June 345. Athanasius returned again from exile in 346 and performed his episcopal functions for more than a decade. But George, another Cappadocian, was appointed to replace him in 349, and in 356 Athanasius was again removed from his see: George came to Alexandria, and until December 361 he was the officially recognised bishop of the city. After George was lynched, the theological opponents of Athanasius elected a successor who laid claim to the see of Alexandria for the last dozen years of Athanasius' life—and occupied it for several years after his death.

This checkered career, which was in fact considerably more complicated than it appears in brief summary, not only depended on political and theological alignments within the Christian church in the East, but also reflected a kaleidoscope of political changes. For, between 328 and 373, the balance of political power changed constantly as a series of emperors ruled and divided the Roman Empire.

Until 337 Constantine was sole emperor of an undivided empire. From the summer of 337 until the spring of 340, his three surviving sons divided the empire into three: Constantinus, the only emperor whom Athanasius ever knew well (from his exile in Trier in 335–337), claimed a general hegemony, but controlled only Britain, Gaul, and Spain; Constantius ruled the whole of the East in an arc from Cyrenaica to Thrace; and Constans, situated between his elder brothers, administered Italy, Africa, and most of the Balkans, including Greece. In 340 Constantinus invaded the territory of Constans, and on his defeat Constans became master of all his territory. In 350 Constans was killed and the usurper Magnentius tried to take control of all that he had ruled. In this attempt he was unsuccessful, and by the late summer of 353 Constantius had reunited the whole of the empire under a single régime. To help in governing such an expanse of territory, he appointed two Caesars, Gallus, who resided in Antioch from 351 to 354, and Julian, whom he sent to Gaul in the winter of 355/6. In 360/1, no longer content with his subordinate status, Julian asserted his equality and independence, but a civil war was averted by the death of Constantius on 3 November 361. For the next twenty months, as sole emperor, Julian set out to undo the Constantinian reformation, until he died in battle in Persia. In June 363 the Christian Jovian, elected as emperor to extricate the Roman army from danger, reversed Julian's religious policies. When Jovian soon died, the brothers Valentinian and Valens became joint emperors and, in the summer of 364, partitioned the Roman Empire between them, after agreeing that neither would interfere in the affairs of the other. Athanasius died before either Valentinian or Valens, and hence before the accession of Theodosius marked the end of the Constantinian empire, under which the whole of his long episcopal career had been played out.

Athanasius' vicissitudes between 328 and 373 were throughout closely linked to these political changes. But his dealings with Constantine, who had become ruler of the East in 324 and was thus the first emperor whom he encountered as bishop, are better attested than most parts of his career after 337, largely because his *Defense against the Arians* gives so full an account. Investigation of Athanasius' career, therefore, may most appropriately begin with a juxtaposition of the details of his political struggles between 328 and 337, so far as they can be ascertained, with his selective and often misleading presentation of the same events.

The new bishop wrote at once to Constantine announcing his election, which he represented as a unanimous choice by the people of Alexandria, and he quoted a decree of the city-council as proof.[1] The shocked Melitians proceeded to elect a bishop of their own. From the start of his episcopate, therefore, Athanasius faced a war on two fronts—in Egypt, against the Melitians and a rival bishop of Alexandria who claimed his see, and outside Egypt, against the allies of Arius, who wished to complete his rehabilitation by securing his return to Alexandria.

The struggle was long and complicated. Athanasius, like Alexander before him, refused requests from both Eusebius of Nicomedia and Constantine himself that he receive Arius and his followers back into communion (*Apol. c. Ar.* 59.4–6). He also used force against the Melitians. They thereupon sent a delegation of bishops to Nicomedia to request imperial permission to meet peaceably.

Eusebius befriended the delegation at court, obtained them an audience with Constantine, and in the summer of 330 formed an alliance with them which proved powerful enough ultimately to send Athanasius into exile.[2]

Soon after this alliance had been made, and allegedly at the instigation of Eusebius, some Melitians accused Athanasius of demanding that they supply linen tunics to him, as if to do so formed part of their tax obligation to the state (*Apol. c. Ar.* 60.1/2). Probably withdrawing to the Thebaid (*Index* 2),[3] Athanasius sent two priests to court to plead his case (*Apol. c. Ar.* 60.3/4). After his return to Alexandria, as he was traveling through the Mareotis, there occurred an incident which was to haunt Athanasius for two decades. His trusted henchman, the priest Macarius, smashed the chalice and overturned the altar used by one Ischyras, a priest ordained by Colluthus, whose pretensions to be a bishop the Council of Alexandria in 324 had rejected (*Apol. c. Ar.* 63.1–4).

In the winter of 331/2, presumably summoned by the emperor (or conceivably at his own request), Athanasius appeared before Constantine to face four charges (*Festal Letter* 4.5; *Apol. c. Ar.* 60.4; *Index* 3). The Melitians reiterated the charge of extortion and alleged that Macarius had broken the chalice of Ischyras on the orders of Athanasius. It was also claimed that Athanasius had been elected bishop below the canonical age and that he had bribed Philumenus, who was *magister officiorum* at the time of the Council of Nicaea—a charge which may be connected with the fact that one of Constantine's bodyguard was accused of plotting to assassinate the emperor.[4]

Constantine listened to both sides and dismissed the charges against Athanasius, who returned to Alexandria in triumph before Easter (which fell on 2 April in 332) after writing an exultant letter from court to the Christians of Egypt (*Festal Letter* 4; *Index* 3). Soon afterward he visited the Libyan Pentapolis (*Index* 4), probably to ensure that Arius gained no foothold there. The intervention provoked Arius into committing some act of indiscretion which was construed as schism and infuriated the emperor, who denounced him in a long and abusive letter designed for publication.[5]

Arius' allies continued to try to dislodge the bishop of Alexandria. The Melitians wrote to Constantine repeating the charge that Athanasius had ordered Macarius to break the chalice of Ischyras, and they now added the more serious charge that he had arranged the murder of Arsenius, the bishop of Hypsele (*Apol. c. Ar.* 63.4). In the spring of 334, the emperor instructed his half-brother Dalmatius, who was residing at Antioch and administering the East with the title of *censor,* to investigate the charge of murder (*Apol. c. Ar.* 65.1) and to bring the matter before a council of bishops which was to meet at Caesarea in Palestine.[6] Eusebius of Nicomedia traveled to Syria for the projected council (*Apol. c. Ar.* 65.4), and the Melitians in Egypt made preparations.[7] Athanasius, however, refused to attend. Instead, having traced Arsenius and discovered him alive and in hiding at Tyre, he wrote to the emperor, who canceled the Council of Caesarea and reaffirmed his confidence in Athanasius (*Apol. c. Ar.* 65.3/4, 68).

The enemies of Athanasius soon made yet another attempt to unseat him. Eusebius of Nicomedia persuaded the followers of Melitius, Colluthus, and Arius to write a joint letter to Constantine making several charges against Athanasius, including new allegations that he had used violence to secure compliance with his wishes and to coerce opposition within Egypt. Constantine ordered a council of bishops to meet in Tyre to put an end to the protracted dispute. The *comes* Flavius Dionysius, a former governor of Syria, was to supervise the conduct of the council and to keep order, and all interested parties were to attend, whether they wished to do so or not.[8]

When the council opened, probably under the presidency of Flacillus, the bishop of Antioch,[9] his accusers depicted Athanasius as an overbearing prelate who systematically employed violence in the affairs of the church. Callinicus, the Melitian bishop of Pelusium, and Ischyras repeated the charge that Athanasius had ordered a chalice to be smashed and a bishop's throne destroyed. In addition, they asserted, Athanasius had wronged both their persons. He had often imprisoned Ischyras, and he had once persuaded the prefect Hyginus to imprison him with a false accusation of throwing stones at the emperor's image. He had deposed Callinicus, who was undoubtedly a bishop of the catholic church since he had been in communion with Alexander of Alexandria; had replaced him with the priest Marcus, simply because Callinicus refused to communicate with him until he could clear himself of the suspicion of breaking the chalice; and had arranged for Callinicus to be arrested by soldiers, tortured, and tried. Five other Melitian bishops (Euplus, Pachomius, Isaac, Achilleus, and Hermaeon) also complained of violence against their persons: having obtained election as bishop by trickery, Athanasius had assaulted and imprisoned them for their honest belief that his election was invalid.[10] The Melitians justified their conduct concerning Arsenius on the grounds that the charge of murder, though in fact mistaken, was a reasonable deduction from the known facts that Plusianus, a bishop under Athanasius and doubtless acting on his orders, had burned Arsenius' house, beaten Arsenius himself, and kept him bound in a hut. The Melitians contended that when Arsenius then disappeared, it was reasonable to conclude that he had been murdered on Athanasius' instructions.[11]

Athanasius and his Egyptian supporters contested the charges. The council, therefore, decided to send a commission of enquiry to the Mareotis. Its composition inevitably produced bitter controversy. The majority chose six members, each of whom the Egyptian bishops at the council rejected as biased—Theognis of Nicaea, Maris of Chalcedon, Theodorus of Heraclea, Macedonius of Mopsuestia, and two young Pannonian bishops, Ursacius of Singidunum and Valens of Mursa, whom Athanasius later alleged to have received their first instruction in the Christian faith from Arius, presumably while he was in exile in Illyricum c. 330 (*Letter to the Bishops of Egypt and Libya* 7). Despite a caution from Dionysius to proceed with fairness, the majority persisted. The commission took Ischyras and went to Egypt. Here too written protests were registered relating to the conduct of the commission and to the facts of the case (*Apol. c. Ar.* 73.2–81.2).

While the commission was conducting its investigation in Egypt, the Council of Tyre adjourned to Jerusalem, where the same bishops dedicated the magnificent new Church of the Holy Sepulchre in mid-September and once again admitted Arius to communion as a holder of orthodox theological views.[12] They then returned to Tyre and completed their business. The commission of enquiry produced a summary of their findings. They complained that Athanasius had removed potential witnesses, but they found the charge that Macarius had broken the chalice of Ischyras on his orders to be sustained by adequate and convincing evidence. The council accepted the report and deposed Athanasius, who had already departed from Tyre (*Apol. c. Ar.* 82.1; *Apol. ad Const.* 1.3)—on a raft, secretly and under cover of darkness in order to evade the soldiers guarding the harbor.[13]

The grounds stated for Athanasius' deposition comprised four counts: first, his flight betrayed his guilt; second, his refusal to present himself at Caesarea in 334 showed contempt for both emperor and church councils; third, he had brought a gang of ruffians to Tyre, who disrupted the business of the council while he abused his fellow bishops; and fourth, the commission sent to Egypt had found the charge of breaking the chalice abundantly proven.[14] The council received the Melitians into communion, reiterated the orthodoxy of Arius, and appointed a new bishop of Alexandria (*Hist. Ar.* 50.2). Unfortunately, no evidence reports his name. He might conceivably have been Pistus, who had long been associated with Arius,[15] or else John Archaph, the Melitian leader since the death of Melitius and bishop of Memphis. However, if either of these men had in fact been nominated by the council, Athanasius would surely somewhere have let slip some jibe about the abortive and hence discreditable nomination. It is more probable, therefore, that Athanasius was replaced by Heraiscus, whom a papyrus attests as the Melitian bishop of Alexandria in the summer of 335[16]— and about whose very existence Athanasius preserves a studied silence in all his writings.

Athanasius' enemies could guess his destination. Six leading bishops, therefore, took the decisions of the council to Constantinople in person—Eusebius of Nicomedia, Theognis of Nicaea, Patrophilus of Scythopolis, Eusebius of Caesarea, Ursacius of Singidunum, and Valens of Mursa (*Apol. c. Ar.* 87.1). They arrived in the imperial capital to find that the emperor had already, in effect, annulled their carefully planned condemnation and deposition of Athanasius.[17]

Athanasius arrived in Constantinople on 30 October (*Index* 8). Constantine happened to be absent from the city. As the emperor returned on 6 November, Athanasius accosted him, informed him that his enemies were again attempting to disgrace him on false charges, and begged to be allowed to confront them in his presence. Constantine granted the request and summoned the bishops at Tyre to come to court at once so that the case of Athanasius could be decided fairly. He did not yet know (he wrote) what the council might have decreed, but he suspected that hostility had obscured the truth, and he informed the bishops that they needed to prove their impartiality (*Apol. c. Ar.* 86.2–12): he thus, by implication, rendered null and void the condemnation which the Council of Tyre had pronounced against Athanasius after his departure.

Within a few hours after Athanasius had accosted Constantine and persuaded him to write this letter, Eusebius of Nicomedia and his five companions arrived from Tyre, as did five Egyptian bishops (*Apol. c. Ar.* 87.1/2). The enemies of Athanasius could see that there was now little point in presenting the decisions of the council to an emperor who had disallowed them in advance. A new charge was needed. Eusebius accused Athanasius of treasonably threatening to prevent the grain ships from sailing from Alexandria to Constantinople. Constantine demanded an answer to the new charge, uttering threats. Athanasius bewailed and denounced the slander: how could a private citizen who was a poor man be so powerful? Eusebius swore that the bishop of Alexandria was rich, influential, and unscrupulous (*Apol. c. Ar.* 9.3/4). He doubtless also reminded Constantine of Athanasius' long intransigence toward Arius, whose orthodoxy the Council of Jerusalem had recently reaffirmed. When Athanasius lost his temper and warned Constantine that God would ultimately judge between them, the emperor sent him to Trier.[18] He did not, however, depose him from his see or formally try him: he merely suspended him from his duties pending further investigation.[19] Athanasius left Constantinople for Trier on 7 November (*Index* 8) still technically bishop of Alexandria.

The exile of Athanasius in 335 was not the normal exile imposed by an emperor on a bishop who had been condemned and deposed by a church council.[20] Although Constantine gave the decisions of councils of bishops legal force, forbidding provincial governors to countermand them, on the grounds that the priests of God were more trustworthy than any magistrate,[21] and thereby bound himself too to accept the decisions of councils, he nevertheless reserved to himself the right to decide whether a particular gathering of bishops was a properly constituted council whose decisions were to be regarded as divinely inspired. Moreover, he both claimed and exercised the right to summon a council of bishops, to refer matters to it, and to define its agenda. Thus he felt himself empowered to acquit a bishop of any criminal charges made against him, but not to convict him: the conviction and consequent deposition of a bishop were the exclusive right and prerogative of a council of his peers. Constantine's treatment of Athanasius in 331/2 and 333/4 falls into this pattern precisely. In 331/2 he summoned Athanasius to court, heard him at Psammathia, and dismissed the charges against him. Under no circumstances, however, would the emperor have pronounced him guilty and deposed him. Had he decided that there was a *prima facie* case against Athanasius, he would have convened a council of bishops to try him—as in fact he did in 333/4 when he first instructed the *censor* Dalmatius to investigate the charge that he had ordered the murder of Arsenius, then summoned a council of bishops to meet in Caesarea, but dissolved the council as soon as he was convinced of Athanasius' innocence. On 6 November 335 Constantine disallowed the verdict of the Council of Tyre, which had not reached him, on the grounds that the council had not acted in accordance with the normal canons of fairness and impartiality—and the subsequent banishment of Athanasius to Gaul did not alter that ruling at all.

Twenty years later Athanasius provided a tendentious, but not totally misleading, description of the situation during his first exile:

> As a result of slander by the Eusebians,[22] [Constantine] sent the bishop to Gaul temporarily on account of the savage hostility of those who were plotting against him—this the blessed Constantinus, the present emperor's brother, made clear after the death of his father, as is shown by his letters—but he was not persuaded to send the Eusebians the bishop whom they themselves wanted: on the contrary, he both prevented them though they wished [to send one] and restrained them with a terrible threat when they attempted [to do so]. (*Hist. Ar.* 50.2)

Although the bishops at Tyre had named a successor to Athanasius, the emperor refused to accept the validity of this appointment or to install the designated successor in Alexandria (*Apol. c. Ar.* 29.3). Such actions imply that Constantine considered the deposition of Athanasius to be null and void.

The anomalous situation persisted as long as the emperor lived. Despite riots, despite a request from the monk Antony, Constantine refused to recall Athanasius. In letters to the church of Alexandria and to Antony, he justified his refusal by describing Athanasius as a troublemaker whose condemnation by a council of bishops he could not simply set aside at his own whim. At the same time, however, in a show of evenhandedness, he checked the Melitians when they tried to occupy the places to which the Council of Tyre had given them title, and he exiled John Archaph.[23] Until Constantine died, Athanasius' status remained highly ambiguous. The decisions of the Council of Tyre had no legal force: therefore Athanasius was still the rightful bishop of Alexandria. On the other hand, the emperor had exiled him to Gaul, where he was compelled to remain until the emperor should decree otherwise.

The account which Athanasius gives of his career as bishop from 328 to 335 in his *Defense against the Arians* is not, and was not intended to be, complete and straightforward. It does, however, purport to be a truthful account, and it quotes a plethora of documents to illustrate the esteem in which Constantine held Athanasius and the dishonesty of the enemies who attacked him. Although Athanasius probably composed the *Defense against the Arians* in approximately its present form in 349, he had compiled the dossier of documents relating to his career between 328 and 335 no later than 338, and had almost certainly drafted the extant account of these years before the summer of 341.[24] Its historical value is immense, for without the *Defense against the Arians* the true course of Athanasius' dealings with Constantine could never be reconstructed. Nonetheless, it is both necessary and instructive to ask how Athanasius selected the facts and marshaled the documents in order to present himself in a favorable light.

The introduction is compressed and obscure. Athanasius passes rapidly from the origin of the Melitian schism (306) to the alliance between Eusebius of Nicomedia and the Melitians (in 330). He is at pains to conceal the fact that the Council of Nicomedia in December 327 pronounced Arius orthodox and readmitted him to communion. A covert allusion to that council has nonetheless escaped his vigilance. He complains:

> Five months had not yet passed, and blessed Alexander died; but the Melitians, who ought to have remained quiet and to have been grateful that they had been received back at all, like dogs unable to forget their vomit, began again to disturb the churches. (59.3)

What are these 'five months'? Either a lacuna must be postulated in an otherwise sound text, or the five months represent the period between the Council of Nicomedia in the winter of 327/8 and the contest over who should be elected bishop of Alexandria after the death of Alexander on 17 April 328.[25] Athanasius wishes to establish the character of each of his two groups of adversaries at the outset. Melitius was a schismatic whom Peter had deposed in a council of Egyptian bishops for many misdemeanors, including sacrifice during persecution (59.1). Nevertheless, the ecumenical council at Nicaea received the followers of Melitius back into communion at the same time as it definitively branded Arius and his followers as heretics (59.3). Athanasius, therefore, claims that he had been prepared to accept the Melitians until they allied themselves to the Arians, with whom no possibility of compromise existed (59.4/5). Throughout his career Athanasius proclaimed a single simple principle when dealing with those whom he considered Arians: 'the heresy which attacks Christ has no communion with the catholic church' (60.1).

Athanasius is even briefer on the accusations against him in 330/1 and 331/2. The accusations are described merely to introduce two letters of Constantine: the first imperial letter, 'condemning Ision [who was one of the accusers] and summoning me to appear before him,' has unfortunately dropped out of the text as transmitted in the manuscripts (60.3), but the second, written in 332, survives in full (61/2). Constantine wrote to the congregation of the catholic church in Alexandria urging them to love one another and to put aside all hatreds. He bitterly denounced those who were disturbing the peace of God's people (that is, the Melitians). Although the wicked have wasted the emperor's time and deserve to be expelled from the church, they have not prevailed against the bishop of Alexandria. Athanasius, so the emperor asserts as his firm conviction, is truly a man of God.

Athanasius now turns to the troubling matter of the broken chalice (63/4). The Melitians had made no headway in the Mareotis and all the churches were at peace, when a certain Ischyras, a known malefactor, tried to lead his village astray by pretending to be a priest. The properly ordained priest of the place informed Athanasius, who was visiting the area, and he sent the priest Macarius with him to summon Ischyras. The two of them found Ischyras lying sick and instructed his father to tell him to desist from doing what had been reported to them. When Ischyras recovered, he joined the Melitians, and they communicated with the Eusebians, who then concocted the story that Macarius had broken a sacred chalice together with the story that Arsenius, whom they themselves were hiding, had been murdered on Athanasius' orders. Ischyras, who was not a priest at all, came to Athanasius in distress at the calumnies invented by the Melitians and submitted an apology in writing. It deserves to be quoted in full:

> To blessed *papa* Athanasius, Ischyras greets you in the Lord.
>
> When I approached you, lord bishop, wishing to belong to the church, you reproached me for what I had said before, as if I had taken this step of my own volition: for this reason, I present to you in writing this defense, so that you can know that I did so because violence had been done to me and blows laid upon me by Isaac, Heraclides, Isaac of Letopolis, and those with them. Taking God as my witness for this, I humbly submit that I know full well that you did none of the things which they have alleged. For neither did any breaking of a chalice occur nor did an overturning of the holy table take place, but they, by using violence on me for this purpose, compelled me to make all these allegations. I have made this defense of myself to you and have handed it over to you in writing, choosing and claiming my right to be one of those who gather together under your authority. I pray that you flourish in the Lord. (64.1/2)

Ischyras presented his declaration to Athanasius in the presence of six priests from different villages in the Mareotis, three deacons from Alexandria, and three from the Mareotis (64.3). It is a very significant document. Given Ischyras' persistence in his accusation over many years, this retraction is much more likely to have been obtained by violence than the original complaint against Athanasius.[26] One internal feature appears to stamp it as undoubtedly fraudulent. Ischyras here proclaims that no cup was smashed, no altar overturned. Now Athanasius' main line of defense against this charge of sacrilege was to argue that, since Ischyras was not a properly ordained priest, his hut cannot have contained either a consecrated chalice or an altar; that the presence of a catechumen at the time of the alleged assault proved that the eucharist was not being celebrated; and that Ischyras himself was so ill that he was confined to bed and hence unable to conduct divine service at the relevant time.[27] The implication of this line of defense is that Ischyras was assaulted, even if the assault did not technically involve sacrilege.

Another line of reasoning also leads to the conclusion that an assault did in fact occur. Ischyras was a follower of Colluthus, who styled himself a bishop and may have been a dissident Melitian (12.1, 76.3),[28] and he was acting as priest of a conventicle of Colluthians in the Mareotis close to Alexandria. Athanasius himself admits that when he heard of Ischyras as he was touring the Mareotis, he sent the priest Macarius to deal with him (63.3): it must be suspected that Macarius was not merely instructed to summon Ischyras, as Athanasius claims, but to take appropriate measures—and hence that the Melitians were in substance correct to assert that, when Macarius broke up a service conducted by Ischyras, he did so on Athanasius' orders.

Athanasius deals next with the charge that he murdered Arsenius. Constantine ordered the *censor* Dalmatius to investigate, but the agents of Athanasius discovered Arsenius and produced him before Paul, the bishop of Tyre. Constantine then stopped 'the court of the *censor*' (which must be identical with the abortive Council of Caesarea in 334, which Athanasius nowhere mentions), and ordered Eusebius and his accomplices, who were on their way to the East, to return (65.1–4). Athanasius quotes the full text of five letters:

(1) Alexander of Thessalonica to Athanasius congratulating him on the exposure of the plot of John Archaph;
(2) Pinnes, priest of the monastery of Ptemenkurkis in the Antaeopolite nome, to John warning him that the agents of Athanasius have discovered that Arsenius is alive and asking him not to accuse Athanasius;
(3) Constantine to Athanasius expressing indignation at the charges brought by the 'perverse and lawless Melitians' and urging him to publish this vindication of himself;
(4) Arsenius to Athanasius submitting to his authority and requesting to be admitted to communion with the catholic church;
(5) Constantine to John accepting his reconciliation with Athanasius and inviting him to come to court. (66–70)

The Council of Tyre receives even more lavish treatment. That was necessary because, when successive Councils of Antioch between 338 and 341 reiterated the earlier verdict, they appealed to the findings of the commission of enquiry which visited the Mareotis in September 335 as having established that Athanasius was indeed guilty of sacrilege because Macarius had broken the chalice of Ischyras on his orders.[29] Athanasius needed to discredit the Council of Tyre, not because its verdict was the legal basis of his exile in either 335 or 339, but lest Christians everywhere regard the sacrilege of which the Council of Tyre found him guilty as automatically disqualifying him from discharging the functions of a bishop. Since Ischyras became a bishop in the Mareotis and in that capacity set his name to yet another condemnation of Athanasius in 343,[30] bare denial of the crime would not suffice. Athanasius needed to discredit the process by which he had been found guilty.

Athanasius depicts the Council of Tyre as conducted with violence and by a secular official. The *comes* Dionysius was sent with a bodyguard for the Eusebians, Macarius was sent to Tyre bound and in military custody, and Athanasius was compelled to attend and dragged about by soldiers (71.1/2, 72.1, 82.1). When the council met, the *comes* presided, the Melitians accused, and the Arians sat in judgement: Athanasius, therefore, withdrew from them 'as from an assembly of treacherous men' (Jeremiah 9.2). To bear out his assertion that the Council of Tyre proceeded improperly, Athanasius quotes an array of documents to prove each of the central points:

(1) A list of his clergy which Melitius submitted to Alexander.[31] Since this list does not contain the name of Ischyras, he cannot have been a priest: therefore Athanasius' accuser ought never to have received a hearing—as Athanasius pointed out at the time (72.6).

(2) A submission made by sixteen priests and five deacons of the church of Alexandria to the commission of enquiry (73). Since the commission brought with them Ischyras, but not Macarius or Athanasius, the clergy of Alexandria requested to be present during their investigations: by refusing this request, the commissioners have revealed their partiality, and the clergy loyal to Athanasius are entering a protest in order to contest their findings before a future 'genuine council.'

(3) A letter of the clergy of the Mareotis (fifteen priests and fifteen deacons) to the Council of Tyre (74/5). The clergy explain that Ischyras was certainly not a priest: he claimed to have been ordained by Colluthus, but a council held at Alexandria in the presence of Ossius of Corduba had declared his ordination invalid. The charges are all fraudulent, since no chalice was broken, no altar overturned either by Athanasius himself or by any of his associates, and the commissioners are proceeding improperly, obtaining evidence against Athanasius only because Philagrius, the prefect of Egypt, is threatening witnesses with violence.

(4) A submission of the same, dated 8 September 335, to Philagrius, the prefect of Egypt; Flavius Palladius, *curiosus palatinus ducenarius;* and Flavius Antoninus, *biarchus centenarius* of the praetorian prefects (76). The clergy of the Mareotis assert on oath that Ischyras is no priest, that he has no church, and that no chalice was broken, and they ask the addressees to forward their declaration to the emperor.

(5) A letter of the bishops of Egypt to the whole council (77). Athanasius' supporters claim that the council is dominated by his enemies, that their own testimony is unjustifiably rejected, and that the proposed membership of the commission of enquiry is improper.

(6) A letter of the same forty-eight bishops to Flavius Dionysius, repeating the

same complaints and requesting him to intervene (78).

(7) A letter in the name of all the bishops of the catholic church present in Tyre to Dionysius asking for the case of Athanasius to be referred to the emperor (79).

(8) A letter of Alexander of Thessalonica to Dionysius objecting to the membership of the commission of enquiry (80).

(9) A letter of Dionysius to Eusebius and his associates (81: quoted only in part). Dionysius informs the bishops of the protests by Athanasius and Alexander and reminds them of his earlier advice that members of the commission be chosen by unanimous vote.

One vital document is missing. The full minutes of the interrogations which the commissioners conducted would show how, though the commissioners prompted, though the prefect uttered threats, though soldiers brandished drawn swords, witnesses nevertheless testified that Ischyras was lying ill at the time of the alleged assault, that the charges against Athanasius were false. The enemies of Athanasius accordingly suppressed the minutes. To no avail, since Rufus, who made the record, can vouch for their contents. Extracts, however, were later sent to Julius, the bishop of Rome, and he transmitted them to Athanasius, whose enemies are now furious because he obtained and read what they wished to conceal (83).

Athanasius has mentioned his flight from Tyre. Before he continues his story, he digresses to denounce the bishops who repaired from Tyre to Jerusalem (in fact, on the emperor's pressing invitation) and readmitted Arius to communion. He quotes the beginning of their synodical letter to show how those who condemned him were prepared to overturn the decisions of the 'ecumenical council' (84). And he explains how Ischyras was set up as a bishop in the Mareotis, quoting a letter of the *catholicus* to the *exactor* ordering that a church be built for him. It was a reward for making his false accusation (85).

To conclude, Athanasius returns to himself. He quotes the letter in which Constantine angrily summoned the bishops from Tyre, summarises the interview in which the emperor exiled him to Gaul, and quotes the letter of 17 June 337 in which Constantinus Caesar commended him to the Christians of Alexandria (86/7). By a singular coincidence, the letter of 6 November 335 survives in two versions, for the text given by Athanasius not only shows minor divergences of wording from the version which Gelasius of Cyzicus reproduces, but also lacks phrases and even sections which Gelasius quotes.[32] What is the explanation for the discrepancies? On general grounds, it might seem obvious that it would have been foolish and risky for Athanasius to tamper with a document which many of his contemporaries had seen, and hence that Gelasius, who was writing c. 475, must have interpolated and rewritten the genuine text preserved by Athanasius.[33] That diagnosis will not account for the actual variants. Moreover, since the letter was overtaken by events very soon after its composition (probably within twenty-four hours), it is unwise to assume that it circulated at all widely until the publication of the *Defense against the Arians* gave it currency.

The passages which stand in Gelasius alone contain some genuinely Constantinian phrases which recur in other speeches or letters of the emperor,[34] and the minor variants in at least one passage betray clear evidence that Athanasius has tampered with the text, if only at a superficial level. Gelasius' Constantine writes:

As I was entering, after an imperial progress, our eponymous and all-fortunate Constantinople...

The corresponding passage in Athanasius reads:

As I set foot in our eponymous and all-fortunate *patria* of Constantinople (he happened at the time to be riding a horse)...

Despite modern editors who print the parenthesis as if it were part of Constantine's letter,[35] the words 'he happened at the time to be riding a horse' clearly cannot have stood in the original document, but must be an editorial addition by Athanasius. More important, since Constantine's *patria* was in the Balkans, he is not likely to have called his new city of Constantinople his *patria* without making the metaphor or conceit obvious.[36] Furthermore, the imperial *processus* is independently attested: Constantine was at Nicopolis on 23 October 335,[37] and Athanasius had been in the capital since 30 October waiting for his return (*Index* 8). On technical grounds, therefore, Gelasius deserves the preference in this passage.[38]

The fact that Athanasius omits the concluding sentence in Gelasius need have no sinister significance: some of the documents quoted in the *Defense against the Arians* are curtailed, and Athanasius could have left it out without any imputation of bad faith.[39] But a long section in the middle of the letter offers substantive divergences which cannot so easily be explained away. The text in Athanasius offers a brief account of the exchange which ensued after the bishop accosted the emperor:

So I neither spoke to him at that moment of time nor admitted him to conversation. But as he continued to ask to be heard, while I refused and almost ordered him to be driven away, with greater freedom he claimed that he wanted nothing else from us except your arrival, so that he could lament what he has suffered out of necessity with you present. (86.8)

Gelasius presents an Athanasius who is 'in grief and mourning' when he confronts Constantine:

We saw the man so humbled and cast down that we fell into unutterable pity for him when we realised that he was that Athanasius, the holy sight

---

31

of whom is sufficient to compel even the pagans to worship the God of the universe.

The Constantine of Gelasius refers in angry but inexplicit language to his summons to Athanasius in 331 and his dismissal of the charges against him then and continues:

> But now a second time, speaking more freely, he cries out that a second assault has been made on him worse than the first, requesting nothing of us except your arrival to us, which he has requested so that he can lament what he has suffered out of necessity with you present.[40]

The text quoted by Gelasius does not mince words when describing the bishop's pitiable condition when he accosted the emperor or the violence of his asseverations. In Athanasius' version of the letter, the sharp phrases are softened and made vaguer. It may be concluded that Athanasius has suppressed and altered phrases and clauses which he found painful to recall or impolitic to reproduce.[41]

'Violence begets violence.' The chance find of a papyrus undoes much of Athanasius' pleading on his own behalf. A private letter survives, never intended for publication, from the Melitian Callistus in Alexandria to two priests at a Melitian monastery in the Upper Cynopolite nome.[42] On 20 May 335 (Callistus relates) the bishop of Letopolis came to dine in the camp with the bishop Heraiscus, who is attested only here, but whom the context identifies as the Melitian bishop of Alexandria.[43] Supporters of Athanasius came to seize Heraiscus and his guests, but they were hidden by soldiers in their living quarters. The supporters of Athanasius, however, came across four Melitian monks, whom they beat and almost killed. They then raided the hospice where the Melitians from outside Alexandria were lodging, and kidnapped the five whom they found there until the *praepositus* of the camp ordered their release. The *praepositus* apologised to Heraiscus for the attack, in which soldiers of the *dux* and of the camp had participated, but he did not allow the Melitians to see their bishop nor the bishop to leave the camp. It was Athanasius' policy to send bishops who would support him to Tyre, but to detain his opponents in Alexandria, by force if necessary. He shut one bishop in the meat-market, a priest in the prison of the camp, and a deacon in the main prison of the city. Besides these explicitly reported facts, the letter seems to assume that Heraiscus himself had for some time not been at liberty to leave the camp.

Despite his protestations of innocence, Athanasius exercised power and protected his position in Alexandria by the systematic use of violence and intimidation.[44] The papyrus of 335 documents in detail one small episode in which he coerced his opponents and used violence in an attempt to prevent them from attending a church council. That was not an isolated misdemeanor, but a typical example of the means by which bishops of Alexandria maintained their power in the Christian Roman Empire. If the violence of Athanasius leaves fewer traces in the surviving sources than similar behavior by later bishops of Alexandria like Theophilus, Cyril, and Dioscorus, the reason is not that he exercised power in a different way, but that he exercised it more efficiently and that he was successful in presenting himself to posterity as an innocent in power, as an honest, sincere, and straightforward 'man of God.'

IV

A JOURNEY TO CAPPADOCIA

CONSTANTINE DIED ON 22 MAY 337. WITHIN FOUR WEEKS OF HIS death, an imperial ukase restored all exiled bishops to their sees. The order was issued in the name of all the emperors (presumably including the Caesar Dalmatius, as well as the three sons of Constantine), but Constantius had no part in undoing his father's policies. The initiative belonged to Constantinus, though he doubtless acted on the advice of the exiled bishop of Alexandria, who had been resident in his capital of Trier since the winter of 335/6.

Athanasius refers to the restoration of the exiled bishops as a joint action of Constantinus, Constantius, and Constans (*Hist. Ar.* 8.1). Yet he nowhere quotes the formal act which had legal force. Instead he quotes a private letter of recommendation which Constantinus wrote in his name alone on 17 June 337 'to the people of the catholic church of the city of Alexandria.' Athanasius (the letter recalled) had been sent to Gaul as a temporary measure and partly for his own safety. Constantine had always intended to restore the bishop to his proper place, but death prevented him from fulfilling his intention. His son and successor, therefore, gave effect to his wishes and was sending the great man back to his welcoming flock (*Apol. c. Ar.* 87.4–7; *Hist. Ar.* 8.2).

Athanasius left Trier at once. But he did not travel to Alexandria by the quickest or most direct route. There was political and ecclesiastical business to perform on the way. Constantius must be conciliated, or at least mollified, and Athanasius had an audience with him at Viminacium in the province of Moesia Superior (*Apol. ad Const.* 5.2). The outcome of the interview is unknown; indeed, the bare fact of its occurrence is known only because Athanasius let slip a single passing allusion to it many years later. The historical context, however, is clear.

Constantius was on his way from Constantinople to confer with his brothers in Pannonia.[1] The three sons of Constantine were proclaimed Augusti on 9 Sep-

---

34

tember 337, presumably when they met together: shortly before that date Dalmatius, their colleague as Caesar, and all other possible dynastic rivals had been killed, most of them in Constantinople, with Constantius conniving at or at least not preventing their slaughter.[2] When he met Athanasius, therefore, Constantius had weightier matters on his mind than ecclesiastical politics. The empire, divided in 335 into four parts, one for each of the Caesars, now needed to be reallocated between the three sons of Constantine. In the event, it was Constans, strategically situated between his older brothers, who emerged with a large increase of territory.[3] Constantinus claimed primacy in the new imperial college, but even if his two younger brothers acknowledged his pre-eminence (which is not at all certain), it can have represented little more than an empty formality.[4] Constantius acquired the diocese of Thraciae, but soon the Persian war, which his father had bequeathed him, required his constant attention. For a dozen years from 338, Constantius prosecuted war on the eastern frontier: Antioch was his principal residence, and he usually spent his winters in Syria, his summers on campaign in Mesopotamia.[5] In 337, however, before he returned to Syria—and perhaps even before he conferred with his brothers—another military emergency had claimed Constantius' attention. Constantine had reconquered territory north of the Danube, originally annexed by Trajan, but abandoned during the tumultuous years of the mid–third century.[6] Soon after his death these conquests were again overrun, even though Constantius campaigned against the Sarmatians, apparently in 337, and was believed by loyal subjects to have won a victory over them.[7]

Athanasius was keenly aware of Constantius' pressing political and military preoccupations, and he made full use of his opportunity. Some years later his enemies at the Council of Serdica described his activities during the summer of 337 with a vivid sense of outrage:

> He reached Alexandria from Gaul after a very long time . . . Throughout the whole of his return journey he overturned churches, restored condemned bishops, promised to some hope of returning to their sees, and consecrated unbelievers as bishops by means of fisticuffs and murder by pagans, even though the existing bishops were alive and remained guiltless [of any crime]. He paid no respect to the laws and pinned all on desperation, so that he seized the churches of Alexandria by force, by murder, by war.[8]

The sober facts behind this diatribe are that Athanasius aided his friends and opposed his enemies in a context of violence. Athanasius himself later unwittingly identified one of the episodes about which complaint was made. Alexander, the aged bishop of Constantinople, who had held the see of Byzantium, later Constantinople, for twenty-three years, died in the summer of 337.[9] Athanasius was in Constantinople shortly after the disputed election which followed Alexander's death. The Christians of the imperial capital were almost evenly divided between those who fervently upheld the Nicene formula and those who were sympathetic to the views of Arius: the former supported Paul, a young priest who had recently come to the city; the latter the elderly Macedonius, who had long been a deacon of their church. Alexander left a document comparing the two men, in which he declared a strong preference for Paul as a teacher and a virtuous man. Paul was duly elected and consecrated. Since the supporters of Paul did not wait for their choice to be ratified by the bishops of adjacent sees, as custom demanded, it seems probable *a priori* that Athanasius was one of the required trio of bishops who consecrated Paul as bishop of Constantinople. When Constantius returned from Pannonia, he was enraged at the election and had it overturned. A council of bishops from the surrounding provinces deposed Paul and replaced him with Eusebius of Nicomedia, even though Macedonius, whom Paul had advanced to the priesthood, supported his bishop (*Hist. Ar.* 7.1).[10]

By this juncture Athanasius had left the imperial capital. He traveled posthaste, but found time to intervene in ecclesiastical matters in Syria, Phoenice, and Palestine.[11] The beneficiaries of his assistance (it may be conjectured) included Asclepas, the bishop of Gaza: he had been exiled in 326, he was now entitled to return to his see, and he subsequently joined Athanasius in exile in Rome. Athanasius entered Alexandria again on 23 November 337 (*Index* 10).[12] His enemies had perhaps already taken the first steps toward deposing him and installing a successor, for a council of bishops met during the winter of 337/8, probably in Antioch while Constantius was in the city,[13] to depose Athanasius and name a new bishop of Alexandria.

The central and unshakeable testimony for the abortive attempt to depose Athanasius in the winter of 337/8 is provided by the synodical letter of a council of bishops held in Alexandria to exonerate him—a council sometimes unhappily misdated to 339.[14] This council of bishops from the Egyptian provinces met in the Egyptian capital in 338 and declared Athanasius innocent of the charges which his enemies had brought against him. In order to vindicate himself, Athanasius later quoted the synodical letter of this council, which indicates, at least in outline, the dangers which beset him after his return from exile (*Apol. c. Ar.* 3–19).

The party of Eusebius (so they are styled) convened a council of bishops (3.2). Since the Alexandrian letter voices no complaint about the membership of the council at Antioch, it was probably a large and representative conclave of bishops from throughout the eastern provinces. The charges against Athanasius included both old ones, which the Council of Tyre had investigated, and new ones relating to Athanasius' behavior during and after his return from the West. The council found Athanasius guilty on at least some grave counts, deposed him from his see, and appointed Pistus to replace him as bishop of Alexandria (*Ep. enc.* 6.1). A letter, to which the assembled bishops appended their names, then communicated the decisions of the council to other bishops and to each of the three emperors (*Apol. c. Ar.* 3.5–7, 19.4/5).

The council resuscitated the old suspicion that Athanasius' election in 328 was invalid. The synodical letter complained that

> after the death of the bishop Alexander, when a certain few made mention of the name of Athanasius, six or seven bishops elected him secretly and *sub rosa.* (6.4)[15]

But that need not have been a formal charge in 338. The formal grounds for the deposition of Athanasius probably comprised three counts. First, Athanasius had ordered the priest Macarius to break the chalice of Ischyras and to overturn his altar (11.1–4). This charge had been thoroughly investigated by the Council of Tyre: that council sent a commission of enquiry to the Mareotis; the commission collected evidence on the spot and found the allegations to be proven (17.6). Second, Athanasius was responsible for deaths and murders in Alexandria after his return (3.5–5.5). And third, he had sold grain supplied by Constantine for the maintenance of widows in Egypt, appropriating the proceeds for his own pocket (18.2).

Athanasius did not of course intend to accept the verdict of a hostile council: he sought vindication from a friendly one. Eighty bishops from the Egyptian provinces met in Alexandria. Athanasius had presumably summoned them as soon as he heard that his enemies were convening a council to try him, but it met after Constantius had written to him endorsing the findings of the Council of Antioch (18.2). Although no source attests the fact, Athanasius must have taken the synodical letter which vindicated him to present to the emperor. It was in fact his own composition, drawing on the dossier of documents which his *Defense against the Arians* was later to quote in full.[16]

The bishops at Alexandria, in their letter addressed 'to the bishops of the catholic church everywhere,' complain that the council which has deposed Athanasius is no council of the church, but a conspiracy designed to compass his death by means of imperial anger (3). Athanasius has killed no one, has handed no one over to the executioner, has caused no one imprisonment or exile. Sentence was passed on the men in question by the prefect of Egypt while Athanasius was still in Syria (5.2–4). Athanasius' enemies are heretics (5.5–6.2), and their leader, Eusebius, not only has clearly broken the law of the church by abandoning the see of Berytus for Nicomedia and now Nicomedia for another see (in fact, Constantinople), but was also rightly deprived of his status as bishop in 325 for fomenting heresy (6.6–7.3). How can such men presume to sit in judgement on Athanasius? The accusations against him are a plot by Arian madmen.

The longest section of the letter goes over charges made at the Council of Tyre (11–17). The allegation that Athanasius murdered Arsenius also receives prominence (8.4/5, 9.5–10.3). Since Arsenius was still alive, he could serve as an example of how baseless the charges against Athanasius were. The chalice of Ischyras receives a much longer discussion. Like the later *Defense against the Arians,* the letter of the Council of Alexandria in 338 argues that Athanasius cannot have ordered Macarius to break a holy chalice belonging to Ischyras or to overturn his altar, because Ischyras was a follower of Colluthus, not a validly ordained priest, and because the building where he claimed to celebrate the sacraments was not a church. The central contention, however, is less that the charges made in 335 against Athanasius were false than that the Council of Tyre was improperly constituted, proceeded improperly, and rendered an improper verdict. The commission of enquiry was biased, the bishops of Egypt in 335 rejected its members as Arians and enemies of Athanasius, and it conducted its enquiry in an illegal manner. Among the council's members was Eusebius of Caesarea, who ought to have been disqualified for sacrificing during the persecution (8.1–3). And the council was not autonomous:

> How do they dare to call it a council, over which a *comes* presided, [where] a *speculator* was present and a *commentariensis* ushered us in instead of deacons of the church? (8.3)

This passage and its subsequent amplification in the *Defense against the Arians* provide the only basis for the conventional (but false) picture of the *comes* Dionysius presiding over the Council of Tyre and guiding its deliberations from the chair.[17]

The ancient accusation continues with an amplification which undercuts its stark picture of secular domination:

> [Dionysius] spoke and those present were silent, or rather obeyed the *comes,* and the removal of the self-styled bishops was prevented by his advice. He gave orders, we were dragged in by soldiers, or rather, when Eusebius and his party gave the orders, he meekly put their decisions into effect. (8.3)

Similarly, another passage complains that in the Mareotis the prefect of Egypt acted in exactly the same way as Dionysius at Tyre:

> Just as there was a *comes* there with a military escort, who allowed nothing to be said or done contrary to what they were resolved on,[18] so too here the prefect of Egypt with his retinue was terrorising all those belonging to the church and permitting no one to give evidence truthfully. (14.4)

On a less hostile representation of the same facts, Dionysius kept order at the council and enforced the decisions made by the majority of the bishops of Tyre. The supporters of Athanasius at Tyre asked the *comes* to overrule the council, but he refused (*Apol. c. Ar.* 78–81). It was a total travesty of the facts to represent Dionysius' refusal to intervene as coercion of the council.

In the event, according to the letter, it was Arian slanders which secured the removal of Athanasius. Since no charge could be proven against Athanasius, even though the *comes* was prejudiced and used violence against him, the bishop fled to Constantine and complained, whereupon the emperor summoned the bishops from Tyre. But when Eusebius and his associates arrived, they made no mention of the charges investigated at Tyre, alleging instead that Athanasius had tampered with the supply of grain from Alexandria to Constantinople. And Eusebius swore that the rich and powerful bishop had become omnipotent in Egypt. Yet God was gracious and Constantine lenient: Athanasius was not executed but exiled (9.1–4).

The letter of the Council of Alexandria was accompanied by documents to bear out its contention that the proceedings of the Council of Tyre were improper and its verdict invalid. The text of the letter explicitly appeals to seven such documents, and Athanasius' *Defense against the Arians* preserves five of them:

(1) the letter of Ischyras to Athanasius (64, cf. 17.6),
(2) a letter of Constantine to Athanasius about the affair of Arsenius (68, cf. 9.5, 17.2),
(3) the protest of the clergy of the Mareotis in September 335 (73–76, cf. 17.1),
(4) the letter of Alexander of Thessalonica to Dionysius (80, cf. 16.1),
(5) the synodical letter of the Council of Jerusalem in September 335 (19.2: quoted in part at *Apol. c. Ar.* 84).

To the letter were also attached two other documents which do not survive—extracts from the *ephemerides* of the prefect of Egypt for August 335 (5.4) and a testimonial on behalf of Athanasius by the bishops of Libya, the Pentapolis, and Egypt which appears to have denied the accusation of embezzlement (19.1). Moreover, the letter appears to utilise, without explicitly citing them, another seven letters written between 333 and 335 which the *Defense against the Arians* also quotes in full.[19]

The arguments and the technique of documentation show the hand of Athanasius,[20] and in fact, years later, in an unguarded moment and in another context, he confessed his authorship of the council's letter. The *Defense before Constantius* protests that

> I did not write to your brother except [on the occasions] when the Eusebians wrote to him against me and I was compelled to defend myself while I was still in Alexandria, and when, at his command that I prepare copies of the holy scriptures,[21] I produced and sent them. (*Apol. ad Const.* 4.2)

The defense of himself against the Eusebians to which Athanasius refers here is clearly the letter of the Council of Alexandria in 338. Athanasius sent a copy of it to Constans (and presumably, therefore, a copy to Constantinus), and in reply Constans asked Athanasius to send him copies of the Bible. That was a clear gesture of sympathy and encouragement, doubtless intended to recall Constantine's similar request to Eusebius of Caesarea.[22] This request to supply Greek texts for use in the new city of Constantinople constituted official recognition of Eusebius' standing as a biblical scholar with a lifelong interest in the text of the Bible.[23] Although there is no reason to think that Athanasius had similar academic and scholarly interests, Constans' request may, nevertheless, have had an effect on the textual transmission of the Greek Bible: the fourth-century Codex Vaticanus of the Old and New Testaments and Apocrypha could be one of the codices which Athanasius sent to the West, since its Alexandrian origin seems certain and its precise contents and their order correspond exactly to the canon of scripture which Athanasius later laid down in his Easter letter of 367 (*Festal Letter* 39).[24]

The letter does not contain all that Athanasius wished to say. The final salutation is missing, and the letter, as extant, closes with a reaffirmation that Athanasius is still the bishop of Alexandria and a warning against the schismatic Melitians, who still vex and harass the church:

> For they make improper ordinations, even of virtual pagans, and they do such things as we are ashamed to write, but which you can learn from those sent by us who will also give you this letter. (19.5)

Copies of the letter were dispatched to the metropolitan bishops of important provinces, and perhaps to many others: they were taken by trusted priests, who performed the delicate task of discrediting the man whom the Council of Antioch had named to replace Athanasius.[25]

The reaction of one important bishop stands on record.[26] Julius, the bishop of Rome, received the letter of the Council of Antioch, brought by a priest and two deacons, which informed him that Pistus was now bishop of Alexandria. Soon afterward priests arrived in Rome from Alexandria bearing the letter which exculpated Athanasius. They informed Julius that Pistus was an Arian who had been ordained (presumably as priest) by Secundus of Ptolemais, whom the Council of Nicaea had excommunicated for heresy.[27] The envoys from Syria could not deny the facts. Julius treated Pistus' ordination by Secundus as an absolute bar to his election as bishop: 'it was impossible for the ordination by Secundus the Arian to have validity in the catholic church,' and to accord it any recognition would be to 'dishonor' the great and holy Council of Nicaea (*Apol. c. Ar.* 24). Moreover, when Julius confronted Macarius, Martyrius, and Hesychius, who brought the synodical letter of the Council of Antioch, with Athanasius' envoys, they let slip an injudicious remark which Julius was able to construe as a request that he convene a new council and that he write both to Athanasius and to Eusebius and his associates inviting them to come to Rome so that a just verdict could be rendered in the presence of all (*Apol. c. Ar.* 22.3).[28] Many other bishops, probably the majority, must have reacted to the appointment of Pistus in the same way.

As the sequel shows, the choice was soon acknowledged to be indefensible.

Constantius undoubtedly encouraged the enemies of Athanasius and may well have attended part of the council which deposed Athanasius in the winter of 337/8. But the bishops formally communicated their decisions to him by letter (*Hist. Ar.* 9.1), and he then wrote to Athanasius. All that is known for certain about this letter, to which the surviving evidence contains a single, barely perceptible allusion, is that it reproached the bishop of Alexandria for embezzlement (*Apol. c. Ar.* 18.2). Presumably, however, it also summoned Athanasius to court. The bishop dared not disobey, and soon departed from Alexandria with the letter which he had written on his own behalf in the name of the assembled bishops of Egypt.

The evidence for Athanasius' journey to the court of Constantius in the spring of 338 is mainly indirect, since he preserves an almost total silence about it in his accounts of his own career. In the *Defense before Constantius,* however, he bases an argument on what he said to Constantius on the three occasions when the emperor had granted him an audience:

> What place or what time does my accuser state, when he has falsely been alleging that I said such things? Or in whose presence was I so mad as to utter such things as he has wrongly accused me of saying? Or who supports his accusation and provides witness? For 'what his eyes have seen,' a man ought also to 'say,' as the holy scripture has recommended (Proverbs 25.7). My accuser will find no witness for what never happened, but I have your piety as a truthful witness that I am not lying. For, knowing the excellence of your memory, I ask you to recall the speeches which I offered on several occasions when you granted me an audience, for the first time in Viminacium, for the second in Caesarea of Cappadocia, and for a third in Antioch, [and to recall] whether I ever spoke ill even of the Eusebians after they had done me harm, whether I denounced any of those who had wronged me. If I did not even denounce those against whom it was my duty to speak, what madness would have possessed me to slander one emperor to another emperor and to bring brother into conflict with brother? I beseech you, either have me refuted face to face or condemn the slanders, and imitate David, who says: 'I have cast out the man who spreads tales secretly against his neighbor' (Psalm 101 [100].5). (*Apol. ad Const.* 5.1–4)

The dates and occasions of the first and third audiences are certain. The first, at Viminacium, can have occurred only in the summer of 337 while Athanasius was on his way from Trier to Alexandria, which he entered on 23 November 337.[29] The third is well attested: in 346 Athanasius went to Syria and saw Constantius in Antioch before returning to Alexandria.[30] But what was the date or the occasion of the second?

The *Defense before Constantius* clearly indicates that the audience in Caesarea occurred between the first audience and the third, while the movements of Athanasius and Constantius between 337 and 346 circumscribe very narrowly the range of possible dates. It must have occurred before Athanasius fled from Alexandria to the West on 16 April 339. But when precisely? A second interview with Constantius before Athanasius returned to Alexandria has often been deduced.[31] But that is surely impossible if Athanasius had returned from exile in the autumn of 337: Constantius cannot have reached Antioch, where he spent the winter of 337/8, much earlier than the end of October,[32] while Athanasius reentered Alexandria on 23 November (*Index* 10). Hence, even in default of confirmatory evidence, the audience in Caesarea would have to be dated to 338, when the emperor went to Cappadocia to supervise the restoration of the pro-Roman Arsaces as ruler of Armenia.[33] But an appearance of Athanasius before Constantius is a necessary sequel to what is known about the Councils of Antioch and Alexandria in the winter of 337/8.

Reticence, prudence, or dissimulation prevented Athanasius from including in any of his numerous apologias on his own behalf an explicit account of his journey to Cappadocia, his appearance before the emperor at Caesarea, and his return to Alexandria. His enemies had no similar motives for silence, and the letter of the eastern bishops at Serdica in 343 complains about his conduct during this journey:

> Afterward Athanasius, traveling through different parts of the world, seducing some people, and deceiving by means of his dishonesty and pestilential flattery innocent bishops who were ignorant of his crimes or unaware of certain of his activities in Egypt, disturbed peaceful churches by begging testimonials from each of them or created new churches for his own support just as he wished. Yet this had no effect against a judgement consecrated long before by holy and distinguished bishops. For the commendation of those who were not judges at the council, never had the judgement of the council [in their possession], and are known not to have been present when the aforesaid Athanasius was being heard, could neither aid nor benefit him.[34]

The complaint relates to Athanasius' conduct after his return to Alexandria in 337 but before his arrival in Rome: whereas an earlier passage had denounced the circumstances of his return in 337, the continuation of this passage complains about his deception of Julius and other Italian bishops. Can the allusion, therefore, be to Athanasius' activities between his flight from Alexandria in the spring of 339 and his arrival in Rome?[35] Hardly. Neither time nor the circumstances of Athanasius' flight permit. In 339 he left Alexandria 'secretly and surreptitiously' (as the same letter puts it), and he fled the territory of Constantius as fast as possible in order to avoid arrest and possible death (*Ep. enc.* 6.3). And once in safety (he may have traveled by way of Africa), he proceeded within a few weeks to Rome, where he knew he would find an important ally. The eastern bishops allude, therefore, not to Athanasius' activities in 339, but to his canvassing of support among the bishops of Palestine, Phoenice, and Syria on his journey to and from Constantius' court in the spring of 338.

This journey provides the context for Athanasius' tenth *Festal Letter*, written for Easter 338, which in this year fell on 26 March (30 Phamenoth). This letter has produced some strange theories from modern scholars who have mistakenly believed that the transmitted text contains a large lacuna: one held that it is a conflation of the *Festal Letters* for 337 and 338, another that there are hidden lacunae in addition to the obvious one in the *editio princeps* and hence that the letter is a miscellany of diverse fragments.[36] But neither the date of the letter nor the integrity of the text transmitted in a Syriac translation admits of any doubt whatever.[37] Athanasius wrote the tenth *Festal Letter* shortly before Easter 338—and there is no reason to imagine that he composed (or began) it in Trier the preceding spring or summer. It was Athanasius' custom to notify the churches throughout Egypt of the date of the next Easter long in advance by means of a very brief communication, then to send a much longer homiletic letter, the 'festal letter' proper, as the Easter season approached.[38] Accordingly, he must have written the tenth *Festal Letter* in late January or February 338.

The letter makes clear that its writer is in Alexandria (11). But it opens with a reference to Athanasius' recent exile in Gaul:[39]

> Even when I traveled so far from you, my brethren, I did not forget the custom which obtains among you, which has been transmitted to us by our [spiritual] fathers, nor was I silent and failed to notify you of the time of the annual holy feast, and the day of its celebration. For although I was hindered by those afflictions of which you have doubtless heard, and severe trials were laid upon me, and a great distance separated us, while the enemies of truth followed our tracks, laying snares to discover a letter from us, so that by their accusations they might add to the pain of our wounds, yet, since the Lord strengthened and comforted us in our afflictions, we were not deterred, even when held fast in the midst of such machinations and conspiracies, from stating and making known to you our saving Easter feast, even from the ends of the earth. (1)

The main theme of the letter, incessantly reiterated, is God's constant protection of his true servants. Athanasius produces the predictable biblical precedents to encourage his flock in time of trouble—Hananiah, Azariah, and Mishael in Babylon (Daniel 3.8–31), Israel leaving Egypt, David hunted by King Saul, Elisha (2 Kings 6.13–17), Esther, Paul, and above all Christ. Athanasius insistently proclaims his confidence in God's protection. The enemy may employ every device in order to ruin him, but the man who is in Christ will obtain the victory. His tone, however, is gloomy and worried—totally unlike the triumphant letter which he wrote in 332 from the court of Constantine after his acquittal at Psammathia (*Festal Letter* 4). The mood of the letter for Easter 338 is hardly what should be expected from a man who had recently returned from exile as a hero. It reflects not the euphoria of Athanasius' return to Alexandria, but the gravity of the perils facing him after his enemies again condemned and deposed him. Athanasius puts on a brave face:

> O beloved friends! if from affliction comes comfort, from labors rest, from sickness health, from death immortality, then it is not seemly to be distressed by what comes upon mankind for a brief period, then it is not right to be downcast because of the tribulations which occur, then it is not proper to be afraid if the gang who attack Christ conspire against true belief. On the contrary, we should please God all the more in such circumstances and consider such things as a testing and practise for a virtuous life. For how can anyone display patience except after labors and sorrows? Or how can anyone be tested for fortitude without an assault from his enemies? (7)

> For the enemy draws near in afflictions and trials and labors, doing everything in his endeavor to overthrow us. But so long as the man who is in Christ enters into battle against the foes and sets patience against anger, humility against arrogance, virtue against wickedness, he wins the victory and exclaims: 'I can do all things through Christ who strengthens me' (Philippians 4.13). (8)

Yet the tone and contents of the letter betray the unconscious fears of a man who had been accused of capital crimes and who knew that he must soon do battle with his enemies.[40] Athanasius probably composed it immediately after the Council of Alexandria and before he departed for the imperial court, which had moved from Antioch to Caesarea in Cappadocia by the time he arrived.

The *Letter to Serapion* which stands in the Syriac corpus of *Festal Letters* between the eleventh and thirteenth letters probably also belongs in the same historical context.[41] Athanasius wrote it as a supplement to an Easter letter which he had just sent to all the bishops in Egypt. One section has a clear relevance to Athanasius' struggle to retain his see:

> Because some Melitians, being come from Syria, have boasted that they had received what does not belong to them, I mean, that they also were reckoned in the catholic church, on this account, I have sent to you a copy of the letter of our fellow ministers in Palestine so that, when it reaches you, you may know the fraud of the pretenders in this matter. For, because they boasted, as I have said before, it was necessary for me to write to the bishops in Syria, and immediately those in Palestine sent us a reply, having agreed in the judgement against them, as you may learn from this example.

There is no other evidence for these dealings of Athanasius with the bishops of Syria and Palestine. But it is hard to believe that they have nothing to do with the attempts to unseat him between the autumn of 337 and the spring of 339: Melitians had suffered from the violence of Athanasius' partisans before the Council of Tyre, and it was doubtless Melitians who complained of his use of violence after his return and provided the evidence on which he had been deposed at Antioch.

Athanasius' defense of himself before Constantius and his diplomatic offensive effectively neutralised his condemnation by the hostile council in the winter of 337/8. He returned to Alexandria still bishop of the city in the early summer of 338, and immediately persuaded the monk Antony to come to lend his prestige to his own cause. At the request of the bishops of Egypt, Antony descended from his mountain and visited Alexandria (July/August 338), where he denounced Arians, converted pagans, and cast out a demon, departing on the third day after his arrival with public ceremony.[42] The visit of Antony was clearly arranged and orchestrated by Athanasius to demonstrate his popularity in Alexandria. That such a demonstration was needed showed the fragility of his hold on power. The visit of Antony probably followed closely upon the arrival of a new prefect of Egypt, whose task was to supervise the expulsion of the bishop of Alexandria.

Failure had not deterred the enemies of Athanasius. They determined to make no mistake the next time. An embassy from Alexandria arrived at the imperial court requesting that Philagrius be reappointed prefect of Egypt in place of Theodorus (*Hist. Ar.* 9.2). The ambassadors clearly belonged to the opposition against Athanasius, for Philagrius had assisted the commission of enquiry in 335, while Theodorus was the prefect whom the Council of Antioch in the winter of 337/8 accused of executing and exiling men on the orders of Athanasius (*Apol. c. Ar.* 5.4). The petition, welcome enough to Constantius and perhaps inspired by him, was granted, and Philagrius entered Alexandria as prefect for the second time, to immense rejoicing.[43] He brought with him the eunuch Arsacius, and he could be relied upon to enforce the planned deposition of Athanasius (*Hist. Ar.* 10.1).

Another council of bishops met at Antioch during the winter of 338/9 and again condemned and deposed Athanasius. The emperor Constantius was present, so that Athanasius was able to complain that his successor was sent 'from court' (*Ep. enc.* 2.1). The council again raked up the charge of ordering the breaking of the chalice of Ischyras, on which the Council of Tyre had found Athanasius guilty. And they again condemned Athanasius for his conduct when he returned to Alexandria in 337: many perished in rioting when he entered the city, and Athanasius had assaulted some and handed others over to be condemned by the prefect. But the charge of embezzlement which the Council of Alexandria had controverted (*Apol. c. Ar.* 18.2) was dropped: hence it may be inferred that Athanasius had successfully disproved the allegations when he appeared before the emperor. On the other hand, a new offense was alleged, though the charge was one of which others were more guilty than Athanasius. The Council of Antioch found Athanasius' return to his see improper and contrary to normal procedure, on the grounds that he had returned on his own initiative without the sanction of a council of bishops.[44] In Athanasius' case, impropriety could be established only if the verdict of the Council of Tyre were assumed to be valid—a most dubious proposition. It must accordingly be suspected that the invocation of a rule which another Council of Antioch had explicitly formulated in 327 or 328 was designed primarily to disqualify not Athanasius,[45] but other bishops whom Constantinus had restored in 337, all of whom had indubitably been condemned and deposed by councils whose verdicts the father of the emperors had endorsed and ratified.

Once it had deposed Athanasius, the Council of Antioch cast about for a suitable and plausible successor. Pistus, to whom Julius (and doubtless many other bishops) had taken exception the previous year, clearly would not do. Eusebius of Nicomedia decided that Eusebius of Emesa was the best candidate, but the latter declined to offer himself, either on principle or out of diffidence.[46] The council thereupon selected Gregory, who was untainted by any scandal, to be the new bishop of Alexandria.[47] Gregory was a Cappadocian like Philagrius, and the new bishop knew that he could rely upon the prefect. He wasted little time in going to Egypt to take possession of his see. On 16 March 339 an attempt was made to arrest Athanasius, and on the following day he went into hiding in the city. On 22 March Gregory entered Alexandria as its bishop. Finally, on 16 April Athanasius fled the city and left Egypt (*Index* 11).

V

ATHANASIUS IN ROME

ATHANASIUS SOON BROADCAST TO THE WORLD HIS VERSION OF HIS expulsion from Alexandria by means of an *Encyclical Letter* sent to a large number of bishops. He began with a salutation to 'his fellow ministers in every place' and drew their attention to his 'dreadful and insupportable sufferings' (1.1). Athanasius compared his expulsion to the rape of the Levite's wife by the sons of Belial (Judges 19.22–30), and he urged Christians everywhere to bestir themselves and to lend aid with no less eagerness than the ancient tribes of Israel had of old, so that the affront to the dignity and honor of the church might be avenged. The *Encyclical Letter* promises to give a brief factual account of recent events, which the bearers of the letter can amplify. It will show how the outrage perpetrated in Alexandria in the spring of 339 surpasses any outrage ever inflicted on the church—even when the Roman state persecuted it (1.2–1.9).[1] Athanasius' account of recent events in Alexandria is predictably tendentious, and either anger or calculation has made him depart from strict chronological order in his professedly straightforward narrative.[2]

The bishop of Alexandria explains that he was occupied in peaceful worship as usual, his congregation was rejoicing at the services and making progress in godly living, and all the bishops of Egypt were abiding in perfect peace and harmony, when the prefect suddenly and unexpectedly published an edict declaring that a certain Gregory, a Cappadocian, was coming from court to replace Athanasius as bishop (2.1). The Christians of Alexandria protested that the deposition of Athanasius was uncanonical, the result of Arian machinations, and they assembled in order to resist. Philagrius, the Arian prefect and fellow countryman of Gregory, set out to install the new bishop by means of bribery and violence. He promised large rewards to gangs of pagans, Jews, and ruffians; armed them with swords and clubs; and set them to attack the Christians in their churches. These thugs perpetrated atrocities worse than any Greek tragedian had ever depicted: a church and its baptistery were set on fire; holy virgins were stripped and raped; monks were beaten and trampled, even killed; altars were desecrated by pagan sacrifice; the scriptures were burned; Jews and pagans bathed naked in the holy baptistery and tried to make virgins and ascetics deny their Lord. Then, while Gregory made a wonderful and glorious entry into the city, the prefect's gangs were permitted, as their reward, to plunder the church. On a Friday in Lent he went into a church with the prefect and pagans: when he saw that the congregation was disgusted with his violent entry, he induced the prefect in a single hour to whip and imprison thirty-four virgins, matrons, and well-born men (2.2–4.5).

Gregory and his supporters next seized the other main church of Alexandria, where Athanasius was staying, hoping to capture and kill him. Athanasius, however, mindful of the precept 'If they pursue you in this city, flee to another' (Matthew 10.23), removed himself. His enemies showed no respect even for Easter Sunday, but imprisoned Christians on the very day when Christ had liberated mankind. By means of such violence, Philagrius seized the churches of Alexandria and handed them over to Gregory and the Arian madmen, so that the people of God and the catholic clergy were now compelled either to participate in the impiety of the Arian heretics or not to attend church at all. Gregory, moreover, acting through the prefect, scourged and tortured sailors—clearly, though Athanasius does not admit it, either in an attempt to prevent the escape of Athanasius or in revenge for it. Gregory also persuaded his savage ally the prefect to send Constantius a decree, purporting to come from the people of Alexandria, which condemned Athanasius in outspoken language: it was drafted by an apostate, and its signatories are pagans, the votaries of idols and Arians (5.1–6). In short, Athanasius protests again and again, the church is being persecuted as it has never been persecuted before.

The *Encyclical Letter* was not written as mere propaganda, nor primarily as apologia. Athanasius had a very practical end in view—to persuade the bishops who received the letter not to recognise his successor as bishop of Alexandria. Gregory is an Arian, a bishop of Arians alone, a substitute for the unfortunate Pistus, whom everyone had earlier rejected after Athanasius wrote about him (2.3/4, 3.1, 4.1, 6.1/2). When he entered Alexandria, Gregory behaved in every way like Caiaphas before Pilate (4.3). The attempt to place him on the bishop's throne in Alexandria is a ploy of the Eusebians that threatens every bishop. If it succeeds, then no bishop can feel confident that a successor will not suddenly arrive to replace him by imperial fiat (6.1–7). Accordingly, all bishops who wish to preserve the true faith must show solidarity and refuse to recognise Gregory as the bishop of Alexandria, even if he swears that he is no Arian (7.1–8).

The *Encyclical Letter* pursues its practical aim fiercely in its final chapters of passionate pleading. Athanasius knew that the bishop of Rome would not recognise Gregory, since Julius had proposed the previous year that a council be held to consider the case of Athanasius, presumably when he received the letter of the Council of Alexandria (7.2, cf. *Apol. c. Ar.* 24.2/3). But how many other bishops would follow Julius' lead? Even if the western episcopate did, the majority of eastern bishops needed persuasion, and hence the *Encyclical Letter* addresses itself primarily to eastern bishops who had taken no part in Athanasius' deposition. There must have been many bishops with no direct stake in the conflicts within the Egyptian church who doubted whether the supersession of Athanasius really did endanger the canons and the faith of the whole church. It was for their benefit that Athanasius emphasised that Eusebius and his associates belonged to the heresy of the 'Arian madmen' whom they had so often repudiated and condemned.

The *Encyclical Letter* is not history, and it would be perverse to complain that Athanasius' account of his replacement as bishop of Alexandria lacks both precision and objectivity. Nevertheless, the nature of the work must be borne in mind continually if it is to be used as evidence for what happened in Alexandria in the spring of 339. On the whole, Athanasius is rather vague about precisely what happened at which church in the city. He does not name 'the church and the holy baptistery' which were set on fire (3.3), nor the church which was plundered (4.2), though he strongly implies that it was the same edifice in both cases, and he writes as if the church in which he was residing were the only other important church in the city (5.1). Nor does the *Encyclical Letter* supply a precise date for most of the events it describes. Athanasius slides swiftly from a Friday during Lent (4.4), which the *Festal Index* implies to be Friday, 23 March, the day on which Gregory entered Alexandria (*Index* 11),[3] to 'the Sunday of the holy festival' (5.3), that is, Easter Sunday, 15 April, the day before Athanasius escaped from the city. It appears that Athanasius' narrative in fact refers to three buildings: the church which was burned and plundered was the Church of Dionysius,[4] the church where Athanasius resided was the Church of Theonas (*Index* 11), and the church where violence was used on Easter Sunday was the Church of Quirinus (*Hist. Ar.* 10.1).

It is a much more serious matter that Athanasius suppresses the fact that there was violence on both sides. It is not necessary to believe Athanasius' enemies when they later charged him with hiring pagans to burn the Church of Dionysius and defile its altar.[5] But it is highly improbable that his partisans failed to resist the imposition of a new bishop with all the force that they could muster. The most significant falsification, however, concerns the author of the *Encyclical Letter* himself. Athanasius depicts himself as a peaceable pastor of his flock against whom no one bore a grudge or voiced a complaint, an innocent ejected from his see by emperor and governor suddenly, unexpectedly, and without warning (2.1). The Melitians and their long-standing complaints are thus conveniently forgotten, and in his carefully written account of his actual expulsion, Athanasius avoids any mention of his successful struggle against the attempt to oust him a year earlier.[6] The presentation is deliberately slanted and selective. Constantius was indeed present at the Council of Antioch which appointed Gregory bishop of Alexandria in place of Athanasius. Hence Athanasius' allegation that Gregory came 'from the court' does not entirely lack plausibility (2.1). But his implicit suggestion that Gregory was actually appointed by the emperor is totally misleading. Athanasius had been deposed and Gregory was appointed in his place by a council of bishops convened and conducted according to due form. Athanasius was never willing to admit that: the central tenet of his repeated apologias on his own behalf was to dispute the validity of his successive depositions, not only in 335 and twice after his return from Trier, but on all other occasions during the next two decades.

When Athanasius left Alexandria, he betook himself to Rome, probably without delay. In order to avoid arrest he needed to escape from the territory of Constantius with all haste, and he knew that Julius, the bishop of Rome, was a firm supporter. Athanasius, therefore, may be believed when he wrote nearly twenty years later that 'he sailed to Rome' (*Hist. Ar.* 11.1), even though his enemies in 343 predictably complained about the secrecy of his departure and his destination.[7]

Although no explicit evidence directly attests the date at which Athanasius arrived in Rome, and it has often been supposed that he reached the city late in 339,[8] the indirect evidence that he arrived in early summer is strong. That is the date which Athanasius assumes in the account of his dealings with Constans which he composed for Constantius in 353 (*Apol. ad Const.* 4.1–3). It is also the date implied by the long letter which Julius wrote in 341 on behalf of Athanasius (*Apol. c. Ar.* 21–35). In this letter answering a letter from the 'Dedication Council' of Antioch, which met in January 341,[9] Julius ridicules the council's accusation that he has infringed canon law by being in communion with Athanasius (27.1–29.1). He protests that he is perfectly entitled to communicate with a bishop whose deposition appears to be questionable. Then he turns to the significance of Athanasius' presence in Rome:

> In addition to all this, he stayed here for a year and six months waiting for your presence or the presence of those who wished to come. By his presence he provided a refutation of [you] all, because he would not have been here had he not been fully confident. For he did not come of his own accord, but after being summoned and receiving a letter from me like the one which I wrote to you. (29.2)[10]

In the context, the period of eighteen months to which Julius refers can hardly be anything other than the time which elapsed between Athanasius' arrival in Rome and the letter which Julius is controverting.[11] Since the 'Dedication Council' met in January 341, it follows that Athanasius reached Rome in June or July 339.

It was doubtless in Rome immediately after his arrival that Athanasius wrote the *Encyclical Letter.*[12] But that was not the only letter he wrote during the summer of 339 in quest of political support. A disingenuous passage of the *Defense before Constantius* unintentionally discloses that in 339 Athanasius wrote a letter which soon became politically embarrassing:

> After departing from Alexandria, I did not go to the court of your brother, nor to any others, only to Rome. Entrusting my cause to the church (for I was concerned for this alone), I spent my time in public worship. I did not write to your brother except [on the occasions] when the Eusebians wrote to him against me and I was compelled to defend myself while I was still in Alexandria, and when, at his command that I prepare copies of the holy scriptures, I produced and sent them. [I say this because] in my defense I must tell the truth to your piety. So, after three years had passed, in the fourth year . . . (4.1–3)

This passage requires very careful exegesis. Athanasius is here giving an account of his dealings with Constans between his departure from Alexandria in April 339 and his first audience with the western emperor, which occurred more than three full years either after he left Alexandria or after he arrived in Rome. (The passage can be interpreted in either of these two ways—though not in any way which makes Athanasius count the three years from his first letter to Constans in 338.)[13] Defending himself against the charge of treasonable communication with Constans, Athanasius considers separately his audiences and his correspondence with the western emperors. In 339 there were two: Constantinus resided in Trier and ruled Gaul, Spain, and Britain, while Constans ruled Africa, Italy, and most of the Balkans and resided in Illyricum.[14] The logic of the passage quoted ineluctably implies that Athanasius wrote to Constantinus as well as to Constans.

On his own presentation, when he left Alexandria in 339, Athanasius went to Rome and there devoted himself to the worship of God. (When Athanasius states that he entrusted his case to the church, he alludes to Julius, the bishop of Rome, but he refrains from naming him, presumably for reasons of tact.) Athanasius proclaims emphatically that he did not go to the court of Constans or 'to any others.' Who are these 'others' whom Athanasius did not approach? The answer is clear from the context and from the official propaganda of the 340s. In the spring of 340, Constantinus invaded Italy and was killed near Aquileia. There followed a purge of his supporters, in which his praetorian prefect Ambrosius, the father of the future bishop of Milan, appears to have perished.[15] After the death of Constantinus, his memory was abolished. The defeated and disgraced Augustus became an 'unperson' who had officially never existed. Already on 29 April 340 Constans coldly instructed the praetorian prefect Marcellinus to cancel the immunities from taxation granted by 'the enemy of the state and of ourself.'[16] In the East, however, Constantius did not abolish the memory of his dead brother at once, since the preface to the so-called *Itinerarium Alexandri* expresses the wish that the emperor, about to invade Persian territory, may surpass the successes of the *maximi Constantini,* his father and brother.[17] But when he abolished it, he did so effectively: the name of Constantinus was erased from public inscriptions in Asia as well as in the provinces ruled by Constans, and even on coins already in circulation.[18]

Libanius' panegyric on Constantius and Constans (probably composed in 344/5) faithfully reflects the official line that Constantine had only ever had two sons—who are now ruling the empire jointly in harmony and concord.[19] The *Defense before Constantius* consistently adopts the same line: whatever Athanasius really thought of Constantinus, he was obliged, if he wished to persuade Constantius, to pretend that Constans was his one and only brother. His phrase 'any others' is a generalising plural of the type commonly found in literary works of the fourth century: it designates solely and precisely Constantinus. This part of Athanasius' defense is thus both straightforward and factually correct: in 339 he went to Rome and did not travel to the court of either of the two emperors then ruling in the West.

Athanasius continues, however, by protesting that he did not even write to Constans except on two occasions. The first was in 338 when he sent him a copy of the synodical letter of the Council of Alexandria (*Apol. c. Ar.* 3–19)—and this passage of the *Defense before Constantius* discloses in passing that it was indeed Athanasius himself who composed that letter.[20] On the second occasion, he sent Constans copies of the Bible which the emperor had requested him to prepare, presumably when he replied to Athanasius' first letter. Neither from the context nor from external probability can it be deduced with certainty whether Athanasius wrote this second letter before or after he left Alexandria. But there is something significant which Athanasius does not say. He does not protest that he did not write either to Constans or to 'any others.' Now Athanasius certainly wrote to Constantinus at least once, since he sent him too a copy of the synodical letter of the Council of Alexandria in 338. Moreover, Constantinus had befriended him during his exile in Trier, and he wrote a personal letter recommending him to his Alexandrian congregation to take with him as he returned from exile in 337 (*Apol. c. Ar.* 87.4–7). Hence it may be deduced with certainty that Athanasius wrote to Constantinus when he arrived in Rome.

When Constantinus invaded Italy in the spring of 340, Athanasius' letter came to be construed as something less innocent than an exiled bishop's plea for assistance. It was alleged that Athanasius had encouraged Constantinus to attack his brother.[21] The allegation may have been completely untrue, yet it was plausible. Constantinus was the only son of Constantine whom Athanasius knew personally. This friendship, so helpful in 337, became a political liability when the emperor of Gaul attempted to remove his brother from power. Athanasius' association with Constantinus must surely be one of the reasons why more than three years elapsed before Constans showed any interest in his cause.

In Rome, despite his claim to have spent all his time in public and private devotions while entrusting his case to the church, Athanasius did not fail to use his opportunities to seek lay as well as clerical support. Again, the only specific and trustworthy evidence comes from Athanasius himself. His *Defense before Constantius* reveals that certain prominent personages in Rome bestowed on him 'favors,' whose nature he declines to specify. Defending himself against the charge of treasonable correspondence with Magnentius in 350, Athanasius dismisses as preposterous the idea that he could ever have written a letter to the usurper:

> What sort of opening would I affix to my letter if I had written to him? 'Congratulations on murdering the one who honored me, whose favors I can never forget'? 'I welcome your killing of my friends who were very firm and devoted Christians'? 'We admire your slaughter of those who received us nobly in Rome, the emperor's aunt of blessed memory, the aptly named Eutropia, Abuerius that noble man, the faithful Sperantius, and many other good men'? (6.5)

Abuerius and Sperantius are otherwise unknown,[22] but Eutropia, the daughter of Constantius (emperor from 293 to 306) and Theodora, was the wife of Virius Nepotianus, consul in 336, and the mother of Julius Nepotianus, who was proclaimed Augustus at Rome in June 350.[23] She was doubtless killed when the generals of Magnentius suppressed her son's short-lived rebellion. As an imperial relative, Eutropia was presumably capable of soliciting emperors on Athanasius' behalf. It must be suspected that between 339 and 342 Athanasius approached many other prominent figures at Rome besides the trio whom the *Defense before Constantius* names. He names Eutropia, Abuerius, and Sperantius only because they were later killed on the orders of Magnentius. By the early fifth century it could be asserted that while in Rome Athanasius told aristocratic ladies of the city about the monks of Egypt and thereby gave an initial impetus to the beginnings of monasticism in the West.[24]

It was not enough for Athanasius to publicise his expulsion from Alexandria in 339, to write to the emperors Constantinus and Constans, and to seek support from prominent Christians in the Roman aristocracy. He saw that political activity alone would probably never suffice to restore him to his see. He needed to elevate his struggle to the ideological plane. In his *Encyclical Letter* he claimed that his deposition represented an attack on the doctrinal orthodoxy of the whole church (1.6–8, 7.3). It was necessary to prove that claim at the theological level. The bishop of Rome had supported him in 338 and welcomed him when he arrived in Italy in 339: he could clearly be relied upon to continue to uphold his cause.[25] But Athanasius realised that ultimate success in his own struggle depended on producing proof that more was at stake than the restitution of a single proud prelate. It seems highly probable that he pursued this aim by means of his *Orations against the Arians,* which he began to compose c. 340.[26]

Athanasius' three *Orations against the Arians,* though separate speeches according to their title, form a substantial theological treatise with a continuous, though largely non-cumulative, argument from beginning to end.[27] An introduction stresses the importance of the undertaking (1.1–10). Arius may be dead, but the heresy which he sired is alive and flourishing. Athanasius sets out the main features of Arius' theology: he quotes the first seven lines of Arius' *Thalia,* drawing attention to and ridiculing his use of the Sotadean metre, and gives a sketch of Arius' theology which repeats the letter of Alexander of Alexandria denouncing Arius and his doctrines which Athanasius himself had composed many years before. Athanasius poses the general issue as a dilemma: which of the two theologies, Christian or Arian, sets forth Jesus Christ as truly God and Son of the Father? There follows a long discussion of the nature of Christ's sonship. But the bulk of the work concentrates on expounding the biblical texts which Arius and others had adduced to support their theological positions (especially Proverbs 8.22–25, which contains the favorite proof text: 'the Lord created me the beginning of his ways'). The Arian heresy, Athanasius proclaims, is crafty and deceitful when it pretends to have the support of the scriptures (1.1). He argues at length that each passage adduced by the Arians, when it is correctly interpreted, supports orthodox, not heretical, beliefs.

Biblical exegesis thus provides both the connecting thread of the arguments of the *Orations against the Arians* and their substance. Athanasius throughout contrasts two firmly defined sets of views about the relationship between God the Father, God the Son or Logos, and the Holy Spirit.[28] The Arians espouse the false view that the three persons of the Trinity are totally unlike one another (1.6), that the Son is unlike the Father and alien to him, foreign to the Father with respect to essence, 'foreign to the essence of the Father' (1.6, 1.9, 1.17, 2.43, 3.14). In contrast Athanasius presents orthodox Christology as holding that the Son is like the Father (1.21, 1.44, 1.52, 2.17, 3.10, 3.11, 3.20), indeed like him in all things (1.21, 1.40, 2.18). That appears to prefigure the ultimate rapprochement in 359/60 between Athanasius and the 'theological conservatives' of Asia Minor[29]—and may suggest that he composed the *Orations against the Arians* with a view to convincing the bishops of Asia Minor in the 340s that, whatever the personal merits of his own case, they were aligning themselves with a party which embraced a fundamentally false theology.

Although the introduction presents the Arian heresy as the last of all 'which has now emerged as the precursor of the Antichrist' (1.1, cf. 1.7), the *Orations against the Arians* have no explicit indication of their date beyond references to Arius as dead (1.3) and Constantius as living and reigning (1.10, 3.25). This merely establishes that the work was written between 337 and 361, and a date between 356 and 360 has sometimes been advocated.[30] But the *Orations* conspicuously fail to defend the term *homoousios,* which became the theological watchword of Athanasius and his allies in the early 350s.[31] The named targets of the *Orations* are Arius himself, Eusebius of Nicomedia (1.22, 37), and Asterius, the sophist and sacrificer (1.32, 3.2, 3.60). Moreover, Athanasius seems to treat this trio as if they were the only Arians rash enough ever to have committed their opinions to writing (2.24). That fits the circumstances of 339 or 340 excellently, when Athanasius had an obvious motive for establishing himself as the theological champion of orthodoxy against the Arian heretics who had expelled him from Alexandria. When he decries the followers of Arius as deriving their perverse doctrine from the teaching of Eusebius (1.27), he probably names his main political adversary.

A further indication that Athanasius was writing in Rome in 339 or 340 can be deduced from his method of attacking his theological enemies. He appears to quote Arius' *Thalia* from memory—the first seven lines verbatim followed by a rather vague and probably not very accurate summary based on the old letter of Alexander, which he himself had composed in the bishop's name (1.5/6).[32] On the other hand, Athanasius quotes nine extracts from Asterius as if taking them from a complete text.[33] The contrast is easily explicable if Athanasius was indeed writing in Rome in 339 or 340. His fellow exile Marcellus of Ancyra surely brought a copy of Asterius with him to Rome: he had been deposed and exiled in 336 for injudicious remarks made in a long attack on Arius and 'Arians' such as Eusebius of Caesarea and Narcissus of Neronias, which pilloried the treatise of Asterius which the *Orations against the Arians* quote.[34]

VI

JULIUS AND MARCELLUS

ATHANASIUS ARRIVED IN ROME WITH ONLY A FEW TRUSTED SUPPORT-
ers from Alexandria, and his cause received no obvious advancement until the
arrival of another exile lent color to his claim that Christian orthodoxy was endangered. Marcellus is attested as bishop of Ancyra as early as 314,[1] and in 325
at Nicaea he showed himself an implacable and outspoken foe of Arius.[2] In 335
Marcellus refused to subscribe to the decisions of the Councils of Jerusalem and
Tyre, which readmitted Arius to communion and pronounced that his views fell
within the limits of permissible Christian doctrine.[3] Moreover, when these councils declared that Marcellus should forfeit his see unless he recanted and communicated with Arius, he hastily composed a tract of some ten thousand lines to
demonstrate that not only Arius but also his most prominent supporters were
patent heretics, and he presented it to Constantine.[4] That step proved his undoing. Constantine convened a council of bishops in Constantinople in July 336,
which declared Arius orthodox yet again, deposed Marcellus, and appointed
Basil to be bishop of Ancyra.[5] Marcellus departed into exile.

In 337, under the amnesty decreed by Constantinus for all exiled eastern
bishops (*Hist. Ar.* 8.1), Marcellus returned to Ancyra amid scenes of violence.
Houses were burned, there was fighting in the streets, and Marcellus repossessed
his church by force: his enemies later complained that priests of the opposing
faction were dragged naked to the forum, Basil was ejected from the sanctuary
and thrown into the street clutching the consecrated host, and holy virgins were
stripped and exposed to public gaze.[6] The bishops who had condemned
Marcellus in 336 reacted quickly. The aged Eusebius of Caesarea was requested
to take up his pen, and he wrote two books *Against Marcellus* and three books
of *Ecclesiastical Theology* to demonstrate, with copious documentation, that
Marcellus was an irredeemable heretic, his views by turn Sabellian and Jewish.[7]
Eusebius addressed the *Ecclesiastical Theology* to Flacillus, the bishop of

Antioch: the same Council of Antioch that appointed Gregory bishop of Alexandria probably also deposed Marcellus and reappointed Basil bishop of Ancyra.[8] Marcellus departed into exile again. But, unlike Athanasius, he did not come to Rome immediately. Indeed, it seems that the exiled bishop of Ancyra did not arrive in Rome until the spring of 340[9]—a coincidence of date which suggests that he first went to Illyricum, perhaps to the court of Constans, and came to Rome only after the death of Constantinus.

Julius soon took up the cause of Marcellus as well as that of Athanasius. He wrote to the eastern bishops complaining not only that Athanasius and Marcellus had been unjustly deposed, but also that the bishops of the East were causing disorder in the church by abandoning the decisions of the Council of Nicaea. Julius proposed, therefore, that they (or at least some of them) come to Rome by a stated day for a joint council of both eastern and western bishops, presumably under his own presidency.[10] Julius' letter was taken to Antioch by the priests Helpidius and Philoxenus (*Apol. c. Ar.* 20.1). They did not receive an immediate answer: on the contrary, they were compelled to wait in Antioch until January 341 (*Apol. c. Ar.* 25.3), when a council of ninety-seven bishops assembled to dedicate the great octagonal church which Constantine had begun.[11] Constantius was present on 6 January 341 when the council dedicated the church (*Syn.* 22.2, 25.1),[12] and he may have attended the sessions in which the bishops considered Julius' complaints. Part of the groundwork for the council had probably been laid by Acacius, bishop of Caesarea in Palestine since the death of Eusebius in May 339: it seems likely that his lost *Contra Marcellum* was written in 340/1,[13] and hence stands in the same relationship to Marcellus' condemnation in 341 as Eusebius' *Against Marcellus* and *Ecclesiastical Theology* to the preceding condemnation in 339.

The theological deliberations of the 'Dedication Council' cannot be reconstructed.[14] No ancient narrative reports their course, and in his work *On the Councils of Ariminum and Seleucia*, Athanasius merely quotes three documents relevant to the council out of context to show how the Arians keep changing their theology. Nevertheless, despite its tendentiousness, something may be deduced from Athanasius' presentation of these three documents. His first quotation begins:

> Neither are we followers of Arius (for how, as bishops, could we follow a priest?) nor have we recognised any creed beside that handed down from the beginning. On the contrary, after appointing ourselves examiners and assessors of his creed, we admitted him to communion rather than followed him, as you will learn from what is said. For we have learned from the outset to believe in one God, etc. (*Syn.* 22.3–5)

The creed which follows avoids the word *ousia* or any of its compounds when defining the relationship between God the Father and God the Son, and it appears to take aim at Marcellus by asserting that the Son remains king and God forever (*Syn.* 22.5/6).[15] Moreover, the brief extract quoted by Athanasius ends in bitter sarcasm: 'and if it needs to be added, we also believe in the resurrection of the flesh and the life everlasting' (*Syn.* 22.7). Athanasius specifies that his quotation comes from a letter written by the council: since the passage clearly answers the charge that the bishops are Arians, it should come from the council's letter to Julius. The fact that Julius, in his answer to it, avoided the theological issue shows that he found nothing positively offensive in this credal statement.

Athanasius' second quotation comprises a much longer and much more explicit creed, duly concluded with anathemas, which declares that the Son is the 'exact image of the godhead, essence, will, power, and glory of the Father' (*Syn.* 23.2–10).[16] The bishops at Antioch cannot have been unaware that Marcellus had attacked the definition of the Son in terms of the 'image' of the Father as utterly incompatible with the central Nicene proposition that he is of the same *ousia* as the Father.[17] There could be no doubt, therefore, what the reaction of Julius would be to such an affirmation. Eusebius of Nicomedia, who had guided his party within the church for many years, knew better than to send a document containing it to Julius, Athanasius, and Marcellus: this creed comes from the synodical letter which the 'Dedication Council' circulated to eastern bishops, a majority of whom were sympathetic to its theology.

Athanasius also quotes a creed submitted to the council by Theophronius of Tyana, which styles the Son 'perfect God of perfect God and existing alongside God in substance (*hypostasis*),' and which ends with an anathema on anyone who shares the views of Marcellus, Sabellius, or Paul of Samosata (*Syn.* 24.2–5). It may be inferred that Theophronius had himself been suspected of sharing the views of Marcellus and that he submitted this creed in order to prove his orthodoxy in the eyes of the council.[18] When Athanasius says that 'they all subscribed to it after accepting the fellow's creed' (*Syn.* 24.1), he is being grossly tendentious: the rest of the bishops accepted Theophronius' creed as proof of his orthodoxy without in any sense adopting it as an authoritative statement of correct doctrine.[19]

More is known about the council's actions relating to Athanasius and Marcellus, since Sozomenus provides a summary of the letter which the council sent to Julius,[20] and Julius' reply survives entire (*Apol. c. Ar.* 21–35). The letter of the Council of Antioch to Julius was presumably the work of Eusebius of Nicomedia. It was stylishly written but with legalistic arguments, both ironical and threatening towards the bishop of Rome. The bishops at Antioch rejected Julius' suggestion of a joint council. The bishop of Rome indeed enjoyed prestige and honor as the occupant of an ancient see founded by the apostles. But Julius' proposal was presumptuous, based on the accident of Rome's political importance (25.2), not on the merits of the case or on ecclesiastical practise, according to which the western church ought to accept the verdict of the eastern church in its internal matters and *vice versa,* just as had happened in the past with Paul of Samosata and Novatian (25.1). Moreover, the day named was impossibly early, especially since the Persian war required eastern bishops to stay in their endangered provinces (25.3/4). Julius' harboring of Marcellus and Athanasius violated the basic principle of canon law that the divinely inspired decision of a church council could not be overturned by a subsequent council (22.1, 22.6, 29.3). Julius, therefore, was setting a council at nought and fanning the flames of discord in the church (25.1, 34.1): he must either withdraw from communion with Marcellus and Athanasius (whose crimes the letter reiterated) or himself forfeit communion with and recognition by the eastern church (34.3–5).

The priests Helpidius and Philoxenus had been compelled to remain in Antioch until January 341. They then took to Rome the letter of the council to Julius (21.2). Julius had already prepared his riposte. A council of fifty bishops from Italy and perhaps from western provinces outside Italy met on the date proposed for the joint council and endorsed a letter of rebuttal which Julius had prepared.[21] The letter, duly taken to the east by the *comes* Gabianus (20.3), was addressed to 'Dianius, Flacillus, Narcissus, Eusebius, Maris, Macedonius, Theodorus,[22] and those who with them have written to us from Antioch.' It essayed a full defense of Marcellus and Athanasius—whose viewpoint it faithfully reproduces almost throughout.[23]

Julius begins with a complaint about the tone of the letter which he has received (21.2–5)—a topic to which he reverts throughout his own letter. It was disputatious and unfriendly, insulting even when it purported to compliment. Julius deals first with the propriety of holding another council to reconsider the charges against Athanasius and Marcellus. Such a procedure, he fallaciously claims, was sanctioned long before by the Council of Nicaea (22.2).[24] More recently, when the priest Macarius and the deacons Martyrius and Hesychius came from the Council of Antioch in 338 and were confronted by priests from Alexandria who contested their assertions, they agreed that Julius should convene a council so that a just decision might be reached in the presence of all: the eastern bishops ought to come to Rome as their trusted envoys had agreed was right and proper (22.3–5). Furthermore, the charge that Julius was dishonoring a council of bishops was one of which the eastern bishops were far more guilty than he. The Arians were condemned by three hundred bishops at Nicaea—a verdict which the eastern bishops have now dishonored and set aside (22.2, 23.1). For as bishop of Alexandria they appointed one Pistus, who was trebly disqualified: he had been excommunicated both by Alexander of Alexandria and by the Council of Nicaea, and he had been ordained to the priesthood by Secundus of Ptolemais, who had himself been excommunicated at Nicaea (24.1–4). If 'the decisions of councils must be regarded as valid,' as the recipients of the letter had stated (22.6), then it was wrong for a mere handful of bishops to overturn the decision of the great council of three hundred bishops from everywhere, wrong that those whom the whole world had proscribed and rejected as heretics should now be received back into communion (23.1–3).

Julius' complaints about the synodical letter from Antioch occupy more than a third of his own letter (21.2–26.3). The rest justifies his reception of Athanasius and Marcellus into communion. He considers their cases separately. About Athanasius, he has received discordant reports: the synodical letters from Eusebius and his allies in 338 and 341 frequently contradict each other, while a letter of many bishops from Egypt and elsewhere (that is, the letter of the Council of Alexandria in 338) states that all the accusations against Athanasius are false (27.1/2). On the basis of the evidence at his disposal, Julius dismisses the charges against Athanasius.

Julius has (he states) carefully examined the *hypomnemata* of the commission of enquiry which visited the Mareotis in 335 (brought to Rome by Martyrius and Hesychius in 338). He pronounces in favor of Athanasius' protests that the commission acted unfairly, illegally, and with patent bias. The accuser Ischyras was in the Mareotis, but not Athanasius or Macarius (27.4). Julius appeals to the letter of Alexander of Thessalonica, Athanasius' letter to the *comes* Dionysius, and the declaration written in Ischyras' own hand in which he unreservedly withdrew his accusations (all supplied by Athanasius), and he appeals to the priests and deacons who accompanied Athanasius to Rome (28.1–3). But the *hypomnemata* themselves provide Julius' central argument.[25] Athanasius has shown from the documentary record that there was one catechumen 'in a small cell' with Ischyras when Macarius committed the alleged offense, that 'Ischyras was then lying ill behind the door.' Consequently Ischyras cannot possibly have been standing and celebrating the eucharist. Further, Ischyras was not a priest, since his name does not appear in the list of Melitian clergy submitted to Alexander (28.4–7).[26] Julius, therefore, is justified in refusing to condemn Athanasius: he regards him as still a bishop; indeed, he invited him to come to Rome (29.1/2) and proposed that an impartial council be held to consider his case (30.1). Those who have 'acted against the canons' of the church are those who sent Gregory from Antioch to Alexandria, a distance of thirty-six *mansiones* on the *cursus publicus*,[27] and installed a foreigner as bishop of Alexandria by military force (29.3). Julius waxes eloquent on the atrocities committed by Gregory in Alexandria, predictably echoing and apparently copying Athanasius' own account in the *Encyclical Letter* (30).

As for Marcellus, Julius explains that he had, at his request, submitted a statement of his beliefs in the form of a letter to the bishop of Rome (32.1). In this statement, which is preserved by Epiphanius,[28] Marcellus declared that he was writing to clear himself of the imputation of heresy brought by some of those whom he himself had convicted of that charge at the Council of Nicaea. Since his adversaries refused to come to Rome, even though Julius had sent priests to them and Marcellus himself had waited a year and three months in Rome, he was submitting a statement of his theological beliefs to Julius, written in his own hand, in order to expose the falsity of the charges against him. Marcellus accuses his enemies of dividing the Father and the Son, as a logical consequence of which they must either suppose the existence of two Gods or else relegate God the Son to the non-divine created order. Marcellus protests that he, in contrast, respects holy scripture and believes in one God and his only-begotten Son, Jesus Christ, the indivisible power of God. 'I believe, therefore,' Marcellus continues—and quotes in its entirety what seems to be the traditional baptismal creed of the church of Rome.[29] He concludes by asking Julius to forward a copy of his letter when he writes to the eastern bishops. When he wrote in the name of the Council of Rome, Julius duly appealed to Marcellus' submission as proof that he was as orthodox in 341 as he had shown himself to be in 325 (32.2–4). Why should he refuse to communicate with such a man?

Julius accuses the eastern bishops of creating schism (32.4). Other bishops besides Athanasius and Marcellus have been unjustly expelled from their sees and are in Rome, while many Egyptian bishops have been prevented from coming to the Roman council (33.1). In Alexandria and Ancyra, violence and oppression have followed the expulsion of Athanasius and Marcellus: bishops are being beaten and imprisoned, some have been forced to perform burdensome civic liturgies, others exiled solely for their refusal to communicate with Gregory and his Arians (33.2/3). Julius is distressed at the sufferings of his brothers in Christ, and his proposal for a joint council was designed to 'set right and heal' an unfortunate situation (33.4). He expresses the hope that the majority of the eastern bishops will disown the petty hatreds of the small cabal who have caused the present dissension, and cease from strife. Julius reiterates his proposal for a general council where the issues can be settled with everyone present.[30] The cases of Marcellus and Athanasius involve a see founded by the apostle Paul and a see with which bishops of Rome have traditionally had close ties. Nor are they the only bishops who have been deposed: other bishops and priests from different places have arrived in Rome with very similar tales of woe. Julius accordingly calls upon the eastern bishops to put an end to the persecution of bishops and priests, and to allow the churches to recover their bishops so that they may rejoice in the Lord always (34/5).

Julius was writing in the summer of 341. The exiled bishops recently arrived in Rome had presumably been deposed either by the 'Dedication Council' itself in January 341 or, as seems more probable, by the earlier Council of Antioch in 338/9 which had deposed Athanasius. The exiles came (Julius specifies) from Thrace, from Syria Coele, from Phoenice and Palestine (33.1)—to be precise, Lucius of Adrianople (in the province of Thracia), Cyrus of Beroea and Euphration of Balaneae (in Syria Coele), Hellanicus of Tripolis (in Phoenice), Asclepas of Gaza (in Palestine), and perhaps others.[31]

Complete obscurity envelops the effect of Julius' letter on the fortunes of Athanasius and Marcellus. That cannot be accidental. When he came to write his *Defense against the Arians* and *History of the Arians*, Athanasius no longer had any desire or inclination to explain how Constans was persuaded to intervene on his behalf, or how his cause was associated for some years with that of the bishop of Ancyra, whom he later abandoned in order to obtain permission to return from exile.[32] Marcellus simply disappears from view until the Council of Serdica in 343. In his letter to Julius, which he presumably composed in the summer of 341, Marcellus declared that he was about to leave Rome.[33] He did not disclose his intended destination. It may have been the court of Constans, and Marcellus may have approached the western emperor in person with a request to intervene on his own behalf and on behalf of other exiles. However, another full year elapsed before Constans took up the cause of Athanasius, and he did so only when another exile with greater political influence arrived at his court. In 342 the fortunes of Athanasius became linked closely to those of Paul of Constantinople.

VII

THE INTERVENTION
OF CONSTANS

ATHANASIUS FINALLY RETURNED TO EGYPT IN 346 AS A RESULT OF
political pressure from Constans, who threatened his brother with war unless he
agreed to the return of the bishop of Alexandria and other eastern bishops in
exile in the West.[1] When Constans was killed early in 350, Athanasius lost his
imperial protector, and, when the Council of Sirmium condemned him in 351,
the charges included high treason.[2] It was alleged, with a certain *prima facie*
plausibility, that during his exile Athanasius had fomented enmity between
the two Augusti. It is a matter of some historical importance, therefore, to discover precisely what dealings Athanasius had with the emperor who ruled the
western empire from 340 to 349. On the other hand, it is not at all easy to unravel the facts, since the only ancient writer who gives anything remotely resem-
bling a complete account of any aspect of these dealings is Athanasius himself.
Consequently, it will be worthwhile to set out the relevant evidence and the deductions which can be elicited from it systematically rather than chronologically.

The *Defense before Constantius* has the form of a speech to be delivered to
the emperor in person. Even though Athanasius neither delivered it before
Constantius nor ever intended to do so, he wrote the original version of the
speech (which comprises the first eighteen chapters of modern editions, apart
from a couple of later additions) with the emperor in mind throughout as the
primary audience whom he needed to convince, and it seems that he sent it to
him in the summer of 353.[3] Athanasius composed his defense against the charge
that he had turned Constans against the eastern emperor with a careful regard
for what Constantius knew about his dealings with his brother. That severely
circumscribed his ability to misrepresent facts which were (or might be) known
to Constantius. What therefore does the original *Defense before Constantius* of
353 reveal about Athanasius' dealings with Constans?

*   *   *

Four chapters of the *Defense before Constantius* (in the division of the text devised by modern editors) deal with the charge that Athanasius caused enmity between 'the most pious Augustus of blessed and eternal memory' and his brother (2–5). The first of these comprises a *captatio benevolentiae*: although the falsity of the ecclesiastical charges made by Athanasius' accusers, already proven in the *Defense against the Arians* to be malicious inventions (1.1–4), means that the charge cannot be taken seriously, Constantius has shown that he possesses the imperial virtue of patience by giving Athanasius the opportunity to reply and set forth the truth (2). And the last of the four chapters devoted to the charge concludes the refutation with an *a priori* argument based on the interviews which Constantius has been gracious to grant Athanasius: if he did not complain to Constantius about his enemies when he had every reason to do so, it is plainly ridiculous to imagine that he ever slandered him to his brother Constans (5).[4] The two intervening chapters present and deal with Athanasius' interviews with Constans.

Athanasius was not deeply imbued with traditional Greek rhetorical culture, and never shows any familiarity with the traditional literary genres except philosophy.[5] Hence neither the structure of the original *Defense before Constantius* of 353 nor its individual parts correspond to the precepts of generations of theorists which underlie the structure of so many works by fourth-century Christian writers.[6] Athanasius' account of his dealings with Constans cannot be called a *narratio* in the technical sense in which that term is used by ancient rhetorical handbooks. Where theorists prescribed an initial *narratio* of the facts of the case (usually brief), followed by an ample elaboration of arguments based upon them,[7] Athanasius throughout combines and interlaces narrative and argument.

Despite his lack of literary polish, Athanasius' native intelligence and familiarity with the world made him capable of forceful pleading on his own behalf. He chose a specific logical structure for this section of his speech. He first discusses his audiences with the dead emperor geographically in order to prove that he never saw him alone—and hence never had the opportunity to slander Constantius privately. Then he reviews his dealings with Constans, including written communications, in chronological order to prove that he saw him only when summoned to court, never on his own initiative or at his own request. Hence if historical deductions are to be teased out of these chapters, what Athanasius says about where he had audiences with Constantius must be analysed separately from what he says about their dates and occasions.

Athanasius sets a somewhat strident tone for his exposition:

> I truly blush with shame to defend myself against such charges, which I think that not even my accuser himself will repeat in my presence. For he knows perfectly well both that he himself is lying and that I neither went mad nor took leave of my senses even so far as to expose myself to the

suspicion of having let any such thing enter my mind. For this reason I would not have replied to any others who asked me in case my listeners might suspend their judgment, if only for the duration of my speech of defense. But to your piety I defend myself in a clear and loud voice, and stretching out my hand, as I have learned from the apostle, 'I call on God as my witness and stake my life on it' (2 Corinthians 1.23). As it is written in the histories of the kings [of Israel], 'the Lord is my witness, and his Christ is my witness' (1 Samuel 12.5). (Permit me too to utter these words.) I never on any occasion spoke ill of your piety before your brother Constans of blessed memory, the most pious Augustus. (3.1–3)

He then proceeds to develop an argument designed to prove that he must be innocent of the charge because he never saw or conversed with the emperor Constans alone:

I did not incite him, as my accusers falsely allege. On the contrary, whenever I entered his presence, he himself spoke of your generosity—and he spoke of it even when the embassy of Thalassus came to Poetovio while I was in Aquileia. The Lord is my witness how I kept recalling your piety and kept saying what I wish God may reveal to your soul, so that you may condemn the calumny of those who are slandering me before you! Bear with me as I say this, most generous Augustus, and freely grant me your indulgence. For that lover of Christ was not so light-minded nor was I of such a character that we could discuss such matters between us, that I could slander brother to brother or speak ill of an emperor before an emperor. I am not mad, emperor, nor have I forgotten the divine utterance which says: 'Do not curse the king in your thoughts, and do not curse a rich man in the secrecy of your bedchamber; for a bird of the air will carry away your utterance and a winged messenger will report your words' (Ecclesiastes 10.20).

If even what is said in private against you who are kings [and emperors] is not concealed, it is surely incredible that I should have spoken against you in the presence of an emperor and with so many in attendance. For I never went alone to see your brother, nor did he ever converse with me alone. I always entered his presence with the bishop of the city where I was and other bishops who happened to be there: we saw him together and we departed again together. On this matter Fortunatianus, the bishop of Aquileia, can bear witness, and Father Ossius is capable of speaking, as are Crispinus, the bishop of Patavium;[8] Lucillus of Verona; Dionysius of Elis;[9] and Vincentius, the Campanian bishop.[10] And since Maximinus of Trier and Protasius of Milan have died, Eugenius too who was *magister* can bear witness. For he stood before the veil and heard the requests I made of Constans and what he graciously said to me. (3.3–7)

What Athanasius says about the places where he had an audience seems clear enough. He was always accompanied by the bishop of the city where the audience occurred and other bishops who happened to be on hand. And his exposition is structured on the assumption that the audiences occurred in the three cities of Aquileia, Trier, and Milan. For his audience or audiences in Aquileia, Athanasius can produce a bevy of witnesses: not only Fortunatianus, the bishop of the city (who is attested as bishop of Aquileia from 343 to 357),[11] but also the bishops Ossius, Lucillus, Dionysius, and Vincentius. For the audiences in Trier and Milan, the testimony available was not so direct and impressive, since Maximinus and Protasius, who were the bishops of these cities in the early 340s, had both died several years before 353.[12] Athanasius appeals, therefore, to Eugenius, who was either *magister officiorum* or *magister admissionum* at the relevant times—and clearly, in Athanasius' opinion, still alive when he composed the original *Defense before Constantius* in 353.[13] Eugenius' political influence is also known from Libanius, who complained to Julian in 362 that the tiny Eugenius became great under Constans and used his power to seize the estates of Aristophanes of Corinth.[14]

One other matter in the passage quoted requires comment before proceeding further. Who was Thalassus, and why did he come to Poetovio? The first question is easy to answer. Thalassus in Athanasius' speech and the Thalassus whom Zosimus names as an envoy sent by Constantius to Magnentius in the summer of 351 are obviously the same man as the Thalassius who is well attested as the praetorian prefect charged with administering the East under the titular authority of the inexperienced Caesar Gallus.[15] Thalassius died during the winter of 353/4, but when Athanasius originally wrote this passage, he was alive and the *de facto* ruler of the eastern provinces including Egypt. It is not so immediately obvious why Thalassius came to Poetovio while Athanasius was in Aquileia, but there is a plausible historical context in the winter of 344/5 which will explain why Athanasius mentions him here: it was (it seems) in answer to the embassy of Thalassius that Constans threatened his brother with war if he did not agree to the restoration of Athanasius and Paul of Constantinople.[16] For the present, it will suffice to observe that, while Athanasius implies that Constans received the embassy of Thalassius at Poetovio, he states categorically that he himself was in Aquileia at the time—where it is known that he resided during the spring of 345 (15.4; *Index* 17).

Although it is established that Athanasius had audiences with Constans only in the three cities of Aquileia, Trier, and Milan, the passage of the *Defense before Constantius* analysed so far reveals nothing whatever about the number of interviews, either in total or in each city, and very little about their dates and occasions. To discover how many audiences there were and when they occurred, it is necessary to turn to the continuation of the passage already quoted, which is evasive and slippery in the extreme:

Although this is sufficient for proof, permit me nonetheless to set out an account of my travels, so that from these facts too you may condemn those who baselessly slander me.

After departing from Alexandria, I did not go to the court of your brother, nor to any others, only to Rome. Entrusting my cause to the church (for I was concerned for this alone), I spent my time in public worship. I did not write to your brother except [on the occasions] when the Eusebians wrote to him against me and I was compelled to defend myself while I was still in Alexandria, and when, at his command that I prepare copies of the holy scriptures, I produced and sent them. [I say this because] in my defense I must tell the truth to your piety. So, after three years had passed, in the fourth year[17] he wrote ordering me to present myself before him. (He was then in Milan.) When I enquired into the reason (for I did not know, the Lord is my witness), I learned that certain bishops had gone to court and requested him to write to your piety so that a council might be held. Believe me, emperor, it happened like this; I am not lying. So I went down to Milan and experienced great generosity; for he graciously saw me and said that he had written and sent to you asking for a council to be held.[18]

I was still residing in the aforementioned city when he sent for me again [to come] to Gaul, since Father Ossius was going there too, so that the two of us could travel [together] from there to Serdica. After the council, he wrote to me while I was residing in Naissus, and after going up to Aquileia I then remained there [until] the letters of your piety reached me there. And after being summoned again from there by your departed brother, I went to his court in Gaul and so came to your piety. (3.8–4.5)

This long passage proceeds in chronological order except for the digression on Athanasius' written correspondence with Constans. Athanasius returns to his main argument with the assertion that he had no dealings with Constans for three full years: the logic of the passage entails that he must mean three full calendar years from his arrival in Rome (or at least from his departure from Alexandria), not three years from his correspondence with Constans in 338.[19] In the fourth year of his exile, that is, no earlier than the summer of 342, Athanasius was summoned by Constans to Milan, because 'certain bishops' had already persuaded him to write to Constantius proposing, or demanding, a council of both eastern and western bishops (4.3). Who were these 'certain bishops'? The plural could, as in the preceding reference to the emperor Constantinus as anonymous 'others,' designate a single individual. But, whether Athanasius in fact intended to refer to one or more bishops here, an easy identification of the date and occasion offers itself. For it was during the year 342 that Paul of

Constantinople arrived at the court of Constans in Trier, and the western emperor decided to take up the cause of all the exiled eastern bishops.

Eusebius of Nicomedia, who had orchestrated the campaign against Athanasius and his allies as bishop of Constantinople since c. October 337, died before he received (or at least before he was able to answer) the conciliar letter which Julius sent from Rome on behalf of Athanasius and Marcellus in the late spring or summer of 341.[20] Paul, whom Eusebius had replaced in 337, thereupon attempted to recover his see. He left his place of exile in Pontus and returned to Constantinople. At the same time, the Christians of the city opposed to Paul elected Macedonius as bishop. News of this reached Constantius while he was wintering in Antioch. He ordered the *magister militum* Hermogenes, who was perhaps already on his way to take up an appointment in Thrace, to expel Paul from Constantinople. When Hermogenes arrived in the city and tried to carry out the emperor's orders, a mob burned the house where he was lodging, dragged him out, and lynched him. Constantius himself then came post-haste across Asia Minor in the depths of winter: he ejected Paul and punished the city by halving its supply of free grain. When he returned to Antioch, he left Macedonius as bishop of the city.[21]

The riot in which Hermogenes perished belongs to the beginning of 342.[22] Expelled from Constantinople, Paul betook himself to Trier, whose bishop Maximinus had already shown his goodwill and political support. That is made clear by the complaints voiced against Maximinus by the eastern bishops at the Council of Serdica in 343:

> He refused to receive our episcopal colleagues whom we had sent to Gaul; he was the first to communicate with the wicked and reckless Paul of Constantinople; and he was himself the cause of such a disaster because Paul was recalled to Constantinople, on whose account many murders were committed. He himself was the cause of so many murders, who invited Paul, who had earlier been condemned, to return to Constantinople.[23]

There appear to be three distinct charges made here against Maximinus, which should be considered in chronological order, since the eastern bishops appear to conflate three separate episodes for rhetorical effect. First, Maximinus was the first to recognise Paul as bishop of Constantinople. If the word 'first' is to have real content, then this charge must relate to Paul's first tenure of the see of Constantinople in 337. Paul must have written to Trier immediately after his election—doubtless with the encouragement and perhaps at the instigation of Athanasius. Second, Maximinus caused slaughter in Constantinople by summoning Paul to the city in the winter of 341/2. And third, Maximinus refused to communicate with the bishops Narcissus of Neronias, Theodorus of Heraclea, Maris of Chalcedon, and Marcus of Arethusa when they went to Constans at

Trier. Socrates plausibly states that these bishops went to Gaul after Constans had written to Constantius demanding that a delegation of three bishops be sent to justify to him the deposition of Paul and Athanasius.[24] The approximate date of the embassy is fixed as 342 by the creed which the four bishops brought with them and which both Athanasius (*Syn.* 25.2–5) and Socrates quote.[25] The precise date can hardly be earlier than the autumn of 342, since time must be allowed for Paul to reach Trier, for Constans to write and Constantius to react, and for the delegation to travel from Antioch to Gaul. Constans' presence in Trier is not in fact explicitly attested during the summer of 342, but the city was one of his normal residences, and it seems that during this summer he settled Franci in Toxandria at the mouth of the Rhine—which implies that he passed through Trier both before and afterward.[26]

In 359 Athanasius alluded to the embassy of the four bishops in a typically cryptic fashion. The Arians (he proclaimed) showed their vacillating inconsistency by composing another creed only a few months after the 'Dedication Council': they sent it to Gaul with Narcissus, Maris, Theodorus, and Marcus, who presented it to Constans and everyone there 'as if sent from a council' (*Syn.* 25.1). Athanasius' chronology is vague and misleading: the 'few months' are not a couple of months (as an unwary reader might suppose), but about a year and a half (from January 341 to the summer of 342). Nevertheless, Athanasius' ridicule documents two important facts about the embassy of the four bishops. It was sent by a council of bishops (which presumably met at Antioch), and it was sent to Constans as well as to Maximinus and other bishops ('all those there'). Furthermore, Athanasius quotes the creed which the four bishops took to Gaul. It makes an obvious attempt to parry the objections of Marcellus and the like to previous creeds of Antiochene councils: although the statement of beliefs avoids the crucial term *ousia,* the anathemas reject as heretical the idea that the Son is 'of different substance *(hypostasis)* and not of God' (*Syn.* 25.2–5).[27]

The reception, fate, and sequel of the embassy of the four eastern bishops to Trier are all alike unknown. Late in 342, however, Constans summoned Athanasius to an audience in Milan.[28] Paul and Maximinus of Trier had exercised effective persuasion. The western emperor had become the champion of all the eastern bishops who were in exile in the west, convinced that their deposition imperiled Christian orthodoxy. Constans wrote again to his brother, presumably in the winter of 342/3, insisting on a joint council of eastern and western bishops (*Apol. ad Const.* 4.4). Constantius acceded reluctantly to his demands, and a day was at last set for the bishops of both brothers' domains to meet at Serdica, close to the border between them. Athanasius no longer stood alone: his cause enjoyed the firm support of the western emperor, it was joined to that of other bishops, and he had convinced both the western emperor and most western bishops that his cause was indeed the cause of orthodoxy.

In this context it will be appropriate to look forward to the other three audiences with Constans which Athanasius records. The emperor's movements establish their approximate dates.[29] Shortly after the first audience in Milan late in 342, Constans crossed the Alps into Gaul, sped north-west, and reached Boulogne by 25 January, whence he made a famous winter crossing of the English Channel.[30] The second audience was in Trier, when Constans interviewed Athanasius and Ossius together before they set off for the Council of Serdica. The emperor's presence in Trier is certified on 30 June 343,[31] but the interview probably occurred some weeks later.

In his chronological survey Athanasius does not explicitly mention the third audience—precisely because it was the embarrassing one, the audience after which Constans threatened his brother with war. But his statement that 'after going up to Aquileia I then remained there' (*Apol. ad Const.* 4.5) can be combined with his earlier admission that he had an audience at Aquileia (3.7) and his later disclosure of the fact that both he and Constans were in Aquileia at an Easter (15.4) to date the third interview to the early months of 345, a year in which Easter fell on 7 April (*Index* 17).

The final interview occurred in Trier after Athanasius received a letter from Constantius permitting him to return to Alexandria. Since the emperor's letter was written from Edessa (*Apol. c. Ar.* 51.6) no earlier than the summer of 345, while Athanasius reentered Alexandria on 21 October 346 (*Hist. ac.* 1.1; *Index* 18), the date must fall between the end of summer 345 and the middle of the following year. But the evidence of the Theodosian Code appears to indicate that Constans was at Sirmium in Pannonia on 5 March 346 and at Caesena in north Italy on 23 May.[32] Hence, if Athanasius needed to travel to Trier to see Constans, the audience presumably occurred in the autumn of 345 or, at the latest, during the winter of 345/6.

To conclude this chapter based principally on what Athanasius says about his audiences with Constans in the *Defense before Constantius*, it may be helpful to set out in schematic form the dates and places which have been deduced from what he says separately about the places where they occurred and their sequence:

342, autumn	Milan
343, c. July/August	Trier
345, late winter/spring	Aquileia
345, autumn	Trier

VIII

THE COUNCIL OF SERDICA

CONSTANS FIRST WROTE TO CONSTANTIUS REQUESTING A COUNCIL IN the spring or early summer of 342.[1] When the Council of Serdica met in the late summer of 343, virtually eighteen months had passed—a period which corresponds closely to the one year and six months which Socrates reports as intervening between the summoning and the meeting of the council.[2] The council confronted a controversial agenda, and East and West regarded the problems it was to discuss from totally different perspectives. The western bishops (as they later declared) saw three central tasks before them: to rescue holy faith and pure truth from those who had violated them; to decide whether the bishops deposed in the East since 337 had been justly or unjustly condemned; and to enquire into charges that in the East churches had been desecrated and clergy maltreated, tortured, even killed for supporting the cause of right.[3] The eastern bishops predictably took a different view—and showed extreme reluctance to attend a council which they were well aware was taking place at the insistence of the western emperor.

Constans had summoned Athanasius, who was still in Italy, to come to Gaul, so that he and Ossius might travel together to Serdica.[4] In the summer of 343 Athanasius duly came to the imperial court at Trier, then set out with Ossius for Serdica with the emperor's blessing (*Apol. ad Const.* 4.4). The bishop of Alexandria and the bishop of Corduba were accompanied by their allies and other exiled eastern bishops, including Paul of Constantinople. Further, despite Athanasius' assertion to the contrary on a later occasion (*Hist. Ar.* 15.3), it should probably be assumed that both a general and a high civilian official accompanied them,[5] if only to secure supplies and safe transport for the western bishops. However, any officials who may have escorted the bishops faded discreetly into the background before they reached Serdica. For it was clearly intended that the western bishops should present themselves, in contrast to the

71

eastern contingent, as independent of the secular authority, and their choice of dispersed lodgings in Serdica appears to have reflected this difference.[6]

The eastern bishops came slowly and reluctantly. Their leaders, Theodorus of Heraclea, Narcissus of Neronias, Stephanus of Antioch, Acacius of Caesarea, Menophantus of Ephesus, Ursacius of Singidunum, and Valens of Mursa (George of Laodicea did not come), made sure that their party had an agreed position. They assembled in the East, even though Ursacius and Valens occupied sees in provinces belonging to Constans, and they held preliminary synods in several cities to concert policy.[7] Finally, the eastern bishops reached Philippopolis, the most westerly large city in Constantius' domains along the great highway which led from Constantinople to northern Italy. Here they assembled in the autumn of 343 under the watchful eyes of three trusted servants of Constantius: the military *comes* Strategius Musonianus, the *castrensis* Hesychius, and the *comes* Philagrius, who, as prefect of Egypt in 339, had installed Gregory as bishop of Alexandria (*Hist. Ar.* 15.3; *Index* 15). Philagrius (it is plausibly alleged) laid down the tactics which the eastern bishops should adopt: they were to insist that the bishops whose cases were to be reviewed should not sit as members of the council until their status was resolved.[8]

Neither group of bishops constituted a completely solid bloc. Despite the close supervision of Philagrius, two eastern bishops, Arius from Palestine and Asterius from Arabia, bolted from the palace in Serdica, where the eastern bishops were housed, allegedly under close supervision, in order to discuss matters with their western colleagues.[9] Moreover, the easterners suffered from numerical inferiority. In all, approximately one hundred and seventy bishops attended the council (*Hist. Ar.* 15.3), but out of this total the eastern contingent accounted for only seventy-six,[10] whereas there were more than ninety western bishops present at Serdica, not including the exiles (some of whom subscribed the western synodical letter):[11] at any church council, where the minority was expected to assent to the will of the majority or face excommunication, that was a fatal weakness, unless waverers could be detached from the party of Athanasius. The eastern bishops knew of trouble enough in certain western churches, for after the council they included among the addressees of their synodical letter Donatus, the Donatist bishop of Carthage; the schismatic bishop of Salonae in Dalmatia (whose name is not known); three Campanian bishops, Fortunatus in Naples, Desiderius, and Eutychius; and the clergy of the church of Ariminum.[12] At Serdica itself, however, neither schism in Africa nor dissidence in Italy dented the unanimity of the western bishops. And they possessed an inestimable moral and political advantage: humble adherents of Paul and Athanasius (and perhaps of Marcellus) had made their way to Serdica, a reminder and threat of violence.[13] The council ran its stormy and predictable course.

The eastern bishops took their stand on the principle invoked in their letter from Philippopolis, and steadfastly refused to sit as members of a council which included Athanasius and the other exiles.[14] The western bishops had already written to reject this argument: they could not now break off communion with bishops whom they recognised and who were both present and ready to submit to an investigation of the charges against them, which they were confident of being able to disprove.[15] Ossius, who was to preside at the council, either by virtue of seniority (he had been a bishop for nearly fifty years) or because the emperors had named him (or both), craftily proposed an apparent compromise. He invited the enemies of Athanasius to come to the church where he was lodging in order to present their complaints to him privately. If they did so, they could be confident that he would render a just decision on the merits of the case: if Athanasius was shown to be guilty, he would be expelled from communion by Ossius; if he was found innocent, and his enemies still refused to accept him, then Ossius would urge him to return to Spain with him (*Hist. Ar.* 44.2/3). The eastern bishops were not taken in. The verdict of Ossius deliberating alone and privately was just as predictable as that of the western bishops sitting in formal conclave. The eastern bishops made a counter-proposal (if they had not made it already). Five of the six members of the commission which went to the Mareotis in 335 were still alive and present: they proposed that they and an equal number of western bishops go again to the scene of Athanasius' alleged crimes to establish the truth definitively. Ossius, Protogenes, and the rest in turn declined this offer.[16]

The two parties at Serdica never met together as a single council. Many days passed, and the ecclesiastical wrangling continued.[17] Suddenly the political situation changed. A letter arrived from Constantius announcing a victory over the Persians. It provided both motivation and an excuse for the eastern bishops. They abruptly left Serdica and returned to Philippopolis, sending a lame apology through Eustathius, a priest of the Serdican church (*Hist. Ar.* 16.2/3). Before they departed, however, they excommunicated their principal opponents and addressed a long synodical letter, duly subscribed by more than seventy bishops, to Gregory of Alexandria, Amphion of Nicomedia, named dissidents in the West, and 'all our fellow priests throughout the world, priests, deacons, and all who are bishops under heaven in the holy catholic church.'[18]

The bulk of the letter consists of explicit and abusive denunciations of Marcellus of Ancyra, Athanasius of Alexandria, Paul of Constantinople (this section, unfortunately, is almost entirely lost in a lacuna), Asclepas of Gaza, Lucius of Adrianople, and their western friends Ossius, Protogenes of Serdica, Maximinus of Trier, Gaudentius of Naissus, and their ringleader Julius of Rome, who first (they complain) opened the door of communion to the eastern criminals and boldly defended Athanasius without listening to his accusers and the witnesses against him. The letter is a well stocked and irreplaceable repository of allusions to episodes and alliances about which writers favorable to those denounced chose to remain silent.

Before he welcomed them into communion, Protogenes had attended and accepted the decisions of councils of bishops which condemned Marcellus and

Paul—the former on no fewer than four occasions.[19] The majority at Serdica included the bishops Dionysius of Elis and Bassus of Diocletiana, the former despite an earlier condemnation by many of the same bishops, the latter despite a criminal record for which he had been deported from Syria. Among them too was Aetius of Thessalonica, whom Protogenes had often accused of many offenses, refusing to communicate with a bishop who had maintained and continued to maintain concubines.[20] And Asclepas of Gaza had gone to Constantinople to support Paul: hence he shared part of the blame for the perpetration of a thousand murders which stained altars with human blood.[21]

The letter waxes eloquent on the heresy of Marcellus, 'a pest more damnable than all heretics,' who combines the falsehoods of Sabellius with the wickedness of Paul of Samosata and the blasphemy of Montanus. It reviews the career of Athanasius from the assault on Ischyras to the time of writing, with frequent descriptions of the violence which he had ordered or caused. And it levels specific charges against the other bishops exiled from the East and their western allies: Paul, Asclepas, and Lucius were guilty of sacrilege and incitement to murder, and Maximinus was 'himself the cause of so many murders' because he was the first to communicate with Paul and encouraged him to return to Constantinople from exile. Nor does the letter confine itself to recent events. Not only is Paul derided for inconsistency in subscribing to the deposition of Athanasius in 335,[22] but Athanasius is similarly ridiculed for accepting the deposition of Asclepas many years before,[23] and Ossius is reprehended for attacking a certain Marcus, now deceased (who seems to be otherwise unknown); for protecting condemned criminals; for being an inseparable friend of Paulinus, formerly a bishop in Dacia, who was convicted of writing magical books and now lives openly with concubines and prostitutes; and for associating with Eustathius of Antioch and Cymatius of Paltus before their deposition in 327.[24]

The eastern bishops profess a tender concern for the unity and orthodoxy of the holy catholic church and for ecclesiastical tradition. Accordingly, because of the conduct of those who disrupt the unity and peace of the church, the council has considered it proper and necessary to take disciplinary action:

> We openly charge you, most dearly beloved brothers, that none of you, misled by anyone, at any time communicate with those expelled from the holy church, that is, Ossius, Protogenes, Athanasius, Marcellus, Asclepas, Paul, Julius, or any of those condemned, or their allies who communicate with them either in person or by letter. Hence you must neither ever write to them nor receive letters from them. It remains, dearest brothers, to ask you to take thought for the unity and perpetual peace of the church, and to choose holy bishops of unsullied faith and holy life, rejecting those who, because of their crimes, have been stripped of the episcopate and wish to recover again the place which they deservedly lost for their misdeeds.[25]

Moreover, since Ossius and his friends endanger the catholic and apostolic faith, the eastern bishops deemed it necessary to attach to their letter, whose recipients they invited to subscribe their own names, a definition of that imperiled orthodoxy. The creed which they enounce is identical with that of the Council of Antioch in 342 taken to Constans by Narcissus, Maris, Theodorus, and Marcus, with a few additional anathemas.[26] These two creeds have an old-fashioned air, for they simply ignore the theological issues which the new term *homoousios* had raised.[27] They were highly suited, and hence presumably designed, to be the basis of a theological compromise. Moreover, the anathemas of 343, the new as well as those taken over from the creed of 342, set out to allay western fears of heretical tendencies:

> Those who say that the Son is from 'that which was not,' or is from another *hypostasis* and not from God, or that there was a time or period when he was not, the holy catholic church condemns as heretics. Similarly also, those who say that there are three Gods, or that Christ is not God, or that before the ages he was neither Christ nor Son of God, or that the Father and Son and Holy Spirit are the same, or that the Son is unbegotten, or that the Father did not beget the Son by his choice or will, the holy and catholic church anathematises.[28]

The repudiation of Arius from 342 is here complemented by anathemas which condemn Marcellus and rebut any suspicion that the eastern bishops hanker after the Origenist doctrine of three *hypostaseis* in the divine triad.[29] On the theological front at least, the eastern bishops adopted a moderate stance permitting the possibility of compromise.

The western bishops acted aggressively on both the personal and the theological fronts. The main section of their synodical letter opens with a partisan denunciation:

> The Arian heretics have often committed many rash acts against the servants of God who preserve the true catholic faith. Pushing their bastard doctrines, they have tried to persecute the orthodox. And now they have attacked the faith so violently that it does not escape the religious piety of the most clement emperors.[30]

The letter then reviews the course which the Council of Serdica has taken: in the past the Eusebians had made false charges against Athanasius and Marcellus, but were unwilling to substantiate them before Julius, the bishop of Rome; now their persistent refusal to attend meetings of the council at Serdica, to which they had been invited not once or twice, but many times, followed by their flight, has broadcast to the world their malice and mendacity. They came with accusations of violence enhanced by theatrical devices—exiles carrying their iron and chains, relatives and friends of those still in exile or who had died in exile, bishops with fetters on their necks on behalf of others. In fact, it was they who used force: they would have killed certain bishops had they not escaped, while Theodulus, the bishop of Traianopolis, has actually perished in a vain attempt to elude their hostility. The victims of the Arians could exhibit real wounds and scars. Orthodox bishops, who deserved credence, had produced reliable evidence of the use of armed soldiers and gangs with clubs, the threats of magistrates, the stripping of virgins, the burning of churches, the imprisonment of God's servants. The Arians themselves, however, made false accusations: Theognis of Nicaea had tried to inflame the emperor against Athanasius, Marcellus, and Asclepas, but his former deacons had produced Theognis' letters, which were read out for the whole council to hear. The heretics, therefore, came to Serdica with guilty consciences and fled in fear that the truth would come out.[31]

The letter next addresses the substantive questions which the council was convened to consider. The western bishops review the charges against Athanasius, Marcellus, and Asclepas: they ridicule Ischyras as an unreliable witness; they defend Marcellus on the grounds that he did not assert the heretical views attributed to him, but only proposed them as hypotheses for discussion; and they claim that the acts of the Council of Antioch which deposed Asclepas (in 327) prove him irreprehensible. The verdict which they render is clear-cut. Athanasius, Marcellus, Asclepas, and 'those who minister to God with them' are innocent and pure, and should be received back by their congregations as bishops instead of Gregory, Basil, and Quintianus. Theodorus, Narcissus, Acacius, Stephanus, Urscacius and Valens, Menophantus and George, however, are all deposed from their sees and expelled altogether from fellowship with the faithful. Let them be anathema, let no one communicate with them! For light cannot communicate with darkness, nor Christ with Belial.[32] The western bishops then appealed to the recipients of the letter to show their approval of the decisions made at Serdica by subscribing their names[33]—a plea which was heeded, so that some versions of the letter soon had the names of almost three hundred signatories attached.[34]

Two of the four versions of the synodical letter which survive conclude with a rambling, outspoken, and incautious statement of how western bishops viewed the theological problems at issue.[35] This statement has justly been characterised as a 'polemical broadside.'[36] It begins by excommunicating any who doubt that Christ is God or that he is Son in the fullest sense of each word, as do those two vipers begotten of the Arian asp, Ursacius and Valens, who, while professing themselves Christians, assert that both the Son and the Holy Spirit were crucified and killed, died, and rose again, and that the *hypostaseis* of Father, Son, and Holy Spirit are different and separate. In contrast, the western bishops assert that 'there is only one *hypostasis*, which the heretics themselves call *ousia*, of Father, Son, and Holy Spirit,' and they go on to argue, in a manner which sometimes betrays the influence of Marcellus, against the eastern supposition that the Son had some sort of personal existence independent of the Father.

As a result, by stressing the oneness of Father, Son, and Holy Spirit sharing a single *hypostasis*, the western bishops fail to make clear how the persons of the Trinity can be regarded as separate in any comprehensible sense.[37]

Despite all its statements of what 'we believe,' this theological manifesto was not intended as a formal creed to be circulated separately, nor is it plausible to argue that it was composed later as a 'separate polemical guide to clergy' to counter a lost document submitted after the council by Ursacius and Valens.[38] Both internal criteria and external evidence indicate rather that it was drafted as part of the synodical letter, but that the western bishops decided to omit this section of the draft from the final form of the letter which they officially adopted and endorsed.[39] For Athanasius, who was in a position to know, claimed in 362:

> The council made no such definition. Some people argued that, since [the creed of] the Council of Nicaea was insufficient, we should write about a creed, and made a rash attempt to do so. But the holy council gathered at Serdica was enraged: it decided that nothing more should be written about a creed, that it was satisfied with the creed acknowledged by the fathers at Nicaea, because it lacks nothing, but is full of piety, and that a second creed should not be issued, lest the creed written at Nicaea be considered invalid, and a pretext be given to those who wish to compose credal formulas frequently.[40]

The theological statement, even though discarded, soon began to embarrass its proposers. Ossius and Protogenes wrote to Julius in Rome protesting that it had been designed to elucidate obscurities in the Nicene creed, not to replace it.[41]

In the context of 343, one feature of the letter deserves special emphasis. Athanasius, Marcellus, and Asclepas were not the only exiled bishops exculpated by their western colleagues. Others were there too, to whom this long document alludes, but whom it does not name.[42] One was Lucius of Adrianople, who appears among the sixty or so original signatories to the council's decisions.[43] A more important omission was Paul of Constantinople, one of the main targets of the eastern bishops in their letter, who pointedly and accurately denounce him as a former bishop of Constantinople.[44] The silence of the western synodical letter about Paul does not prove his absence from Serdica, still less that the western bishops in 343 did not restore him together with Athanasius and Marcellus.[45] It indicates, rather, that even his supporters could not produce a plausible defense of his actions, especially of his uncanonical return to Constantinople in the winter of 341/2, which had provoked riots, the lynching of a general, and imperial punishment for the city.[46] The silence of the western bishops was a prudent tactical one, which has misled many ecclesiastical historians over the centuries into omitting Paul from their accounts of the Council of Serdica and denying that the council discussed his status. Socrates, however, states explicitly, presumably taking the information from Sabinus of Heraclea, that the council restored Paul together with Athanasius and Marcellus.[47]

The general letter addressed to churches everywhere was supplemented by letters to specific recipients. The western bishops acknowledged the moral leadership of the bishop of Rome. They wrote to Julius, therefore, requesting him to make their decisions known throughout Italy, Sicily, and Sardinia. A full report of the council was unnecessary, since Julius could read the accompanying documents and question the representatives whom he had sent to Serdica, the priests Archidamus and Philoxenus, and the deacon Leo. The bishops at Serdica, however, considered it necessary not only to summarise their findings briefly, but also to subjoin the names of the seven bishops whom they had formally deposed lest any western bishop communicate with any of them unawares. They also allude to an episode not mentioned elsewhere. Valens (they allege) abandoned his own church of Mursa and attempted to take over the church of Aquileia: in the riot which his attempt provoked, the bishop Viator was knocked down and so badly trampled underfoot that he died two days later.[48]

Athanasius' supporters in Egypt had contrived to convey letters to the western bishops, which were brought by Alexandrian clergy.[49] The bishops replied with almost identical letters to the church of Alexandria and to the churches throughout Egypt and Libya.[50] These letters naturally concerned themselves almost exclusively with Athanasius, whose proven innocence (they proclaim) ought soon to produce his restoration to Alexandria. But the western bishops at Serdica could also announce that they had received the exiled priests Aphthonius, Athanasius the son of Capito, Paul, and Plution into communion and acquitted them of the charges made by the Eusebians. In addition, they wrote to the churches of the Mareotis, who had complained of intolerable repression. They urged them not to be saddened, but to rejoice at persecution. Since the holy and great council has pronounced Athanasius completely guiltless and deposed his enemies, their tribulations must soon come to an end.[51]

The western bishops considered other problems besides doctrine, the status of exiled bishops, and the oppression of their adherents in the East. They devised a formula for ensuring that East and West celebrated Easter on the same day. Previously the computations used at Rome and Alexandria had sometimes produced different dates, even though both churches adhered to the rules laid down at Nicaea. That had happened in 343 precisely, when Rome celebrated Easter on 3 April, Athanasius and the Alexandrian church on 1 Pharmouthi (27 March).[52] At Serdica, a table of Paschal dates for the next fifty years was adopted, which the bishops of Rome and Alexandria were to announce to the churches in their jurisdictions (*Index* 15).[53]

The western bishops also debated a variety of disciplinary problems of pressing practical concern. These debates are known from the so-called canons of the Council of Serdica, which passed into early collections of canon law and hence acquired enormous authority in later centuries.[54] Their immediate effect is less easy to estimate: even though Gratus, the bishop of Carthage, appealed to their authority at an African council probably held in 345,[55] the canons appear to have been otherwise unknown in the West, except at Rome, until their sudden rediscovery and employment toward 420.[56]

The Serdican canons pose extremely serious textual problems, since the Greek and Latin canons that survive appear to constitute two divergent recensions of a document which did not collect and reproduce the formally ratified, subscribed, and promulgated decisions of the council, but rather summarised the minutes of the original discussions. The 'canons' of the Council of Serdica are thus radically different in nature from the canons which survive from the Council of Nicaea in 325 or the Councils of Arles (314), Ancyra (314), Antioch (probably 328), and Laodicea (probably c. 340), or even the canons of the Council of Gangra (probably c. 355), which merely reproduce and divide into sections the synodical letter of the Paphlagonian bishops.[57] The Serdican 'canons' have the form of proposals, mostly by Ossius, who presided and presented motions for approval: these proposals are sometimes followed by amendments by a second speaker, and the formula whereby the council signified its assent is not entirely uniform.[58]

Four principal problems worried the western bishops and recur throughout the canons: the translation of bishops and clergy from one city to another, the appointment of bishops, appeals against ecclesiastical decisions, and episcopal visits to the imperial court.[59] In addition, two canons which have dropped out of most of the Latin manuscript tradition address themselves to the problems of the church of Thessalonica, where the bishop Aetius, present at the council, confronted a difficult situation, since a certain Musaeus and Eutychianus claimed to be bishops and were ordaining priests. Presumably, both Musaeus and Eutychianus had been elected in opposition to Aetius: the council laid down that they should be received into communion as laymen, but that the priests whom they had ordained could retain their status.[60] It should be suspected that similar local problems lie behind many of the decisions of general applicability made at Serdica. In particular, the canons which provide that disputes between bishops of a province should be decided either within the province or by appeal to the bishop of Rome may have been motivated by disputes in Africa.[61] For Ossius and Alypius, the bishop of Megara, betray the motivation of the canons which prohibit bishops from going to court and compel them to intercede with the emperor by sending a deacon whom the bishop of Rome and bishops on the main roads shall have the power to intercept. Too many bishops (they complain) have been going to court, especially African bishops who spurn the salutary counsels of Gratus, the bishop of Carthage: in future, appeal by bishops to the emperor should be allowed only in cases of real oppression, such as of beggars, widows, and orphans.[62] It is relevant that one of the recipients of the eastern synodical letter was Donatus, who claimed the metropolitan see of Carthage. The church named after him had attained dominance in Numidia under

Constantine, who attempted repression systematically between 317 and 321, tolerated virtually open schism when he went to war against Licinius, and then reintroduced repressive measures at the end of his reign.[63] No disturbances are known for a decade after Constantine died, but Constans commenced another attempt to stamp out the Donatist church within a few years of the Council of Serdica.[64] The canons of the council, which are firmly dated to the period of apparent peace, reveal that the silence of the surviving sources is misleading. There was no real peace in the African church under Constans, merely a lull in hostilities.

Ossius and his allies had not forgotten the political and diplomatic context of the Council of Serdica. The emperors Constantius and Constans had summoned the bishops of East and West to assemble together. Since the single council envisaged by the emperors had never convened, each emperor was now free to accept the decisions of the bishops from his own territories. It was necessary, therefore, for both parties to report to both emperors. No record survives of any such report which the eastern bishops made: their leaders presumably went to congratulate Constantius on his Persian victory in person, and reported orally—and the predominantly pro-Athanasian sources that survive had no motive to preserve any letter they may have written to Constans. In their letters to Julius, to Alexandria, and to the Mareotis, the western bishops allude to a report 'to the most blessed Augusti' which was given wide currency (Julius was sent a copy).[65] If an identical report was sent to both emperors, it must have been a formal and factual account of the council. The western bishops also wrote a letter specifically designed to be read by Constantius alone, whose tenor differed greatly from their letters to sympathetic clerics.[66]

Constantius' piety and propensity to do good (the western bishops protest) will ensure that he grants their reasonable request to stop the persecution of the catholic church:

> Let your clemency provide and decree that all magistrates everywhere, who have been entrusted with the governing of provinces, whose sole care and concern should be for public business, refrain from surveillance of religion, and in future cease to presume, encroach, claim to decide the cases of clerics, and to vex and harry innocent men with various harassments, threats, violence, or acts of intimidation.[67]

The emperor has a duty to allow his subjects to enjoy liberty, to live as they please, to be catholics and Christians rather than heretics and Arians, to have the bishops and priests whom they choose to teach them, and to celebrate with them the divine mysteries. The writers proclaim their loyalty: all is quiet and modest, there will be no suspicion of rioting, of muttered opposition. They beseech Constantius to restore to their places the distinguished clergymen who are in exile or confinement. Arianism is 'a novel and terrible plague,' a recent invention of Eusebius of Nicomedia, Eusebius of Caesarea, of Narcissus, Theodorus, Stephanus, Acacius, and Menophantus, and of the two ignorant and improper youths Ursacius and Valens. Anyone who communicates with them becomes a partner in their crime and will suffer eternal punishment when the day of judgement comes.

IX

ATHANASIUS AND
THE MARTYRS OF ADRIANOPLE

AFTER THE COUNCIL OF SERDICA, PRACTICALLY THREE YEARS PASSED before Athanasius reentered Alexandria. For it was clear that the exiled bishops whom the western council had restored could not resume secure possession of their sees until the eastern emperor agreed to their return. A certain amount is known about the ecclesiastical negotiations between East and West after the Council of Serdica and about Constantius' dealings with Athanasius after he had accepted the Serdican decisions and agreed to allow him to return.[1] But what did Athanasius do between the council and the first letter which he received from Constantius in the summer of 345? As with his journey to the court of Constantius in 338,[2] it seems that Athanasius has been successful in concealing significant activities which he subsequently wished to obliterate from the historical record. The *Defense before Constantius* conveys the impression, which the *Festal Index* converts into asserted fact, that after the council Athanasius retired from the border-city of Serdica to Naissus and remained there uninterruptedly until he moved to Aquileia, which he had reached by the Easter season of 345: specifically, in 344 'being at Naissus on his return from the council, he there celebrated Easter,' and in 345 'having traveled to Aquileia, he kept Easter there' (*Index* 16, 17, cf. *Apol. ad Const.* 4.5). There is no reason to doubt that Athanasius celebrated Easter 344 in Naissus and Easter 345 in Aquileia. The falsification of history comes in the suggestion or assertion that he went nowhere else. For there is irrefragable evidence in his own writings that Athanasius set foot in the territory of Constantius during this period—and a strong possibility that he crossed illegally into the eastern empire not merely once, but twice.

The *History of the Arians* eloquently describes the misdeeds of the villainous and cowardly eastern bishops immediately after the Council of Serdica. Their cruel and vicious attacks on laymen and right-thinking bishops who opposed them far surpassed their previous wrongdoing:

> Since the people of Adrianople did not wish to communicate with [the eastern bishops] because they were fleeing from the council and were guilty of misdemeanor, they sent a report to the emperor Constantius and caused ten laymen from the imperial factory there to be beheaded, with Philagrius, the *comes,* again present and aiding them in this too. (The tombs of these men are outside the city: we too have seen them as we passed by.) Then, priding themselves on their great success, because they had fled to avoid being convicted of making false accusations, they persuaded the emperor to put their wishes into effect. They caused two priests and three deacons to be banished from Alexandria to Armenia. Arius and Asterius,[3] the one the bishop of Petra in Palestine, the other bishop in Arabia, who had bolted from them, they not only banished to Upper Libya, but caused to suffer violence. As for Lucius, the bishop of Adrianople, when they saw that he used great freedom in denouncing them and exposed their impiety, they caused him again, as before, to be bound neck and hands in iron chains: in this manner they sent him into exile, where he perished, as they know. They removed the bishop Diodorus, but when they saw that Olympius of Aeni and Theodulus of Trajanopolis, both bishops from Thrace and good and orthodox men, hated heresy, on the first occasion the Eusebians brought false charges and the emperor Constantius wrote, and on the second they reminded [him of them].[4] The rescript ordered them not only to be expelled from their cities and their churches, but also to suffer capital punishment wherever they were found . . . They wished to show in Alexandria that they deserved to be feared, and they caused an order to be issued that the harbors and gates of the cities be watched, in case they returned to their churches on the strength of the permission from the council. They caused orders to be sent to the magistrates at Alexandria concerning Athanasius and certain named priests, that if either the bishop or any of them should be found to have set foot in the city or its territory, the magistrate should be permitted to behead those who might be discovered. (*Hist. Ar.* 18.2–19.4)

Athanasius here passes in rapid review a series of actions taken against himself and Lucius of Adrianople, both restored by the Council of Serdica, and against certain eastern bishops who were coerced and punished for displaying sympathy for their exiled colleagues. Since Athanasius himself provides the main (and sometimes the only) evidence for each of these episodes, each needs to be examined separately.

First, the trouble at Adrianople (18.2). Ten workers in the imperial arms factory at Adrianople, which was a large and important producer of weapons and shields,[5] were executed for insulting the eastern bishops as they returned from

Serdica. There would have been a considerable interval between the arrest and execution of the *fabricenses* if Constantius were still in Syria when he was consulted about their punishment. However, the emperor may have come to Constantinople in the autumn of 343.[6] The date of the execution has some relevance to determining when Athanasius might have seen the tombs of the executed men by the side of the road leading out of the city. The arrest, banishment, and death in exile of the bishop Lucius appear to be later than and entirely separate from the execution of the *fabricenses* (19.1). Lucius had been with the western bishops at Serdica:[7] there is no evidence independent of Athanasius bearing on his arrest, but the obvious inference from what he says is that Lucius returned to Adrianople after the council and was arrested for this clearly illegal action. Athanasius also adduces the death of Lucius in the *Defense of His Flight* (3.3), but there he provides no specific detail at all about it.

Second, the exile of two priests and three deacons from Alexandria to Armenia (18.3[a]). This is known only from this passage and a later one in the *History of the Arians* where Athanasius records that Constantius permitted them to return in the early summer of 344 (21.1).

Third, Arius and Asterius (18.3[b]). The Palestinian bishop Arius and the Arabian bishop Asterius came to Serdica with the eastern bishops, but broke ranks by associating with the western party: as a result, according to Athanasius, they were incarcerated in the *palatium* where the easterners were lodging (15.4). Yet their names appear among the original subscriptions to the western synodical letter,[8] they added their names and salutations to the council's letter to the churches of the Mareotis,[9] and the western bishops state that they attended a session of the council and informed it of their maltreatment.[10] On the other hand, according to Athanasius, they were sent into exile in Libya Superior. It seems to follow either that they left Serdica with the rest of the eastern bishops before the western synodical letter was composed and subscribed or that they were later apprehended and arrested in eastern territory.

Fourth, the deposition of Diodorus (19.2[a]). Since Diodorus subscribed the western synodical letter at Serdica as bishop of Tenedos in the Asian province of Insulae,[11] while Athanasius can find nothing more serious to complain about than his deposition and replacement (*Hist. Ar.* 5.2), it may be conjectured that he went to the West before the council and stayed there.

Fifth, Olympius of Aeni (in the province of Rhodope) and Theodulus of Traianopolis (19.2), the bishops of two small neighboring cities on the Thracian shore of the Aegean Sea. Since Athanasius couples the names of Olympius and Theodulus, it may be inferred that both had been excommunicated by the eastern bishops at one of the gatherings which they held before they reached Serdica:[12] Athanasius had earlier observed that the eastern bishops used Musonianus and Hesychius to terrorise and plot against any victims whom they chose (*Hist. Ar.* 15.3). Olympius and Theodulus then fled to escape arrest, and Theodulus died either before or during the council.[13] Olympius, on the other hand, played some part in the debates at Serdica and appears to have secured himself a safe refuge whatever the outcome of the council: it was at the suggestion of Olympius that Ossius proposed that any bishop who had suffered violence and had been expelled unjustly because he agreed with the beliefs of the worldwide church or defended truth should be allowed to remain in the city where he had taken refuge until he could return to his own city or until the wrong done to him was remedied.[14] What Athanasius says about the actions of the Eusebians is compressed and obscure, but he appears to distinguish between two consultations of Constantius, the first before the council, the second after: that perhaps lends support to the hypothesis that Constantius visited Constantinople in the autumn of 343.

Sixth, Athanasius himself (19.3–4). Athanasius' complaints imply that his enemies expected or feared that he might sail to Alexandria. The only rational motive for sending a proclamation to officials in Alexandria allowing them to behead either the bishop or any of the priests named therein is that they suspected that Athanasius might go to Egypt. How did such a suspicion arise? That it had some basis in fact is confirmed by a reference to this period in Athanasius' *Defense of His Flight*, written in 357:

> They caused Theodulus and Olympius, bishops from Thrace, and us and priests of ours to be sought out in such a way that, if we had been found, we would have suffered capital punishment. Perhaps we would have been killed thus, if we had not escaped contrary to their expectation on that occasion too. For that is the import of the letters given to the proconsul Donatus against Olympius and his friends and to Philagrius against us. (*Fug.* 3.4–5)

To what earlier occasion or occasions does Athanasius here refer? The end of the passage could refer to his expulsion by Philagrius from Egypt in 339.[15] But the flight of the bishops Theodulus and Olympius and the mention of Donatus, who can only be the proconsul of Constantinople,[16] anchor the rest of the passage to the period of the Council of Serdica. Moreover, the order to search out Athanasius and his priests *prima facie* belongs to the months after the council. Nor does the mention of Philagrius contradict this hypothesis. He accompanied the eastern bishops to Serdica (*Index* 15),[17] and he executed the *fabricenses* at Adrianople who had refused to communicate with the same bishops after the council (*Hist. Ar.* 18.2). It is a legitimate deduction that Athanasius entered eastern territory at this juncture in order to assist Lucius in resuming possession of his see.

When did Athanasius see the tombs of the men executed at Adrianople? The natural assumption made by all who have so far expressed an opinion is that he must have passed through Adrianople as he returned to Alexandria in 346.[18] But in 346 Athanasius went to Rome (*Apol. c. Ar.* 52.1) before going to the court of Constantius in Antioch (*Apol. c. Ar.* 54.1): hence it seems overwhelmingly probable that he traveled from Rome to Syria mainly by sea, not overland through the Balkans.[19] On the other hand, if Athanasius accompanied Lucius when he returned to his see, it seems possible that he saw the tombs then. But he speaks of seeing the tombs as he 'passed through': since Adrianople lies on the great highway leading through the Balkans to Constantinople, it is at least equally possible that he saw them on his way to that city in 344 in the company of his friend Paul of Constantinople, who reoccupied his see in the second half of the year 344. It is again Socrates, with his knowledge of affairs in the city, who describes Paul's second illicit return to his see and his third expulsion.[20]

When Constantius in Antioch heard that Paul had returned to Constantinople and was again comporting himself as bishop of the city, he ordered the praetorian prefect Philippus to expel him. Philippus, remembering the fate of Hermogenes, went about his task skilfully. He concealed the real purport of his instructions from the emperor and proceeded to the baths of Zeuxippus as if to perform routine official business. From there he summoned Paul with a show of honor, saying that he needed his advice. Paul came. But when he arrived, the prefect produced his imperial instructions. Paul accepted what Socrates calls 'his condemnation without trial': Philippus had called his bluff and outsmarted him, and he perceived how untenable was his usurped position in face of the armed force of the prefect. Philippus quickly had Paul led into the imperial palace and from there bundled aboard a waiting boat. The bishop was sent to Thessalonica, his native city and the closest large port in the territory of Constans, and forbidden to set foot in the eastern parts of the Roman Empire— in other words, he was deported from the territory of Constantius. In Constantinople, Philippus then restored Macedonius as bishop: in the riot which accompanied his reinstatement, more than three thousand people were killed, either by soldiers or crushed underfoot. Paul soon left Thessalonica and, according to Socrates, sailed by way of Corinth to Italy.

Although Socrates narrates this episode before the Council of Serdica, his implied date has no authority.[21] On the contrary, the name of the praetorian prefect who expelled Paul from Constantinople establishes a clear *terminus post quem* for the episode. Since Domitius Leontius is attested as the praetorian prefect of Constantius until 6 July 344,[22] Philippus cannot have become prefect before July 344, though his predecessor may have retained office for some time after his latest attestation. Elsewhere, Philippus is first securely registered as praetorian prefect on 28 July 346.[23] Nevertheless, the sequence of ecclesiastical events firmly fixes the expulsion of Paul (and hence the start of his prefecture) to the autumn of 344 or the early winter of 344/5.[24] Paul had perhaps been in Constantinople for several weeks before Philippus deported him.

X

RETURN TO ALEXANDRIA

THE SYNODICAL LETTER OF THE WESTERN COUNCIL OF SERDICA WAS taken to Antioch by the bishops Vincentius of Capua and Euphrates of Cologne, who also carried the council's request to Constantius to allow the exiled eastern bishops to return and a letter from Constans commending the exiles to his brother. They reached Syria toward Easter 344, which in this year fell on 15 April. For reasons which remain obscure, Stephanus, the bishop of Antioch, attempted to discredit the two envoys. Using priests as intermediaries, he hired a prostitute to spend the night with Euphrates. The plan misfired when the woman saw that her intended bedmate was an elderly bishop calmly asleep and totally unaware of what was happening: instead of making the false accusation which Stephanus' agents expected, she began to shout and complain of violence. By daybreak the matter was public knowledge in the city, a crowd gathered, and officials from the imperial palace needed to intervene. During the investigation, the brothel-keeper identified the priests who had hired the woman's services from him, and they implicated Stephanus. As a result, Stephanus was deposed and Leontius became bishop in his place.

Such is Athanasius' account of the immediate diplomatic sequel to the Council of Serdica (*Hist. Ar.* 20.2–5). It is both incomplete and tendentious. Theodoretus has a more detailed narrative full of specific detail, combining fictitious elaboration of the same original story with authentic local tradition, which has supplied him with some basic facts about the episode which Athanasius glosses over.[1] Theodoretus reports that the two bishops were accompanied by the general Salianus, who must be the Flavius Salia attested by papyri as *magister equitum* and ordinary consul in 348.[2] Moreover, since a bishop could be deposed and replaced only by a council of bishops, Theodoretus must be correct in stating that Stephanus was condemned and deposed by a council of bishops: since this council met at Antioch not long after Easter 344, it seems likely, on chronological grounds, that it is identical with the Council of Antioch which met in the summer of 344 and adopted the so-called long creed (*Syn.* 26).[3]

This 'long creed' reflects the political circumstances of its composition, and its tone has aptly been characterised as one which 'breathed the spirit of appeasement.'[4] The document comprises the creed and anathemas adopted by the eastern bishops at Serdica, followed by eight explanatory paragraphs designed to assuage a western audience. These paragraphs carefully avoid the term *ousia* and deny that the Son is of a different *hypostasis* from the Father: although the persons of the Trinity are admitted to be three *prosopa* and three objects *(pragmata),* the strongest emphasis is laid on the unity of the godhead. The eastern bishops proclaim that the Son is 'like the Father in all things,' and set out to be conciliatory on the main theological issues. On the other hand, they criticise at length and with outspoken frankness both Marcellus of Ancyra and his pupil Photinus, who had recently been elected bishop of Sirmium—his name deformed to 'Scotinus,' the dark and shadowy one instead of the light-bringer.[5] Not long after the council met, probably in September 344, Constantius too made a conciliatory gesture: he ordered the release of the Alexandrian clergy exiled to Armenia and sent instructions that the clergy and laity in Alexandria loyal to Athanasius no longer be harassed (*Hist. Ar.* 21.2, cf. *Index* 16).

The Council of Antioch sent four bishops to convey its synodical letter to the West: Demophilus, Eudoxius, Martyrius, and Macedonius from Cilicia (*Syn.* 26.1). But some delay intervened, perhaps not unconnected with the attempt of Paul to reestablish himself as bishop of Constantinople in the second half of 344.[6] Moreover, the bishops may have been accompanied by the *comes* Thalassius, who came to the court of Constans while the emperor was at Poetovio—an event which caused Athanasius, the only ancient writer who mentions it, some embarrassment when he defended himself against the charge of fomenting hostility between Constans and his brother (*Apol. ad Const.* 3.3).[7] The eastern bishops received an answer from their western colleagues at the Council of Milan, which met in the early months of 345, while Constans was either present or at least close at hand.[8]

The proceedings of this council are not at all well documented. The lack of information is admittedly not unusual at this period, but the Council of Milan was more interesting and significant than most councils, because it witnessed important changes of theological attitude and personal allegiance. The western bishops condemned Photinus, and although they refrained from condemning Marcellus, they ceased to support him as they had hitherto. Athanasius himself had withdrawn from communion with Marcellus before the council; Marcellus prudently declined to force the issue and absented himself from the council.[9] The Pannonian bishops Ursacius and Valens, whose sees lay in the territory of Constans, denounced the Arian heresy and requested to be accepted into communion by the western bishops. The political advantages of such a change of allegiance were obvious, and Ursacius and Valens were allowed to make their peace with the western church. The eastern envoys, however, did not like the manner in which the council performed the ritual denunciation of Arius and his heresy: they refused to assent to the document which it drew up and angrily stormed out.[10] The fragmentary reports of the Council of Milan (it will be observed) contain no reference at all to the reinstatement of Athanasius.

Constans now intervened with decisive effect. He had written to Athanasius while the latter was still in Naissus, and Athanasius implies both that Constans granted him an audience in Aquileia and that he and Constans were both in Aquileia at an Easter (*Apol. ad Const.* 4.5, 15.4). Constans, therefore, interviewed Athanasius at Aquileia in the spring of 345, when Easter fell on 7 April, either shortly before or shortly after the Council of Milan.[11] Moreover, he wrote a letter which contained an explicit threat of civil war:

> Athanasius and Paul are here with me. From questioning them I have discovered that they are being persecuted for the sake of piety. Accordingly, if you undertake to restore them to their episcopal thrones, expelling those who are vainly clinging to them, I shall send the men to you. But if you were to refuse to take this action, be assured that I will come in person and restore them to the thrones which are theirs, even against your will.

Such is the extract quoted by Socrates:[12] the letter from which he quotes was known to the other ecclesiastical historians of the fifth century and should not be dismissed as a forgery.[13]

Rufinus, presumably here translating Gelasius of Caesarea, produces a paraphrase of the same extract which makes three significant changes to the original: Paul of Constantinople has disappeared, the diplomatic language has been made harsher, and a threat to punish Athanasius' enemies has been added.[14] Both Philostorgius and Theodoretus report that Constans wrote to his brother in very similar tones.[15] Admittedly, Theodoretus may be mistaken when he states that the general Salia and the bishops Vincentius and Euphrates brought a threatening letter to Antioch early in 344.[16] But Constans wrote to his brother immediately after the Council of Serdica (*Hist. Ar.* 20.2) as well as in 345, and the earlier letter was milder in tone than the later. Sozomenus specifically records two letters, the first requesting Constantius to restore Athanasius and Paul, the second telling him 'either to receive the men or prepare for war.'[17] If Theodoretus has confused the milder letter of 343/4 with the later and more hostile letter of early 345, that in no way impugns the authenticity of Socrates' quotation. Moreover, though Philostorgius too reports a letter which demanded the return of Athanasius alone,[18] he supplies a detail which strongly suggests that he is paraphrasing the same letter as the one from which Socrates quotes: it was taken to Constantius by the *comes rei privatae* Eustathius—who is attested in that office on 15 May 345.[19]

Athanasius himself provides unwitting and unwilling confirmation that the letter from which Socrates quotes is authentic. His *Defense before Constantius* refers allusively and with obvious embarrassment to an occasion when 'the embassy of Thalassius came to Poetovio' while he was in Aquileia (*Apol. ad Const.* 3.4). No other writer or surviving document explicitly mentions this embassy. But Athanasius' presence in Aquileia fixes the date as lying between the summer of 344 and the following summer, and the fact that the *Defense before Constantius* refers to the embassy in a context where Athanasius is defending himself against the charge that he had fostered discord between the dead Constans and his brother indicates clearly, albeit indirectly, that Constans gave Thalassius a truculent answer. The interlocking details provided separately by Athanasius, Socrates, and Philostorgius suggest that Eustathius took the letter of which Socrates quotes a part to the eastern emperor together with the synodical letter of the Council of Milan.

Constantius yielded. Fortune (or the hand of God) provided the decisive argument. Gregory, who had replaced Athanasius as bishop of Alexandria in 339, died on 26 June 345 (*Hist. Ar.* 21.1/2; *Index* 18). Since the normal procedure of an episcopal election in Alexandria would have produced no result other than the reelection of Athanasius, the emperor bowed to necessity. He wrote from Edessa to Constans, and also to Athanasius, who was still at Aquileia (*Apol. ad Const.* 4.5), in the following terms:

> The generosity of our gentleness has not allowed you to be buffeted and tossed as if by the wild waves of the sea for long. Our unwearying piety has not abandoned you while you have been deprived of your ancestral hearth and stripped of your belongings and wander in savage wildernesses. Even if I have for a long time deferred communicating the purport of my intentions, because I expected you to appear before us of your own accord and to ask for relief from your toils, nevertheless, since fear has perhaps prevented the fulfilling of your intention, we have accordingly dispatched to your gravity letters full of bounty, so that you may hasten without fear to provide your presence speedily to our sight, in order to obtain your desire, to experience our generosity, and to be restored to your home. For this purpose I have on your behalf requested my lord and brother Constans, the victorious Augustus, to give you permission to come, so that you may be restored to your homeland with the consent of us both, receiving this as a pledge of our favor. (*Apol. c. Ar.* 51.2–4)

That is the language of diplomacy which veils, though it does not quite conceal, the emperor's insincerity. When it suited him, Athanasius could quote the letter as evidence of Constantius' respect, even affection, for him (*Hist. Ar.* 22/3). But he can have had no illusions about the emperor's true feelings, for he knew how Constantius' new expression of sympathy for his sufferings contrasted with his actual policy towards him since 339. Whether it was sincere or devious, however, the letter of Constantius unconditionally promised Athanasius that he could return to Alexandria. It must be assumed that Paul of Constantinople received a letter couched in similar terms, even though nothing precise is known about the date of his return.

Athanasius returned during the summer and autumn of 346, a full year after Constantius' first letter permitting him to do so. Why the delay? Either Athanasius did not trust Constantius and asked for guarantees, or else there was dispute and negotiation about the terms of his return. Constantius wrote two further letters urging Athanasius to come to his court. The first requested him to come with all speed by means of the *cursus publicus*, without worry for himself, without distrust and fear, so that the emperor could send him to Alexandria (*Apol. c. Ar.* 51.5). The second lamented Athanasius' slowness in responding to his original letter written a year earlier, and it reiterated his request for the bishop to come to him. Constantius sent it by the deacon Achitas, who added his own exhortation (*Apol. c. Ar.* 51.6–8). Various high officials seconded the emperor's request by writing too: Athanasius names the *comites* Polemius, Datianus, Bardio, Thalassius, Taurus, and Florentius, adding that he was readier to believe their assurances of friendship than to believe those of the emperor (*Hist. Ar.* 22.1).[20] Confirmation that matters were not quickly settled between the imperial brothers comes from the consular fasti. The two halves of the Roman Empire had different consuls for 346: in the East Constantius proclaimed himself (for the fourth time) and Constans (for the third time), but there is no good evidence that this imperial consulate was accepted in the West, at least until very late in the year.[21]

During the autumn of 345, Athanasius was summoned by Constans to the court at Trier (*Apol. ad Const.* 4.5).[22] It would be worth knowing exactly why Constans required his presence, or how his visit impinged on negotiations between the two emperors. But the diplomatic exchanges of 345/6 will always remain shrouded in secrecy. Athanasius preferred to emphasize the public stages of his triumphant return.

From Trier, Athanasius probably returned to Aquileia. When his return to Alexandria was finally agreed upon, he went to Rome, where Julius provided him with an eloquent testimonial to take to the church at Alexandria (*Apol. c. Ar.* 52/3),[23] and where he presumably did not fail to renew his contacts with sympathetic Christians in the Roman aristocracy. From Rome Athanasius went to Syria, where he presented himself before Constantius. He will have traveled mainly or entirely by sea, either via Brundisium, Greece, and the south coast of Asia Minor or through the Straits of Messina to Cyprus.[24] When Athanasius reached Antioch, according to the *History of the Arians,* the emperor promised, under an oath and with God as witness, never again to listen to slanderous accusations against him (*Hist. Ar.* 22.2, cf. *Apol. ad Const.* 4.5). Whether that is true or not, Constantius certainly rescinded all existing measures against the bishop of Alexandria.

The emperor wrote to Nestorius, the prefect of Egypt, and to the *dux* of the province to ask for the return of all letters in their offices pertaining to Athanasius (*Apol. c. Ar.* 56.1; *Hist. Ar.* 23.3). The *decurio* Eusebius retrieved the documents—and presumably supplied copies to Athanasius on his return. In letters to the prefect of Egypt and to the *praesides* of the provinces of Augustamnica, Thebais, and the two Libyas, Constantius restored freedom from civic liturgies to the clergy loyal to Athanasius without removing that privilege from other clerics (*Apol. c. Ar.* 56.2/3). He wrote a circular letter to the bishops and priests of the catholic church everywhere announcing the pardon of Athanasius and the restoration of full privileges to the clergy loyal to him: after 'a brief season' of 'the trials inherent in the human condition,' the bishop has obtained release 'by the will of the Supreme Power' (*Apol. c. Ar.* 54.2–5). Constantius also furnished Athanasius with a letter of commendation to the Christians of Alexandria which encouraged them to respect the unanimity and peace of the church and discreetly warned them against disturbance and sedition (*Apol. c. Ar.* 55).

In Antioch Athanasius pointedly rebuffed Leontius and celebrated services with the Eustathians in private houses.[25] Then he traveled south through Syria, Phoenice, and Palestine. In Laodicea he met and formed a friendship with the priest Apollinaris, who thus earned the hostility of George, the bishop of his city.[26] In Jerusalem Maximus convened a provincial council which welcomed him and sent him on his way with yet another impressive testimonial (*Apol. c. Ar.* 57). As Athanasius approached Alexandria, people flocked out of the city to greet him. On 21 October 346 he received a warm welcome from 'the people and all those in authority' fully one hundred miles outside Alexandria (*Hist. ac.* 1.2; *Index* 18). He was escorted to the city in honor and glory, and his triumphant progress into Alexandria resembled less the return of an exiled bishop than the *adventus* of a Roman emperor.[27]

In stark contrast to Athanasius' restoration and resumption of power in his native city stands the fate of Marcellus, once his partner in misfortune and close ally.[28] Marcellus too had been rehabilitated at Serdica in 343, but thereafter his western supporters gradually came to accept the eastern view that his doctrines were, by the standards now applicable, irretrievably heretical—and Marcellus himself refrained from contesting the point in any way which might embarrass Athanasius.[29] It is unlikely that he returned to Ancyra after the Council of Serdica, as Socrates and Sozomenus allege.[30] Moreover, the fact that Marcellus' erstwhile supporters failed to defend him at Milan in 345 implies that Constans did not insist upon his return to the East with Paul and Athanasius in 346. After 349 a return was out of the question until the winter of 361/2, when Julian restored all eastern bishops exiled under Constantius.[31] Presumably Marcellus availed himself of the opportunity, since a conventicle of his supporters in Ancyra submitted a creed to Athanasius in 371, in which they described themselves as 'the clerics and others in Ancyra of Galatia who assemble for worship with our father Marcellus.'[32]

Marcellus cut a pathetic figure as he dragged out his existence until he died at the age of ninety or more, sixty years after his first attestation as a bishop in 314.[33] Perhaps he was already suffering from senility when the western bishops dropped him in 345. Marcellus seems to have occupied the last thirty years of his life in futile attempts to clear himself of the stigma of heresy.[34] All to no avail, for he was formally condemned at the Council of Constantinople in 381.[35] To his credit, Athanasius refused to join in the chorus of condemnation, even though Basil of Caesarea requested him to do so.[36] When the young and zealous Epiphanius asked Athanasius about Marcellus, he neither defended him nor showed any hostility, but merely 'revealed by the smile on his face that he was close to wickedness, but that he treated him as having acquitted himself.'[37] Athanasius' smile may have had a personal rather than theological significance.

XI

THE CONDEMNATION OF
349 AND ITS CONTEXT

DURING HIS EXILE, ATHANASIUS HAD CAREFULLY MAINTAINED CON-
tact with the Egyptian church and his supporters in Alexandria. He continued to
notify the Christians of Egypt each spring or summer of the date of Easter in the
following year, and he sent a full *Festal Letter* to be read in Lent whenever it was
possible for him to do so.[1] Clergy came to Serdica from Alexandria and the
churches of the Mareotis and read out before the western bishops letters describing the sufferings of Athanasius' supporters in Egypt at the hands of Gregory
and his supporters.[2] When the council had finished its business, the western
bishops wrote to the church of Alexandria, to the churches of the Mareotis, and
to the Christians of Egypt and Libya as a whole to announce the reinstatement
of their metropolitan,[3] while Athanasius himself sent a letter to his own church
and one to the churches of the Mareotis subscribed by some sixty other bishops.[4] Moreover, it is clear both from the complaints made at Serdica and from
the actions of Constantius after the council that Athanasius' supporters were
active and powerful in the city—indeed, the emperor was afraid that
Athanasius, like Paul in 341/2 and again in 344, might attempt to resume possession of his see without waiting for official permission.[5]

Athanasius' careful attention to his supporters in Egypt through the seven
long years of exile brought political benefits when he returned to Alexandria in
346. Although Gregory enjoyed an opportunity to build up an opposing system
of power and patronage for six of these years, there is no sign that he succeeded
in weakening the power of the exiled patriarch. Athanasius complained of violence used on his supporters in the docks of Alexandria in 339 (*Ep. enc.* 5.5), but
any success that his opponents may have attained within the city proved only
temporary. In October 346 both magistrates and populace turned out to greet
their returning bishop (*Index* 18).

It is less easy to assess the balance of power between the supporters and opponents of Athanasius outside Alexandria. In the Egyptian countryside, the un-easy coexistence of Melitians and churches loyal to Athanasius continued. In the 320s Melitius had named a total of thirty-four Melitian bishops, including him-self, in the list of his clergy which he submitted to Alexander (*Apol c. Ar.* 71.6). That was clearly the total number of Melitian bishops at that time. In 335 Athanasius took a phalanx of forty-eight bishops loyal to himself to the Council of Tyre—a number which happens to correspond exactly to the number of nomes in Egypt, if only by accident.[6] During Athanasius' exile, Serapion of Thmuis was presumably entrusted with the task of keeping the bishops in the Egyptian *chora* loyal in the face of pressure and inducements to support Gre-gory. In 338 Athanasius had instructed Serapion to ensure that the churches throughout Egypt observe the recently introduced custom of a forty-day fast before Easter and informed him of the names of newly appointed bishops.[7]

During Athanasius' second exile, there were few defections, if any, and it seems that the Melitian episcopate went into a gradual but steady decline. Only a handful of bishops from Egypt attended the Council of Serdica in 343, and all those Egyptian bishops who subscribed the eastern synodical letter were known Melitians and enemies of Athanasius—Ischyras of the Mareotis, Eudaemon of Tanis, Callinicus of Pelusium, Isaac of Letopolis (probably not at Serdica, since Eudaemon seems to have subscribed for him), and Lucius of Antinoopolis.[8] The *Festal Letter* which Athanasius wrote shortly after his return in October 346 for Easter 347 closes with an appendix in which he lists sixteen recently appointed bishops in order that the recipients of the letter may know 'to whom to write and from whom to receive letters' (*Festal Letter* 19.10). By 348 the total number of Egyptian bishops loyal to Athanasius had almost doubled from 335: no fewer than ninety-four appended their names to a copy of the western synodical letter from Serdica (*Apol c. Ar.* 49.3 Nos. 149–242).

Equally significant, the *Festal Letter* for 347 reveals Melitian defections to the Athanasian side—Arsenius at Hypsele, apparently Isaac at Nilopolis, Isidorus at Xois, and Paulus at Clysma. Furthermore, even though Athanasius complained bitterly that Melitians cooperated with Arians in 356 (*Letter to the Bishops of Egypt and Libya* 21/2), and the *Festal Letters* for 365, 367, and 369 contain sustained attacks on the Melitians, especially for their extravagant cult of the martyrs,[9] only two Melitian bishops appear to have attended the Council of Seleucia in 359.[10] It seems clear that by the later 360s the Melitians of the Nile Valley were no more than a rural rump of 'old believers,' who had priests and monks but no ecclesiastical organisation, the bishops of the early days having died or defected without being systematically replaced.[11]

The restoration of tax privileges to the clergy loyal to Athanasius was not contingent on the removal of existing privileges from the Melitian clergy and clergy who had supported Gregory (*Apol c. Ar.* 56.2/3). In places where there were rival bishops, both now enjoyed exemption from civic liturgies. Probably to the period immediately after Athanasius' return should be assigned the

Hermopolite land registers, the surviving parts of which list the citizens of one of the four wards of Hermopolis in the Thebaid with the size of their landholdings in the nome and citizens of Antinoopolis who owned land in the Hermopolite nome.[12] Not only do these lists yield to sophisticated analysis to produce a picture of landholding patterns in a peasant society,[13] but they include four bishops—Dios of Hermopolis, who owned more than one hundred and twenty arourae, and three bishops from Antinoopolis: Arion, whose election Athanasius confirmed in 347; Ammonianus (or Ammonius), who had previously shared the see with Tyrannus (now presumably dead); and Macarius, who, by a process of elimination, must be the successor of the Lucius who attended the Council of Serdica as the Melitian bishop of the city.[14]

The restoration of Athanasius probably also occasioned changes in the local administration to reflect the new constellation of power. The chance survival of the archive of papers which Flavius Abinnaeus took to Philadelphia when he retired as commander of the fort at Dionysias in the Arsinoite nome gives a glimpse of vicissitudes which may have beset many officials in Egypt in these years.[15] After a long military service in the Thebaid, Abinnaeus had escorted ambassadors of the Blemmyes to Constantinople in 336, where the emperors Constantine and Constantius gave him the honorary rank of *protector*. Abinnaeus then escorted the Blemmyes back to their native land. Next, he brought recruits from the Thebaid to Constantius at Hierapolis in Syria (presumably in 339 or 340) and received an imperial letter of appointment as prefect of the Ala Quinta Praelectorum and commander of the fort at Dionysias.

In Egypt the bureau of the *dux et comes* Valacius refused to act on the letter because other men had produced similar letters. Abinnaeus thereupon submitted a petition to the emperors, to which he clearly received a favorable reply, since he had already assumed his post as *praepositus* at Dionysias by 29 March 342.[16] During the course of the year 344 Valacius sent Abinnaeus a brusque letter of dismissal,[17] which the latter prepared to contest by traveling to court: two letters of 1 and 2 February 345 promise to reimburse him for expenses in furthering the interest of others besides himself.[18] Again, Abinnaeus was successful. But he may not have needed to present himself at court. Probably in 345 Valacius was thrown from his horse and died from the accident within three days:[19] by 1 May 346 Abinnaeus had obtained reinstatement, and he remained at his post until at least February 351.[20] Valacius had helped Gregory in Alexandria, allegedly whipping monks and assaulting bishops and virgins in order to secure cooperation with the anti-Athanasian bishops (*Hist. Ar.* 12.3). It is tempting to see in Abinnaeus a Christian who sympathised with Athanasius and perhaps even supported him actively in the Arsinoite nome, and to attribute a large part of his difficulties with Valacius to their different political and ecclesiastical allegiances.[21]

Athanasius had enjoyed the goodwill and political support of monks in rural Egypt from the very start of his episcopate.[22] In 336, after he departed into exile in Trier, Antony wrote to Constantine on Athanasius' behalf, and after his return he demonstrated his support of the embattled bishop by visiting Alexandria during the summer of 338.[23] The years following 346 saw a strengthening of this alliance. When Antony died c. 355, he divided his clothing among Athanasius, Serapion of Thmuis, and his own disciples.[24] Much further up the Nile from Antony's Outer Mountain, the Pachomian communities of the Thebaid exhibited equal loyalty to the restored metropolitan of Egypt, and some Pachomian monks traveled to Alexandria in 346 in order to welcome him back.[25] On the other hand, the letter which Athanasius wrote some weeks before Easter 354 urging the monk Dracontius to allow himself to be consecrated as a bishop may be a sign that the monks of Egypt wished to retain a certain independence of action by remaining outside the ecclesiastical hierarchy controlled by the metropolitan of Alexandria.[26]

Athanasius also had considerable political support outside Egypt. He could count on the continuing goodwill of the emperor Constans and the western bishops. Moreover, two of his oldest enemies changed sides and began to confess him innocent of all the charges ever brought against him. In 347 a council of western bishops met in Rome and condemned Photinus.[27] Ursacius of Singidunum and Valens of Mursa came, fearful that their frequent condemnations of Athanasius would become the cause of their own deposition, even though they had expressly repudiated 'Arian' ideas at the Council of Milan two years earlier. They approached the bishop of Rome and submitted to him a letter written in Valens' own hand which he and Ursacius subscribed jointly in the presence of Julius: the two Illyrian bishops declared that all the accusations which they had ever made against Athanasius were false and lacked any basis. The bishop of Rome formally accepted this declaration, and the council over which he was presiding admitted Ursacius and Valens to communion.[28]

As the two Pannonian bishops were returning home, they met the priest Moses, who was taking a message from Paulinus, the bishop of Trier, to Athanasius: at Aquileia they gave him a copy of their submission to Julius and a brief letter of salutation to the bishop of Alexandria expressing confidence in him.[29] Moses (it appears) took the two documents with him from Aquileia to Alexandria: that at least seems to be the most suitable hypothesis to explain how Athanasius could say that copies of the two letters of Ursacius and Valens, one of which was addressed to himself, were sent to him by Paulinus of Trier (*Apol. c. Ar.* 58.1; *Hist. Ar.* 26.2). Paulinus (it may be deduced) had written to Athanasius to announce that he had just been elected bishop in place of the deceased Maximinus.[30]

Athanasius appeared secure. But Constantius had allowed the restoration of Paul and Athanasius to Constantinople and Alexandria only out of political weakness and necessity, presumably judging that the military situation in Mesopotamia made it impossible to resist his brother's threat to restore the two bishops by force. Paul and Athanasius were soon again in peril. The bishop of Constantinople was the more vulnerable and was therefore attacked first, probably in the early months of 349.

Paul was accused by Macedonius, who had been elected bishop of Constantinople in place of Eusebius in the winter of 341/2, but had of necessity yielded place to Paul when he and Athanasius were restored. An accusation implies a trial, and the trial of a bishop implies a council of bishops. Paul was condemned, deposed, and sent to Constantius at Singara in iron fetters: Constantius sent his praetorian prefect Flavius Philippus to arrest Paul and convey him safely to court.[31] Paul was taken to Emesa (presumably accompanying the court there), and from Emesa he was sent into exile at Cucusus in Cappadocia, remote in the Taurus Mountains (*Hist. Ar.* 7.1, 3–6).[32]

The council which condemned Paul is known only from a single obscure allusion in the *History of the Arians* which Athanasius wrote several years later. It was probably, for reasons of prudence, not held in Constantinople itself, but in a nearby city such as Nicaea or Nicomedia, whose bishops were firmly in the opposite camp in ecclesiastical politics.[33] Some time later, probably in the autumn of 349, a council was held at Antioch which condemned and deposed Athanasius. This council stands on explicit attestation in the *Ecclesiastical History* of Sozomenus:

> Those who rejected the creed of Nicaea very assiduously exerted themselves in the palace to expel from their churches all those who had been removed from office by them on the grounds that they were heterodox and had, while Constans was still alive, endeavored to bring the two halves of the empire into conflict with each other, because Constans had threatened his brother with war if he did not receive them back, as has been explained before. They particularly accused Athanasius: because of their excessive hatred of him, they did not refrain from open hostility even when Constans was still alive and when Constantius was pretending to be his friend, but assembled in Antioch—Narcissus the Cilician, Theodorus the Thracian, Eugenius of Nicaea, Patrophilus of Scythopolis, Menophantus of Ephesus, and others, about another thirty in all—and wrote to bishops everywhere to the effect that Athanasius had returned to Alexandria in violation of the laws of the church, without having been pronounced innocent at a council, only through the partisan activity of those who shared his opinions. They exhorted [the recipients of the letter] not to communicate with or write to Athanasius, but to George, who had been elected by them.[34]

The context of this notice is both mistaken and confused. Sozomenus presents the Council of Antioch which deposed Athanasius as a consequence of the death of Julius, and jumbles up a series of events in what seems almost a random order: the death of Magnentius (353), the rebellion of Silvanus (355), the Jewish revolt (352), the execution of Gallus (354), Constantius' visit to Rome (357), and the death of Julius (352).[35] But what Sozomenus reports about the council itself points to a date before January 350—and appears to derive from the council's synodical letter, which he will have found in the collection of anti-Athanasian conciliar documents compiled by Sabinus of Heraclea in the 360s.[36]

Sozomenus supplies the names of the principal bishops who attended, and he can hardly be mistaken over the content of a letter whose date clearly puzzled him.[37] Moreover, the existence of such a council can be confirmed from Athanasius himself. The structure of the *Defense against the Arians* necessitates a somewhat complicated hypothesis to explain the genesis of the work. Despite some rewriting at the end, the bipartite shape and overall argument of the *Defense against the Arians* indicate that it is basically a document composed between 347 and 350.[38] When most of the last two chapters, which allude to events of 357, is removed, the *Defense* presents a coherent case which makes perfect sense in the context of 349—and at no later date. Athanasius relies heavily on the palinode of Ursacius and Valens in 347: after they withdrew their retraction of the charges against him in 350/1, that would have been an extremely lame central argument around which to construct a case. Consequently the hypothesis that Athanasius composed the *Defense against the Arians* in approximately its present form in 349 for submission to the Council of Antioch, which Sozomenus reports, both solves a serious literary problem and explains the motivation of the work.

Although it is certain that Athanasius did not leave Egypt to attend this council in Antioch, he may have sent trusted envoys to Syria with the *Defense against the Arians* to present to the assembled bishops. The work has two quite separate parts. The second is a reworking of the defense which Athanasius had elaborated for Julius at Rome nearly a decade earlier and deals with Athanasius' career under Constantine.[39] The first part extends the same method of argumentation to Athanasius' career after 337. It quotes documents at length, linking them together with brief commentary in order to present Athanasius as one whose conduct has been thoroughly investigated and thoroughly vindicated. The main documents quoted are:

(1) the letter of the Council of Alexandria in the early months of 338 (3–19);
(2) the letter of Julius in 341 replying to the synodical letter of the 'Dedication Council' at Antioch (21–35);
(3) three letters of the western bishops at Serdica: the first a letter addressed specifically to the church of Alexandria (37–40), the second a letter in almost identical terms to the bishops of Egypt and Libya (41), the third the synodical letter to bishops of the catholic church everywhere—with no fewer than two hundred and eighty-three names appended as signatories (42–50);[40]

(4) eight letters relating to Athanasius' return to Alexandria in 346, including six written by Constantius (52–57);

(5) the letters of Ursacius and Valens to Julius and Athanasius withdrawing their charges against Athanasius (58).

The overall argument is that bishops of independent judgement, councils of bishops unswayed by petty animosities, and even the emperor Constantius himself all agree that the charges made against Athanasius in the past have all been proven baseless. The previously composed second part of the *Defense* complements the arguments of the first by reviewing the struggles of Athanasius against Melitians and Arians in the early years of his episcopate, from 328 until his restoration by Constantinus in 337.

Athanasius lays particular stress on the change of mind by Ursacius and Valens, who have preferred a brief embarrassment to eternal punishment for calumny (88.3). The introduction and peroration make the circumstances of composition clear. Athanasius begins by expressing surprise that he needs to defend himself once more, that his enemies, who have so often been confounded, assert that his whole case ought to be tried yet again. That is arrant nonsense: 'My cause needs no further judgment, for it has been judged, not once or twice, but many times' (1.1). Athanasius reels off a list of councils which have vindicated him: a council of almost a hundred bishops in Egypt, a council of more than fifty bishops at Rome, the great Council of Serdica convened 'at the command of the most pious emperors Constantius and Constans'—councils whose verdicts Ursacius and Valens have confirmed by repenting of their former slanders. There is, therefore, no need to rehash yet again matters which so many distinguished bishops have investigated and upon which they have often pronounced an unambiguous verdict (1/2). After this introduction, Athanasius proceeds to quote documents *in extenso* with relatively brief linking comments until he reaches his peroration, which proclaims that everyone who knows the facts can see that the charges are false and that so many bishops have been right to pronounce him innocent (88, 90).[41]

Whether or not the *Defense against the Arians* was in fact laid before it, the Council of Antioch condemned and deposed Athanasius. But before its verdict could be enforced or George installed as bishop of Alexandria, political conditions changed with startling suddenness.

XII

THE USURPATION OF
MAGNENTIUS

CONSTANS WAS NOT A POPULAR AND WIDELY RESPECTED RULER. WRIT-ing in 361, Aurelius Victor charged him with rabid pederasty, headlong avarice, and the employment of corrupt ministers.[1] More serious, he alienated both high civilian officials and his military high command, and on 18 January 350 his most successful general was proclaimed Augustus at Autun.[2] The new emperor who replaced Constans was a surprising choice. Magnentius, born at Amiens of a Breton father and Frankish mother, had begun his career as a common soldier: on normal criteria, therefore, he was doubly disqualified from the imperial purple.[3] Constans fled and tried to reach the Mediterranean to take ship to Italy, but he was caught at Helena, south of Narbo, and killed.[4] Magnentius soon controlled Rome and Italy, where Fabius Titianus, who had served Constans faithfully for nearly ten years as praetorian prefect of Gaul, became *praefectus urbi* on 27 February.[5] Magnentius crossed from Gaul to north Italy and seized Emona and the passes through the Julian Alps leading to the Balkans.[6] He failed, however, to gain control of the Illyrian portion of Constans' domains. Constantina, a daughter of Constantine probably resident in Rome, helped to put up the *magister peditum* in Illyricum as emperor on 1 March: despite later innuendo, Vetranio was proclaimed emperor, not to challenge Constantius, but to forestall a second real rebellion.[7] Moreover, the usurper's hold on Rome was fragile. Julius Nepotianus, the son of Constantius' sister Eutropia, was proclaimed emperor on 3 June, though suppressed by Magnentius' forces before the month was out.[8]

Initially at least, Magnentius hoped to gain recognition from Constantius as ruler of the West, and he attempted negotiations with Vetranio and Constantius to that effect.[9] It was perhaps the rebellion and suppression of Nepotianus which convinced him that war was unavoidable. In July or August 350 (so it seems) Magnentius ceased issuing coinage in the name of Constantius as his senior colleague and proclaimed his brother Decentius Caesar in Milan.[10] The usurper no longer aspired to join the Constantinian dynasty, but to supplant it. Nevertheless, he sought political legitimacy by marrying Justina, a girl who appears to have been a great-granddaughter of Constantine.[11]

Magnentius' policies and propaganda reflected both the weakness of his position as a usurper and his claim to replace an incompetent and corrupt régime. He depicted himself from the outset as the 'liberator of the Roman world,' the 'restorer of liberty and the state,' the 'preserver of the soldiers and the provincials.'[12] A little later, after the rebellion of Nepotianus and its suppression, coins of the Roman mint proclaimed 'liberty restored for the second time' (bis restituta libertas) and 'the renewal of the city of Rome' (renobatio urbis Rome)—phrases with a long history and traditional appeal.[13] The coinage of Trier promised 'recovery of successful times' (fel(icium) temp(orum) reparatio), and one issue associated this traditional theme with a reverse depicting Magnentius in military dress standing on a galley holding Victory on a globe and the labarum with its Christogram.[14] The usurper compared himself to Constantine, who, unlike his unfortunate sons, had enjoyed great political and military success, which he attributed to his conversion to Christianity.[15] Despite the chorus of vituperation after his death, which depicted him as a pagan as well as a tyrant, Magnentius was a Christian.[16] Nevertheless, as one who challenged an established ruler, he needed to seek political support wherever he could find it.

Constantine had declined to extend to the West the prohibition of sacrifice and the spoliation of pagan temples which he ordained in the East after his defeat of Licinius.[17] Constans extended the prohibition to Italy in 341,[18] and Firmicus Maternus urged him to seize temple treasures—a process which may have begun in the West by 350.[19] For, in the suburbs of Rome itself, the ancient confraternity of the Arval brethren ceased to use the baths attached to the sanctuary of the dea Dia—which implies that they also ceased to perform their annual rites of worship of the goddess.[20] Magnentius appears to have rescinded his predecessor's prohibition of pagan sacrifice, since Constantius in 353 ordered that 'nocturnal sacrifices allowed on the authority of Magnentius be abolished and the wicked license be rejected in the future.'[21] Such official toleration of sacrifice looks like a clumsy attempt to curry favor with pagan aristocrats.

Magnentius secured Africa very quickly[22] and made overtures to known dissidents in the East. Magnentius' approach to Paul proved fatal to the imprisoned bishop. Paul was starved for six days in a small, dark cell, then strangled, allegedly on the orders of the praetorian prefect Philippus. Philagrius, who was then *vicarius* of Pontica, wrote to friends of Athanasius to tell them what had happened (Hist. Ar. 7.3–6). Athanasius attributes his motive to chagrin at not being permitted to supervise the murder himself, but it seems more likely that he wrote to Egypt by way of warning.[23]

For his approach to Athanasius, Magnentius chose his envoys carefully—

two bishops, probably both Gallic, and two men who are otherwise totally unknown. The bishops were Servatius of Tongres and Maximus, whose see is uncertain: both had attended a Gallic council in the 340s which probably reaffirmed the decisions of the Council of Serdica.[24] They were accompanied by Valens, the leader of the embassy, and Clementius: it can safely be assumed that both were military men and, since they came to Egypt by way of Libya, that they had helped to secure Africa for Magnentius. The four were, at least ostensibly, traveling as ambassadors to Constantius. For their reception in Alexandria, as for the whole episode, Athanasius provides the only evidence—clearly disingenuous, but nonetheless revealing (*Apol. ad Const.* 9/10). Athanasius was accused in 351 of treason not only for turning Constans against his brother before 350, but also for writing to Magnentius. The *Defense before Constantius* addresses this charge and attempts to rebut it (6–11). In the course of some tortuous pleading, Athanasius gives what appears to be a straightforward account of his reception of Magnentius' envoys.

The envoys, according to Athanasius, brought no letter addressed to him by the usurper—so how could he have written to a man whom he did not know? The bishop of Alexandria was afraid that he was marked out for death as a friend and admirer of the murdered Constans. He had recently received a letter from Constantius promising no less benevolence with his brother dead than before his murder (10.1), and he repulsed the envoys' advances, taking care to advertise his loyalty in public. He appeared before the populace of Alexandria in the presence of the *dux* Felicissimus, the *catholicus* Rufinus, the *magister privatae* Stephanus, the *comes* Asterius, Palladius, who later became *magister officiorum*, and the *agentes in rebus* Antiochus and Evagrius. He announced: 'Let us pray for the safety of the most pious Augustus Constantius.' All the people with one voice shouted in reply: 'Christ, come to the aid of Constantius,' and continued to pray for some time.

The public display of loyalty can hardly be gainsaid. But what happened in private? Athanasius' enemies later produced a letter which they alleged he wrote in 350 to Magnentius. Athanasius claimed that it was a clever forgery:

> Even if [my accuser] displays letters similar to my own, he does not have certain proof. For there are forgers who have often imitated even the hands of you emperors. The imitation does not establish the genuineness of the document, unless my normal scribes also authenticate the letters. I wish again to ask those who have slandered me the following questions: Who provided these letters? When and where were they discovered?[25] For I had men who wrote [my letters], while [Magnentius] had men to receive them from those who carried them and to hand them to him. Our [scribes] are present: order [those who received letters for Magnentius] to be summoned (for it is quite possible that they are alive) and learn about these letters. (11.2/3)

It is extremely difficult to divine where the truth lies. The hysterical tone of much of Athanasius' argument on this issue inevitably raises suspicions. But would so canny a politician have taken the risk of entrusting a secret letter to envoys who might be arrested and searched? On the other hand, Athanasius may have written a letter which Magnentius answered. It would have been entirely in character for him to repeat in 349 the strategy which had defeated at least some of the earlier attempts to unseat him—the strategy of appealing to allies in the West. If Athanasius was condemned and deposed by a council of eastern bishops who met in Antioch in 349,[26] then it can be inferred with a high degree of probability that he wrote to Constans imploring his protection. The *Defense before Constantius* could not admit this damaging fact without thereby acknowledging that Athanasius had engaged in treasonable correspondence—with Constans, if not with Magnentius. If Constans had not answered the letter before 18 January 350, Magnentius may be supposed to have written to Athanasius in the early months of 350 assuring him of his support in the hope that the bishop of Alexandria would respond by detaching Egypt from its allegiance to Constantius.

Magnentius had some reason to expect Athanasius to welcome, or at least not to repulse, his overtures. For the praetorian prefect Philippus was already on his way to install George as bishop in Alexandria in his place when news reached the East that Constans was dead. But Constantius too was a canny politician. He sensed the danger and acted as soon as he heard of the death of his brother. He immediately sent the *comes* Asterius and the *notarius* Palladius to the *dux* and prefect of Egypt with orders overruling or countermanding Philippus' instructions (*Hist. Ar.* 51.4). And he wrote personally to Athanasius. Constantius was alert and skilful enough to know when weakness dictated a strategic withdrawal. He simply denied any desire to remove Athanasius from the see of Alexandria:

> It will not have escaped your prudence that I always prayed that every success attend my late brother Constans. Your wisdom will easily be able to judge with how great a sorrow I was afflicted, when I learned that he had been murdered by the vilest treachery. Since there are some who at the present time are trying to alarm you by so lamentable a tragedy, I have accordingly decided to send the present letter to your reverence, urging you to teach the people, as befits a bishop, to conform to the established religion and according to custom to spend your time in prayers with them, and not to believe any rumors which may reach you. For it is our resolve that, in accordance with our wishes, you be bishop in your own place for all time. (*Apol. ad Const.* 23)[27]

The emperor added in his own hand the salutation 'the godhead preserve you for many years, beloved father,' and his letter was in Athanasius' hands before the envoys from Magnentius arrived in Alexandria (10.1). Constantius was using diplomatic guile, not expressing his real wishes. Athanasius can hardly have been deceived, but he decided, doubtless out of calculation rather than loyalty or trust in the emperor's assurances, to spurn the overtures from Magnentius—however much he might inwardly hope for the defeat of Constantius. For his part, the emperor was determined to turn his attention back to ecclesiastical politics as soon as the impending civil war permitted.

Constantius was in Edessa when news came of the death of Constans, and Shapur's third siege of Nisibis compelled him to spend the summer and autumn of 350 defending Roman Mesopotamia.[28] It was late in the year before he crossed Asia Minor and advanced into Europe. At Serdica his forces mingled with those of Vetranio, who resigned the imperial purple at Naissus in a carefully staged ceremony on 25 December.[29] Constantius then probably began to reside in Sirmium, and gave serious thought to the future of the Constantinian dynasty.

Since Constantius had no issue, his heir presumptive was his closest male relative. Gallus was the second son of Julius Constantius, a much younger half-brother of Constantine, who emerged as a power at court late in his reign, was given the title of *patricius,* and held the ordinary consulate in 335.[30] After the death of Constantine, Julius Constantius and his eldest son were killed in the dynastic bloodbath which removed actual and potential rivals of the sons of the late emperor. The eleven- or twelve-year-old Gallus was spared, on grounds of age and because his sister was married to the emperor Constantius (*Hist. Ar.* 69.1), and with him his still younger half-brother Julian.[31] While Eusebius, the bishop of Constantinople, lived, Gallus and Julian stayed in Nicomedia under his supervision. Subsequently, Constantius sent them to a remote imperial estate at Macellum in Cappadocia, where for six years they were isolated, closely confined, and entrusted (it appears) to the spiritual care of the George who was to replace Athanasius as bishop of Alexandria.[32] Since Constantius' marriage was still childless, he realised that he needed to employ his cousins to stabilise his own throne. Gallus was summoned to court, invested with the purple on 1 March 351, and sent to Antioch to administer the East with the rank of Caesar.[33]

The course of the campaign between Constantius and Magnentius in Pannonia can be reconstructed in outline, although many details remain unclear.[34] The opposing armies wintered far apart: Magnentius close to the passes through the Julian Alps into Italy, Constantius in Sirmium preparing to march westward. It appears that in the spring of 351 Constantius' generals attempted to break through into Italy but were repulsed. When Magnentius sought to pursue his advantage and occupied Siscia,[35] they were able to regroup and force a decisive battle at Mursa while Constantius awaited the outcome in safety at Sirmium. On 28 September 351, the forces of Constantius won a clear but costly victory after enormous losses on both sides.[36] Magnentius fled to Aquileia and blocked the crossing of the Julian Alps. Constantius consolidated his control of the Balkans, winter came on, and it seems that in the following campaigning season the emperor needed to do battle with the Sarmatians before he could enter Italy.[37] Aquileia was still under Magnentius' control on 28 July 352,[38] but the forces of Constantius broke through into the north Italian plain in August, the whole of Italy rapidly came over,[39] and on 26 September 352 Constantius' nominee became *praefectus urbi* at Rome: he was Naeratius Cerealis, the maternal uncle of the Caesar Gallus.[40]

Magnentius retreated to Gaul in the hope of maintaining his régime there. But it was vain for Magnentius and his Caesar Decentius to hope for the safety which their coinage proclaimed.[41] In the summer of 353 the forces of Constantius crossed the Alps, and in Trier a certain Poemenius raised the standard of rebellion in the name of Constantius.[42] A battle at Mons Seleucus doomed the usurper. Magnentius committed suicide at Lyon on 10 August 353, Decentius at Sens eight days later.[43] Constantius proceeded to Lyon and repealed Magnentius' unpopular enactments.[44] He then traveled south to Arles for the winter, where he celebrated his *tricennalia* (presumably on 8 November 353).[45]

In the East, Gallus was not a success. Although he suppressed a Jewish rebellion (apparently in 352),[46] he soon embroiled himself in bitter conflicts both with the people of Antioch and with the officials whom Constantius had sent to the East.[47] The Caesar forgot that Constantius intended him to be a mere figurehead, necessary for political and dynastic reasons, but with the real power vested in experienced administrators whom he himself had appointed.[48] By 354 the situation had become intolerable and embarrassing. While Constantius busied himself on the upper Rhine, Gallus was persuaded to come to court. When the Caesar reached Poetovio, he was arrested, stripped of the imperial purple, tried secretly for high treason, and executed at Pola.[49]

The problem of how to rule so vast an empire still remained. And there were serious problems in Gaul as well as the permanent danger of Persian attack in Mesopotamia. In August 355 the Frank Silvanus was proclaimed emperor. Although officers of Constantius assassinated him a month later, the Rhine frontier was breached in the autumn and Cologne sacked.[50] Constantius, residing in Milan after a spring campaign against the Alamanni, proclaimed Gallus' younger brother Julian Caesar on 6 November 355 and sent him to Gaul with a carefully selected staff of high officials.[51]

The posthumous reputation of Constantius was fixed for later generations of Christians by Athanasius, especially in his *History of the Arians,* by Hilary of Poitiers in his *Against Constantius,* and by Lucifer of Caralis: all three damned him as an 'Arian,' a persecutor, a devil incarnate, or even an Antichrist.[52] This hostile picture does not correspond either to the complicated realities of ecclesiastical politics or to the sentiments of the majority of eastern Christians during Constantius' lifetime. A letter from an important bishop illustrates how he was widely respected as a worthy successor of his father.

Cyril of Jerusalem probably composed his *Catechetical Lectures* in 348 while he was still a priest:[53] these lectures, delivered to prepare catechumens for baptism, provide a systematic exposition of Christian doctrine, marshaled around the local baptismal creed of Jerusalem. Cyril's theology is couched in somewhat old-fashioned language, and it has been claimed that 'he began as an anti-Nicene conservative, strongly opposed to Marcellus of Ancyra.'[54] But Cyril was aware enough of controversial issues to repudiate firmly (if anonymously) tenets associated with the name of Arius,[55] and his theological views were close enough to the intent of the Nicene creed, first to cause him political difficulties with his eastern colleagues between 357 and 361, then to win him a lasting reputation for orthodoxy. After a career of vicissitudes,[56] Cyril was accepted at the Council of Constantinople in 381: he died in secure possession of the see of Jerusalem in 387, and his writings were thereafter regarded as a repository of sound theology.[57] Yet the earliest stages of his career reveal a bishop allied to the enemies of Athanasius.

Cyril was elected bishop of Jerusalem in succession to Maximus, the ally of Athanasius (*Apol. c. Ar.* 57), who either died or was deposed—or possibly, given the divergent reports, died when about to be deposed by the Council of Antioch which condemned Athanasius in 349. Cyril was the nominee, or at least enjoyed the support, of Acacius of Caesarea, and Jerome later alleged that he became bishop by expelling Heraclius, whom the dying Maximus had designated as his successor.[58] Within a very few years Cyril wrote to Constantius to describe a miraculous happening in Jerusalem on 7 May 351.[59] On that day an enormous cross of light appeared in the sky, stretching from Golgotha to the Mount of Olives: it was brighter than the sun, remained for several hours, and was seen by everyone in the city. Cyril felt impelled to announce to the emperor this sign of divine approval of his rule, a heavenly sign more powerful (he proclaimed) than the discovery of the true cross in Jerusalem in the reign of Constantine.

Cyril's motives were no doubt in part at least self-serving, for such a manifestation of divine approval in Jerusalem might favorably dispose the emperor toward the city and its bishop. It is more significant that Cyril flatters Constantius in the fashion of any Christian panegyrist as a true believer from birth, as a theological expert, as a divinely appointed and inspired guardian of the church. And he closes with the following salutation:

> May the God of the universe preserve you with your whole house for us for many peaceful yearly cycles in health, adorned with every virtue, displaying your customary loving concern *(philanthropia)* for the holy churches and the Roman Empire, glorious with greater rewards of piety, Augustus, most God-loving emperor.

Cyril's letter will have reached Constantius some time before the decisive battle against Magnentius. The emperor's coinage was invoking the aid of God by proclaiming, in the familiar phrase which evoked his father's battle against

Maxentius at the Milvian Bridge, 'in this sign you will conquer' *(hoc signo victor eris)*.[60] Whatever else was in his mind, Cyril clearly intended to win imperial favor by predicting a victory which he implicitly presented as inevitable. Valens of Mursa is reported to have achieved the same result by the more mundane method of employing swift messengers so that he could be the first to inform Constantius when the victory was won—with the result that Constantius frequently declared that he owed his victory more to the intercession of Valens than to the valor of his army.[61]

XIII

SIRMIUM, ARLES,
AND MILAN

ALTHOUGH THE COUNCIL OF SIRMIUM MET LATE IN 351,[1] ONE IMPOR-
tant preparatory step had been taken before the Battle of Mursa, probably in the
spring. Basil of Ancyra interrogated Photinus about his theological views in the
presence of eight officials of Constantius, some of very high rank: they included
Taurus, the future consul of 361; Datianus and Cerialis, who held the consulate
together in 358; and Thalassius, the praetorian prefect of Gallus—which implies
that Gallus and his prefect had not yet left court to reside at Antioch.[2] These dig-
nitaries attended, not as judges to try Photinus,[3] but as witnesses to the accuracy
of the record of the interrogation made by shorthand writers, who produced
three sealed copies, one for Constantius, one for the *comites* themselves, and one
for use by the council of bishops destined to decide whether the theology of
Photinus was orthodox or heretical. This preliminary investigation must not be
confused with the council proper, whose decisions were to provide the basis for
Constantius' attempt to enforce his ecclesiastical policies in the newly conquered
West.

The Council of Sirmium took three decisions which were announced in a
single synodical letter. First, it condemned and deposed Photinus, replacing him
with Germinius from Cyzicus,[4] and Marcellus of Ancyra was (as before) associated with his disciple in the condemnation. Second, the council reiterated the
creed originally drawn up at Antioch in 342. To the original text of the creed
and its repudiation of the most notorious views associated with Arius were now
added twenty-six brief anathemas to replace the complex formulations of the
'long creed' of 344: a few rejected the caricature of Arius' views current in the
West, but the majority proscribed the views of Marcellus and Photinus, though
without naming the pair.[5] Third, the Council of Sirmium again condemned and
deposed Athanasius.

This crucial fact nowhere stands on fully explicit record. Yet Sulpicius

Severus speaks of a joint condemnation of Photinus, Marcellus, and Athanasius in a context which can hardly refer to any occasion other than the Council of Sirmium,[6] and a condemnation of Athanasius by the council is a necessary hypothesis, both *a priori,* since his deposition by the Council of Antioch in 349 had been set aside,[7] and in order to explain the subsequent course of events. For it was to controvert his condemnation by a council of hostile bishops shortly after 350 that Athanasius originally composed his *Defense before Constantius,*[8] and the evidence directly pertaining to the Councils of Arles in 353/4 and Milan in 355 strongly implies that it was the synodical letter of the Council of Sirmium which was placed before the western bishops for their signatures, and that that letter contained both a creed and a joint condemnation of Marcellus, Photinus, and Athanasius.[9]

The Council of Sirmium wrote to Julius, the bishop of Rome, but he died on 12 April 352 before he could take any action.[10] It thus fell to his successor Liberius, who was consecrated in May 352,[11] to find the correct diplomatic response. Liberius acted as his predecessor had a dozen years earlier.[12] He appointed himself as an arbitrator in the dispute between Athanasius and his enemies, and sent three priests from Rome to Alexandria. In his letter of 357, which constitutes the only clear evidence for his action, Liberius claims that he was motivated by a desire for peace and concord between the churches, and that he had invited Athanasius to come to Rome so that a decision could be made in accordance with ecclesiastical discipline, with a threat to cut him off from communion with the church of Rome if he refused.[13] The invitation can hardly be doubted, but in 357, when writing to the eastern bishops after his capitulation to the demands of Constantius, Liberius had reason enough to misrepresent the tenor of his letter of 352. At the earlier date, he cannot have threatened to excommunicate Athanasius, since such a threat would have been tantamount to accepting the validity of his deposition by the Council of Sirmium. Rather, he invited both parties to come or to send representatives to Rome.

Athanasius declined to come. Instead, as in 338, he convened a council of Egyptian bishops, seventy-five or eighty in number, which reiterated his innocence, adding for good measure that this Council of Alexandria was attended by a larger number of bishops than were present at the Council of Sirmium.[14] When this letter was transmitted to Italy, Liberius convened a council of Italian bishops, presumably at Rome, to which he read the letter from Alexandria.[15] The council reviewed the case of Athanasius, and it seems that it requested Constantius to convene a larger and more representative council at Aquileia: such at least is the implication of an allusion in a partially preserved letter which Liberius wrote to Ossius in late 353 or early 354, where he refers to a request by Italian bishops to Constantius to convene a council at Aquileia.[16]

It had long been Athanasius' strategy to associate his own cause with the defense of true faith. Hence it is plausible to conjecture that he wrote the work compendiously known as *On the Council of Nicaea* in response to Liberius' letter of 352 in order to put the Council of Nicaea and its creed at the centre of ecclesiastical controversy.[17] The work opens like a letter:

> You have done well in telling me of the question you put to those who were advocating the views of Arius, among whom were both some of the accomplices of Eusebius and very many brothers who believe what the church teaches. I welcome your Christ-loving vigilance which well exposed the impiety of their heresy, but I am astounded at their shamelessness. Although the Arian arguments have been shown to be rotten and futile, and they themselves have been condemned by all for every perversity, nevertheless, even after this they have been complaining like the Jews, and saying: 'Why did those who assembled at Nicaea use terms not in scripture, "from the essence" and "of the same essence" *(homoousios)*?' You, as a learned man, showed that they were talking nonsense in spite of their subterfuges of this sort. (1.1/2)

Athanasius compares the Arians at length to the Jews who killed Christ, then observes:

> Knowing this, I would have made no reply to their questions. But since your friendliness has asked to be informed of what was done at the council, I have not delayed. By reply I have told [you] how it happened then, showing briefly how destitute the Arian heresy is of pious wisdom and how they only frame evasions. (2.3)

Athanasius gives a brief and selective account of the Council of Nicaea, concentrating on the phrase 'from the essence' and the word 'of the same essence.' He points out how Eusebius of Caesarea accepted them as part of the church's faith and the tradition of the fathers (3/4). He quotes Eusebius' embarrassed letter to his congregation in an appendix to prove that Acacius, the successor of Eusebius, knows this perfectly well and is therefore acting inconsistently in rejecting these terms (3.5, cf. 33). That should be an allusion to Acacius' role at Sirmium, though Athanasius nowhere refers explicitly to the council.

On the Council of Nicaea comprises four main sections. First, Athanasius discusses in what sense Christ is the Son of God. He poses a dilemma between the adoptive and essential senses of the word, and ridicules Arian attempts to find a third sense: the choice lies between the teaching of the Sadducees and Paul of Samosata, which Athanasius expounds, and catholic doctrine (6–17). Next, Athanasius argues that the phrase 'from the essence' and the word 'of the same essence' embody that teaching and were chosen by the Council of Nicaea precisely in order to contradict 'the impious phrases of the Arians' and to preserve the true sense of the scriptures (18–24). Third, Athanasius quotes Theognostus, Dionysius of Alexandria, Dionysius of Rome, and even Origen to demonstrate that the Council of Nicaea did not invent the phrases which the Arians have impugned (25–27).[18] Finally, Athanasius closes his argument by objecting to

Arian use of the term 'unoriginate' *(agenetos)* as borrowed from pagans and theologically misleading (28–32).

In the manuscripts of *On the Council of Nicaea,* there then follow not only the letter which Eusebius of Caesarea wrote from Nicaea to his congregation in Palestine justifying his acceptance of the creed of 325 (33), but also a sheaf of other documents in which Arius and his allies are condemned:

(1) the deposition of Arius by Alexander of Alexandria in a letter of Alexander to the clergy of Alexandria and the Mareotis, recited by him in their presence, asking them to subscribe to his circular letter excommunicating Arius, followed by that letter and its subscriptions (c. 320);

(2) a letter of the Council of Nicaea to the churches in Egypt condemning Arius (325);

(3) a letter of Constantine to the church of Alexandria announcing the condemnation of Arius at Nicaea (325);

(4) the letter of Constantine exiling Arius, brought to Alexandria in 333;

(5) the long and abusive letter which Constantine wrote to Arius and his fellow Arians at the same time;

(6) Constantine's letter to the church of Nicomedia announcing the deposition of Eusebius of Nicomedia and Theognis of Nicaea (c. October 325);

(7) Constantine's letter to Theodotus.[19]

This dossier builds up a coherent case. Athanasius argues that the creed of the Council of Sirmium in 351 expresses heretical ideas which the Council of Nicaea condemned long before. It has often been observed that the Nicene creed and its key term *homoousios* become prominent in theological debate only in the 350s.[20] On the known facts, it can plausibly be claimed that it was Athanasius who brought it into prominence by sending his *On the Council of Nicaea* to the bishop of Rome in 352. He had devised a potent rallying-cry.

Athanasius also needed to wage war on another front. He realised that Constantius would try to enforce the decisions of the Council of Sirmium as soon as political conditions permitted. Accordingly, on 19 May 353, when he knew that Constantius would soon invade Gaul, Athanasius sent Serapion of Thmuis, four other bishops, and three priests of Alexandria to court with a present for the emperor (*Hist. ac.* 1.7; *Index* 25). Sozomenus reports that they had instructions to attempt to conciliate Constantius if at all possible, to reply to calumnies against Athanasius if it proved necessary, and to take any other measures they might deem appropriate for the welfare of the church and the bishop of Alexandria.[21] These envoys probably carried with them the original version of Athanasius' *Defense before Constantius.*

Although the speech nowhere explicitly mentions the Council of Sirmium, Athanasius' oblique and tendentious allusions to it suggest that he originally wrote to parry the charges on which the council had condemned and deposed him. Athanasius presents himself as the victim of a hostile plot (1.1). His enemies, who are rank Arians (6.2, 11.1), have written to the emperor (2.1)—that is, to put their letter in its proper historical context, which Athanasius conceals, they have written to Constantius to inform him officially of the decisions of the council. Athanasius answers in the literary form of a speech designed to be recited before Constantius, as if the emperor were conducting a formal trial of Athanasius in the presence of the accuser to whom the speech refers several times.[22] The literary form may be artificial, but the charges against the bishop of Alexandria were real enough.[23]

It would be naive to suppose that what Athanasius selected for refutation comprised the whole of the case against him. A sentence in Socrates may imply that Athanasius was charged with disturbing all Egypt and Libya.[24] And Athanasius himself reveals that ecclesiastical offenses, including the old charge of sacrilege, formed part of the indictment. Against these he rested his case on the letters quoted in the first part of the *Defense against the Arians* and the palinode of Ursacius and Valens. The prooemium of the speech presents as the basis of the whole argument the assumption that Constantius loves truth and God, that Athanasius is innocent of all suspicion, and that his accusers are proven calumniators (1).

In the original *Defense before Constantius,* Athanasius concentrated on three 'slanders': that he had fostered enmity between Constans and his brother; that he wrote to the usurper Magnentius; and that he showed disrespect for Constantius by using the newly constructed Great Church in Alexandria before it was formally dedicated. Athanasius had some explaining to do, and his rebuttals of the charges, for all their vigorous eloquence, are often convoluted and evasive.[25] His answer to the first charge was twofold. First, he protested that neither he nor Constans had ever spoken a harsh word to the other about Constantius, and he argued that he never spoke with Constans alone and in secret, so that the content of their conversations can easily be verified from the bishops or the high official who between them heard every word uttered during these audiences. Second, he gives an extremely compressed account of his dealings with Constans down to 346, and appeals to what he said to Constantius at the three audiences to show that he never spoke evil of his adversaries (2–5). The answer to the charge of treasonable correspondence with Magnentius had to overcome the inconvenient fact that a letter of Athanasius had been produced. The bishop dismissed it as a forgery and argued on *a priori* grounds that it was absurd to imagine that he could have written to someone whom he had never met. Could he have begun (he asks) by congratulating Magnentius on the murder of his own benefactor, of the pious Christians who had welcomed him as an exile in Rome? Magnentius was a devil or demon, untrustworthy to his friends: he broke oaths, sinned against God, and employed magic (6–12).

The third charge was easier to rebut. Athanasius had not dedicated the Great Church, since it was illegal to do so without Constantius' instruction; he had merely used it as an emergency measure because of the size of the crowds flocking to worship at Easter. During Lent many worshippers had almost been crushed in the existing small churches: at Easter itself Athanasius wished to avoid unnecessary suffering and death. There were good precedents for using an unfinished church: Alexander had used the Church of Theonas while it was still being built for similar reasons, while Athanasius had seen the same happen in Trier and Aquileia—where Constans himself attended the service (15.4). Athanasius then justified his action on more general practical grounds and ended with a long peroration in which he prayed that Constantius might live long and perform the dedication: the church was ready, it only required his presence, and it was the wish of all that he come to Alexandria to dedicate it (14–18).

The *Defense before Constantius* was overtaken by events long before it reached the emperor in whose presence Athanasius had composed it to be recited. Four days after the envoys who carried it sailed from Alexandria, the *palatinus* Montanus arrived with a letter inviting Athanasius to come to the imperial court (*Apol. ad Const.* 19.4; *Index* 24; *Hist. ac.* 1.8). Athanasius seized on a reference in the letter to his own request to come to Italy as a pretext for rejecting the invitation. He had never made such a request. Had he done so, he would have been grateful to the emperor for granting it. But, since he had in fact not done so, it would be wrong for him to abandon his duties to visit one who granted his requests on behalf of the church even while he was absent. Athanasius protested in a written reply that he was ready to obey, but that since Constantius had issued no peremptory command, only an invitation based on misinformation or a misapprehension, he had concluded that the emperor did not really wish him to come (*Apol. ad Const.* 19.4–21.4).

Constantius had met his match in diplomatic evasion, but he was not yet willing to take the risk of attempting to supplant Athanasius by force. He turned his attention to obtaining acceptance of the Council of Sirmium in the West. Some agents of this policy can be identified.[26] The most prominent and most active were Saturninus, bishop of Arles; Paternus of Périgueux; and Epictetus, the young bishop of Centumcellae on the Italian coast north of Rome.[27] Saturninus and Paternus were Gauls themselves and established bishops, but Epictetus appears to have been an easterner imposed by Constantius after September 352 (*Letter to the Bishops of Egypt and Libya* 7; *Hist. Ar.* 75.2).[28] Auxentius, who became bishop of Milan in 355 and retained the see until his death in 374, came from Cappadocia (*Hist. Ar.* 75.1) and was alleged to have received ordination as a priest from Gregory in Alexandria.[29] And the name of Zosimus, who replaced Maximus as bishop of Naples, probably also in 355, suggests that he too was of eastern origin.[30]

Another bishop who played a prominent role, if only briefly, was Potamius, the first bishop of Lisbon known to history. Unfortunately, there is little fourth-century evidence for his career except the biased and unreliable *Libellus precum* composed by two followers of Lucifer of Caralis more than twenty years later, and it is difficult to reconcile what contemporary writers report about the conduct and beliefs of Potamius in the late 350s with the orthodoxy of those works which survive.[31] According to the two Luciferians, Potamius was orthodox in his beliefs until he was bribed with the promise of a *fundus fiscalis:* after Ossius of Corduba had denounced him to all the Spanish bishops as an impious heretic, he complained to Constantius, who then summoned Ossius to Sirmium in 357.[32] Whatever the truth of these allegations, or of the story in the same document that he died before he could enjoy his reward, Potamius was at court in the summer of 357: there he put pressure on Liberius,[33] and his name and that of Ossius stand in the heading of the 'blasphemy of Sirmium' as its joint authors.[34] Moreover, a Gallic bishop writing in the autumn of 357 denounced a 'letter of Potamius' from which he quoted the heterodox proposition that the incarnation made God passible.[35]

Significantly, that is the total of western bishops who are attested as active supporters of Constantius' attempts to win western acceptance of the Council of Sirmium. The small number reflects more than paucity of evidence: it indicates an almost complete lack of enthusiasm for the decisions of the Council of Sirmium among the bishops of Italy, Gaul, and Spain. Constantius was compelled to obtain acceptance of those decisions by coercion and threats, and the acceptance thereby extorted represented no more than a sullen, grudging, and temporary acquiescence. Even if there was as yet no groundswell of active support for Athanasius or the Nicene creed, the vast majority of Gallic and Italian bishops showed their deep reluctance to endorse the decisions of their eastern colleagues by staying at home when Constantius convened councils at Arles and Milan.

While Constantius was spending the winter of 353/4 at Arles, a council of bishops met there, perhaps before the end of 353.[36] The membership of the Council of Arles is nowhere fully described, but those known to have attended are predominantly eastern and Gallic bishops (with envoys from the bishop of Rome), and their total number was undoubtedly small.[37] No new creed was formulated at Arles. The only ancient narrative source which describes the proceedings speaks of an imperial edict ordering that bishops who refused to subscribe to the condemnation of Athanasius be driven into exile. The same writer discloses that the document presented to the council for acceptance and signature was a letter which condemned Marcellus and Photinus as well as Athanasius—and which must be the synodical letter of the Council of Sirmium. Paulinus, the bishop of Trier, who assented to the condemnation of Marcellus and Photinus, but not to that of Athanasius, was exiled.[38] Two legates had been sent from Rome: one of them, to Liberius' intense shame, accepted the decisions of the council, though the other refused to do so.[39] The rest of the bishops, 'compelled by fear and a faction,' signed the document presented to the council.[40]

Constantius was not willing to allow his aim of obtaining western assent to the decisions of the Council of Sirmium to be frustrated by the mere absence of potential signatories from the Council of Arles (or later from the Council of Milan). At Nicaea in 325 his father had sent officials to set the creed before each bishop at the council individually for signature, and after the Council of Serdica more than two hundred bishops who had not been present added their names to the western synodical letter. Constantius now combined these two precedents. In a process which lasted several years, officials took copies of the Sirmian decisions, as subscribed at Arles, and subsequently at Milan, to individual bishops in Italy,[41] and then in Gaul, Spain, and Britain, and compelled them to add their names under threat of exile. Finally, in 356 the document was presented to the bishops of Egypt for their approval (*Letter to the Bishops of Egypt and Libya* 5/6). It is Athanasius who describes most fully and explicitly the procedure used after the Councils of Arles and Milan. Although he describes at first hand what happened in Egypt, his description is valid also for the West:

> Immediately instructions and letters came here to the prefect that the grain be taken away from Athanasius and given to those who hold the views of Arius, and that those who wish should be allowed to harass those who worship with him. And there was a threat against the magistrates if they did not worship with the Arians. This was the preliminary to what was done later through the *dux* Syrianus. To the parts [of the empire] outside [Egypt] also went orders, and *notarii* and *palatini* were sent from city to city both to the bishops and to the magistrates carrying threats, so that the magistrates should apply pressure and the bishops should either enter into communion with the Arians and write against Athanasius or themselves endure the penalty of exile, while the congregations who worshipped with them knew that there would be imprisonment, violence, beatings, and confiscation of their property [if they did not comply]. (*Hist. Ar.* 31.2/3)

It seems that the policy succeeded, at least in the short run. Decurions who received an imperial command that they compel their local bishop to comply or else themselves suffer financial loss (31.6) could not remain totally indifferent. Such indirect pressure secured widespread compliance: bishops throughout the West succumbed to the demand that they either subscribe to the document presented to them or forfeit their see. Athanasius' account rings true (31.4–6)—except for his final claim that 'every place and every city was filled with fear and disorder as bishops were dragged around, while the magistrates watched the tears and groans of the congregations.'

Liberius remained aloof and defiant, and Constantius himself wrote to the people of Rome complaining about the conduct of their bishop.[42] Liberius responded politely, then, after an exchange of letters, requested the emperor to convene yet another council in a letter taken to Milan by the Sardinian bishop Lucifer of Caralis, the Roman priest Pancratius, and the deacon Hilarius.[43] The envoys appear to have passed through Vercellae, where they enlisted the support of the bishop Eusebius, formerly a priest at Rome, who soon became a staunch supporter of the cause of Athanasius.[44]

Constantius called another council, which met at Milan in 355, probably in July and August, with the emperor again close at hand to keep a watchful eye on the proceedings.[45] Again the attendance was small. Socrates indeed asserts that more than three hundred western bishops came.[46] But his figure is implausible in itself, and his testimony is outweighed by the direct evidence of a letter from the Council of Milan to Eusebius of Vercellae: the letter, which urged Eusebius to attend in order to join in the whole world's condemnation of the heretics Marcellus and Photinus and the sacrilegious Athanasius, was followed by thirty subscriptions commencing with the names of Caecilianus (who seems to be otherwise unknown), Ursacius, and Valens.[47] The council opened with a demand that those present subscribe to the condemnation of Marcellus, Photinus, and Athanasius as set out in the synodical letter of the Council of Sirmium.[48] According to Sulpicius Severus, Eusebius and Lucifer refused and were deposed. Dionysius, the bishop of Milan, agreed to put his name to the condemnation of Athanasius, provided that the council discuss doctrinal matters. Ursacius, Valens, and the rest demurred. The emperor was consulted and repeated his demand that the decisions of Sirmium be accepted entire. Dionysius refused and was exiled: the easterner Auxentius replaced him.[49] Besides Dionysius, the Council of Milan also condemned Lucifer and Eusebius for refusing to add their names to the document placed before them, and all three bishops departed into exile in the East.[50]

One episode at the Council of Milan is of particular importance. Writing within three years of the council, Hilary of Poitiers reported that when Eusebius of Vercellae was pressed to sign the condemnation of Athanasius, he replied that agreement ought to be reached first on the orthodoxy of the bishops present since he had heard that some were 'polluted with heretical corruption.' He then produced a copy of the Nicene creed and professed himself willing to fulfill the demands made of him if everyone subscribed this creed. Dionysius of Milan took the paper and began to append his assent. Valens snatched the pen and paper from his hand, shouting that that was not on the agenda. The episode became known and provoked resentment in the city. The bishops, therefore, repaired to the imperial palace and—here, unfortunately, the fragmentary narrative breaks off.[51]

The historicity of the episode has recently been denied.[52] Yet it is *a priori* probable that the allies of Athanasius would try to shift debate from his guilt or innocence to the Nicene creed: Athanasius had proclaimed as early as 339 in his *Encyclical Letter* that his deposition then imperiled the orthodoxy of the whole church, and he had recently (it seems) sent Liberius his *On the Council of Nicaea* to make the same case on purely theological grounds.[53] What more natural than that Liberius and other Italian bishops should publicise the Nicene creed? Moreover, two other items of evidence support the story. In his work *On the Councils,* Hilary protests that he heard the Nicene creed only shortly before his exile: the context is tendentious and cannot be pressed to mean that he first heard the creed at the council which exiled him in 356, but it is perfectly consonant with Hilary's first hearing the creed recited and discussed in 355.[54] And Athanasius' circular *Letter to the Bishops of Egypt and Libya,* written in the spring of 356, alludes very clearly to the Council of Milan. It warns the bishops against accepting a creed which is about to be circulated for their signatures under threat of exile, and contrasts this Arian creed with the creed of Nicaea, the touchstone of orthodox belief (*Letter to the Bishops of Egypt and Libya 5/6*).

Pressure was now put on Liberius, who had avoided attending the council. The eunuch Eusebius came to Rome and urged Liberius in secret and diplomatically to subscribe the Sirmian decisions (*Hist. Ar.* 35.2–40.3). When the bishop continued to refuse, Constantius ordered the prefect of the city to arrest him and send him to the imperial court in Milan (during the autumn of 355).[55] There he had an audience with the emperor, of which a record, doubtless somewhat embroidered, has been preserved: if this purported transcript can be believed, the interview was acrimonious on both sides, and Epictetus of Centumcellae was present to add his voice to the attempt at persuasion.[56] When Liberius persisted in his recalcitrance, he was sent to Beroea in Thrace until such time as he should agree to append his name too to the synodical letter of the Council of Sirmium (*Hist. Ar.* 41.3). In his place, the archdeacon Felix was consecrated bishop of Rome by the prescribed trio of bishops (*Hist. Ar.* 75.3). The consecration probably took place in Milan, and the consecrators of Felix included Acacius of Caesarea, who happened to be at court.[57] The clergy of Rome had all sworn a joint public oath never to accept any other bishop as long as Liberius lived, but in the event they all (including the future bishop Damasus) acknowledged Felix as their legitimate bishop.[58]

When Liberius capitulated to Constantius' demands in 357, he was allowed to return, and Felix left the city, though without (it seems) forfeiting episcopal status.[59] Felix had proven more adept than Liberius at frustrating the emperor's wishes: he retained a reputation for never having sullied the faith of Nicaea,[60] and his name was allowed to stand in the official records of the Roman see as a legitimate bishop, not an interloper.[61] When Liberius died in 366, the dissensions in the Roman church broke out in a violently contested election: Damasus was elected bishop, but fighting between his partisans and those of his rival left one hundred and thirty-seven bodies in the basilica of Sicininus in a single day.[62]

While the Council of Milan was still in session, Constantius acted to expel Athanasius from his see. The imperial *notarius* Diogenes arrived in Alexandria during August 355 and began to try to dispossess Athanasius by political means. After four months he gave up and left the city on 23 December 355 (*Apol. ad Const.* 22; *Hist. ac.* 1.9). On 6 January 356 the *dux* Syrianus and the *notarius*

Hilarius entered the city with a large body of troops. Athanasius asked the *dux* whether he had orders from the emperor: when he denied having any, Athanasius asked him or Maximus, the prefect of Egypt, to write to Constantius on the grounds that he possessed a letter (the letter of 350, which he produced) promising him secure enjoyment of his see. Athanasius' request was supported by his clergy, his congregation, and a large part of the city. Syrianus proceeded carefully. He agreed to the request and bided his time for another twenty-three days. Then, suddenly, during the night of 8/9 February he occupied the Church of Theonas (*Apol. ad Const.* 25; *Fug.* 6.1; *Hist. ac* 1.10; *Index* 28).

Athanasius escaped and left Alexandria. Perhaps he went to Libya, for he later claimed that he started to travel to the court of Constantius until he was stopped, first by news of the arrest of Liberius and the exile of bishops by the Council of Milan, then by a report of the persecution of bishops in Egypt and Libya (*Apol. ad Const.* 27.1–4). But events in Egypt required that he not abandon the sources of his political support. Force was being used in Alexandria and throughout Egypt to secure compliance with the deposition of Athanasius: of the ninety bishops loyal to him, sixteen were exiled, some fled, and others conformed to the new policy (*Apol. ad Const.* 27.1–28.4; *Hist. Ar.* 54–80). Resistance proved tenacious, especially in Alexandria. On 12 February the laity of the city entered a long, formal protest at the violence of Syrianus (*Hist. Ar.* 81). The supporters of Athanasius retained the city churches until June, when the new prefect Cataphronius and the *comes* Heraclius dispossessed them and handed the churches over to the supporters of George. George himself arrived eight months later, on 24 February 357. His hold upon his see was never secure and did not last long. On 29 August 358 the largely Christian populace attacked him in the Church of Dionysius and almost lynched him. Just over a month later (on 2 October) George left Alexandria. The supporters of Athanasius seized all the churches of the city a few days later. However, although the *dux* Sebastianus ejected them and restored the churches to the supporters of George on 24 December 358, and although the *notarius* Paulus arrived on 23 June 359, published an imperial edict on George's behalf, and used coercion to drum up support for him, George himself did not attempt to return to Alexandria for more than three years (*Hist. ac.* 2.2–5; *Index* 29).[63]

Athanasius remained in hiding for the rest of the reign of Constantius. After his initial flight, he returned to Alexandria and hid there during at least part of 357 and 358—presumably emerging when his partisans controlled the city in the autumn of the latter year. Thereafter, he wandered among the monks of Lower and Upper Egypt, a fugitive from the emperor and his agents, but apparently never in danger of betrayal to the authorities. Constantius, no longer constrained by the necessities of diplomacy, gave vent to his feeling of annoyance toward Athanasius in letters to the city of Alexandria and to Aezanes and Saezanes, the rulers of the kingdom of Axum.

The emperor flattered the city of Alexander, but informed the people that

Athanasius was an outlaw who deserved to be apprehended and killed. He denounced the outlawed bishop as a low-born impostor who had achieved power by deceit:

> Most of those in the city were blinded, and a man who comes from the lowest depths of society obtained authority, tricking into falsehood those who desired the truth as if they were blindfolded, never providing fruitful discourse, but corrupting their minds so that they were dull and useless. His flatterers shouted and applauded, they were astonished [with admiration] and are probably still murmuring secretly.[64] Most of the simple folk took their cue from them, while matters went downhill with everything being overwhelmed as if in a flood. The man who led the crowd (how could I describe it more accurately?) was no different from the artisans, and the only benefit which he gave to the city was not to throw its inhabitants into pits. (*Apol. ad Const.* 30.3/4)

The Alexandrians should welcome the excellent and learned George, turning their minds from mundane to heavenly matters and living in peace with good hope for the life hereafter.

Constantius warned the princes of Axum too against Athanasius, and asked them to send Frumentius, whom Athanasius had ordained as bishop, to Alexandria, so that George could investigate his conduct and beliefs as a bishop, reappoint him if they proved to be sound, and then send him back to spread true doctrine in the lands beyond the southern frontier of Egypt (*Apol. ad Const.* 31). In this letter, which Athanasius quotes to illustrate the danger which compelled him to flee, Constantius states a central feature of his conception of his role as a Christian emperor: he felt that he had a duty to spread true belief both inside and outside the borders of the Roman Empire.[65] Official ambassadors are known to have gone to the Axumitae and Homeritae, since a constitution of 15 January 357 preserves part of Constantius' instructions to Musonianus, the praetorian prefect of the East, limiting their free maintenance to one year.[66] And inscriptions found at Axum not only attest a king of kings named Aeizanas and his brothers Saizanas and Adephas, but also imply that the ruler Ezana, who is presumably identical with Aeizanes (or Aezanes), converted to some form of monotheism after his accession.[67]

XIV

APOLOGIA, POLEMIC,
AND THEOLOGY

IN FEBRUARY 356, AS IN THE SPRING OF 339, ATHANASIUS ESCAPED arrest when his church in Alexandria was seized. A picturesque story was later told of how he remained concealed for six years, his whereabouts unknown, through the agency of a devoted virgin.[1] The truth is more interesting and more complex, though few precise details are known.[2] Since Athanasius was an outlaw whom the authorities strenuously sought to apprehend, he must have moved about constantly until he resumed possession of his see after the death of Constantius.

Athanasius passed his third 'exile' in concealment either in the city of Alexandria itself or among the monks of the Egyptian countryside, with whom he had close and long-standing ties of friendship. Antony himself had supported Athanasius by writing to Constantine in 336 and by visiting Alexandria in 338, and his followers remained well disposed toward the bishop regardless of his political and ecclesiastical vicissitudes.[3] Pachomius had supported Athanasius at the time of his disputed election in 328, and Athanasius visited the Thebaid shortly afterward (*Index* 2). After their founder's death the Pachomian communities regarded Athanasius' cause as their own, and the abbot Theodore declared that in his generation God had raised up three great leaders—Antony, Pachomius, and Athanasius. It was not without cause, therefore, that the *dux* Artemius searched Pachomian monasteries in Upper Egypt on suspicion that the fugitive bishop might be concealed there.[4]

In February 356 Athanasius left the city and (it appears) traveled through the desert toward Cyrenaica (*Letter to the Bishops of Egypt and Libya* 5, 7; *Apol. ad Const.* 27.1), then turned back and returned to Alexandria when the initial search for him, which was conducted with vigor and violence (*Index* 29), had died down. There he remained in hiding for some time (*Index* 30). He did not stay in the city continuously, but he was in Alexandria again in 360, when another determined attempt was made to apprehend him by the prefect Faustinus and the *dux* Artemius, who instituted a search, entered a private house, and tortured the virgin Eudaemonis, with whom Athanasius had secretly been lodging (*Index* 32).[5]

During his exile Athanasius kept up a constant correspondence with friends and allies,[6] even though he may not have been able to send a *Festal Letter* for all of the Easters between 358 and 361.[7] Two letters of some historical importance which survive from the many Athanasius must have written in these years deserve brief comment. They are addressed to monks. One accompanied a brief account of the sufferings of Athanasius and the church which refuted the Arian heresy (probably a lost work): Athanasius requests an immediate return of his manuscript, which no one is to copy or transcribe.[8] The other warns monks not to welcome to their monasteries any visitors who associate with the Arian party, even if they profess to repudiate the views of Arius himself.[9] Significantly, this letter was inscribed on the walls of a monastery at Thebes.[10] The two letters are political as well as pastoral documents in which Athanasius looks forward to the day when 'the slaves of Antichrist' will be overwhelmed as the servants of Pharaoh once were at the crossing of the Red Sea.

Athanasius wrote more in his years of 'exile' between 356 and 362 than in any other period of his life. These years also witnessed profound theological changes within the eastern church.[11] Were Athanasius a different type of man or writer, or had he not been an outlaw, it might have been possible to chart in his writings the changes of ecclesiastical alliances and to follow the moods of the eastern church in the tumultuous years between 357 and 360. For the most part, however, the exiled Athanasius of these years looked backward in bitterness rather than forward and ruminated on the grievances of the past in order to explain (and discredit) the persecution of the present. Nevertheless, his writings reveal a sudden realisation, late in 359, that those whom he had long denounced as heretics as well as personal enemies could be won over as allies in ecclesiastical politics.

Athanasius wrote his long *Letter to the Bishops of Egypt and Libya* from an unknown location (perhaps the Nitrian Desert) shortly after his expulsion from Alexandria.[12] The letter was designed to dissuade its recipients from subscribing to the synodical letter of the Council of Sirmium which had deposed Athanasius and drawn up a creed. Athanasius is typically allusive in his references to the target of his criticisms, but he reveals enough to make the identification certain. Some Arians had written concerning the faith, threatening exile and other punishments and seeking to overturn the creed of Nicaea:

> They disturb and confuse everything, and not even so are they satisfied with their actions. For every year, like men writing their wills, they meet and pretend to write about the faith, so that in this too they tend to de-

serve ridicule and disgrace, because their decisions are rejected not by others, but by themselves. (6)

That is a tendentious but unmistakeable allusion to the Councils of Arles in 353/4 and Milan in 355. Athanasius contrasts the Arian party, the enemies of Christ, who are few in number but wish their view to prevail, with the orthodox who uphold the tenets of the ecumenical Council of Nicaea. Who are the former? Secundus from the Pentapolis, who has often been removed from the priesthood; George of Laodicea, the eunuch Leontius of Antioch, his predecessor Stephanus, Theodorus of Heraclea, Ursacius and Valens, Acacius, Patrophilus, and Narcissus, men deposed at Serdica; Eustathius of Sebasteia, Demophilus, Germinius, Eudoxius, and Basil; Cecropius of Nicomedia, Auxentius of Milan, the impostor Epictetus of Centumcellae, and above all George of Cappadocia, a man with the character of a public executioner, who has been hired as bishop of Alexandria despite his ignorance of the Christian faith and his rumored devotion to idols (7). And who are the orthodox? The confessor Ossius, Maximinus of Trier and his successor Paulinus, Philogonius and Eustathius, successive bishops of Antioch, Julius and Liberius of Rome, Cyriacus from Moesia, Pistus and Aristaeus from Greece, Silvester and Protogenes from Dacia, Leontius and Eupsychius from Cappadocia, Caecilianus from Africa, Eustorgius of Italy, Capito of Sicily, Macarius of Jerusalem, Alexander of Constantinople, Paederos of Heraclea, the great Meletius, Basil, Longianus, and the other bishops of Armenia and Pontus, Lupus and Amphion from Cilicia, Jacob of Nisibis, and other bishops from Mesopotamia (8). The long list, designed to impress the country bishops of Egypt and Libya, reveals Athanasius' isolation: too many of his champions were dead when he wrote, and even Ossius and Liberius were soon to accept a creed other than the Nicene formula.

The *Letter to the Bishops of Egypt and Libya* is well constructed and maintains an optimistic tone. Athanasius begins with a general warning against false prophets, the Devil, and rejection of paths of scripture, and follows with a specific warning against Arian attempts to subvert the creed of Nicaea. The second part of the *Letter* attacks the Arian position on doctrinal grounds and from scripture. Athanasius concludes by urging the bishops to stand firm for true faith against the unholy alliance of Arians and Melitians, and declares his conviction that when 'our gracious emperor' hears of what is happening, he will stop the persecution (23, cf. 5, 19).

Athanasius adopted the same optimistic assumption about Constantius when he added a long continuation to the *Defense before Constantius* which he had originally composed as a practical measure of self-defense in 353.[13] But now he found it increasingly hard to sustain the pretense that imperial benevolence was being systematically frustrated by the emperor's servants. As Athanasius described his resistance to attempts to remove him in 353 and 355 (*Apol. ad Const.* 19–22), then his expulsion and the installation of George (24–28), and finally Constantius' denunciations of him (29–31), he repeated his contention that Constantius' agents were exceeding, even disregarding, his orders. He protested that the emperor, who was pious, patient, and kind, disapproved of the exile of aged bishops and the torturing of virgins (29.2). Yet a note of exasperation creeps in as Athanasius contemplates the possibility that officials may kill him on the authority of the emperor's letters (32). Athanasius knew what Constantius' attitude toward him really was, and he had known it for a long time. Perhaps he composed the final version of the *Defense before Constantius* in the hope of deterring subordinate officials and civilians in Egypt who might be tempted to arrest him.[14]

The distress which Athanasius felt at being compelled to leave Alexandria, the firmest bastion of his political support, surfaces in the closing chapters of the *Defense before Constantius*. Also in 357, Athanasius wrote a *Defense of His Flight*, which, unlike the *Defense before Constantius* and the earlier *Defense against the Arians*, never underwent a fundamental revision (though Athanasius did add at least one sentence to the original version).[15] The work appears to have been composed in the summer or autumn of 357.[16] Athanasius refers to events in Alexandria of May and perhaps June 357 (6/7), but consistently assumes that Leontius is still bishop of Antioch (1.1, 26.6): although the exact date of Leontius' death is not known, news that he was fatally ill had already reached Eudoxius while he was in Rome with the emperor in May.[17] It is not known what title Athanasius himself gave the work. The title in the Greek manuscripts ('concerning those who were reproaching his flight in persecution') does not go back to the author, but represents an inference from what the text reveals about the occasion of composition:

> I hear that Leontius, who is now at Antioch, Narcissus of the city of Nero, George, who is now at Laodicea, and the Arians with them are spreading much gossip and slander about me and charging me with cowardice because, when I was sought by them to be killed, I did not deliver myself up to be surrendered into their hands. (1.1)

The opening sentence reveals clearly the circumstances which impelled Athanasius to write: the slanders may have been inspired by Leontius, Narcissus, and George of Laodicea, but the whispering campaign was dangerous because it coincided with, and was intended to make easier, an attempt to win Alexandria away from the departed bishop. His replacement, George, was in Alexandria when Athanasius wrote, as were Aetius and Eunomius.[18] It was a critical time for Athanasius. The charge of cowardice might stick and impair his authority. There were alarming precedents in the opposition which arose in Carthage when Cyprian withdrew during the Decian persecution in 250/1,[19] and in the Melitian schism, which began precisely because Melitius stepped in to perform the duties of an absent bishop of Alexandria.[20] Athanasius' *Defense of His Flight* meets that challenge, and it is reasonable to assume that he wrote it for immediate circulation in Alexandria.

Athanasius begins by impugning the motives of his accusers, and concludes by attacking their characters and praising God for frustrating their machinations. They imitate the Jews who killed Jesus, so that it is insincere for them to complain when their intended victim escapes their clutches (2.1). Leontius, whom Constantius installed as a bishop by force (in 344), is a eunuch who castrated himself in order to live freely with the young woman Eustolium and was expelled from the priesthood for doing so; Narcissus has been deposed by three church councils; and George of Laodicea has been both expelled from the priesthood and, at the Council of Serdica, deposed from his episcopal see (26.2–4). Each has his own vices, but they share the common stain of heresy, being no Christians, but Arians (27.1).

The main argument of the *Defense of His Flight* is twofold: Athanasius is a victim of persecution, and it is right to flee persecution if one can.[21] Athanasius presents the attack on himself as part of a systematic attack, sustained over many years, on all who have upheld truth and fought the Arian heresy. He names victims from earlier years: Eustathius of Antioch, Euphration of Balaneae, Cymatius of Paltus, Carterius of Antaradus, Eutropius and Lucius of Adrianople, Marcellus of Ancyra, Cyrus of Beroea, Asclepas of Gaza, the Thracian bishops Theodulus and Olympius, Athanasius himself long ago, and Paul of Constantinople, whom the praetorian prefect Philippus killed (3.3–6). Next, Athanasius names those now in exile for refusing to accept either the Arian heresy or the calumnies against him: Liberius of Rome, Paulinus of Trier, Dionysius of Milan, Lucifer of Caralis, Eusebius of Vercellae, and the venerable Ossius of Corduba (4.2–5.2). Athanasius then summarises the outrages which George of Cappadocia (as he always styles him) has perpetrated in Alexandria and Egypt, with emphasis on his use of torture and the exile of more than thirty bishops (6.1–7.5).

Athanasius himself has escaped: the real complaint of his adversaries is that their wicked designs have been frustrated (8.1). He has fled to avoid persecution: in doing so, he has followed biblical precept and biblical examples. Jesus himself both hid when enemies sought him and instructed his disciples to flee. For God allots each man a time which he does not know: it is wrong, therefore, to offer oneself to one's persecutors. The saint who is persecuted should wait for God to reveal his appointed time: that is not cowardice, but a sign of fortitude. Athanasius illustrates and buttresses his argument with examples from scripture—not only Jesus himself, but also Jacob, Moses, David, Elijah, and the apostles Peter and Paul (8.2–23.2). Athanasius applies the general rule to himself by describing Syrianus' attempt to arrest him and the remarkable escape by which divine providence delivered him. To surrender himself now would be to act contrary to scripture (24.1–26.1).

Athanasius' *Defense of His Flight* provides yet another touchstone for assessing his literary culture. At first sight, the work appears to have antecedents and obvious models in Greek philosophical literature (such as Plutarch's *On Exile*) and in Christian writings (such as Tertullian's *On Flight under Persecution*). On closer examination, however, it is hard to discover any clear literary affinities between Athanasius' work and earlier extant works of a similar type, whether pagan or Christian. Nor does the *Defense of His Flight* show any obvious influence of traditional Greek methods of composition or use any *exempla* other than biblical ones. The *Defense of His Flight* gives no support at all to the notion that Athanasius owed much to Greek rhetorical theory in his apologetical works. On the contrary, the matrix of Athanasius' mind was and remained biblical. The *Defense of His Flight* is steeped throughout in biblical language and biblical modes of thought. In this work too Athanasius' style of expression reflects the vigor of his native intelligence rather than the influence of pagan literary culture: it is rough and forceful rather than polished and urbane.

The *History of the Arians* has an evil reputation as 'the solitary monument of a less noble spirit which Athanasius has left us, the one work which we would gladly believe to have come from any other pen.'[22] That verdict implicitly denies the tendentious quality evident in Athanasius' other writings: the *History of the Arians* merely states outright much that Athanasius deemed it politic to suppress or to veil when he was writing to defend or justify himself to a neutral or hostile audience. The *History of the Arians* was addressed, if indeed it had a definite audience, to monks sympathetic to the author.[23] As it stands, the text begins abruptly, without introduction and with a reference back to what precedes (1.1: 'They themselves [the Melitians] soon fulfilled the purposes for which they had contrived these things'). A lacuna is usually postulated.[24] It would have to be one of considerable compass, since the *History* appears to continue the narrative of the second part of the *Defense against the Arians*. Perhaps, therefore, the *History of the Arians* is the surviving part of a work which Athanasius never completed or intended to publish in its present form. Its composition may be assigned to the closing months of 357. At the time of writing, Athanasius knew that Liberius had capitulated (41.3/4) and that Ossius had died repenting on his deathbed of setting his name to the 'blasphemy' of Sirmium (45.4/5); yet he assumes that Leontius of Antioch is still alive and that Eudoxius is still bishop of Germanicia (4.2).[25]

The *History of the Arians* is political satire or political caricature. It deserves to be compared to works like Synesius' *On Kingship,* which attacks the ministers of the emperor Arcadius, and Procopius' *Secret History* of the reign of Justinian.[26] Like them, it is opposition literature in an age of panegyric and ceremonial laudations. Here too, however, Athanasius shows no signs of familiarity with the techniques of invective and vituperation developed in a long Greek and Latin literary tradition. Instead of deliberate and conscious art, he uses native wit. The product is all the more lively and effective for being spontaneous.

Athanasius had shown his talent for such writing in miniature when he wrote to Serapion of Thmuis long before to tell him how Arius died.[27] In this brief epistle, essential facts which fix the date of the episode are stated succinctly: Athanasius was not in Constantinople when Arius died, but the priest Macarius was—and the emperor Constantine. Arius drew up a dishonest creed and swore that he had never held the views for which Alexander had excommunicated him. The emperor commented: 'If your creed is orthodox, you have done well to swear; but if your creed is impious, although you have sworn [that it is not], may God judge your case according to your oath.' The Eusebians tried to compel Alexander of Constantinople to receive Arius into communion. Alexander prepared to resist and prayed; as Arius was being escorted to his church, he retired to a latrine to relieve himself—and dropped down dead. The story has clearly been made more stylised and pointed than a straightforward narrative would naturally be. Some of the most colorful details may be suspect, and Athanasius has invented the dialogue for himself, yet the narrative fits perfectly into the known historical framework: Arius died in July 336 while the Council of Constantinople was attempting to vindicate his orthodoxy.[28] The *History of the Arians* exhibits the same talents and techniques on a large scale.

The underlying assumption of the *History of the Arians* is that Athanasius is a victim of a systematic policy of persecution mounted by the Arians against Christ and his true believers ever since the days of Constantine, and that this policy has been rendered possible only by secular support. Constantine himself was duped by slanderous accusations and worked upon by his female relatives, so that Eustathius and many of his clergy were exiled for insulting his mother, Helena (4.1). Eutropius of Adrianople was ruined through the agency of Basilina (5.1), and Marcellus of Ancyra came to grief because Eusebius and his associates had access to the emperor through the women of the palace (6.1).[29] High officials too supported the heretics. Philagrius installed Gregory as bishop of Alexandria in 339 (9.3–10.2), and he was *vicarius* of Pontica when Paul of Constantinople was murdered at Cucusus: he was so disappointed that the praetorian prefect Philippus had forestalled him in despatching the exiled bishop that he disclosed details of the murder (7.5). But it is Constantius above all who has fostered the persecution of orthodoxy and interfered improperly in the affairs of the Christian church. Athanasius denounces the emperor as the enemy of Christ, as Antichrist, worse than the biblical villains Saul, Ahab, and Pontius Pilate (67/8). Athanasius produces a litany of family treacheries which even the tirades of the emperor Julian never surpassed. Constantius slaughtered his uncles and his cousins, he refused to pity his relatives or his father-in-law, whom he killed while still sleeping with his daughter,[30] and he gave Olympias, the intended bride of his brother Constans, in marriage to a barbarian (69.1).[31] His actions, toward his family as well as toward the church, show that he is an unjust ruler with wicked subordinates (69–73).

The connecting thread of the *History of the Arians* is Athanasius' career from 337 onward. The relation of the introductory chapters to the rest is clouded by the chapter on Paul of Constantinople, which Athanasius appears to have added carelessly to an existing text (7). Without this chapter, Athanasius proceeds smoothly from the general recklessness of the Melitians and Arians as allies in the 330s (1–3) to bishops deposed and exiled under Constantine (4–6); he then makes the transition to himself by means of the restoration of bishops by the sons of Constantine in 337, and quotes the letter of Constantinus to the church of Alexandria (8). The discussion of Paul, though full of valuable historical details, interrupts its context both logically and chronologically.[32]

The introduction to the *History* already exhibits one of the characteristic features of the work: Athanasius' use of invented dialogue to ridicule his adversaries. Any Melitian or Arian who wishes to become a bishop is told to adopt un-Christian views and not to worry about character: 'that suffices to recommend you and to win the emperor's friendship' (3.4). Athanasius had a good eye for plausible caricature, and some of his inventions have imposed themselves on the historical tradition.[33] More serious, Athanasius' tendentious narrative has unduly influenced both the ecclesiastical historians of the fifth century and modern reconstructions of his career.

Athanasius' primary techniques in the *History of the Arians* are suppression and distortion. He makes no allusion here to his audiences with Constantius at Viminacium and Caesarea in Cappadocia (*Apol. ad Const.* 5.3), no allusion to his audiences with Constans (*Apol. ad Const.* 3/4), and no open allusion to his journeys into eastern territory in 343 and 344—though a reference to his seeing the tombs of the supporters of Lucius at Adrianople in 344 has escaped his vigilance (18.2).[34] Nor, predictably, is there any reference to his alliance with Paul of Constantinople or to the letter which Constans wrote in 345 threatening to restore the pair by force[35]—only to the earlier letter which Constans wrote very shortly after the Council of Serdica on behalf of all the exiled bishops (20.2). And there is naturally no hint of the shifts and compromises of 345 and 346 whereby Athanasius and Paul returned to their sees while Marcellus of Ancyra remained in exile.[36]

The omissions are matched by tendentious misrepresentations. Athanasius never admits that his enemies proceeded against him in due form or that he was ever condemned by a properly constituted council of bishops: an innocent reader of the *History of the Arians* might conclude that it was only Athanasius' allies who habitually convened church councils. On Athanasius' presentation, it was Constantius who replaced him with Gregory: the emperor sent Philagrius to Egypt as prefect with the eunuch Arsacius, and he sent Gregory to Alexandria with a military escort (10.1). Gregory himself had not been ordained a bishop according to proper ecclesiastical procedure: he arrived from court with military pomp as if entrusted with a post in the secular administration, and he received letters from the emperor and magistrates with extreme joy, but refused letters from the monk Antony (14.1/2). Similarly, the eastern bishops came to the Council of Serdica under the protection of the *comes* Musonianus and the *castrensis* Hesychius, expecting them to manage the conduct of the council: when things went badly for them, they fled and concocted the excuse that they needed to congratulate Constantius on his victory over the Persians (15.3–16.2). In contrast, the western contingent consisted only of bishops, with Ossius as their leader (15.3). Athanasius presents the Council of Sirmium in 351 as a cabal which persuaded Ursacius and Valens to return like dogs to their vomit, then approached Constantius and so inflamed him with anger that he turned against Athanasius and forswore his oaths (29/30). Athanasius cannot resist quoting Constantius' flattering letter of 350, and he cannot gainsay its reference to the death of Constans; yet he quotes it in the context of his return from exile in 346 (24). Hence he can slide easily over Magnentius' overtures to him and the embarrassing accusations which the *Defense before Constantius* had rebutted.[37]

Athanasius did not set out to write a full or impartial narrative. For his career between 337 and 346, he drew on the existing account in the *Defense against the Arians,* sharpening and exaggerating as well as supplying additional details. For more recent events, he marshaled his account around the theme of Constantius as a persecutor. Throughout he selected, emphasised, and developed striking episodes. As a result, the *History of the Arians* is a systematically deceptive work. When the course of events has been reconstructed from other evidence, the distortions can be recognised and the skill of the caricaturist can be admired. Yet an accurate reconstruction of the complicated ecclesiastical politics of the years between 337 and 357 could not be deduced from the *History of the Arians,* even though Athanasius includes many details and individual episodes which can be found nowhere else in the surviving record.

Athanasius describes briefly the outrages which attended and followed his expulsion in 339: a mob of herdsmen and dissolute youths armed with swords and clubs attacked the Church of Quirinus; worshippers were killed, beaten, and insulted; bishops were exiled or wounded, monks scourged; Gregory appropriated alms for his own use, and the *dux* Valacius lent him aid—until his horse bit and threw him with fatal results (10, 12–14). But recent events occupy the most space: almost half of the *History of the Arians* is devoted to the persecution of Athanasius and the orthodox in Alexandria and Egypt between 353 and 357 (47–81).

First, with a great deal of rhetorical elaboration, Athanasius denounces Constantius for his unsuccessful attempts to oust him. He then describes in some detail the Arian seizure of the churches in Alexandria in 356 and the violence used both then and later. In all this he emphasises the role of secular officials. In June 356 it was the *comes* Heraclius, the prefect Cataphronius, and the *catholicus* Faustinus who instigated a crowd of pagan youths to attack the Church of Theonas and to seize and burn the seats, the bishop's throne, the altar, and the curtains (54–56). Later it was the *dux* Sebastianus, a notorious Manichee, the prefect, and the *catholicus* who assisted the Arians in insulting virgins, procuring the death of Eutychius by scourging, plundering the poor, and exiling priests and deacons (59–61).

Next, again with much rhetorical elaboration, Athanasius describes the persecution in the rest of Egypt, which he compares to the 'Great Persecution' in the reign of Constantius' grandfather Maximian (64.2). Here he is at pains to establish that, without the aid of external power and persecution, the Arian heresy would long ago have withered and died: refuted, cast down, shamed by the truth, it coerced with violence, with the lash, and with imprisonment. Sebastianus wrote to the *praepositi* and the military authorities everywhere, and they exiled all the true bishops, replacing them with holders of impious doctrines: Athanasius names a total of twenty-six exiled bishops, of whom ten were so aged that they had been ordained by Alexander before his death in 328. Some of these suffered violence, some were sent to hard labor in stone-quarries. Laymen too were banished, monasteries destroyed, private houses robbed (72). The new bishops were young, wanton pagans, not yet even catechumens, men with two wives, chosen because of their wealth and civil power (73)—all of which showed that 'puny Constantius' was no Christian, but the image of the Antichrist (74.1).[38] From denunciation of Constantius, Athanasius slides easily to denigration of the Melitians, his original foes in Alexandria in the early years of his episcopate (78/9). Finally a documentary appendix quotes two formal protests which the Christians of Alexandria submitted on Athanasius' behalf in February 356 (81: the first has been lost in transmission).

Athanasius naturally devoted much space to the vicissitudes of his own career between 339 and 346 (8–28). He also selected the cases of Liberius and Ossius for special treatment. Liberius resisted the blandishments of the eunuch Eusebius and refused to condemn Athanasius: the *History of the Arians* invents a speech of firm defiance. When Liberius then refused to accept the bribe previously dangled before him as an offering at the shrine of Saint Peter, Eusebius was annoyed and induced the emperor to summon the bishop from Rome. Despite resistance in the city, Liberius was dragged before Constantius, whom he defied. After two years of exile, however, he succumbed to the fear of being murdered, and subscribed (35–41). The aged Ossius also resisted bravely and doggedly. Yet he too was eventually broken by imprisonment and violence. After being detained a whole year at Sirmium, Ossius agreed to hold communion with Ursacius, Valens, and their associates, although he still would not subscribe against Athanasius (42–45). That corresponds to the truth. Liberius left Rome in autumn 355, saw Constantius at Milan, and was exiled to Beroea in Thrace: when he subscribed to the decisions of the Council of Sirmium of 351, he was allowed to return to Rome, which he reentered on 2 August 357.[39] Ossius (it may be inferred from Athanasius) never subscribed to the decisions of the Council of Sirmium of 351: he put his name to the 'blasphemy' of 357. Again, the distortion is recognisable, but the original reality could not be recovered from Athanasius' depiction of it alone.

In every section of the *History*, Athanasius employs the technique of invented speeches or invented dialogue. He uses it most effectively, not in long speeches such as that put into the mouth of Liberius, but in short, snappy sentences which lampoon his opponents' motives. Three examples of some historical importance will illustrate. First, the Arians approached Constantius in 338/9 as the patron of their heresy:

> Spare the heresy. You see that all have deserted us: few of us are left. Start to persecute, for we have been abandoned even by these few and are isolated. Those whom we compelled after these men had been banished, the exiles have again persuaded on their return to take sides against us. Write then against them all, and send Philagrius as prefect of Egypt for the second time, for he can persecute properly, since he has already shown it in practise, and especially because he is an apostate. And send Gregory as bishop to Alexandria, for he too can sustain our heresy. (9.2/3)

Second, the eastern bishops at Serdica in 343:

> We came for one result and see another. We arrived with *comites* and the trial is proceeding without *comites*: we are being completely condemned. You all know our orders. The Athanasians possess the records from the Mareotis by which he is cleared and we are put to shame. Why then do we hesitate? Why do we delay? Let us invent excuses and depart, lest by remaining we be condemned. It is better to flee in shame than to be convicted and condemned as false accusers. If we flee, we can still champion our heresy in some way: even if they condemn us for fleeing, we still have the emperor as our patron, who will not allow us to be expelled from our churches by our congregations. (15.5)

Third, Constantius to the bishops who refused to condemn Athanasius or hold communion with heretics at Milan in 355:

> Whatever I wish, let that be considered a binding rule [of the church]. The so-called bishops of Syria agree with me when I speak thus. Therefore, either obey or you too will become exiles. (33.7)

It is inconceivable that either the eastern bishops or Constantius used such words: the former cannot have styled themselves heretics, nor can the latter have questioned their right to be called bishops. Athanasius puts into the mouths of his adversaries what he believes their real reasoning to have been—in his own words.[40] Such invented utterances in the *History of the Arians* fall into a pattern of painting Constantius as an Arian emperor and the principal patron of the Arian heresy.

Athanasius is unfair to Constantius. That must be conceded. But what here is the reality which he distorts? It will not suffice to challenge Athanasius' characterisation of the Arian emperor and his motives, while accepting most of his narrative of imperial actions.[41] For the distortions vitally affect the narrative:

when Athanasius has systematically avoided reporting the decisions of eastern church councils (or at least has avoided reporting them as such), then it becomes no easy matter to define Constantius' role in ecclesiastical politics. Nevertheless, two guiding principles of imperial policy can be discerned, which Constantius inherited from Constantine. First, the emperor both showed an interest in defining true belief and believed that God had given him the duty of propagating it. Constantius attended councils which discussed credal matters, and took part in attempts to define an acceptable orthodoxy: if he overstepped the mark in promoting a homoean creed in 359,[42] that may be a sign of his exasperation with disputing bishops—and permits no inference back to his policy in earlier years. Second, Constantius both consistently observed and explicitly reasserted the principle that a bishop could be condemned and deposed only by a council of his peers, whatever the charge.[43] The principal defect of the *History of the Arians* as history is that it consistently denies this central fact.

Athanasius is also inconsistent. His constant complaint that the emperor interferes in the affairs of the church is not in fact directed against interference as such, but against imperial actions of which he disapproves. He commends the imperial restoration of exiled bishops in 337 (8.1), which was clearly uncanonical and condemned as such by contemporaries: bishops deposed by a council of bishops ought to be reinstated only by a similar body or court.[44] Athanasius implicitly asserts that emperors have a right to overrule church councils—provided that they do so in the interest of orthodoxy rather than heresy. Instead of the complexities of the real world of the fourth century, the *History of the Arians* propounds a simplistic disjunction:

> If there is a decision by bishops, what concern has the emperor with it?
> But if it is merely a threat from the emperor, what need in that case for the
> so-called bishops? (52.3)

Athanasius avoids the real ambiguities and vicissitudes of his career in order to make the false and barefaced claim that he has never been condemned by an ecclesiastical verdict, only persecuted for his devotion to Christ by imperial fiat (1.2).

The content of theological discussion changed radically around 360 and rendered the debates of the 340s and 350s out-of-date. Until c. 360 controversy centred on Christology; thereafter the issue became one of trinitarian theology. What is the relation of the Holy Spirit to the Father and the Son? The problem was posed, debated, and solved to the satisfaction of the vast majority of the theologically aware very quickly.[45] When the Council of Constantinople met in 381, the issue was dead. And so was the classic 'Arianism' which Athanasius opposed throughout his long episcopate, at least as an intellectual force within the Greek-speaking eastern empire. If those who rejected the *homoousion* tended to subordinate the Son to the Father, *a fortiori* they so subordinated the

Holy Spirit as to lose any sense of equal persons in a threefold godhead.

Athanasius acutely saw and seized upon this flaw while he was in exile. Serapion wrote to him in the desert about certain Christians who held views which appear to derive from indoctrination by Aetius and Eunomius, who were active in Alexandria c. 357. These *tropici* (as Athanasius calls them) forsook the Arians, but still continued to assert that the Holy Spirit is a creature, a ministering spirit, a superior type of angel.[46] Athanasius wrote a long letter, then two briefer ones, to Serapion setting out his doctrine of the Holy Spirit. He had always assumed a trinitarian position. Now he made it explicit. The long letter disproves the deductions which the *tropici* have made from their proof-texts (Amos 4:13; 1 Timothy 5:21), then transcends their dilemma that the Spirit must be either creature or son, and finally argues the case for 'the holy and indivisible Trinity' from scripture and the tradition and life of the church. Athanasius argues with force and clarity. But some of those who wished to use his arguments found the exposition too long. Athanasius accordingly composed a briefer letter which distills the longer treatment into a more systematically anti-Arian format: here Athanasius argues first that the Son is not a creature, then that the Spirit is not a creature either. Finally, in response to a further letter from Serapion informing him that the *tropici* were still employing their dilemma, Athanasius supplied the brief refutation which his second letter had omitted. These *Letters to Serapion* show Athanasius at his best, in the lofty realms of theological speculation, where he always retains a tone of hard-headed moderation.[47] They are also a valuable document for the intellectual life of Alexandria, where theological argument was an everyday occurrence.

Athanasius' 'letter on the councils which took place at Ariminum in Italy and Seleucia in Isauria' spans the two realms of polemic and theology. Athanasius was writing in the late autumn of 359: although he later (apparently after 3 November 361) added a postscript containing the exchange of letters between Constantius and the Council of Ariminum (55), and a passage in the middle of the work which quotes the creed of the Council of Constantinople (January 360) and discusses the Council of Antioch held in the spring of 360 (30/1), most of *On the Councils* was written after he received news of the Council of Seleucia (which broke up on 1 October), but before he learned of Constantius' reception of the envoys from the Council of Ariminum.[48] Athanasius wrote *On the Councils of Ariminum and Seleucia* for a very immediate and very practical purpose—to make common cause with the homoeousians of Asia Minor. It would be optimistic to suppose that the work had an immediate impact, or even that it reached Athanasius' potential allies before events overtook it. But it marks a significant change of position: Athanasius was now seeking an alliance with bishops who had condemned and deposed him in 351, and whom he had recently been denouncing as Arians in virulent language.

The work falls into three entirely separate parts. The first comprises a brief account of the two councils, every bit as tendentious as the *History of the*

Arians, though somewhat less abusive. Athanasius makes great play with the 'dated creed' of 22 May 359 (3/4), as if the catholic faith had suddenly been revealed on a specified day of the current year. And he reiterates his long-held view that any council which considers the faith is either futile or dangerous, since it will either repeat the Nicene creed or subvert it (5–7). The account of the Council of Ariminum contrasts the dishonesty of those who framed and presented the 'dated creed' with the firm letter of the council to Constantius defending the Nicene creed and deposing Ursacius, Valens, Gaius, Germinius, and Auxentius (8–11). For events at Seleucia, Athanasius provides a summary narrative without documents, and contrasts the resolution of the bishops at Ariminum with the fickleness of Eudoxius, Acacius, and their allies who disown the Council of Nicaea (12.1–14.3).

The second section of *On the Councils* argues that the Arian heresy which the majority at Seleucia has condemned in 359 is in all important respects identical with the heresy of Arius himself and his original sympathisers, which the Council of Nicaea condemned. Athanasius had long believed this thesis: now he quotes Arius himself (selectively and at length), Eusebius of Nicomedia, Eusebius of Caesarea, Athanasius of Anazarbus, George of Laodicea, and the sophist Asterius (also at some length) to show that the Acacians of 359 are advocating precisely the same doctrines (15–19). And he quotes a long series of creeds to show how the Arians have tried to replace the Nicene formula for many years (21–28). Athanasius' comments on the documents are misleading, for not all are creeds, and he presents them all as due to mere whim, ignoring their political and theological contexts. The documents quoted are the following:

(1) part of the synodical letter of the Council of Jerusalem in 335, which readmitted Arius;
(2) part of the letter which the Council of Antioch in 341 wrote to Julius of Rome;
(3) the creed from the synodical letter of the same council;
(4) a creed submitted to the same council by Theophronius of Tyana;
(5) the creed drawn up at Antioch in 342 and sent to Constans in Gaul;
(6) the 'long creed' drawn up by the Council of Antioch in 344;
(7) the creed and anathemas of the Council of Sirmium in 351;
(8) the theological manifesto drawn up at Sirmium in 357, in the names of Ossius and Potamius.[49]

In Athanasius' exposition, all these documents are the work of the same group of bishops, perennially dissatisfied with their existing creed. The only alternative, Athanasius urges, is to acknowledge the Council of Nicaea.

The third section of *On the Councils of Ariminum and Seleucia* addresses itself to the key words *homoousios* and *homoiousios.* Athanasius argues against Eudoxius and Acacius that if the Son really is 'like' the Father (as they assert), then he must also be of the same essence.[50] He defends the Nicene term, but also claims that there is no serious difference between calling the Son *homoousios* with the Father and defining the relationship as *homoiousios*. Accordingly, those who prefer the latter term are neither Arians nor heretics, but should be treated like brothers who have a friendly disagreement. Athanasius compares the two terms in conciliatory tones, arguing amicably but firmly that the Council of Nicaea chose the correct word (32–54).

Athanasius was thus not unaffected by the theological changes of the late 350s. By late 359 he welcomed as allies men who had long been enemies. His vocabulary shows an internal shift which reflects his change of attitude. In all of his earlier writings, including the *History of the Arians*, the word 'Arian' denotes anyone who condemned Athanasius and who was not a Melitian—a category which originally coincided with those who also thought that Arius should not be treated as a heretic. But *On the Councils of Ariminum and Seleucia* restricts the term 'Arian' to homoeans and anomoeans. The Athanasius who returned from exile in 362 was ready to cooperate with men who had deposed him, and he was prepared to forget the condemnation at Sirmium in 351, reiterated in 353/4 and 355, which had dominated both ecclesiastical and imperial politics for the greater part of the sixth decade of the fourth century.

XV

NEW THEOLOGICAL
CONTROVERSIES

THE THEOLOGICAL COALITION IN THE EAST WHICH HAD SO OFTEN condemned Athanasius from 335 to 351 changed suddenly and unexpectedly in the late 350s. A powerful catalyst was added to the theological brew which had been steeping in the same controversies for twenty years—and reaction soon produced new combinations and alignments. The radical doctrines of Aetius and Eunomius shattered the broad alliance of bishops in Asia Minor, Syria, and Palestine which had united to condemn Athanasius, Marcellus, and Photinus and to propose a series of creeds which sought to modify the Nicene formula without formally repudiating it.

Aetius was born c. 313, and poverty compelled him to support his family as a goldsmith.[1] He studied in Antioch, Anazarbus, Tarsus, in Antioch again, and finally in Alexandria, where he learned medicine and Aristotelian philosophy. Unfortunately, the earlier stages of his ecclesiastical career are known only from Photius' summary of Philostorgius, which presents either unusual vicissitudes or some doubling up of episodes. Three steps stand out. Leontius ordained Aetius deacon in Antioch, where he began to teach. After 351 Aetius became a confidant of the Caesar Gallus, who sent him to his brother Julian in Asia Minor to steer him away from paganism.[2] Then, in 357, Aetius came to Alexandria: he accompanied the new bishop George and was presumably active in attempts to obtain Egyptian acceptance of the creed and condemnations of the Council of Sirmium.[3] When Leontius died, Aetius hurried to Antioch to win over Eudoxius.[4] In 358 Aetius was exiled,[5] then presumably recalled, since he presented his *Syntagmation* in Constantinople in the winter of 359/60—and was promptly exiled again.[6] In January 362 Aetius was recalled by Julian, and died shortly thereafter.[7]

Eunomius was a Cappadocian of humble origin, apparently born shortly before 330, who became a shorthand-writer, then decided to acquire a literary education, first in Constantinople, then in Antioch, and finally in Alexandria, where he became the pupil and disciple of Aetius.[8] He returned to Antioch with Aetius and was ordained as a deacon by Eudoxius. In December 359 (so it appears) he recited his *Apology* in Constantinople, after which, in January 360, he was appointed bishop of Cyzicus.[9] Basil of Caesarea soon took up his pen to refute him and produced his *Against Eunomius:* Eunomius resigned his see in 361 and lived on for more than twenty years, defending himself from time to time (his *Defense of His Apology* belongs to 378).[10]

Aetius and Eunomius were dialecticians, aggressive and skilled in argument, and the latter earned the nickname 'the logic-chopper.'[11] Their innovation was to apply Aristotelian logic, specifically the principles of Aristotle's *Categories,* to Christian theology.[12] Although it has been fashionable to make them both Neoplatonists, and to detect in Eunomius the influence of Iamblichus' exegesis of Plato's *Cratylus,*[13] such hypotheses are neither necessary nor convincing.[14] Still less should Aetius and Eunomius be styled 'Neo-Arians'—a term invented at the beginning of the twentieth century.[15] For terms like 'Neoplatonist' are employed in order to emphasise that philosophers of Late Antiquity who called themselves Platonists (such as Plotinus, Porphyry, and Iamblichus) did not in fact preserve the philosophy of Plato unchanged, but interpreted the teachings of the master on the basis of assumptions and patterns of thought which differed greatly from his. The term 'Neo-Nicene' is entirely appropriate to describe the theology which prevailed in the later fourth century,[16] but the so-called Neo-Arians stand in a very different relationship to their alleged avatar.

Arius died in 336 in circumstances which were embarrassing, degrading, and, by the standards of the age, damning.[17] Henceforward, not even those who had regarded Arius or his views with sympathy ventured to defend him. Marcellus of Ancyra had accused Arius at length of heresy in 335/6, but when Eusebius defended himself and his theological allies against Marcellus in 337/8, he took care that neither his *Against Marcellus* nor his more systematic *Ecclesiastical Theology* ever named Arius.[18] Two decades later, Athanasius depicted Aetius (and by implication Eunomius) as Arians who were reviving and restating the doctrines of the disgraced heresiarch (*Syn.* 38.4). Such a partisan view of their intentions should not be accepted as if it were the result of careful investigation or theological analysis: the opponents of Aetius and Eunomius were usually more concerned to ridicule and discredit them than to describe their views and their intellectual parentage accurately. It should not even be assumed (as it traditionally has been) that the views of Aetius and Eunomius really were fundamentally similar to those of Arius.[19]

Arius and the alleged 'Neo-Arians' need to be understood against their different intellectual backgrounds a generation apart. The theology of Aetius and Eunomius was a new phenomenon, whatever its similarities to some of the propositions which Arius had advanced (or was believed to have advanced). 'Eastern conservatives' like Basil of Ancyra, who had happily admitted Arius to communion when he gave assurances and toned down his views, found the ideas of these new radical theologians completely unacceptable. Aetius and Eunomius used formal logic to unravel and explain a theological mystery which *ex hypothesi* defied the normal rules of syllogistic reasoning.

Liberius had been arrested in the autumn of 355, interviewed by Constantius, and sent to Beroea in Thrace.[20] By the spring of 357, he was ready to compromise. When Constantius visited Rome, both the people and the nobility of the city requested the return of their exiled bishop: the request was granted, and he reentered the city on 2 August.[21] Fragments of the lost historical polemic by Hilary of Poitiers against Ursacius and Valens make clear what Liberius had done to secure permission to return. First, he accepted the condemnation and deposition of Athanasius by writing to the eastern bishops announcing that neither he nor the church of Rome was any longer in communion with Athanasius. This partial acceptance of the decisions of the Councils of Sirmium, Arles, and Milan was deemed insufficient by Potamius and Epictetus, and when Fortunatianus, the bishop of Aquileia, took a copy of the letter to the emperor, he was rebuffed by both the emperor and episcopal colleagues to whom he tendered the letter. Liberius accordingly wrote a second letter to the eastern bishops, in which he reiterated his condemnation of Athanasius and added his acceptance of the creed drawn up by the Council of Sirmium.[22]

When Liberius capitulated, there remained one prominent western bishop who still held out against the condemnation of Athanasius and the creed of Sirmium. The venerable Ossius of Corduba, now almost a centenarian, had prudently avoided the Councils of Arles and Milan, and had declined to subscribe to the synodical letter from Sirmium. Constantius summoned him to court at the same time as Liberius. When Ossius arrived, Constantius urged him to comply. The old man refused in displeasure and grief, but nevertheless obtained permission to return home to his city. Constantius wrote to Ossius more than once, mixing flattery and threats. Ossius remained obdurate and encouraged other Spanish bishops to resist. After some months Constantius sent for Ossius again and had him detained for a whole year in Sirmium, where Germinius could add his constant pleas. Finally, intimidation and harassment broke the aged bishop. Potamius of Lisbon arrived in Sirmium during the summer of 357: although Ossius still obdurately refused to condemn Marcellus, Photinus, and Athanasius or to accept the creed of 351, he was induced to allow his name to be attached, together with that of Potamius, to a theological manifesto in which, for the first time, the creed of the Council of Nicaea was explicitly repudiated (*Hist. Ar.* 42–46).[23]

In the presence of Ursacius, Valens, and Germinius (and perhaps other bishops), Potamius and Ossius drew up a statement which professed to settle the central theological issues of the day.[24] It should be suspected on *a priori* grounds that the document was drafted by Ursacius and Valens, and in fact Phoebadius of Agen presents Ursacius, Valens, and Potamius as its authors.[25] The statement emphasised the uniqueness of God the Father, and hence the subordination of the Son. Since the document is a theoretical statement, rather than a profession of belief, there are no anathemas. The crucial innovation was a proposal to prohibit the contentious philosophical term around which debate had long centered:

> Since some or many have been disturbed about [the term] essence *(substantia)*, which is called *ousia* in Greek, that is, to make it more explicit, [the term] *homoousios*,[26] there ought to be no mention [of it] at all, and no one should employ it, for the cause and reason that it is not contained in Holy Scripture, it is beyond the knowledge of man, and no one can explain the incarnation of the Son.

The nature of this manifesto must not be misunderstood. It was not a creed formally promulgated, formally accepted, and formally subscribed by a council of bishops.[27] Hence it cannot have been presented to other bishops as a document requiring their signature. The manifesto was, to use modern parlance, a 'trial balloon.' The three Illyrian bishops and Potamius wished to use the authority of Ossius to undermine the creed of 325 which he had presented to the Council of Nicaea. They had not entirely miscalculated the theological temper of the East.

Careful preparations had been made. Leontius of Antioch was old and infirm. Eudoxius of Germanicia was one of the bishops in the imperial entourage when Constantius visited Rome in May 357. It appears that Eudoxius learned that Leontius was failing: he invented a plausible excuse, obtained permission to leave court, and sailed to Antioch. There, when Leontius died, Eudoxius was hastily elected and consecrated bishop without the sanction of George of Laodicea, Marcus of Arethusa, or any other leading Syrian bishop.[28] Eudoxius fostered the belief that he enjoyed support from the emperor and palace officials, and he at once began openly to uphold the views of Aetius. He convened a council of predominantly Syrian and Phoenician bishops in Antioch, which accepted and endorsed the Sirmian manifesto, writing a synodical letter to congratulate Ursacius, Valens, and Germinius for their services in promoting correct doctrine.[29]

Even in the church of Antioch, however, there were dissidents. When Eudoxius excommunicated them, George of Laodicea raised the alarm in Asia Minor. Basil of Ancyra had invited the bishops of Galatia to come to his city to dedicate a new church which he had built. George wrote to Macedonius of Constantinople, Basil, Cecropius of Nicomedia, and Eugenius to warn them of the 'shipwreck' at Antioch, where Aetius was now an ordained priest and where Eudoxius was teaching that the Son is dissimilar from the Father.[30] Because of the season and inclement weather, only twelve bishops attended the Council of Ancyra, which met shortly before Easter 358, but it drew up a long and carefully reasoned statement of the case for holding that the Son is of similar essence to the Father. The synodical letter was doubtless mainly the work of Basil himself and Eustathius of Sebasteia, whose names stand first in the subscriptions.[31]

The letter from the bishops at Ancyra addresses their fellow servants in Phoenice and 'the others who hold the same views as we do.' They express surprise that any further clarification of the faith is needed after the definitions provided at Constantinople in 336, at Antioch in 341, at Serdica in 343, and at Sirmium in 351, and after the explanations of the Council of Antioch in 344. The form of their exposition resembles that of the recent document that they set out to denounce and refute. Their central argument is that if the Son really is the son of God, begotten of his Father, not the creature of a creator, then he must be similar to the Father, and specifically must be similar in essence *(homoios kat' ousian)*. They draw the corollary that to affirm that the Son is dissimilar in essence *(anomoios kat' ousian)* is to deny that he is truly Son. Accordingly, the bishops end their letter with a long series of anathemas against that view, capped by a half-hearted anathema on anyone who, 'by saying that the Father is the father of the Son by authority and essence, says that the Son is of one essence or of identical essence *(tautoousios)* with the Father.'[32] The contrast of emphasis is the first open hint of a radical change in theological alliances.

The Council of Ancyra sent ambassadors to the emperor with a request to convene a council to confirm the doctrine established at the Councils of Serdica and Sirmium. Basil of Ancyra, Eustathius of Sebasteia, Eleusius of Cyzicus, and Leontius, who is described as an imperial chaplain, found Asphalius, a priest of Antioch, on the point of departing from court with an imperial letter, presumably commending Eudoxius.[33] After hearing the delegation from Ancyra, however, Constantius wrote to the church of Antioch in a very different strain. He denied that Eudoxius came with his authority and accused him of deceit in the pursuit of power. He denounced Aetius as a virtual atheist and asserted his own belief that 'our Savior is the Son of God and of similar essence to the Father.' And he concluded by urging good men to come forward to defend the traditional faith of the church.[34]

Constantius agreed to Basil's request for another council and proposed Nicaea as its venue. Basil persuaded the emperor that Nicomedia was preferable, and an edict may already have been issued summoning bishops from the whole empire for a council to be held in the autumn of 358 when, on 24 August, an earthquake devastated Nicomedia and damaged nearby cities. Among the dead was Cecropius, the bishop of Nicomedia itself.[35] What happened next is not altogether clear.[36] There were long deliberations and consultations—and doubtless much intrigue within the palace. It is alleged that Basil and his allies succeeded in exiling no fewer than seventy of their opponents, including Eunomius and Aetius, and compelled Eudoxius to withdraw to his native Armenia.[37] Finally, Constantius decided to hold two parallel councils in East and West, presumably because either he or the bishops who had his ear (Ursacius, Valens, and Germinius) thought that separate councils were more likely to produce a correct decision than a single empire-wide council—or at least could be more easily induced to do so. The western council met at Ariminum in July 359,[38] but the date and place of the eastern council were changed more than once: in the autumn of 358 it was expected to meet at Ancyra, then the bishops were summoned to meet at Nicaea in the early summer of 359, but the council was transferred from there to Tarsus, and finally opened in Seleucia in Isauria on 27 September 359.[39] By then, a wide rift had opened between East and West.

The Sirmian manifesto provoked an immediate and hostile reaction in the West. In Gaul Phoebadius, the first attested bishop of Agen in Aquitania, penned a refutation as soon as he learned of this 'deceit of diabolical cleverness.' He examined the main propositions of the manifesto and drew the correct inference that, since it forbade using the phrase 'of one essence,' it outlawed the creed of Nicaea. Consequently (he protested) the new statement of theological principles repudiated Christian tradition, and the authority of the aged and venerable Ossius could not disguise this indisputable fact.[40]

Phoebadius may have sent his work to a Gallic bishop in exile in the East. For there are similarities between his work and one which Hilary of Poitiers probably composed in the winter of 357/8, which have fostered the belief that Phoebadius drew on Hilary.[41] But the assumption that Phoebadius used Hilary would rob his work of its force and immediacy—and at the time of writing Phoebadius had evidently not yet heard of the death of Ossius.[42] It is historically more plausible to date Phoebadius' *Against the Arians* to the autumn of 357 and to explain its similarities to Hilary either as the natural result of two writers from the same cultural background arguing closely similar theses, which draw on the same traditions of theological reasoning, or by the hypothesis that Phoebadius sent a copy of his work to Hilary. Phoebadius presumably knew Hilary before his exile, and there is no difficulty in assuming that Hilary, perhaps only semi-consciously, incorporated phrases of what he had recently read.

Hilary of Poitiers had been condemned in 356 by the Council of Baeterrae, together with Rhodanius of Toulouse, probably because both refused to subscribe the synodical letter of the Council of Sirmium.[43] Hilary was sent into exile in Phrygia. In the winter of 357/8 his position as a Latin-speaking Gallic bishop in exile in Asia Minor gave him the opportunity to play an important political role. He composed (probably during the winter of 357/8) a work of historical polemic against the 'blasphemy of Sirmium.' He surveyed the Councils of Serdica, Sirmium, Arles, and Milan with a newly acquired conviction that the attacks on Athanasius were after all attacks on orthodoxy. He discussed and documented the capitulation of Liberius, he stressed the Nicene creed as the guarantee of true belief, and he arranged his argument as an attack on Ursacius and Valens.[44] Hilary was writing for a western, primarily Gallic, audience, and his work had an immediate resonance.

A council of Gallic bishops met in the spring of 358, condemned the Sirmian manifesto, wrote to Hilary, and asked him pointed questions about recent theological developments in the East.[45] Hilary responded by attempting to forge an alliance between the Gallic bishops and the party of Basil of Ancyra. The long letter to the bishops of Gaul and Britain which Hilary wrote later in 358, and which the manuscripts entitle 'On the Councils, or on the Creed of the Easterners,' constitutes primary evidence for the complicated theological situation at the time of its composition.[46]

Hilary argues at length that the two groups are in fact in agreement, that the terms *homoousios* and *homoiousios* have precisely the same meaning and implications. He admits that the Gallic and eastern bishops harbor mutual suspicions, but sets out to remove western suspicions of eastern credal statements by quoting and expounding the anathemas of the recent Council of Ancyra and the creeds of the Councils of Antioch in 341, of Serdica in 343, and of Sirmium in 351, together with its twenty-seven anathemas. Hilary's apologetical intent emerges from a marginal note which he subsequently appended to a copy of the work sent to Lucifer of Caralis: he suppressed the last five of the Ancyran anathemas, including the proscription of the term *homoousios,* because he quotes only those which were reported to the emperor at Sirmium.[47] For his Gallic audience, Hilary depicts his eastern allies as an embattled minority:

> So great is the danger of the eastern churches that it is rare to find either clergy or laity of this faith (whose quality you are to judge). Great authority has been given to impiety by certain men, and the strength of the profane has been increased by the exiles of bishops of the cause of which you are not unaware. Apart from Eleusius and a few with him, the ten provinces of Asiana, in which I reside, in large part do not know God truly.[48]

With this holy remnant Hilary shares his creed. He may preach one essence, the eastern bishops similarity of essence, but both mean the same and hence agree on theological fundamentals.

In the final section of his long letter, Hilary turns abruptly to the eastern bishops.[49] He congratulates them for resisting heresy and for sending an embassy to court, which rescued the emperor from the error into which the heretics had inveigled him. At Sirmium in 358, Ursacius, Valens, and Germinius had demanded that their letter expounding the terms *homoousios* and *homoiousios* be read aloud. It rejected the former term as philosophically improper, since it precluded sharing of essence; as having been condemned long before by the council which deposed Paul of Samosata; and as having been imposed on the Council of Nicaea by force: it was non-scriptural and should be avoided. To counter this argument, Hilary defends both the term *homoousios* and the Nicene creed: to reject them is to become Arians—and the term *homoiousios* stands or falls with *homoousios.*

No evidence describes how Hilary's letter was received. Yet an immediate and bracing effect may be indirectly detectable. Hilary declared that he had never heard the Nicene creed recited until shortly before his exile in 356, and that claim, despite its tendentious context, must reflect a general lack of familiarity with the creed in the West until the 350s.[50] By 359, however, the western bishops assembled at Ariminum were ready to take their stand on the Nicene creed.[51] Moreover, at least one literary product of the hardening of western opinion owes its origin to the stimulus of the writings which Hilary sent to Gaul. The Spanish bishop Gregory of Iliberris composed *On Orthodox Faith against the Arians,* a work which echoes both Phoebadius and Hilary's historical polemic against Ursacius and Valens.[52] Gregory makes no obvious allusion to the precise historical context in which he is writing: however, the fact that he defends the term *homoousios* at length but ignores the formula 'alike in all things' officially adopted in 359 suggests that he was writing before the Council of Ariminum.[53]

In Rome, also before the Council of Ariminum, the converted grammarian Marius Victorinus embarked upon a more ambitious and arduous enterprise.[54] He began to pen a dense refutation of Arius in which he defended the *homoousion* within a philosophical framework taken from Plotinus and Porphyry, which ultimately, through Augustine, had a great influence on the development of western trinitarian theology. Although Victorinus completed the last of his nine linked treatises against Arius and Arianism only in 363, he probably wrote the first group of four in 358 in reaction against the apparent triumph of 'Arianism' in 357 and to attack the homoeousian views of Basil of Ancyra and his allies.[55]

Victorinus devoted three treatises to refuting Arianism as expounded in two letters by the straw-man Candidus, whom he invented for the purpose. He then turned to a refutation of Arius himself and included in the first of his treatises *Adversus Arium* a bitter attack on Basil. The term *homoiousios* (he protested) was a very recent invention. Why had Basil, his friends, his pupils, and his fellow teachers kept quiet since 325? Even when he was with the emperor in Rome in 357, Basil had heard views which contradicted what he now asserted, but he had disregarded them and had dined with the very men on whom he was now pronouncing anathemas.[56] The ferocity of Victorinus' defense of the absolute necessity of employing the term *homoousios* in theological discourse is an index of the resistance which the western bishops were likely to offer if any attempt was made to persuade them to reject or abandon the key term in the creed of Nicaea.[57]

XVI

THE HOMOEAN CREED

NEITHER CONSTANTIUS NOR THE BISHOPS AT HIS COURT INTENDED
the Councils of Ariminum and Seleucia to enjoy untrammeled freedom of debate.[1] Imperial commissioners were to supervise the councils closely and to influence their proceedings. In 359, as at Arles and at Milan some years before, the
bishops assembled in conclave were expected to ratify a document presented to
them, not to excogitate a new one (*Syn.* 8.2). The document to be presented was
prepared by Marcus of Arethusa and endorsed by a small committee of bishops,
comprising Ursacius, Valens, Basil of Ancyra, Germinius of Sirmium, the Egyptian bishops George of Alexandria and Pancratius of Pelusium, and possibly
Hypatianus of Heraclea. During the vigil before Pentecost, late in the evening of
22 May 359, in the presence of Constantius, this statement of 'the catholic
creed' was set forth and subscribed (*Syn.* 8.3–7).[2]

The text of the creed shows the hand of the drafter in apparent similarities to
the local creed of Antioch, and it is the first creed to include the dead Christ's
descent into hell. But its main feature is an attempt to mediate, to devise a formula which all might accept.[3] In language perhaps first employed by Acacius of
Caesarea,[4] it avoided technical terms and propounded a homoean Christology:

> Since the term 'essence' *(ousia)* was adopted by the fathers [sc. at Nicaea
> in 325] without proper reflection and, not being known by the people,
> causes offense because the scriptures do not contain it, it has been re-
> solved that it should be removed and that in future there should be no
> mention whatever of essence in regard to God, since the divine scriptures
> nowhere refer to essence [when speaking] about Father and Son. But we
> declare that the Son is like the Father in all things, as the holy scriptures
> indeed declare and teach. (*Syn.* 8.7)[2]

This compromise did not satisfy even the original signatories. Valens attempted to omit the phrase 'in all things' in his subscription until Constantius compelled him to include it, while Basil added a gloss explaining that 'in all things' meant not merely in will, but 'in *hypostasis* and in existence and in being.'[5]

The emperor then wrote to the councils to set the agenda for each. The eastern council was instructed first to settle doctrinal issues; then to consider the cases of individual bishops such as Cyril of Jerusalem, who were challenging their deposition or exile, and complaints against bishops in office, such as Egyptian accusations of violence and peculation against George of Alexandria; and finally to send ten envoys to court to report the decisions made.[6] The western council seems, through a bureaucratic oversight, to have been sent exactly the same letter. For Constantius wrote a second letter, on 28 May, in which he bade the Council of Ariminum to concentrate on what concerned it, namely, faith and unity, and to send ten envoys to him to report on the proceedings, but to make no decisions in matters concerning eastern bishops.[7]

Flavius Taurus, praetorian prefect in Italy and Africa since 355, was charged with conducting the western council, and it was rumored that an ordinary consulate would be his reward for success (he became consul in 361).[8] Taurus secured a large attendance. He sent officials throughout Italy, Africa, Spain, and Gaul with warrants for free transport and supplies, and pressing invitations. The bishops came, more than four hundred in number, though those from the Gallic prefecture (except for three impoverished bishops from Britain) are said to have insisted on coming at their own expense, in order to avoid compromising their freedom of action.

The council assembled in July. As soon as the creed of 22 May was read, the bishops split into two camps. The large majority of western bishops denied that any new creed was needed after Nicaea. Accordingly, they reaffirmed the Nicene creed, declared that nothing should be added to it or taken from it, and proceeded to draw up a formal condemnation of Arius and his heretical views.[9] Moreover, they condemned Ursacius, Valens, Germinius, and Gaius (another Illyrian bishop) for disturbing the churches and attempting to subvert the creed of Nicaea.[10] These decisions, of which the last is dated to 21 July 359, they communicated to Constantius in a letter of polite defiance which also contained a request that they be allowed to depart from Ariminum.[11] The letter was taken by a delegation, which presumably left Ariminum in late July. Taurus had instructions to detain the bishops in the city until the business of the council was concluded in a manner satisfactory to the emperor.[12]

Ursacius, Valens, and Germinius had come to Ariminum. Together with their western allies and presumably several dozen other bishops from Illyricum, they formed a sizeable minority of almost eighty. Seeing the majority recalcitrant, they withdrew from the large church where the council was meeting to a nearby building which was unoccupied and took counter-measures.[13] They wrote an effusive letter to Constantius asking that they as defenders of pure doctrine and catholic truth, who had renounced all talk of 'essence' on his orders, be permitted to return home.[14] They wrote too to the eastern bishops, and most of their leaders went as envoys to Constantius—skilful pleaders and practised politicians who proved able to outwit the rival delegation.[15]

Constantius had left Sirmium in June, and he was to spend the winter of 359/60 in Constantinople.[16] It is not known where or when the two delegations from Ariminum met him, but they were received very differently. Constantius welcomed the delegates of the minority, but refused to grant an audience to the others. Coercion was then applied. Constantius departed on a military expedition and ordered the envoys to await his return at Adrianople.

Delay and threats produced the desired result.[17] On 10 October, at the town of Nike in Thrace, Restitutus of Carthage and the other envoys of the majority disowned their decisions at Ariminum, disavowed their excommunication of Ursacius, Valens, Germinius, and Gaius, and subscribed the creed which the other delegation had brought from Ariminum.[18] The formulary which they now accepted was a revision of the creed of 22 May by the Illyrian bishops: it omitted the phrase 'in all things' after 'like the Father,' and it prohibited the use of the phrase 'one *hypostasis*' as well as 'one *ousia*.'[19] The place of this capitulation had been craftily chosen. The new creed expressing the new homoean orthodoxy was subscribed at Nike: hence it could be represented as a 'Nicene' creed, and it is reported that the similarity of name proved capable of deceiving some bishops.[20]

Meanwhile, the Council of Seleucia took an even stormier course.[21] Personalities and grievances were at issue as well as ideas. One hundred and sixty bishops attended,[22] with the *comes* Leonas and Bassidius Lauricius, the *dux* of the province of Isauria, ordered to attend the sessions. The council opened on 27 September 359, and Leonas invited the bishops to declare their views. Dispute began at once. First, there was a request that the proceedings be stayed until all the bishops whose presence was expected should arrive. The absentees included Basil of Ancyra, Macedonius of Constantinople, and Patrophilus of Scythopolis: the latter pair pleaded illness and were perhaps reluctant to face the accusations against them. When Leonas refused to countenance any postponement or delay, some of those present refused to discuss anything until the charges against individual bishops such as Cyril of Jerusalem and Eustathius of Sebasteia were settled,[23] while others contended that doctrinal questions must be debated first. Both sides appealed to imperial letters. When the council began its business, it at once split into two factions. Acacius of Caesarea led the one, with George of Alexandria, Uranius of Tyre, Eudoxius of Antioch, and another forty bishops.[24] The majority were led by George of Laodicea, Sophronius of Pompeiopolis in Paphlagonia, and Eleusius of Cyzicus. The latter group wished to accept the Nicene creed with as little alteration as possible (merely removing the term *homoousios*), while the former proposed to draft a new creed to replace the Nicene definition. Debate dragged on till evening, when Silvanus of Tarsus declared that no new creed was needed, that the creed of the 'Dedication Council' would suffice. The party of Acacius withdrew. The majority then brought forward the creed of 341, read it, and adjourned. The next day, they met in the main church of Seleucia behind closed doors and subscribed the creed.

Acacius and his sympathisers objected that the procedure was technically improper, because the majority had acted in secret conclave. Acacius had his own creed prepared, which he read to Leonas and Lauricius. On 29 September Leonas attempted to convene the whole council again. Macedonius and Basil had now arrived. The party of Acacius refused to sit down with them, arguing that both previously deposed and currently accused bishops should be excluded. The argument was conceded, and those bishops withdrew against whom a formal accusation had been laid. Acacius and his party then entered, and Leonas declared that he had a petition from Acacius. When the assembly fell silent, Leonas read what turned out to be a credal statement.[25] After a preface which combined flattery of Leonas and Lauricius with complaints against their opponents, the Acacians denied that they rejected the creed of the 'Dedication Council.' But since the terms *homoousios* and *homoiousios* had troubled many, while the term *anomoios* had only recently been introduced, they repudiated the terms *homoousios* and *homoiousios* as contrary to the scriptures and anathematised *anomoios*. Instead, they professed that the Son is like the Father, enounced a creed almost identical to the one drafted at Sirmium in May, and excommunicated all who ventured to disagree with it. Acacius and his supporters subscribed the document, but Sophronius objected, and after much inconclusive discussion the third day's session ended.

Debate continued on the fourth day. Eleusius of Cyzicus reiterated that the creed of 341 should suffice,[26] and Acacius was pressed to specify exactly how the Son was like the Father. When he contended that it was in will alone, not in essence, it became clear that the majority disagreed. As the questions continued to provoke heated discussion, Leonas rose and terminated the session. On the following day, he refused to join the bishops. Acacius was satisfied with the outcome. The majority were not. They took up the case of Cyril of Jerusalem, which Constantius' original letter to the council had instructed it to consider. Cyril was in Seleucia and expected to be heard. The bishops of the majority summoned both Acacius, who had presided at the council which deposed Cyril, and the associates of the bishop of Caesarea, who included men under accusation for non-theological offenses. When they failed to appear despite repeated requests, the bishops of the majority deposed Acacius himself, George of Alexandria, Uranius of Tyre, Theodulus of Chaeretapa in Phrygia, Theodosius of Philadelphia in Lydia, Evagrius of Mytilene, Leontius of Tripolis, Eudoxius of Antioch, and Patrophilus of Scythopolis, and suspended a further nine bishops from communion until they should acquit themselves of the charges outstanding against them.[27] They then nominated Anianus to replace Eudoxius as bishop of Antioch. The Acacians retaliated by arresting him and handing him over to Leonas and Lauricius, who exiled him. After a protest to the two officials failed to persuade them to rescind the sentence of exile against Anianus, the majority finally sent the required ten envoys to Constantinople to inform the emperor of the decisions of the council and left Seleucia to return to their cities.[28]

The rival delegation of Acacius reached the emperor first. Constantius showed no less annoyance at the eastern refusal to accept the homoean creed and canceled the exemptions from curial duties and other civic liturgies which some of the offending bishops enjoyed.[29] But he detained the delegates in anticipation that the western bishops at Ariminum would soon capitulate. The envoys who had accepted the creed of Nike returned to Italy and were at first refused communion. But the prefect Taurus and the bishops Ursacius and Valens applied steady pressure: western resolve faltered, then collapsed, and finally Valens (allegedly by dishonesty and outright fraud) induced the last twenty bishops who maintained resistance to accept the new creed. A second delegation left to announce that the western bishops were now united in their acceptance of the new creed.[30] They arrived in Constantinople toward the very end of the year.[31] Similar pressure on the envoys from Seleucia brought similar results. It was argued that only adoption of the homoean creed could provide a bulwark against the obvious heresy of Aetius.[32] When the envoys arrived from Ariminum, the Acacians presented themselves as the legates of the whole Council of Seleucia and warned the westerners of the dangers which Aetius posed.[33] The classic manoeuvre of telling both sets of recalcitrant envoys separately that the other had accepted the homoean creed succeeded. On 31 December 359, representatives of both councils subscribed the creed which established the new imperial homoean orthodoxy.[34]

It now merely remained to ratify the creed before a single council and to expel obdurate dissentients. In January 360 a council which perhaps numbered as many as seventy-two bishops met in Constantinople. Venerable figures such as Maris of Chalcedon and the Gothic bishop Ulfila attended. The majority present were Bithynian bishops, but the dominant influence was that of Acacius.[35] The council promulgated a creed, based on that of Nike, which rejected all earlier creeds and forbade any new ones:

> As for the term 'essence' *(ousia)*, which was adopted by the fathers without proper reflection, and being unknown to the people caused offense, because the scriptures do not contain it, it was resolved that it should be removed and that in future no mention should be made of it at all, since the holy scriptures have nowhere made mention of the essence of Father and Son. Nor should the term 'hypostasis' be used concerning Father, Son, and Holy Spirit. We declare that the Son is like the Father as the divine scriptures declare and teach. But let all heresies, contrary to this document now promulgated, both those which have been condemned previously and any new ones which may arise, be anathema. *(Syn.* 30.8–10)[36]

The council then turned to the pleasing task of condemning the enemies of Acacius.[37] In almost every case, disciplinary infractions were alleged and accepted as proven: they included the offense of a bishop transferring to another see—which the council not only excused in its own members but even committed by replacing Macedonius of Constantinople with Eudoxius of Antioch. Nor did the council show much greater consistency when it deposed Eleusius of Cyzicus and replaced him with Eunomius, while at the same time condemning the latter's teacher Aetius for heresy.[38] The council deposed Basil of Ancyra, who (it was alleged) had tried to turn the clergy of Sirmium against their bishop Germinius and had written to Africa to seek support among the bishops there.[39] It deposed Neonas of Seleucia, Sophronius of Pompeiopolis, Cyril of Jerusalem, and many more.

This purge was conducted by a small council in Constantinople with the approbation of the emperor.[40] Some of its results were unforeseen. Although the bishops in Constantinople appointed Meletius bishop of Sebasteia to replace Eustathius,[41] Meletius was elected by popular acclaim in Antioch to fill the see which the council had left vacant when it transferred Eudoxius to Constantinople. After his election, Meletius rapidly showed himself to be in reality an upholder of the Nicene creed.[42] He was unceremoniously deposed, less than a month after his election,[43] and replaced by Euzoius, who long before had been a close associate of Arius. In consequence, the existing schism at Antioch became still more complicated. There were now three rival and competing 'churches of Antioch.' The officially recognised bishop was the newly appointed Euzoius, who attempted to introduce the anomoean ideas of Aetius. Eustathius had been deposed in the reign of Constantine and died in exile before 337 (*Hist. Ar.* 4.1), but his followers maintained a separate organisation and rejected Meletius as an Arian appointee, even when he defended the term *homoousios*. Meletius, however, could plausibly claim to be the true successor of Leontius, and the Meletians (it is reliably reported) formed the most numerous of the three groups.[44]

Constantius crossed Asia Minor in the early spring of 360 and passed through Antioch on his way to Mesopotamia, where Amida had fallen to the Persians after a long siege in the previous summer. The war against Persia demanded his urgent attention, and the unanimity of doctrine within the church, which his prolonged efforts appeared to have secured, proved fragile. Although the homoean creed promulgated at Constantinople in January 360 (which in fact asserted none of Arius' original tenets) was to have a long life as the 'Arian' creed of the northern barbarians even after they invaded the Roman Empire in the fifth century,[45] within the western empire its fate was linked to the political fortunes of its imperial sponsor. Constantius detained four hundred western bishops at Ariminum for half a year until they subscribed the creed he wished to impose upon them. But the craven acquiescence he extorted was short-lived. In the spring of 360, Gaul and Britain (and probably Spain too) passed out of the political and military control of Constantius, and Hilary of Poitiers soon arrived in the West determined to undo the new eastern orthodoxy.

Hilary played an important (if often obscure) part in the theological debates of these years, but he is still more important as a barometer of changes in the theological atmosphere and the attitude of educated Christians toward Constantius. Writing in 358, Hilary had defended and even praised the creeds of the 'Dedication Council' of 341, of the eastern bishops at Serdica in 343, and of the Council of Sirmium of 351.[46] The fact that all three councils had condemned Athanasius will help to explain why the bishop of Alexandria never names Hilary among the western bishops who were exiled on his behalf. But by 360 Hilary and Athanasius were allies.

Hilary attended the Council of Seleucia, compelled to be present, Sulpicius Severus states, by the *vicarius* and governor who gave him use of the *cursus publicus*.[47] He may have played some part in strengthening the resolve of the majority to resist the imposition of the new creed, though his presence and activities leave no trace at all in eastern accounts of the council.[48] After the council, Hilary went to Constantinople on his own initiative, not as a member of the official delegation.[49] There, apparently in January 360, he composed a brief request for an imperial audience in a desperate attempt to persuade the emperor at the eleventh hour to remain true to the creed of Nicaea.[50]

Hilary's *To the Emperor Constantius* adopts the assumption that Constantius is good, pious, religious—and therefore orthodox.[51] He protests that he himself had been wrongly condemned and exiled, though he waives his right to summon the man responsible, Saturninus of Arles, who was then in the city, and appeals instead, for proof of his innocence, to the absent Caesar Julian and to a letter of Constantius, which was (he says) available.[52] Hilary sets out briefly, respectfully, and with urgency all that conduces to the peace of East and West. Immediate action is needed, for a new creed is about to be written. Hilary beseeches the emperor to allow him to address the council which is now arguing about the creed: he will produce scriptural texts and the words of Jesus himself. In this plea, Hilary is careful never to refer to the Council of Nicaea by name, but he defends the 'council of our fathers' as the key to preserving the church's 'heavenly patrimony.'[53]

Hilary failed to obtain an audience with Constantius. Instead he watched the emperor secure compliance with the creed of Nike and the Council of Constantinople condemn and banish his ecclesiastical allies. Shortly afterward Hilary composed a violent diatribe against the eastern emperor. His *To the Emperor Constantius* contained an implicit threat: after voicing a wish that the emperor's breast should be full of the awareness of divine sayings, Hilary remarks that a ruler who refuses to act as a Christian is an Antichrist.[54] His *Against Constantius* draws the inference which the earlier work had adumbrated. It denounces Constantius as a tyrant who does not deserve to rule because he attacks God and persecutes the Christian church just as much as Nero, Decius, and Galerius ever had, but more craftily: 'we are fighting against a deceitful persecutor, against an enemy who uses flattery, against Constantius the Antichrist.' The East is full of terror or war; Constantius is attacking the faith of the West, he has unleashed his armies on Christ's flock, his tribunes have defiled the holy of holies in Milan, he has brought war to Rome and Toulouse. He is attacking not living mortals, but the fathers who have gone to their eternal rest, the bishops at Nicaea, and even his own father; he is a foe of divine religion; though an heir to his father's piety, he rebels against it.[55]

Hilary's argument, like the rabid denunciations of Lucifer of Caralis and the historical case developed by Athanasius in the *History of the Arians*,[56] had political implications, even if they were only potential when the work was composed: if the eastern emperor was a persecutor, he was a *tyrannus*, and a *tyrannus*, by definition, was unworthy to rule the Roman Empire, whether it was Christian or not. Shortly after Hilary wrote his *Against Constantius*, that corollary ceased to be merely theoretical. Within a few weeks, when the Caesar Julian was proclaimed Augustus in Gaul, the attitude of bishops like Hilary suddenly acquired a very sharp political relevance.[57]

XVII

THE ELDER STATESMAN

WHEN ATHANASIUS WAS EXPELLED FROM HIS SEE IN FEBRUARY 356, he was an isolated figure, with few supporters in the East apart from his devoted following within Egypt. When he returned to Alexandria in February 362, the theological climate of the East had changed completely, and with it Athanasius' position in the eastern church. Between 356 and 362 the exiled bishop was transformed from a proud prelate with a dubious reputation into an elder statesman renowned for his heroic defense of Nicene orthodoxy. In the autumn of 359, his *On the Councils of Ariminum and Seleucia* signaled a fundamental change of attitude, as Athanasius decided to ally himself with the theologians of Asia Minor, whom for twenty years he had stigmatised as 'Arians,' 'Arian fanatics,' and the like.[1] They held conservative views and approved of the successive attempts by eastern councils to define a doctrinal *via media* from the 'Dedication Council' of 341 to the Council of Sirmium a decade later,[2] and those among them who attended the councils which formulated creeds had condemned Athanasius time after time, not only because of his intransigent rejection of their theology, but also because they genuinely (and with good reason) believed that he was guilty of using violence and intimidation to control the Egyptian church.

It must remain a matter of speculation what would have been Athanasius' fate had Constantius continued to rule instead of succumbing to illness in November 361. The military odds were in favor of the eastern emperor: he might well have defeated Julian and then secured empire-wide acceptance of the homoean creed of 359/60 for a period of years. In the event, however, the new official creed of 360 lost its imperial patron within two years, and Athanasius was allowed to return to Alexandria as bishop of the city by a pagan emperor who soon turned to persecuting him—and thus established even more firmly his reputation as a steadfast defender of embattled orthodoxy.

*　　*　　*

152

Julian, who was appointed Caesar on 6 November 355 and sent at once to Gaul, cannot have failed to notice how unpopular was Constantius' policy of requiring bishops to accept the decisions of the Councils of Sirmium, Arles, and Milan. Moreover, a cryptic remark later made by Hilary of Poitiers appears to imply that Julian expressed some sympathy for the victims of the imperial policies that he was obliged to enforce. In January 360 Hilary protested to Constantius that he had been wrongly deposed, and claimed that Julian 'suffered more insult from evil men in the matter of my exile than I did injury.'[3] Hilary appears to mean that his ecclesiastical enemies abused Julian for not treating him with sufficient harshness or rigor when he enforced his deposition by the Council of Baeterrae by exiling him to Phrygia.[4] On *a priori* grounds, it is not fanciful to imagine Julian looking for future allies against the senior emperor long before he was proclaimed Augustus.[5]

After the proclamation in the early months of 360, Julian still kept up the pretense of being a Christian. Ammianus notes both the fact and its motivation:

> So that he might induce everyone to support him with no hindrance, he pretended adherence to the Christian cult, which he had long ago secretly abandoned, engaging with a few who shared the secret in divination, augury, and everything else which the worshippers of the gods have always done. And so that this should be concealed for the meanwhile, on the festival day which the Christians celebrate in January and call Epiphany, he proceeded to their church and departed after praying to the divine power in the normal fashion.[6]

Since no usurper who wished to displace a Christian emperor could succeed if he were a known pagan, Julian maintained an outward show of Christianity as long as Constantius lived. But what stance should a usurper adopt in ecclesiastical politics? That depended on the circumstances of the moment, and in 360/1 it was clear where Julian's advantage lay. At the Council of Ariminum, the majority of western bishops had opposed Constantius' attempts to secure their acceptance of an eastern homoean creed.[7] By his proclamation as Augustus, Julian declared his political independence of Constantius. Accordingly, his subjects could expect him to abandon Constantius' most unpopular policies. Political interest, perhaps even political necessity, thus dictated that Julian pose as a champion of religious freedom, specifically of the freedom of western bishops to adhere to the Nicene creed. Moreover, there is unimpeachable (if indirect) evidence that in 360 and 361 Julian wooed the political support of Christians who were ecclesiastical opponents of Constantius.[8]

Hilary of Poitiers returned to the West, apparently in the spring of 360 and without the permission of Constantius.[9] Probably before the end of 360, a council of bishops met at Paris, with Hilary present. The Gallic bishops addressed a synodical letter to 'all the eastern bishops in various provinces,' from whom Hilary had brought a letter. The Gallic bishops thank God for their own liberation from association with heresy and lament that so many bishops had been compelled to avoid the term *ousia* 'under the authority of your name' because East and West were divided. They defend the use of the term *homoousios* as avoiding Sabellianism while excluding Arianism. The fact that the eastern letter avoids the term *ousia* shows that its writers have been deceived, that the bishops who went from Ariminum to Constantinople were duped, since Hilary reports that they could not be driven to such blasphemy. Accordingly, the council excommunicated Auxentius, Ursacius, Valens, Gaius, Megasius, and Justinus, condemned all the blasphemies subjoined to the eastern letter, condemned all those who had replaced exiled bishops, and excommunicated anyone in Gaul who objected to their decisions. The letter closes by reiterating Gallic adherence to the *homoousion* and by stating that Saturninus of Arles has been deposed by all the bishops of Gaul for crimes in the past and for recent impiety.[10]

The letter is not straightforward, since it appears to envisage two sets of addresses. The Gallic bishops often express themselves as if writing to friends—who must be the bishops of Asia Minor whom Hilary regarded as allies. Yet it seems probable that the letter which Hilary brought is the synodical letter of the Council of Constantinople—and hence that the Gallic bishops are trying to win back eastern bishops from the new official orthodoxy. For in 360 and 361, by means of councils of bishops, Hilary 'condemned the decisions made at Ariminum and restored the faith of the churches to its original state of purity.'[11]

Julian allowed the Gallic bishops to meet in Paris, and perhaps actively encouraged them to do so.[12] It was, moreover, probably in 360 that he first issued an edict allowing bishops exiled by Constantius to return to their cities. This edict is normally dated to the period after Constantius' death on the very reasonable grounds that it reached Alexandria on 8 February 362 and was published there on the following day, whereas the edict restoring pagan temples, which Julian certainly issued after Constantius' death, was published in Alexandria on 4 February (*Hist. ac.* 3.1/2).[13] But it is hard to see what advantages such a policy could bring Julian after he had become sole emperor. Why should he now wish to restore Athanasius to Alexandria when he must have known how effectively he had resisted Constantius? On the other hand, the policy made perfect sense before November 361, for the exiled bishops, both eastern and western, were enemies of his enemy Constantius. The delay in publishing the edict can be explained. For the document which arrived in Alexandria on 8 February was not a copy of the imperial edict itself, but a letter from the *comes Orientis* transmitting its contents. Now the *comes Orientis* was an appointee of Constantius who went on to serve the Arian Valens as praetorian prefect of the East for eight years: Domitius Modestus was a prudent and cautious man who may have hesitated before proclaiming an edict at variance with the official paganism of the new ruler of the East.[14]

As soon as Constantius was dead, Julian ordered his army to sacrifice to the old gods. He canceled all the privileges granted to Christians and the Christian church by Constantine and his sons, and embarked upon a systematic attempt to undo the Constantinian reformation. His religious policy had three main aspects. First, Christians were to be subjected to legal disabilities, but not persecuted outright, since Julian desired to debilitate the church without giving it more martyrs.[15] Second, pagans were to benefit from 'affirmative action,' while paganism as an entity was to be organised along Christian lines as a counter-church. And third, the Jews were to be allowed to live in Jerusalem again and have a temple there in which to worship.[16] But Julian's policy of harassment or covert persecution was doomed to be ineffectual. The Christian church had long been too powerful for the Roman government to suppress it—as Galerius and Maximinus had learned to their cost at the beginning of the fourth century.[17] The ineffectiveness of Julian's attempt to subvert Christianity is perhaps most clearly displayed in his dealings with Alexandria.

George reentered Alexandria on 26 November 361. His timing was unfortunate. Four days later, news came of Constantius' death, and he was imprisoned. A month later, on 24 December, a mob dragged him out of prison and lynched him (*Hist. ac.* 2.8–10). On receipt of the news, Julian jumped to the conclusion that George had been murdered by pagans. He accordingly wrote the city a letter of mild rebuke for killing George, 'the enemy of the gods,' rather than leaving him to be tried and suitably punished. The letter emphasises that the Alexandrians are Greeks and devotees of Serapis, who will in future show themselves worthy of their Greek—in other words, their pagan—character.[18] Julian was sadly deluded about the Hellenism of Alexandria, and also probably about the identity of George's murderers. George's ecclesiastical opponents had as much cause to attack him as the pagans whose shrines he had seized. Since they had forced George to flee the city in 358 and had then taken over the churches from his supporters (*Hist. ac.* 2.3/4), it seems highly unlikely that they were mere spectators when he was killed.

Athanasius was ready to take advantage of the edict which allowed bishops exiled under Constantius to return. On 21 February 362, twelve days after the prefect Gerontius published it in Alexandria, he reentered the city (*Hist. ac.* 3.3) and within a few weeks presided over a small but important council of bishops. Eusebius of Vercellae and Lucifer of Caralis were in exile together in the Thebaid and also ready to act. Eusebius came to Alexandria, conferred with Athanasius, and played a prominent role in the council.[19] The hot-headed Lucifer preferred to go straight to Antioch, where he took the precipitate step of consecrating Paulinus as bishop of the followers of Eustathius, who were in schism not only with the recently appointed homoean bishop Euzoius, but also with the followers of Meletius, who, having been deposed for Nicene tendencies in 360, was also entitled to return to the city under the terms of Julian's edict. Meletius reached Antioch before Lucifer and his supporters had already taken possession of the 'old church':[20] hence the latter's hasty consecration of Paulinus exacerbated existing dissensions and divided the pro-Nicene party in the church of

Antioch into two mutually hostile factions. Athanasius and Eusebius, in contrast, were determined to restore peace, concord, and unity among all who could accept the creed of Nicaea.[21]

The Council of Alexandria met in the spring of 362, probably shortly after Easter, which fell on 31 March. Two primary documents have survived to illuminate its proceedings. The first, transmitted under the title *Epistula Catholica*, appears to be the opening section of the synodical letter of the council: it long languished forgotten among the numerous Athanasian *spuria*, but has recently been recognised as a genuine document of great historical significance.[22] The second document is the so-called *Tomus ad Antiochenos*, which was produced by a small sub-committee after the council in an attempt to persuade the two pro-Nicene groups in the church of Antioch to lay aside their quarrel.[23]

Most of the bishops who attended the Council of Alexandria came inevitably from Egypt and Libya. But the presence of Eusebius of Vercellae, of the Arabian bishop Asterius, and of two deacons representing Lucifer made it much more than a mere provincial council. Its synodical letter was composed jointly by Athanasius and Eusebius—or, to be more precise, Athanasius produced the final version from a draft which Eusebius had prepared before he reached Alexandria.[24] Its tenor is pacific, its aim reconciliation. The letter alludes to the violence suffered by the orthodox in the recent past, but it presents the current situation in the best possible light and propounds a minimal interpretation of orthodoxy. Although the corruption of Arianism has long been present, nevertheless the vast majority of both ordinary Christians and bishops retain the true apostolic faith unsullied. Even if both laity and bishops have been constrained by force or misled with deceptive words, they can now redeem themselves merely by acknowledging the truth of a few basic propositions. These are set out in the broadest of terms. Since it must be accepted 'that as God the Son of God cannot be a creation of God and that the Holy Spirit cannot be reckoned among what is created,' for only divine incarnation, not the presence on earth of a creature or a slave, can make men divine or into God's temples, what every Christian needs for salvation can be stated briefly and succinctly:

> The badge of our faith [is]: the Trinity [is] of one essence *(homoousios)*,[25] true God who became man of Mary. Whoever does not agree, let him be anathema! For this is what the document of the great Council of Nicaea means: that the Son is of one essence with the Father, and that the Spirit is glorified [equally] with the Father and the Son; that as true God the Son of God became flesh, suffered, rose again, ascended into heaven, and will come as judge of the living and the dead, to whom be glory for ever and ever. Amen![26]

The *Epistula Catholica* was designed for an empire-wide audience. The version of which a part survives was addressed to the orthodox bishops of Syria, Cilicia, Phoenice, and Arabia, and Eusebius was charged with taking a letter identical in content to the West.[27] But before he departed, he subscribed his name to the so-called *Tomus ad Antiochenos,* which Athanasius drew up in the name of himself and other bishops, including Eusebius and Asterius, who met after the main council in an attempt to solve the schism in the church of Antioch.

The *Tomus* has the same general aim as the *Epistula Catholica,* but it addresses itself specifically to the situation in Antioch, where it was to be read aloud with both Eustathians and Meletians present in the hope that those who desired peace could ensure that the Lord would be glorified by all together.[28] Hence Athanasius advances a careful (but not carefully constructed) argument which seeks throughout to persuade the followers of Eustathius to enter into communion with the newly returned Meletius and his much larger congregation.[29] The letter praises fellowship, peace, and concord, and voices a prayer that 'if someone still seems to be associating with the Arians, he may abandon their madness, so that everyone everywhere will in future say "One Lord, one faith" (Ephesians 4.5).'[30] And in order to secure that end, the representatives of the council who are being sent to Antioch will join both the congregation in the 'old church' and former Arians with Paulinus and his congregation by requiring of all only that they abjure the heresy of Arius, accept the creed of the holy fathers at Nicaea, and anathematise those who say that the Holy Spirit is a creature and distinct from the essence *(ousia)* of Christ, and also anathematise the heretical ideas of Sabellius, Paul of Samosata, Valentinus, Basilides, and Mani.[31] Moreover, since the theological statement which the western bishops at Serdica in 343 had discussed was known in Antioch, Athanasius deemed it necessary to emphasise that it had been rejected by the council.[32] For the central contention of the whole document is that acceptance of the creed of Nicaea as the sole authoritative creed is both necessary and sufficient to restore harmony to the church.[33]

The *Tomus ad Antiochenos* has the form of a letter written in the name of Athanasius, Eusebius, Asterius, and some seventeen Egyptian bishops to Eusebius, Lucifer, Asterius, and two Syrian bishops, Cymatius of Paltus and Anatolius of Beroea. The apparent oddity of the fact that Eusebius and Asterius are both writers and recipients of the letter is easily explicable: they were deputed to take it to Antioch, read it aloud, and attempt to reconcile the dissident factions.[34] The transmitted form of the *Tomus* reveals what happened to it after Athanasius had composed it. First, in Alexandria, it was duly subscribed by the bishops whose names stand in its heading; in addition, two deacons sent by Lucifer and two by Paulinus added their names in the presence of monks sent by Apollinaris. Moreover, Eusebius appended a very brief doctrinal statement in Latin signifying his agreement with the preceding document, while Asterius added a single sentence to the same effect.[35] Then, in Antioch, Paulinus added a paragraph in which he accepted the trinitarian theology of the *Epistula Catholica* and the *Tomus ad Antiochenos* and uttered the required anathemas.[36]

In Antioch, however, events had moved beyond the situation which the

Council of Alexandria sought to remedy: Eusebius arrived to find that Lucifer had already consecrated Paulinus as the pro-Nicene bishop of Antioch, and as a result he was totally unable to reconcile the two factions. Hence he left for the West with his mission in Antioch unfulfilled, while Lucifer, enraged that Eusebius refused to recognise his consecration of Paulinus, tried to wriggle out of the consequences of his deputies' acceptance of the decisions of the Council of Alexandria, then returned home to Sardinia, where he soon died after founding a schismatic sect of Luciferians.[37] In Antioch itself, Meletius controlled the major churches and was widely recognised as the legitimate bishop of the city by other bishops who attended councils under his presidency.[38] Athanasius, however, refused until his death to enter into communion with Meletius, even when Basil of Caesarea pressed him to do so in order to strengthen the pro-Nicene forces with the churches of Syria and Asia Minor.[39]

The importance of the Council of Alexandria should not be measured by its failure to solve the local problems of the church of Antioch. When Eusebius reached Italy, he entered into alliance with Hilary of Poitiers and Liberius of Rome to undo all the consequences of the western bishops' acceptance of the homoean creed at Ariminum three years earlier.[40] The Council of Alexandria was not an isolated phenomenon. A letter of Athanasius discloses that similar councils were held in 362 in Greece, Spain, and Gaul: those councils, like the Council of Alexandria, decided to pardon those who had fallen and championed impiety, provided that they repented, though excluding them from the clergy, and both to pardon and to acknowledge as clergy those who had not voluntarily furthered the course of impiety, but had acquiesced as a result of necessity and violence, provided that they were able to explain their actions satisfactorily.[41]

Julian realised too late that his subversion of homoean predominance in the East was not weakening the Christian church as he hoped, but strengthening those parts of it which had shown themselves most capable of resisting imperial power. Accordingly, he decided on a change of policy. On 24 October 362, the philosopher Pythiodorus, a native of Thebes, arrived in Alexandria bringing with him an edict from the emperor which ordered Athanasius to leave the city (*Hist. ac.* 3.4; *Index* 35).[42] Julian explained that he had allowed the bishops exiled by Constantius to return to their cities, not to their churches: since Athanasius had reoccupied his episcopal throne, and this was displeasing to the pious people of Alexandria, he must leave as soon as the emperor's letter arrived.[43]

Athanasius did not leave. On the contrary, the local senate submitted a petition requesting that he be allowed to remain. In reply, Julian banished Athanasius not only from Alexandria but from the whole of Egypt, and he wrote to the prefect Ecdicius scolding him for his silence in the matter of Athanasius and commanding him to expel the bishop from Egypt by 1 December. A querulous subscription added in the emperor's own hand to the dictated letter betrays his impotent fanaticism:

It vexes me greatly to be disobeyed. By all the gods, there is nothing I should rather see, or rather hear of as done by you, than that Athanasius has been driven out of Egypt. The infamous fellow! He has had the effrontery to baptise Greek women married to prominent citizens in my reign! Let him be hunted down![44]

Athanasius was not perturbed. He dismissed the imminent persecution by Julian as 'a small cloud which will soon pass,'[45] went up river to the Thebaid (*Index* 35), and again avoided capture by the soldiers sent to arrest him.[46] Julian's death in Persia soon provided him with yet another proof that God intervened actively in human affairs to protect both true faith and Athanasius himself.

As soon as he learned of Julian's death, Athanasius returned secretly to Alexandria by night, and at once set off to the imperial court.[47] The death of Julian had been announced in Alexandria by the prefect Ecdicius on 19 August 363 (*Hist. ac.* 4.1). On 6 September Athanasius embarked and left Egypt to seek an audience with the new emperor, whom he reached before Jovian left Hierapolis (*Index* 35), probably in early October.[48] The emperor received Athanasius with honor and gave him the vital document which past experience warned him he might need for his own protection (*Hist. ac.* 4.4): a letter which complimented him on his sufferings for orthodoxy and instructed him to return to his episcopal duties in Alexandria.[49] Other bishops too approached Jovian, even before Athanasius. The allies of Macedonius asked to be restored to the sees of which anomoeans had dispossessed them. The bishops Basil of Ancyra, Silvanus of Tarsus, Sophronius of Pompeiopolis, Pasinicus of Zela, Leontius of Comana, Callicrates of Claudiopolis, and Theophilus of Castabala presented the petition. Jovian declined to grant their request, observing that he hated rivalry, but loved and respected those who preached concord within the Christian church.[50]

What Jovian meant by concord became clear when he arrived in Antioch and showed favor to Meletius. Under Meletius' presidency a council was held at Antioch which drew up a letter to the emperor. Recalling not only Jovian's desire for peace and concord within the church, but also his insistence on a creed to embody this unity, the assembled bishops declared that they accepted the Nicene creed. They explained, however, that by *homoousios* the fathers at Nicaea had meant that the Son was 'begotten from the essence of the Father,' and that he was 'like the Father in essence' (that word not being used in the normal Greek sense). They condemned both Arius and the anomoeans, and quoted the creed of Nicaea. The signatories of the letter comprised Meletius, Eusebius of Samosata, Titus of Bostra, and another twenty-four bishops from Oriens and Asia Minor.[51]

Athanasius may have felt obliged to make a gesture of friendship toward Meletius, but there was no reconciliation, and the aims of the *Tomus ad Antiochenes* remained unfulfilled.[52] Athanasius acted independently. He presented to the emperor, in response (or so at least he alleged) to his request for a brief statement of catholic doctrine, a letter which had been drawn up by a hastily convened council of bishops in Alexandria before he left.[53] It emphasises the Nicene creed as the touchstone and guarantee of orthodoxy. The holy fathers at Nicaea had condemned Arius and promulgated an orthodox creed. That creed now needs to be reiterated because some who wish to renew the Arian heresy have set it aside: while pretending to confess the creed, they deny it because they interpret away the term *homoousios* and blaspheme against the Holy Spirit by saying that the Holy Spirit is a creature and came into existence through the agency of the Son.

Athanasius must have remained in Antioch for some time, since he did not reenter Alexandria until 14 February (*Hist. ac.* 4.4). Jovian left Antioch in early November, but before he departed, he repulsed the enemies of the bishop. A single page has survived in Coptic translation of a letter which Athanasius wrote from Antioch to his Alexandrian congregation. Athanasius appears to allude to the Council of Antioch: he urges his congregation not to ridicule a document which his erstwhile enemies may publish and to let bygones be bygones. The emperor has shown himself well disposed toward Athanasius despite the complaints which 'Lucius, Berenicianus, and the other Arians' made in Antioch on 30 October 363.[54]

A full account of these complaints and of the emperor's reaction to them has been preserved in a documentary or quasi-documentary form in the corpus of Athanasius' apologetical writings.[55] Lucius, formerly a priest of George in Alexandria, had been elected as George's successor, and was recognised outside Egypt by Eudoxius of Constantinople, Theodorus, Sophronius, Euzoius, and Hilarius.[56] Lucius too was now in Antioch, leading a group of Alexandrians with complaints against Athanasius. They approached the emperor as he rode out of the city to military exercises. He refused to listen. They then approached Jovian a second time, but he brushed aside as obsolete accusations which were ten, twenty, or even thirty years old. On the third occasion, Jovian listened to two representatives from each side. But he still refused to hear ill of Athanasius, whose orthodoxy he had himself verified. Moreover, he asserted Athanasius' right to prevent his opponents from assembling to worship, since they were sectarians and heretics. Significantly, the Arians complained that Athanasius had seized church property (in other words their churches), and one of their number, who was a lawyer, stated that the *catholicus* had seized his houses at Athanasius' instigation. Jovian rebuffed the petitioners again. Later the same day, when Lucius approached the emperor yet again as he returned to the palace, he was rebuffed yet again at the porch of the palace, and the emperor punished the court eunuchs who petitioned him to grant the Arians an audience.

After he left Antioch, Jovian crossed Asia Minor and traveled toward Constantinople, but died in Bithynia of accidental suffocation during the night of 16/7 February 364.[57] A few days later, the army acclaimed as emperor the Pannonian officer Valentinian, who, on 28 March, after pressure from his officers and men, appointed his younger brother Valens joint Augustus with him.[58] The two brothers reorganised the administration of the empire, then, on 4 August at Sirmium, divided the empire between them and parted. Valentinian took the western provinces and most of the Balkans, Valens the East. This division of the Roman Empire closely resembled the earlier division between Constans and Constantius, and the ecclesiastical politics of the decade from 365 to 375 show a strong similarity to those of the 340s. There is, however, one striking and fundamental difference between the two periods: the western emperor Valentinian gave no encouragement or support to eastern bishops who opposed his brother's ecclesiastical policies when they appealed for western assistance in combating heresy in the East.

Valens was later remembered as an 'Arian' emperor who persecuted the Christian church fiercely, and the orthodox ecclesiastical historians of the fifth century duly repeat tales of atrocities—eighty clerics burned on a ship in the Gulf of Astacus near Nicomedia and a massacre at Edessa supervised by the praetorian prefect.[59] But those stories have long (and rightly) been regarded with extreme suspicion: the early and reliable evidence fails to document any real 'persecution' except in Egypt.[60] Valens reinstituted the homoean creed of 360 as the official creed of the Roman Empire in the East, but, unlike Constantius, he did not insist that all bishops subscribe to it in order to retain their sees, merely that they refrain from repudiating or attacking it.[61] Hence a resolute and crafty opponent like Basil, who became bishop of Caesarea in Cappadocia in 370, was able to build up a strong opposition by ensuring the ordination of priests and the election of bishops who accepted the Nicene creed—provided that both he and they took care not to condemn the Council of Constantinople and its creed.[62]

As the emperors left Constantinople in the spring of 364, a council of bishops from Bithynia and the region of the Hellespont who accepted the term *homoousios* sent Hypatianus, the bishop of Heraclea, to the emperors to request permission to meet 'for the correction of doctrine.' Valentinian replied that as a layman he had no right to an opinion on such matters, but the bishops whose concern they were might gather wherever they wished. The Hellespontine bishops then met at Lampsacus and declared the decisions of the Council of Constantinople invalid: they reaffirmed the creed of the 'Dedication Council' of 341 and the formula that the Son is like the Father in essence, they reinstated the bishops deposed in 360, and they wrote to all the eastern churches to that effect. When Valens learned of their decisions, he invited them to be reconciled with Eudoxius, and when they refused, he exiled them.[63]

In the following year, a series of councils met on the south coast of Asia Minor, at Smyrna, in Pisidia, in Isauria, in Pamphylia and Lycia, and decided to send Eustathius of Sebasteia, Silvanus of Tarsus, and Theophilus of Castabala as envoys to the western emperor Valentinian with letters to Liberius and the western bishops generally asking for their aid in the defense of orthodoxy. When the envoys arrived in Italy, Valentinian had already departed for Gaul: they gave up any attempt to see him, and simply presented the letters of the councils and a briefer communication of their own to the bishop of Rome. They protested that they and the bishops who had met at Lampsacus, Smyrna, and elsewhere were defending the orthodox faith of the catholic church as defined by the three hundred and eighteen bishops at Nicaea against the insane attacks of heretics. Liberius received the envoys into communion and gave them a long letter in his name and in that of the western bishops in general addressed to some sixty-six named bishops and 'all the orthodox bishops in the East.'

The bishop of Rome complimented the eastern bishops on their adherence to the creed of Nicaea, the pure 'catholic and apostolic faith' which the West also upheld, and explained that the western bishops in 359 had repudiated it only temporarily at the Council of Ariminum because of deception and compulsion by secular power: the recipients of the letter, therefore, should publicise the fact that the West was now firm in its repudiation of the creed of Ariminum (that is, of the official homoean creed of the East) and of all the blasphemies of Arius. The envoys sailed back to the East by way of Sicily, where a provincial council gave them a similar letter, and presented the letters which they had received in the West to a council at Tyana. This council endorsed the decisions of the earlier Asian councils, welcomed the agreement of the western bishops, and circulated a synodical letter which invited bishops elsewhere in the East both to signify their agreement in writing and to gather on a stated date in Tarsus. This projected large eastern council at Tarsus was clearly intended to ratify and reaffirm the creed of Nicaea. To forestall it, thirty-four bishops hastily met at Antioch in Caria: they proclaimed the need for concord in the church, rejected the creed of Nicaea, and affirmed their adherence to the creed of the 'Dedication Council' as reiterated at Seleucia in 359. The Carian council presumably followed the normal practise of transmitting its decisions to the emperor: at all events, Valens prohibited the planned Council of Tarsus from meeting and issued a general order to provincial governors that bishops who had been deposed under Constantius, then restored to their sees under Julian, be expelled from their churches.[64]

Valens' general policy and the new decree had an obvious relevance to Athanasius in Alexandria. Athanasius had never disguised his disapproval of the homoean creed, and there was a rival claimant to the see of Alexandria in the shape of Lucius, whom the supporters of George had elected to succeed him and who accepted the official homoean creed. On 5 May 365 an imperial order was published in Alexandria which stipulated that bishops who had been deposed and ejected from their churches under Constantius but who had recovered their positions in the reign of Julian should again be expelled from their churches. The edict also threatened with a fine of three hundred pounds of gold any local *curia* which failed to ensure the expulsion of the bishop in its city if he fell under its terms. The leading *curiales* of Alexandria, who were few in number, and the prefect Flavianus urged Athanasius to obey the imperial order and leave the city, but a crowd of Christians demonstrated against the authorities, arguing that the imperial order did not apply to their bishop, since Athanasius had been restored as well as exiled by Constantius and exiled as well as restored by Julian, and owed his most recent restoration to Jovian, not to Julian.[65] Public disorder continued until 8 June, when Flavianus announced that he had written to the emperors reporting on the situation and requesting clarification.

Nearly four months later, on 5 October, Athanasius left his church secretly during the night and went into hiding, just in time to escape an attempt to arrest him by Flavianus and the *dux* Victorinus, in command of a detachment of soldiers. Athanasius remained in hiding for four months.[66] Release came for reasons which had nothing to do with ecclesiastical politics. On 28 September 365 Julian's relative Procopius was proclaimed Augustus in Constantinople. Valens was compelled to break off his journey to Syria to confront what appeared to be a serious challenge to his rule, and the rebellion was not suppressed until the spring of the following year.[67] Like Constantius in 350, therefore, Valens could not take the risk that Egypt might side with the rebel. On 1 February 366 the *notarius* Brasidas arrived in Alexandria with a letter from Valens which invited Athanasius to return to his church and resume his normal functions as bishop. After Brasidas, accompanied by the prefect and the *dux*, had announced the imperial order to the decurions and the people of the city in the prefect's palace, Brasidas led the decurions and a large crowd of Christian to Athanasius' hiding place and escorted him back to the Church of Dionysius (*Hist. ac.* 5.1–7; *Index* 37).

That was almost the end of Athanasius' troubles. On 21 July 366 it is reported that a pagan mob burned the Caesareum (*Index* 38): the episode is isolated and puzzling—unless its correct date is 21 July 365, on which day a great tidal wave caused great destruction in Alexandria and throughout the eastern Mediterranean (*Index* 37). After 365/6 Valens decided to leave Athanasius unmolested. When Lucius returned to Alexandria again, he did so without official support. Athanasius' rival arrived in the city secretly on 24 September 367. After spending the night in hiding, he went to his mother's house. As soon as his arrival became known, a large crowd gathered and denounced his entry into the city. The *dux* Traianus and the prefect Tatianus sent the leading decurions to persuade Lucius to depart. When it became clear that Lucius could not leave his mother's house without being lynched by the crowd, the *dux* and the prefect came with a large number of soldiers and escorted him through a continuous shower of insults to the official residence of the *dux*, where he stayed until the next day. On 26 September Traianus took Lucius to Nicopolis, whence he sent him out of Egypt under armed guard (*Hist. ac.* 5.11–14; *Index* 39).

* * *

Athanasius was at last secure, and on 8 June 368 he celebrated the fortieth anniversary of his consecration as bishop of Alexandria. He marked the occasion by commissioning a documented history of the church of Alexandria from the beginning of the fourth century in order to ensure that his version of events would henceforth be accepted—an enterprise in which he was conspicuously successful. He may also have collected and revised the works which he had composed and recomposed to defend himself against the attacks of his ecclesiastical enemies in the 330s, 340s, and 350s: although the collected edition which survives in mediaeval manuscripts is a posthumous edition, there are signs that Athanasius himself may have made revisions and additions around 370.[68] Athanasius also left his mark on his city with two new buildings. Through Traianus, who had shown his goodwill toward him in 367, he submitted a request to Valens that he be granted imperial permission to rebuild the Caesareum. Valens indicated his official support of Athanasius by granting permission, and rebuilding commenced on 1 May 368 (*Index* 40). On 22 September of the same year, Athanasius began construction in the Mendidion of the church which was to bear his own name: it was completed quickly and dedicated on 7 August 370 (*Index* 41, 42).[69]

Outside Alexandria and Egypt, Athanasius was regarded as an elder statesman whose opinions carried great weight, and Basil of Caesarea wrote to him in flattering terms.[70] Basil pressed Athanasius to join in the struggle for orthodoxy, to become a Samuel for the churches. But Athanasius declined to involve himself in ecclesiastical affairs outside Egypt, and he did not respond to Basil's urgent pleas to heal the schism in Antioch by entering into communion with Meletius.[71] After 362 Athanasius served as a potent symbol of the resolute defense of true faith in the face of heretical oppression, but it may plausibly be argued that he had long been out of touch with current theological debate.[72] He played no significant part either in shaping the Neo-Nicene orthodoxy which was to triumph at the second ecumenical council or in more mundane ecclesiastical politics outside Egypt. The *Letter to the Africans,* which appears to show that Athanasius supported the theological initiatives of Damasus and the bishops of Gaul and Spain, must be pronounced inauthentic.[73] And when, toward the end of his life, Athanasius wrote to Epictetus, he was responding to a letter from the bishop of Corinth, whose acquaintance he may have made as he passed through Greece on his return from seven years of exile in the West a quarter of a century earlier.[74]

XVIII

THE EMPEROR AND
THE CHURCH, 324–361

WHAT DOES THE CAREER OF ATHANASIUS REVEAL ABOUT THE CHRIS-
tian church in the Constantinian empire? This essay in historical reconstruction
has attempted to understand what Athanasius wrote about his career and why
he wrote as he did, and, at the same time, to analyse what he wrote in order to
disentangle the true course of events from the subtle misrepresentations with
which he deliberately covered and obscured his controversial career. What general inferences may now drawn?[1]

Perhaps the most striking feature of Athanasius' career is the interpenetra-
tion of ecclesiastical and imperial politics. In 345 the western emperor Constans
threatened civil war if the eastern emperor Constantius did not agree to accept
the restoration of Athanasius and Paul of Constantinople. The threat may have
been made more gently and less directly in the winter of 343/4 when Constans
sent a letter with the bishops who took the decisions of the Council of Serdica to
his brother. But on this earlier occasion Constantius declined to act—and his refusal may be connected with a recent success in his war with Persia. In 345,
when Athanasius' replacement in Alexandria died, Constantius yielded to his
brother's threats and agreed to allow Athanasius to return to his see, perhaps
partly because of the military situation in Mesopotamia: in 346 the Persians be-
sieged the important city of Nisibis for three months. But in 349, as Constans
was drawing toward the end of an unpopular reign, the eastern bishops who
opposed Athanasius judged the time opportune to remove him again.

The Council of Antioch in 349 cannot have met without imperial permission
(or at least acquiescence): the bishops who attended clearly expected
Constantius to enforce their renewed deposition, and it seems that the emperor
ordered his praetorian prefect Philippus, who had recently arrested Paul in
Constantinople and brought him to court, to go to Egypt to apprehend
Athanasius. But a sudden political change saved Athanasius. Magnentius was

proclaimed emperor in Gaul, Constans was killed, and the usurper made himself master of the whole of the western empire. Magnentius wrote to Paul and Athanasius seeking their support. Paul was killed in prison in remote Cucusus in Cappadocia, but Constantius decided that he must conciliate Athanasius, who was still very much in control of Alexandria. He wrote to assure him of his goodwill, and promised to maintain him in office permanently.

With the defeat of Magnentius at the Battle of Mursa in 351, and still more with his retreat from Italy in 352 and his death in Gaul in 353, Constantius could revert to his earlier policy. The Council of Sirmium in the autumn of 351 on the one hand condemned Athanasius, Marcellus of Ancyra, and Photinus of Sirmium, and on the other propounded a creed of which Athanasius and (as it turned out) the vast majority of western bishops disapproved. When Constantius gained control of Italy, Gaul, and Spain, he attempted to secure acceptance of the decisions of the Council of Sirmium throughout the West: he convened councils in Arles in 353/4 and Milan in 355, and when few eastern bishops attended (no more than thirty or forty on either occasion), he sent imperial officials with copies of the synodical letters, which incorporated the decisions of the Council of Sirmium, to be subscribed by the local bishops individually in their own cities.

This constant involvement of Constantius in the affairs of the Christian church is only imperfectly reflected in the ecclesiastical historians of the fifth century, and is seriously obscured by Ammianus Marcellinus, whose full and often first-hand account survives of the period from the death of Magnentius in 353 to the death of Valens in 378 and its immediate aftermath. Ammianus enjoys a very high reputation as a historian capable of impartiality, who both understood the world in which he lived and faithfully recorded its main features for posterity.[2] There is much that is valid and correct in that assessment, yet a deep and insidious bias can be detected in Ammianus when he writes about Christianity. Ammianus does indeed make favorable remarks about the religion and its humble practitioners, but in virtually every case the favorable comment has the literary function of emphasising a criticism in the immediate context—and of surreptitiously demonstrating the author's fairness and impartiality.[3]

The extant books of Ammianus' *Res Gestae* give what purports to be a complete account of the significant political and military activities of the emperor Constantius from the end of the last campaign against Magnentius in the summer of 353 to his death eight years later (3 November 361). During this period, Ammianus records neither Constantius' presence at any of the several councils for which he was at hand nor the disaffection produced by his attempt to secure compliance with the decisions of the Councils of Sirmium, Arles, and Milan. He does, it is true, allude to a council which had deposed Athanasius in his notice of the arrest of Liberius in 355 'for resisting imperial orders and the decrees of very many of his colleagues.'[4] But this account of the arrest of Liberius raises serious questions about his treatment of Athanasius. Ammianus introduces Athanasius as if he had never mentioned him before[5]—which implies that his account of the 340s omitted the Council of Serdica altogether and achieved the difficult feat of describing the dealings between Constantius and Constans after the council without ever mentioning the bishop of Alexandria. No less disturbing is Ammianus' clear implication that the main charge against Athanasius in the 350s was that of employing illicit divination—the only precise crime specified besides vague charges of harboring improper ambitions and 'other things abhorrent to the rule of the law over which he presided.' Moreover, Ammianus sets the arrest in an incomplete and misleading historical context. He states that Constantius wished to secure Liberius' subscription to the synodical verdict against Athanasius because of the prestige of his see ('the more powerful authority of the bishop of the eternal city'): he makes no mention of the Councils of Arles and Milan, no mention of any attempt to compel other western bishops to accept the deposition of Athanasius, and no mention of any doctrinal dispute.

Ecclesiastical politics also impinged on imperial appointments during the reign of Constantius. The most explicit evidence concerns the career of the Cappadocian Philagrius. Before Athanasius could be removed from his see in 339, it was necessary to ensure that there be a compliant prefect in office who would make no attempt to protect the bishop: accordingly, Philagrius, who had been prefect in 335, when he assisted the special commission from the Council of Tyre in its investigations, was reappointed in the summer or autumn of 338 and served as prefect of Egypt until 340. Two subsequent appointments are known for Philagrius: as a *comes* in 343, he supervised the contingent of eastern bishops who came to the Council of Serdica, and as *vicarius* of Pontica in 351, he was in charge of the exiled Paul of Constantinople.[6]

A general tendency for Constantius to appoint Christians of a particular type to high office can also be detected. Constantius showed a clear preference for Christians over pagans as consuls and praetorian prefects, both offices conferring nobility on a family in perpetuity.[7] Between 337 and 361 the only ordinary consuls who are certainly known to be pagans held office in the West: most were nominated by Constans before 350, while one was appointed by Constantius in 355 as a reward for dynastic loyalty, and perhaps as consolation for his extrusion from the consulate of 338 to which Constantine had designated him.[8] A similar pattern can be detected among praetorian prefects: Constantius appointed only one pagan to this office in the East (in the late 350s).[9] Among Christians, moreover, Constantius gave preference to those who shared his theological inclinations, and his policy was so marked that one modern analysis of his praetorian prefects concludes that 'religious intolerance in part dictated the choice of imperial administrators.'[10]

At a more fundamental level, the career of Athanasius reveals significant facts about the power structure of the Roman Empire. In 350, Constantius decided that he could not risk a civil war in which the bishop of Alexandria might support a challenger to his rule, and Valens made the same calculation in 365/6 when confronted with the rebellion of Procopius in Constantinople. In 356, when Constantius attempted to arrest Athanasius, he was unable to apprehend him. Imperial officials, generals, and troops could prevent Athanasius from performing his normal functions as bishop in the city of Alexandria, and they could sometimes install a rival as bishop in his place, but they were unable to lay hands on Athanasius himself or to eliminate him as a political factor. In 339, Athanasius had escaped to Italy: after 356, he remained at liberty in Alexandria itself, then in the Egyptian countryside until the death of Constantius. Under Julian, Athanasius was similarly able to evade arrest until it was safe for him to return to Alexandria. And under Valens, when Lucius came to replace him with imperial backing, Athanasius retired into hiding within the city and reemerged when the revolt of Procopius compelled the emperor to acknowledge him as the rightful bishop of Alexandria. It is thus clear that in the middle of the fourth century a Roman emperor did not enjoy complete control over Egypt, where a popular bishop of Alexandria could resist his will successfully and with impunity.

It has often been assumed that the Christian church in the reign of Constantine and his sons was subservient to the emperor. The dominant model in recent scholarship of the relationship between the Christian church and the Roman state in the fourth century has been one which was developed by German scholars, especially by Eduard Schwartz, in the late nineteenth and early twentieth centuries—and which appears to take its inspiration from the situation of the church in the Germany of Bismarck and Kaiser Wilhelm II.[11] This model operates with terms such as 'Reichskirche' and 'kaiserliche Synodalgewalt':[12] it holds that the emperor not only convened important councils of bishops, but also either presided himself (as he is often imagined to have done at Nicaea in 325)[13] or appointed an imperial official to preside in his place (the prime example being the *comes* Dionysius at the Council of Tyre in 335).[14] And it reduces the role of bishops at councils such as Nicaea and Tyre to utter insignificance by assimilating them to members of the imperial *consilium,* whose advice was not binding on the emperor. Hence, according to this model, all the decisions made at Nicaea were, strictly speaking, decisions of Constantine alone, since he could have disregarded the merely advisory opinions of the bishops whom he had summoned to the council.[15]

This model has not stood unchallenged. J. N. D. Kelly dismissed as exaggerated Schwartz's view that Constantine imposed on the bishops at Nicaea 'the obligation of finding a formula for the admission of clergy to, or their exclusion from, the new state Church.'[16] And Jean Gaudemet elegantly rejected the notion of Caesaropapism as if it were as implausible as the claim (which no one has ever seriously entertained) that the Roman Empire of the fourth century was a theocracy: the relationship between church and state was one of collaboration in which each party had rights and duties of its own to uphold and perform.[17] But the protests of Kelly, Gaudemet, and others have failed to impair the continuing wide acceptance of the paradigm laid down by Schwartz, which is still dominant in German scholarly writing about the church in the Constantinian empire and often tacitly, or even explicitly, accepted by scholars of other nationalities.[18] It will be worthwhile, therefore, to set out in some detail the model of the relationship between the emperor and bishops which this book partly assumes and partly attempts to establish as valid, and the view which it takes of the status and function of church councils.

In the period between Constantine's conquest of the East in 324 and the accession of Theodosius in 379, neither the emperor nor any of his officials ever presided over or even sat as a member of a council, except in the extraordinary circumstances of 359, when Constantius took an abnormally prominent role in theological debate, a role which had no precedent. In 359 the emperor ordered the bishops of the West and the East to meet at separate councils in Ariminum and Seleucia in order to ratify a creed which had been presented and subscribed in his presence at Sirmium on 22 May, and which thus had his prestige and authority behind it. Hence both the praetorian prefect Taurus at Ariminum and the *comes* Leonas at Seleucia, acting with Bassidius Lauricius, the governor of Isauria, played an active part in securing the compliance of the assembled bishops with the emperor's wishes. However, the historically significant fact is not that the emperor's will eventually prevailed in 359/60, but that it took the prolonged use of strong-arm tactics and deceit to extort from the bishops an acceptance of the official homoean creed, which was both grudging and temporary.

The test-cases for determining normal practise must be the Council of Nicaea in 325 and the Council of Tyre in 335. In the former case, despite the familiar image of Constantine seated among the bishops and presiding over their discussions, the evidence makes it clear that the emperor was not technically a member of the council at all: he took part in its discussions as an interested layman who was present, but he was not a voting member of the assembly. The council proper comprised bishops, priests, and deacons, and it was presided over by Ossius, the bishop of Corduba. In the latter case, there is *prima facie* evidence that Dionysius presided: Athanasius says so, and modern scholars have been very reluctant to disbelieve his testimony. But everything Athanasius says about the Council of Tyre must be evaluated carefully, not taken on trust as if his testimony were impartial. Athanasius consistently tried to discredit the Council of Tyre and its verdict against him in every way possible. Yet in his eagerness to document the bias, partiality, and improper procedures of his enemies, he quotes letters exchanged between Dionysius and the bishops at Tyre which show that the *comes* was not even present at some of the crucial sessions of the council.

In both cases, a distinction must be drawn between the formal opening ceremony and the substantive deliberations of the council. Eusebius of Caesarea attended the Council of Nicaea and has left a brief and tantalising account of the opening ceremony which, though deficient in precise detail, shows that

Constantine played a central role, indeed that the ceremony was to a large degree an act of homage to the emperor by the council.[19] At Tyre in 335, the council opened with a ceremony in which the imperial *notarius* Marianus read aloud a letter from Constantine welcoming the bishops and defining the agenda of the council:[20] there is no difficulty or implausibility in holding that Dionysius presided at the opening ceremony, but then put the substantive matters and the conduct of the council wholly in the hands of the bishops.

Councils met both with imperial permission or at imperial command and without any consultation of the emperor and his officials. There had been councils of bishops even in the days when Christianity was a capital crime,[21] and there is no hint that pagan emperors were ever asked to grant permission for councils to be held in the late third and early fourth centuries. Alexander convened a council which excommunicated Arius, and Arius' supporters held counter-councils which vindicated him without any reference to Licinius until the emperor prohibited councils of bishops from meeting altogether—which may have been a partisan intervention inspired by Eusebius of Nicomedia. It was entirely predictable, therefore, that this long-standing practise should continue under Christian emperors, and there were numerous councils between 324 and 361 which met without seeking imperial permission to do so. The novelty was that after 324 the emperor sometimes summoned a council and set its agenda.

It is not certain that it was Constantine rather than the bishops assembled in Alexandria in the late autumn of 324 who summoned the council which was expected to meet at Ancyra in 325, but it was certainly the emperor who transferred the planned council from Ancyra to Nicaea.[22] Moreover, Constantine set at least part of the agenda and subsequently claimed credit for some of the decisions in which he had participated just as if he were a bishop. For some later councils in his reign, it seems certain that Constantine both summoned the bishops to meet and defined their agenda (which did not prevent them from discussing other matters too)—and on occasion compelled the attendance of both bishops and other interested parties. A papyrus shows the compulsion used to secure attendance at the Council of Tyre in 335, and it was Constantine who both ordered a council to meet at Caesarea in Palestine in 334 to try Athanasius for murder and canceled the council when Athanasius convinced him that the charge was false. Constantine also took the initiative in summoning councils of bishops to meet in Nicomedia in 327/8, in Jerusalem in 335, and in Constantinople in 336: he attended the Council of Nicomedia in December 327 or January 328; he ordered the bishops assembled at Tyre to adjourn to Jerusalem to dedicate the Church of the Holy Sepulchre in September 335, requesting them again to readmit Arius to communion; and he attended the Council of Constantinople in 336, which condemned Marcellus of Ancyra.

On the other hand, it is not necessary to suppose that the bishops who met at Antioch in 327 and deposed Eustathius and other bishops in Syria, Phoenice, and Palestine sought imperial permission before they met. And the councils of Alexandria in 338 and 352, which pronounced Athanasius innocent of the charges on which he had been condemned and deposed, clearly assembled in defiance of the wishes of Constantius, since the councils whose verdicts they disputed had just met with the obvious approval of the emperor, who certainly attended the Council of Sirmium in 351 and probably also the Council of Antioch in early 338. Moreover, Julius did not consult Constans before holding the Council of Rome which exculpated Athanasius and Marcellus in 341: indeed, no bishop of Rome would have seen any need to seek imperial permission to hold a council in Rome under any circumstances. Nor again did Eusebius of Vercellae and Athanasius even consider consulting Julian before they convened the Council of Alexandria in 362.

The agenda of a council might include any or all of three types of business: the adjudication of disputes concerning the status of individuals, the definition of what constituted true doctrine, and disciplinary matters concerning both clergy and laity. Its membership might comprise the bishops of a single province, of several provinces or a region, or, in theory, of the whole empire or whole world. But what if two councils came not merely to different decisions but to opposing ones? The ecclesiastical history of the reign of Constantius provides examples enough of this phenomenon, the clearest cases being the two councils of 338 (Antioch and Alexandria), the two councils of 341 (Antioch again and Rome), and the divided Council of Serdica in 343. There was as yet no agreed procedure for resolving such disputes. Admittedly, the synodical letters and the polemical literature of the middle of the fourth century contain appeals to the ecumenical nature of the Council of Nicaea as endowing its decisions and above all its creed with a supreme and inviolate status,[23] and Athanasius frequently argues that the decisions of a council attended by a large number of bishops ought to prevail over the decisions of a council attended by few bishops, but the earliest clear statement of a formal hierarchy subordinating provincial to regional councils and the latter to ecumenical councils occurs at the very end of the century.[24]

The Council of Nicaea prescribed that the bishops of each province meet twice each year, once in the spring between Easter and Ascension and once in the autumn.[25] These councils sometimes transacted important business: it was a provincial council of the bishops of Narbonensis (so it seems) that deposed Hilary of Poitiers in 356, probably with the Caesar Julian on hand, and the Council of Gangra, whose synodical letter became enshrined in later collections of canon law, was probably an assembly of the bishops of the province of Paphlagonia. Nor did a small attendance prevent the decisions of a council from receiving a subsequent imprimatur as an authoritative source of canon law: the preserved lists of subscriptions to the canons of the Council of Ancyra (314) contain the names of twelve or thirteen bishops; those of the Council of Neocaesarea, eighteen; and those of the Council of Antioch in 328, thirty-two in all, while the heading of the synodical letter of the Council of Gangra names fifteen.[26]

Constantine declared that the decisions of councils of bishops were divinely inspired,[27] and he gave them legal force. In recording this enactment, Eusebius states:

> He put a seal of approval on the rulings of bishops declared at councils, so that the governors of provinces were not allowed to rescind what they had decided, for he said that the priests of God were more trustworthy than any magistrate.[28]

Although Eusebius mentions only the duty of provincial governors to respect and enforce the rulings of church councils, both consistency and Constantine's public pronouncements about the status of the decisions of councils entailed that even the emperor lacked the right to countermand them. That was a startling innovation, since the Roman emperor had traditionally been regarded as the ultimate arbiter of all disputes among his subjects.[29] Constantine denied himself the right to try bishops, who could be condemned and deposed only by a council of their peers. He did on occasion conduct a preliminary examination, which could (and sometimes did) result in the dismissal of the accusation and the acquittal of the bishop. But if he found that there was *prima facie* case, he thereupon convened a council of bishops and submitted the whole matter to them.

Constantine's attested dealings with Athanasius fall into this pattern. It is wrong to describe his hearing of Athanasius at Psammathia in 331/2 as an imperial trial or *cognitio:*[30] had Constantine not dismissed the charges as unfounded, he would not have condemned or deposed Athanasius himself, but would have submitted the case to a council of bishops. Similarly, when Athanasius was accused of murdering Arsenius, Constantine ordered the *censor* Dalmatius to investigate the charge. But he planned no 'trial for murder in Antioch':[31] the 'court of the *censor*' derided by Athanasius was the abortive Council of Caesarea which was instructed to meet in order to render a verdict on the charge of murder. The emperor (or his deputy) merely conducted a preliminary hearing: if he decided that there was a *prima facie* case against the accused bishop, the matter was then referred to a council of bishops who functioned as the court of both primary and ultimate jurisdiction.

After a bishop had been tried and condemned by his peers, it was both proper and necessary for the emperor to enforce his deposition by means of exile, using force if necessary. That was not in itself an innovation by or under Constantine. There was a precedent in the third century when Paul of Samosata refused to accept his deposition by a Council of Antioch: Christians of Italy, acting on behalf of their colleagues in Syria, submitted a petition to the emperor Aurelian requesting him to compel Paul to surrender the church in Antioch.[32] What was new in the Christian empire of Constantine was the automatic enforcement of the decisions of church councils. An Aurelian could have reviewed and reversed the decision of a third-century council: Constantine bound himself in advance to accept and enforce the condemnation of a bishop by his peers meeting as a council. In practise, that did not prevent a deposed bishop like Athanasius (and perhaps Eustathius of Antioch before him) from attempting to persuade the emperor to reconsider his case, but there is only one example between 324 and 361 when a synodical condemnation was openly reversed by imperial fiat—in 337, when Constantinus issued an edict restoring all the bishops exiled under his father. Significantly, the Council of Antioch in 338/9 regarded this restoration as canonically invalid.

The first exile of Athanasius does not neatly fit into this pattern, since it cannot legitimately be regarded as the automatic enforcement of his condemnation by the Council of Tyre.[33] On this occasion, Constantine did not accept the decision of a council. He was persuaded by Athanasius that it had proceeded improperly and unfairly—but before he knew of its verdict. The letter which he wrote to the bishops at Tyre did not overrule their synodical decision. He commanded them to come to him so that he could ensure fair play: in other words, he felt that he had a duty to guarantee due process and thus to aid the council in reaching a just verdict. But that letter, despite its prominence in Athanasius' account of his exile in 335, was immediately overtaken by events. Constantine rendered it null and void when, after the arrival of two delegations from Tyre, one bringing the council's condemnation of Athanasius, the other protesting that it was unjust, he interviewed Athanasius and sent him to Gaul. That action, however, did not reinstate the condemnation of Athanasius by the Council of Tyre as a valid deposition. The emperor refused to allow the successor whom the council had appointed in his place to become bishop of Alexandria: although he was in exile and debarred from the normal exercise of his episcopal functions, Athanasius was technically still the lawful bishop of Alexandria.

The situation of Athanasius in 335–337 was highly anomalous. In contrast, both his exile in 339 and his flight in 356 fit perfectly into the pattern of deposition by a council followed by imperial enforcement of its verdict. In 339 the decision of the Council of Antioch was put into effect at once. In the 350s more than four years passed before Constantius could enforce the deposition of Athanasius by the Council of Sirmium. But the delay did not alter the legal basis of his supersession. Athanasius' eloquence in his *Defense before Constantius* should not be allowed to obscure the fact that the Council of Sirmium had deposed him in 351—nor should his eloquence elsewhere be allowed to obscure the fact that he was often condemned by councils of bishops, whose verdicts he steadfastly refused to accept.

Constantine gave bishops important privileges in the new Christian empire. They could act as judges in disputes between Christians by virtue of the newly introduced *episcopalis audientia*,[34] they could preside over the manumission of slaves in church,[35] and they soon began to act regularly as ambassadors in matters of high political import.[36] In significant ways the Christian bishop was now outside the normal legal system. Theodosius ruled that bishops could not be compelled to appear as witnesses in court.[37] It should not be assumed that this ruling represented an innovation. For the bishop's privilege of trial by his peers, though not explicitly attested until 355, surely goes back to Constantine. On 23 September 355 Constantius wrote to one Severus, whose office is unknown, in the following terms:

> By [this] law of our clemency we forbid bishops to be accused in [secular] courts, lest there be an unrestrained freedom for deranged minds to denounce them, in the belief that [false accusations] will not be punished because of the benevolence of the bishops. Accordingly, if anyone at all lodges any complaint [against a bishop], it is appropriate for it to be examined only before other bishops, so that a suitable and convenient hearing be provided for the investigation of all [relevant matters].[38]

The principle that only a council of his peers could try, condemn, and depose a bishop can be observed in operation in the reign of Constantine, particularly and with the greatest clarity in the case of Athanasius. It also encouraged the formation within the church of coalitions of bishops which functioned much like modern political parties—a broad ideological (or theological) cohesiveness furthered and sometimes hindered by personal ambitions.

Not the least among the privileges which bishops enjoyed was a relative immunity from coercion by secular authorities. No matter what his crime, a bishop could only be deposed and exiled, not legally tortured and executed.[39] This encouraged the development of an attitude of independence and even defiance, which was fully fledged by the end of the reign of Constantius and which had clear political implications. Athanasius, Hilary of Poitiers, and Lucifer of Caralis all argue that because Constantius maltreats the church, he is a persecutor and a tyrant who no longer deserves to be emperor.[40] By the end of the fourth century Christian orthodoxy had been added to the traditional list of virtues required in a legitimate emperor. Athanasius himself thought through the implications of regarding church and state as opposing entities,[41] and it was in the reign of Constantius that the classic antithesis was first voiced in its most familiar form.[42]

Ossius of Corduba, as quoted by Athanasius in the *History of the Arians*, begged Constantius to emulate his brother Constans in granting the church real independence:

> Stop using force, and do not write or send *comites*. Release those who have been exiled, so that they do not perform greater deeds of violence because you are accusing them of using violence. What [action] of this sort was ever taken by Constans? What bishop was exiled [by him]?

When did he ever participate in an ecclesiastical decision? What palatine official of his compelled people to subscribe to the condemnation of anyone?

Stop, I beg you, and remember that you are a mortal man: fear the day of judgement and keep yourself pure for it. Do not intrude yourself into the affairs of the church, and do not give us advice about these matters, but rather receive instruction on them from us. God has given you king-ship, but has entrusted us with what belongs to the church. Just as the man who tries to steal your position as emperor contradicts God who has placed you there, so too you should be afraid of becoming guilty of a great offense by putting the affairs of the church under your control. It is written: 'Render unto Caesar the things that are Caesar's, and unto God those that are God's' (Matthew 22.21). Hence neither do we [bishops] have the right to rule over the world nor do you, emperor, have the right to officiate in church. (*Hist. Ar.* 44.6–8)[43]

Not all Christians took such a favorable view of the ecclesiastical policies of Constans. In 347 there was a violent repression of the schismatic Donatists in Africa. Donatus in fury denounced the emperor's court as the abode of Satan and asked the pointed question which has reverberated through the ages: 'What has the emperor to do with the church?'[44]

XIX

BISHOPS AND SOCIETY

THERE EXIST EXCELLENT STUDIES OF MANY ASPECTS OF THE GENERAL
historical context against which the career of Athanasius must be viewed, such
as imperial legislation relating to Christianity, the place of the church in the
Later Roman Empire, and the Christian bishop in Late Antique society.[1] Modern historians have also produced fine studies which illuminate Athanasius' immediate background, such as the spread of Christianity in the Egyptian countryside, the organisation of the church in Egypt, the early days of Egyptian
monasticism,[2] the wealth of the Christian church in Egypt,[3] the economic activities of the bishop of Alexandria,[4] the role of the bishop of Alexandria in ecclesiastical politics,[5] and the role of Athanasius himself as the leader of the Egyptian
church.[6] And there are two recent surveys concentrating, respectively, on state,
church, and dynasty at the death of Constantine, and on church, law, and society in the reign of Constantius.[7]

There would be no point in attempting here to cover the same ground again
or to reduplicate any of these or similar studies. It may be useful, however, to
emphasise certain features of the position of the Christian bishop in the East between 324 and 361 which help to explain Athanasius' political role in the Roman Empire of his day. His personal character cannot provide an adequate explanation of how or why he became an important political figure. The
prominence of Athanasius and later bishops of Alexandria derives rather from
changes in the political structure of the Roman Empire consequent upon the
conversion of Constantine in 312 and his establishment in 324 of Christianity as
the official religion of the Roman government.[8] The period between
Constantine's defeat of Licinius and the death of Constantius as he prepared to
fight Julian has unique characteristics of its own and cannot be understood or
reconstructed by extrapolation from the better-documented periods which precede and follow it. In 324/5 the Christian bishops of the eastern Roman Empire

suddenly acquired an extremely privileged position in society, which they lost with equal suddenness in 361/2—and which after 363 they recovered only gradually and incompletely.

In the three and a half decades after 324, eastern Christians showed themselves militant and aggressive as they eagerly exploited the opportunities which Constantine gave them. The Roman Empire was now officially Christian, and the performance of the traditional rites of sacrifice was illegal: as in the English reformation of the sixteenth century, there must have been many individuals who consciously set out to profit from the disestablishment of the old religion. In the winter of 361/2, as soon as Constantius was dead, Julian declared the empire officially pagan again and canceled all the privileges which Constantine and his sons had lavished on the church.[9] Although Julian ruled as a pagan emperor for a mere twenty months, his Christian successors did not fully restore the privileges he had abolished. Theodoretus reports that when Jovian reinstated Christian financial and fiscal privileges, he fixed them at one-third of their level under Constantine, and that this reduced level of support had not been increased by his own day, eighty years later.[10]

When Constantine exempted the Christian clergy from public liturgies and initiated a policy of systematic donations to the Christian church from imperial funds, he did so in a way which gave bishops the power to decide in both cases which individuals should benefit.[11] His letter to the proconsul of Africa in the winter of 312/3 declares:

> It is my wish that those persons who, in the province entrusted to you, provide their personal service in this holy worship within the catholic church, over which Caecilianus presides, whom they are accustomed to call 'clerics,' should once and for all be made absolutely free of the obligation to perform public liturgies, so that they may not be drawn away from the worship owed to the divinity by any error or sacrilegious fault, but may rather serve their own law without any hindrance.[12]

Constantine thus defined the catholic church of Carthage, to which he granted exemption from civic liturgies, by reference to its bishop—who of course determined who became a priest or deacon by his control of ordinations within his own diocese. Similarly, shortly after October 324, when Constantine wrote to eastern bishops to encourage them to build churches, he wrote in these terms:

> Concerning the churches over which you yourself preside, or know others who preside in such places, whether bishops, priests, or deacons—remind them to be active in the building of churches, either restoring or enlarging existing buildings or constructing new ones where need requires. You may yourself request, and the rest may request through you, what is needed from governors and the prefect's office. For these have been given

instructions that they are to lend their assistance to communications from your holiness with all eagerness.[13]

Again, Constantine channels his generosity to the church as an institution through the local bishop (or possibly, in this case, the metropolitan bishop of the province).[14]

Imperial subsidies to the Egyptian church had already been established before Athanasius was elected bishop of Alexandria. Since ecclesiastical organisation tended to copy imperial administration, such subsidies were automatically channeled by the governor of the province and by imperial financial officials through the bishop of the capital city of each province. In Egypt, the Council of Nicaea had decreed that the bishop of Alexandria should retain his traditional authority as metropolitan not merely over the reduced Diocletianic province of Aegyptus, but over the whole of Egypt and Libya.[15] The practical effects can be clearly seen in the handling of Constantine's grant of food for the widows and poor in Egypt as tendentiously described in 338 by Athanasius himself:

> Grain was given by the father of the emperors for distribution to widows, separately in the Libyas and to certain [bishops] from Egypt. All the bishops have received this until now, with Athanasius getting no benefit therefrom, except the trouble of helping them. But now, even though they receive it, have made no complaint, and acknowledge that they receive it, Athanasius has been falsely accused of selling all the supply of grain and embezzling the proceeds. (*Apol. c. Ar.* 18.2)

Whether true or false, the accusation assumes that Athanasius in some way controlled the supply of grain for widows throughout the Egyptian provinces.[16] It is hard to believe that bishops failed to see the opportunities for patronage inherent in such a situation.

Imperial subsidies channeled through the bishop of Alexandria provide the background to the mysterious affair of the linen tunics. According to Athanasius, the first charge ever concocted against him was

> an accusation by Ision, Eudaemon, and Callinicus concerning linen tunics, to the effect that I had imposed a requisition on the Egyptians, and demanded it from them. (*Apol. c. Ar.* 60.2)

This is not a tax on linen tunics (as has sometimes been supposed), but a demand that tunics be supplied to Athanasius for distribution to the poor and needy, or else for liturgical use. The charge presupposes an imperial grant of supplies in kind to the church, a grant whose terms permitted the bishop of Alexandria to ask individuals to give him tunics to discharge what was, in strict legality, an obligation to the state or the emperor.[17] The same background illuminates the charge which made Constantine lose his temper and send Athanasius to Trier in

335. His enemies accused Athanasius of 'threatening to prevent the grain from being sent from Alexandria to Constantinople' (*Apol. c. Ar.* 87.1). Athanasius had legitimate access to the Egyptian grain-supply for charitable purposes. But Egypt was one of the main sources of supply for Constantinople: Athanasius was being accused, in part, of wishing to divert to his own purposes grain needed to prevent riots in the imperial city. The exiles of Athanasius made no difference to the institutional arrangements; they merely changed the identity of the bishop who controlled the supplies and their distribution. The *History of the Arians* notes, as a predictable and commonplace occurrence, that after the Councils of Arles and Milan, instructions were sent to the prefect of Egypt that 'the grain be taken away from Athanasius and given to those who hold the views of Arius' (31.2).

In the traditional societies of the Roman Empire in which Christianity originated, grew, expanded, and eventually attained dominance, religious authority was vested in local political élites who normally also formed the wealthiest group in their city. Political and religious authority were indissolubly bound together at all levels, from the emperor as *pontifex maximus* down to the priests and magistrates of small provincial towns.[18] Hence, as Christians became prominent in local society in the course of the third century, they automatically began to hold local magistracies, local priesthoods, and even the provincial priesthood of the imperial cult: the Council of Elvira implicitly sanctioned the practise before the Diocletianic persecution by excluding Christian *flamines* only during the term of their annual office,[19] while Constantine so denuded the imperial cult of what he called 'the contagion of disgusting superstition' that he sanctioned the construction of a temple of the Gens Flavia at Hispellum in Umbria,[20] and the imperial cult continued to function as a focus for the public expression of political loyalty into the fifth century.[21]

The Constantinian reformation severed this immemorial nexus of religious authority, social status, and political power. It thereby created a new type of patron in a society where, outside the family, patronage was the primary form of both political and social relationships between individuals.[22] The officially recognised and designated mediators between the human and the divine were now the Christian bishop and the Christian holy man. The positions of the two categories, however, were structurally different. The holy man acquired status individually through miracles, prophecies, or asceticism, and he typically operated on the margins of society as a patron of poor villagers or as a mediator of conflict in or close to a large metropolis.[23] The Christian bishop, on the other hand, possessed ascribed status, his authority was inherent in his office, and he was at the centre of a web of local patronage. His position thus conferred on him a very real political power which enabled a man who knew how to exploit it to defy the emperor who in theory ruled the Roman Empire. Athanasius of Alexandria is the earliest and most spectacular example of this phenomenon.

X X

EPILOGUE

ATHANASIUS NEVER FORGOT THE CONTROVERSY SURROUNDING HIS election in 328. In order to prevent another disputed election after his own death, he chose a successor and consecrated him at the end of April 373, five days before he died (*Hist. ac.* 5.14).[1] No sooner was Athanasius dead than his choice was ratified by his clergy, his congregation, and the worthies of the city of Alexandria, who elected Peter as their new bishop. But the guarantee of security which Athanasius had effectively enjoyed since 366 did not extend to his successor. As soon as the new bishop was enthroned, the prefect surrounded the church and demanded that Peter come out. But Peter had learned from the example of his predecessor a generation earlier. Although it seems that Peter was arrested, he soon escaped from custody, boarded a ship, and, like Athanasius in 339, sailed to Rome, where he was confident of the support of the bishop.[2] Damasus, who had become bishop of Rome in 366 in an election contested with extreme bitterness and violence,[3] gave him a warm welcome. After his arrival in Rome, again like Athanasius in 339, Peter composed an account of his expulsion from Alexandria, which survives (though not complete) as a long quotation in Theodoretus' *Ecclesiastical History*.[4] With greater plausibility than his predecessor forty-four years earlier, Peter presented his own cause as the cause of endangered orthodoxy, and he gave specific details of his expulsion which, even when allowance is made for exaggeration, indicate that great violence was also used in this attempt to install the emperor's candidate as bishop of Alexandria.

The prefect Palladius, who was a pagan and a worshipper of idols, gathered a crowd and attacked the Church of Theonas. Holy virgins were stripped and beaten with clubs: many were struck on the head and killed, and their bodies were denied proper burial. Lucius entered the city, a man who regarded the position of bishop as a secular honor to be bought with gold, a man who had not been 'elected by a council of orthodox bishops, by the vote of true clergy, or at the insistence of the laity, as the laws of the church prescribe.' He was not escorted by bishops, priests, deacons, laymen, or monks, but by two thoroughly disreputable characters. Euzoius, the Arian bishop of Antioch since 360, had been condemned at Nicaea in 325 together with Arius, while he was still a deacon in Alexandria. Magnus, the *comes sacrarum largitionum*, had burned the main church in Berytus in the reign of Julian, and had subsequently been compelled to rebuild it by Jovian, who spared him from the execution which his crime merited. In Alexandria in 373, Magnus assembled nineteen priests and deacons as if they were guilty of a criminal offense and pressured them to accept Lucius and his homoean creed. When they refused and reiterated their adherence to the creed of Nicaea, he imprisoned (and perhaps tortured) them; when they persisted, he brought them before a crowd of pagans and Jews (so Peter alleges) close by the harbor; when they refused yet again, he deported them to Helipolis in Phoenicia, which was still heavily pagan.

The prefect Palladius forbade the display of sympathy for the exiles: those who lamented their fate, twenty-four in number, including the deacon who had brought letters of communion and comfort from Damasus in Rome, were arrested, imprisoned, tortured, and finally sent to the mines of Phaeno or the quarries of Proconnesus. Repression extended beyond Alexandria itself into Egypt: Magnus sentenced bishops who refused to accept Lucius to serve in their local city councils, and eleven bishops who resisted with exceptional determination were exiled to the Jewish city of Diocaesarea in Galilee.[5] Action was also taken against the monks who supported Athanasius and his chosen successor,[6] and the repression probably continued for some time. For it is reported that Flavius Eutolmius Tatianus, who between 367 and 370 had been prefect of Egypt, then the first *praefectus Augustalis* of the Egyptian diocese, exiled bishops and tortured and burned priests, deacons, and monks after the death of Athanasius— presumably when he replaced Magnus as *comes sacrarum largitionum*.[7]

The bishop of Rome was sympathetic. But effective action depended on the western emperor, and either Valentinian refused to intervene or his attitude was so well known that Damasus and Peter did not think it worthwhile to make a formal request. Lucius remained in Alexandria with the support of the eastern imperial administration until a political and military emergency enabled Peter to return. In the spring of 378 Valens left Antioch to confront the Goths. Almost immediately, Peter returned to Alexandria with a letter from Damasus which reaffirmed the creed of Nicaea and confirmed him as the rightful bishop of the city. His supporters reinstated him and expelled Lucius, who betook himself to Constantinople in search of imperial support.[8] The issue was decided by the defeat and death of Valens at the Battle of Adrianople on 9 August. The senior surviving emperor Gratian appointed the Spaniard Theodosius *magister militum* to command Roman forces in the Balkans, and on 19 January 379 Theodosius became Augustus and ruler of the East. As a westerner, Theodosius was a firm supporter of the creed of Nicaea, and he soon acted to make

Nicene orthodoxy the official religion of the eastern Roman Empire.

A general edict of 27 February 380 declared the emperors' desire that everyone abide in the religion given of old by the apostle Peter to the people of Rome and now preserved by Damasus and by Peter, the bishop of Alexandria and a man of apostolic sanctity. The edict defines catholic Christians as those who believe in the equal divinity of the Father, the Son, and the Holy Spirit, and denounces those who do not as disrespectful and insane heretics who deserve punishment.[9] Theodosius was consistent and thorough in his religious policies. The Council of Constantinople in 381 officially reaffirmed the creed of Nicaea, the emperor enshrined its decisions in law,[10] and he subjected Christians who did not accept the creed of Nicaea and its watchword *homoousios* to legal disabilities.[11] As has long been recognised, these events mark the transition from one distinctive epoch in the history of the Christian church and the Roman Empire to another—the age of Theodosius had replaced the Constantinian empire.

Appendix 1

THE *FESTAL LETTERS*

It was customary for bishops of Alexandria to write a *Festal Letter* as Easter approached, and two recent studies have done much to solve the chronological problems posed by the *Festal Letters* which Athanasius wrote for the Easters during his long episcopate, from the Easter of 329 to the Easter of 373.[1] In 1986 Rudolf Lorenz published a facsimile of the Syriac text of *Letter* X with a German translation, preceded by a brief but incisive discussion of the editorial process which lay behind the Syriac and Coptic corpora and followed by a consideration of the theological content of the letter.[2] In the same year Alberto Camplani presented a thesis at the University of Rome which was subsequently revised and published as a substantial monograph in 1989: it contains a full treatment of the direct and indirect transmission of the *Festal Letters*, of the compilation of the two corpora and the chronology of the *Letters*, and of the value of the *Letters* as a historical source.[3] Fortunately, the most important chronological conclusions at which Lorenz and Camplani (and the present writer)[4] arrived independently of each other largely coincide: hence a summary exposition of the problems of the *Festal Letters* will suffice.

Two basic propositions must be set out starkly and very clearly at the start:

(1) the numbering and the chronology of the *Festal Letters* in the Syriac and Coptic corpora reflect the decisions of an editor or editors who collected the *Letters* after Athanasius' death;

(2) the *Festal Letters* proper, which Athanasius wrote for circulation in Egypt shortly before each Easter, must be distinguished from the brief notifications of the date of the next Easter which he circulated long in advance, probably a few weeks after the preceding Easter.

It is one of the greatest merits of the studies of both Lorenz and Camplani that these fundamental points are allowed due weight.

The original Greek of Athanasius' *Festal Letters* has perished except for a few brief quotations in Cosmas Indicopleustes (10.3–13) and a large part of *Letter* XXXIX, preserved in Greek collections of canon law because it lists the canonical books of the Old and New Testaments (*PG* 26.1434–1440).[5] Apart from quotations, in Syriac and Armenian as well as in Greek, the letters survive in Syriac and Coptic translations, each of which is incompletely preserved:[6]

(1) A Syriac manuscript in the British Library (Add. ms. 14569) preserves the first half of a corpus of the letters together with a scholarly apparatus supplied by an Alexandrian editor not long after Athanasius's death. The text of this manuscript was published by William Cureton in 1848 in a disordered state: it had been acquired by the British Museum in two batches and arrived in London not as a continuous manuscript, but as a collection of single leaves in two instalments.[7] In 1853 Cureton's text, restored to its proper order, was reprinted by Cardinal Mai, together with a Latin version made by Mai on the basis of a literal rendering into Italian by a Maronite scholar in Rome.[8] This Latin version, subsequently reprinted by J. P. Migne (*PG* 26.1351–1432), became the standard 'text' of the *Letters* used in scholarly writing about Athanasius. Unfortunately, Cureton originally overlooked two leaves of the manuscript, which he consequently omitted from his edition. Although he soon noticed his oversight and drew the two leaves to the attention of Henry Burgess, who printed their text as an appendix to his English translation of 1854,[9] the missing portions of *Letters* X and XI were unknown to Mai, and, since Migne too omitted them, they remained unknown outside the English-speaking world until recently, so that far-reaching deductions have sometimes been based on the supposed lacunae.[10] English-speaking scholars have avoided the error because for them the most easily accessible and most widely used version of the *Festal Letters* has long been Jessie Payne Smith's 1892 revision of Burgess's translation, which had already in 1854 incorporated the contents of the two leaves omitted by Cureton.[11]

The manuscript, which breaks off suddenly in the middle of *Letter* XX, has normally been dated to the eighth century or so,[12] but Camplani has produced cogent paleographical grounds for dating it to the tenth century.[13] The translation itself, which renders the Greek very literally and uses *matres lectionis* to reproduce almost all the vowels of the Greek proper names, appears to have been made in the sixth or seventh century.[14]

(2) Fragmentary Coptic codices preserve large parts of seventeen letters throughout the collection which overlap both with the Greek fragments and with the Syriac version of *Letters* I–XX. The fragments known in 1955 were edited with a French translation by L. T. Lefort,[15] whose edition has recently been supplemented with further fragments from the same codices.[16]

Camplani now provides a useful conspectus of the Coptic fragments of the *Festal Letters* which, though dispersed in more than half a dozen modern libraries, come from three manuscripts from the White Monastery, and he uses codicological criteria to place the fragments of letters transmitted without a number.[17] The Coptic translation, Camplani argues, was made during the second half of the fifth century shortly after the death of Shenute of Atripe to be read for edification during Lent and at Easter ('come catechesi prepasquale e pasquale').[18]

Lefort's edition (it should be noted in passing) must be used with some caution. It includes the text of two leaves published in 1938 as part of the *Festal Letter* for Easter 364, which have a different provenance from the manuscripts which preserve the *Festal Letters*.[19] It has been recognised for some time that the content of one of these two fragments (*CSCO* 150.69–70; 151.26–27) indicates that it cannot have been written by Athanasius at all,[20] while Camplani shows that the other (*CSCO* 150.70–71; 151.27–

28) probably comes from a non-festal letter written by Athanasius at Antioch in the winter of 363/4.[21]

The Syriac corpus numbered the *Festal Letters* from I to XLV, but not continuously: the numbers are correlated with the years between 329 (I) and 373 (XLV), but a number was simply skipped wherever a letter was not included for the Easter of the relevant year: hence, in the fully preserved section of the corpus, there are no *Letters* VIII, IX, XII, XV, XVI. Besides the letters themselves, the Syriac corpus includes three scholarly aids:

(1) Before each letter stands a heading which states (a) the day and month of the Easter for which the letter was written according to both the Egyptian and Julian calendars; (b) the year of the Diocletianic era; (c) the consular date; (d) the name of the prefect of Egypt in office at the time; (e) the indiction-year.

(2) Each letter is immediately followed by a subscription, which usually has the form 'here ends the *n*th Festal Letter of holy Athanasius the Patriarch'.

(3) Prefixed to the whole collection is 'an index of the months of each year, and of the days, and of the indictions, and of the consulates, and of the governors in Alexandria, and of all the epacts, and of those [days] which are named "of the gods," and the reason [a letter] was not sent, and the returns from exile.'

The individual entries in the index often also furnish information about Athanasius' activities during the year preceding the relevant Easter (such as: 'In this year he went through the Thebais' [2]).

The Syriac corpus of the *Festal Letters* thus comprises elements of quite disparate origin and value: the letters themselves were written or dictated by Athanasius himself as bishop between 328 and 373, but the introduction (or *Festal Index*), the heading to each letter, and the subscriptions came into existence during a process of editing after Athanasius' death. Since the text of the extant letters nowhere states in any form the year in which it was written, the number and the date of each letter must reflect editorial judgement. There are some patent contradictions between the *Index* and the corpus of letters to which they are prefixed,[22] and both Cosmas Indicopleustes (10.6) and Severus of Antioch (CSCO 102.216) quote from *Letter* XXIX, written for Easter 357, although the *Index* states that Athanasius wrote no *Festal Letter* for the Easters of 357, 358, 359, and 360 (29–32). Hence a serious question inevitably poses itself: are the dates assigned to the *Festal Letters* in the Syriac corpus invariably correct?

The transmitted chronology of the *Festal Letters* stood unchallenged until 1913, when Adolf Jülicher adumbrated a proof that some of the letters must be wrongly dated, a proof which Eduard Schwartz restated clearly and succinctly in 1935.[23] Whereas most of Athanasius' *Festal Letters* either speak of 'the fast of forty [days]' or assume a pre-Easter fast of that duration, a few assume that the fast preceding Easter commences on the Monday of Holy Week (*Letters* I, IV, V, XIV). Since it is impossible that the church of Alexandria varied its practise in this matter inconsistently from year to year, the *Festal Letters* which prescribe a pre-Easter fast beginning on the Monday of Holy Week must be all earlier than those which prescribe or assume a fast of forty days—despite the numbers and dates assigned to them by the ancient editor or editors.

Schwartz explained how the editorial process of producing a corpus almost inevitably led to chronological errors. The editor or editors deduced the date of each *Festal*

Letter from the only evidence available—the date of the forthcoming Easter stated in its text, which was collated with a table of the dates at which Easter was celebrated in Alexandria between 329 and 373. Such collation with a Paschal cycle sufficed to establish the dates of some letters with complete certainty. Since during these years the Alexandrian Easter fell on 11 Pharmouthi = 6 April in 329 alone and on 7 Pharmouthi = 2 April only in 332, *Letters* I and IV must belong to these years. For most letters, however, two or more Easters were theoretically open. The ancient editor or editors were thus compelled to invoke other criteria and to exercise judgement, so that it is in no way surprising if the resulting choice of year was occasionally mistaken.

Ten years after Schwartz had systematically redated the *Festal Letters*, F. L. Cross surveyed the progress of modern scholarship on Athanasius and proclaimed that Schwartz had for the first time rendered an 'intelligent reading' of the *Letters* possible.[24] Schwartz, however, worked almost entirely from the Syriac translation of the *Index* and *Letters* I–XX. In 1953 L. T. Lefort argued that the Coptic fragments furnish a decisive refutation of his attempt at redating.[25] For the Coptic *Letter* XXIV, transmitted with the date of 352, prescribes a forty-day fast with Easter on 24 Pharmouthi = 19 April. Between 329 and 373 the Alexandrian Easter fell on 19 April only in 330, 341, and 352: hence *Letter* II, which refers to 'the fast of forty [days],' cannot be redated to 352, as Schwartz wished, since the only other possible year (341) is securely occupied by *Letter* XIII, which states that it was written in Rome.

Lefort's arguments against Schwartz held the field for thirty years,[26] even though an embarrassing fact seriously damages their cogency. The lemmata to a series of quotations from the *Festal Letters* by Timothy Aelurus, preserved only in Armenian, identify a passage which occurs in the Coptic *Letter* XXIV as coming from *Letter* II of the forty-sixth year of the Diocletianic era (329/30), which would be its correct numbering and date—were Schwartz's redating of the Syriac *Letter* II from 330 to 352 justified. Similarly, the same source identifies a passage which occurs in the Syriac *Letter* XIV as coming from *Letter* III of the forty-seventh year of the Diocletianic era—the very date (330/1) and original numbering to which Schwartz assigned it.[27] Lefort disallowed this evidence as unreliable by attributing to Timothy Aelurus the method which Schwartz attributed to the editor of the corpus and by accusing him of employing it carelessly.[28]

In his edition of *Festal Letter* X, Lorenz invalidated Lefort's central argument and thus established beyond doubt that some letters are wrongly dated in the Syriac corpus (as Jülicher and Schwartz had argued). Lorenz analysed the formulaic wording which Athanasius uses to announce both the six-day and the forty-day fast and showed, on form-critical grounds, that the reference to a forty-day fast in *Letter* XXIV is a later interpolation.[29] Presumably, the editor noticed the discrepancy over the length of the pre-Easter fast between this letter and those immediately preceding it and adjusted the text accordingly. It should be accepted, therefore, that the western practise of observing a forty-day fast before Easter was introduced into Egypt after Athanasius had written *Festal Letter* V for Easter 333, and hence that *Festal Letters* II and III must be redated to reflect this fact. It is a minor matter that opinions still differ on whether the change occurred between 335 and 338 or as early as 333/4.[30]

Lorenz offered a brief 'attempt at an insight into the redaction-history of the collection of festal letters,' in which he stressed the contradictions between the *Festal Index* and the actual contents of the collection of letters which it purports to describe.[31] These contradictions were noted very soon after the publication of the *Festal Index* and *Festal*

Letters: as early as 1853 C. J. Hefele deduced that the *Index* 'originally belonged to another collection of the *Festal Letters* now lost, but was combined with and set at the
head of the surviving collection by a later copyist,'[32] and the relevant sentence is repeated
virtually word for word in his classic history of church councils.[33] In 1892 Archibald
Robertson accepted Hefele's inference and asserted that 'some phenomena might suggest that the *Index* was originally prefixed to another collection of the letters' (one
which lacked *Letters* XIII and XIV), and he deduced from the subscription to *Letter* VII
(which states: 'there is no eighth or ninth [letter], for he did not send them') that 'the
present collection of letters has undergone a recension since its union with the index.'[34] It
is only quite recently, however, that the full significance of the contradictions has been
appreciated. In 1961 V. Peri noted that the *Index* for 340 relates to the notification of
the date of Easter 346: in 345 Athanasius declared that the next Easter should be celebrated on 30 March, not 23 March (*Festal Letter* XVIII), but the *Index* states that it
was in 340 that 'the Arians proclaimed [Easter] on 27 Phamenoth [= 23 March], and
were much ridiculed on account of this error' until they changed the date to 4
Pharmouthi [= 30 March] and in the event celebrated Easter on the same date as the
catholics (*Index* 12).[35]

Camplani has now made the contradictions the cornerstone of a bold and original reconstruction of the process of collecting and editing and of the subsequent transmission of the *Festal Letters,* which appears to explain all the phenomena, especially the
discrepancies.[36] He argues that the Syriac corpus reflects a fusion of two originally separate editions of the *Festal Letters,* and he reconstructs the history of the two original collections as follows:

In Athanasius' lifetime

(1) his *Festal Letters* and brief notifications of the date of Easter were preserved in Alexandria with the exception of certain letters sent from exile;
(2) elsewhere, perhaps at Thmuis, were kept and collected the two notifications (XVII
and XVIII) and various letters, including some sent from exile and the *Letter to
Serapion.*

After Athanasius' death

(1) the letters preserved in Alexandria were collected and put in sequence with the trans-
position of the notifications for the Easters of 340 (now lost) and 346 (*Festal Letter*
XVIII);
(2) the letters preserved elsewhere were also collected and put into sequence with some
transpositions (III and XIV, II and XXIV), and this collection began to circulate in
Egypt.

About 400

(1) the *Index* was added to the Alexandrian collection;
(2) headings were added to each of the letters in the other collection.

In the second half of the fifth century

(1) Timothy Aelurus quoted from a copy of the collection available to him in Alexandria;
(2) the other collection was translated into Coptic but without the heading to each letter;

(3) someone prefixed the Alexandrian *Index* to the other collection.

On this hypothesis, the numbering of the *Festal Letters* in the Syriac corpus derives from an editor outside Alexandria, so that Timothy Aelurus, the bishop of Alexandria, could quote letters with correct numbers and dates, whereas Severus of Antioch and Cosmas Indicopleustes repeated incorrect ones from the non-Alexandrian collection. The Syriac corpus of which the first half survives is translated from an edition which combined the Alexandrian *Index* with the other collection of letters—a collection significantly different from the one for which it was originally composed.

In the present context, it is not necessary to decide on the correct date of every *Festal Letter* of which the whole text or significant fragments survive. It will suffice to tabulate, separately for the brief notifications of the date of the next Easter which survive and the *Festal Letters* proper, the following information:[37]

(1) the number of the *Letter* in the corpus (numbers are omitted for letters which are totally lost),
(2) the Easter to which the late fourth-century editor or editors assigned it,
(3) the other years between 329 and 373 when the celebration of Easter in Alexandria fell on the same day,[38]
(4) either the correct date of the *Letter* where this appears to be certain or the alternative dates adopted by Schwartz, Lorenz, and Camplani where they disagree.

	TRANSMITTED DATE	ALTERNATIVE DATES	CORRECT DATE(S)
(A) 'Notificazioni festali'			
XVII	345	334, 356	345
XVIII	346	335, 340	346
(B) Festal Letters			
I	329	none	329
II	330	341, 352	352
III	331	342, 353	342
IV	332	none	332
V	333	339, 344	333
VI	334	345, 356	356 Schwartz
			345 Lorenz
			334 Camplani
VII	335	340, 346	340 Schwartz
			346 Lorenz
			335 Camplani
X	338	349	338
XI	339	333, 344	339
XIII	341	330, 352	341

	TRANSMITTED DATE	ALTERNATIVE DATES	CORRECT DATE(S)
XIV	342	331, 353	331
XIX	347	358, 369	347
XX	348	337	348
XXII	350	372	350
XXIV	352	330, 341	330
XXV	353	331, 342	353
XXVI	354	343, 365	354
XXVII	355	366	355
XXVIII	356	334, 345	334 Schwartz
			356 Camplani
XXIX	357	none	357
XXXVIII	366	355	366
XXXIX	367	none	367
XL	368	363	?363
XLI	369	358	369
XLII	370	none	370
XLIII	371	none	371
XLIV	372	350	372
XLV	373	351, 362	373

It remains to add brief notes on individual letters where specific arguments supplement the general considerations already applied.

III speaks of 'the fast of forty [days]' (6). Easter fell on 16 Pharmouthi = 11 April in 342 and 353 as well as in 330. But the historical allusions in the text fit 342 far better than 353: Athanasius not only writes of affliction (5), but also as one absent from Alexandria (1). Schwartz accordingly (and rightly) deduced that 'the year 352 is excluded.'[39]

IV records that it was sent from court by an *officialis* of the praetorian prefect Ablabius (5), and 332 is the only year between 329 and 373 when Easter fell on 7 Pharmouthi = 2 April.

VII speaks of 'the fast of forty [days]' and fixes Easter as 4 Pharmouthi = 30 March (11), on which day it also fell in 340 and 346. Although the letter does not explicitly refer to Athanasius' absence from Alexandria, its references to wicked men intruding into the church of the saints and its contention that heretics and schismatics ought not to celebrate Easter (4) would not be inappropriate to either of the alternative dates.

X and all subsequent letters except XIV prescribe a lenten fast of forty days. X fixes the date of Easter as 30 Phamenoth = 26 March, on which day it also fell in 349. Schwartz argued that Athanasius wrote the letter in Trier shortly after Easter 337 for the following year;[40] A. Robertson, that Athanasius began the letter in Trier and failed to revise the introduction when he completed it in Alexandria after his return.[41] But their arguments collapse once a distinction is drawn between Athanasius' notification of the date of Easter 338 in the late spring or early summer of 337 and his *Festal Letter* proper written in the winter of 337/8. Athanasius in fact wrote the *Festal Letter* not only after his return to Alexandria on 23 November 337, but also after a council of hostile bishops met in Antioch to condemn and depose him.[42]

XI fixes Easter as 20 Pharmouthi = 15 April, on which day it also fell in 344. The transmitted year must be correct, since Athanasius was writing before the party of Eusebius had dislodged him from Alexandria (12).

XIII was written from Rome (1): therefore, in 341, not in 330 or 352, when Easter also fell on 24 Pharmouthi = 19 April.

XVII and XVIII are brief communications to the clergy of Alexandria shortly after one Easter giving notice of the date of the next. Since the three successive Easters in question fell on 20 Pharmouthi = 15 April, 12 Pharmouthi = 7 April, and 4 Pharmouthi = 30 March, while XVIII refers explicitly to the decision of the Council of Serdica concerning the date of Easter, there can be no doubt that the letters were written in 344 and 345 respectively in order to make known the dates at which Easter was to be celebrated in 345 and 346. A recent denial of their authenticity is based on a failure to see that they are 'notificazioni festali,' not *Festal Letters* proper.[43]

XIX explicitly refers to Athanasius' return from exile since the preceding Easter (1), so that it was clearly written for Easter 347, even though Easter also fell on 17 Pharmouthi = 12 April in 358 and 369.

The end of XX is lost, but the heading attests its date for Easter as 8 Pharmouthi = 3 April. Although Easter also fell on the same day in 337, the tone of the letter implies Athanasius' presence in Alexandria. It was, therefore, written in 348.

XXVIII, of which both the beginning and end are lost, must be redated from 346 to 334 if VI is to be redated from 334 to 356, as Schwartz proposed.[44]

XL dates Easter to 25 Pharmouthi = 20 April. Easter fell on the same day in 363, when Athanasius was in hiding from the agents of the emperor Julian. The content of the two preserved fragments could suit 363 better than 368.[45]

The substantial Coptic fragments of XLIII are securely identified as such by a brief quotation from the original Greek in Cosmas Indicopleustes. The date of Easter is not preserved: it fell on 22 Pharmouthi in 371, but in no other year between 329 and 373.

The *Letter to Serapion* stands in the Syriac collection of *Festal Letters* between *Letters* XI and XIII with the subscription: 'He wrote this from Rome. There is no twelfth [letter].' Moreover, it explicitly refers to the lengthening of the pre-Easter fast in Egypt from six to forty days:

> I have deemed it highly necessary and very urgent to make known to your modesty . . . that you should proclaim the fast of forty days to the brethren, and persuade them to fast, lest, while all the world is fasting, we who are in Egypt should be derided as the only people who do not fast, but take our pleasure in these days.

The place of the letter in the corpus and the subscription unambiguously imply a date of 339/40. But it is not clear what evidence the editor had for his dating beyond an inference that Athanasius wrote the letter from exile and hence must have written it in Rome for Easter 340. Most recent scholars reject the transmitted date in favor of a slightly earlier one.[46] Following a hint from Duchesne, both Schwartz and Lorenz construed the *Letter to Serapion* as introducing the change in liturgical practise into Egypt, and deduced that Athanasius wrote it in exile in Gaul in the autumn of 336 for Easter 337.[47] But it seems improbable that Athanasius would have tried to introduce such a change in Egypt while he himself was in exile in Gaul: it is surely much more probable *a priori* that he did so on his return, for Easter 338. Moreover, although the *Letter to Serapion* refers to the change, it does not itself read like a document introducing the forty-day fast to a country where it is completely unknown. Peri argued for composition early in 338, noting certain similarities of thought and expression between the *Letter to Serapion* and *Festal Letter* X, which was written for Easter 338, and the fact that its list of new bishops (2) has a close analogue only in the *Festal Letter* for 347 written immediately after Athanasius' second return from exile (XIX.13).[48] On the other hand, Camplani dates the *Letter to Serapion* to the winter of 338/9, supposing that it accompanied or closely followed the copy of *Festal Letter* XI sent to the bishop of Thmuis—which would explain perfectly why it was placed after *Festal Letter* XI in the non-Alexandrian collection of the letters.[49] In either case, whether the letter was written for the lenten season of 338 or 339, it illuminates Athanasius' struggle to retain possession of his see between his first return from exile on 23 November 337 and his second exile in the spring of 339. If the *Letter to Serapion* was indeed written outside Alexandria, as has often been supposed,[50] that would be no argument against dating it to the late winter of 337/8, but confirmation that Athanasius went to the court of Constantius to defend himself very shortly after he had returned to Egypt.[51]

Appendix 2

THE COMPOSITION OF
THE *DEFENSE AGAINST THE ARIANS*

The *Defense against the Arians* has a puzzling structure which calls for explanation:

1–2   Introduction

3–58   Letters on behalf of Athanasius written by the following, with brief connecting remarks:

     3–19   Council of Alexandria (338)

     21–35   Julius, bishop of Rome, to the eastern bishops (341)

     37–50   Council of Serdica (343)

     51   Constantius to Athanasius (three letters of 345/6)

     52–53   Julius to the church of Alexandria (346)

     54–56   Constantius to
                 (1) bishops and priests of the catholic church
                 (2) the church of Alexandria
                 (3) governors in Egypt (all 346)

     57   Council of Jerusalem (346)

     58   Ursacius and Valens to
                 (1) Julius
                 (2) Athanasius (both 347)

59–87   The persecution of Athanasius by Melitians and Arians in the reign of Constantine, quoting many letters and other documents:

     59.6   Constantine to Athanasius (probably early 328)

     60.3   Constantine to Athanasius (331: the letter is omitted in the manuscripts)

     61–62   Constantine to the church of Alexandria (332)

     64   Retraction of Ischyras (shortly after 330)

192

The work thus consists of two main parts, each of which proceeds in chronological order (with only two minor deviations in the second part),[1] yet the second deals with events down to 337, the first with Athanasius' career between 338 and 347.

Why does the work have such a peculiar arrangement? And how and why did Athanasius compose it? R. Seiler distinguished six stages in its evolution:

(1) Athanasius first composed a narrative sketch of his career down to 337, comprising 59.1–5 (Opitz 139.4–140.4), 60.1–3 (140.11–19), 63.1–5 (142.24–143.14), 65.1–4 (144.3–21), 71.1–2 (148.25–149.4), 72.2–6 (151.13–152.7), 82 (161.17–30), 86.1 (164.12–14), 87.1–2 (165.36–166.6), and 88.1 (167.1–4). This sketch certainly existed in 338, since the letter of the Council of Alexandria (3–19) draws on it, but Athanasius had probably already drafted most of it in the autumn of 335 in preparation for his appeal to Constantine in Constantinople.

(2) The Council of Alexandria in 338 had before it both the narrative sketch and almost all the documents quoted in 59–87, but the documents had not yet been integrated into the narrative in their present order. Athanasius combined the separate narrative and documents into a single continuous text virtually identical with the present 59.1–88.1 after Julius made available to him the *hypomnemata* of the commission sent to the Mareotis in 335 (83.4). Julius appears to draw on the second part of the *Defense* in its present form in his letter to the eastern bishops in (21–35). Presumably, therefore, Athanasius composed it for submission to the Council of Rome in 341.

(3) Athanasius composed a third version consisting of 1–50 and 59–88, though without any references to Ursacius and Valens, shortly after the Council of Serdica (probably in 344) for use in persuading Constantius to allow him to return to Alexandria.

(4) A fourth version reflected the *volte face* of Ursacius and Valens in 347 and was composed before they resumed their earlier hostility toward Athanasius in 351: it added 51 and 58 and also references to their change of side in other passages (1.3, 2.2, 20.2, 88.3).

(5) A fifth version added 52–57 some time after 351.

(6) Athanasius added 89–90 in 357 while working on the *History of the Arians,* the content of whose lost first part it largely duplicated. But Athanasius never revised the *Defense* properly for publication either in 357 or later, and it was published in its surviving form after his death in 373.[2]

Seiler's analysis contains much of value and rules out of court H.-G. Opitz's later claim that Athanasius composed the whole of the *Defense against the Arians* in hiding in

357/8 as a unitary work with a single coherent argument.[3] But it suffers from over-subtlety: in particular, the grounds advanced for distinguishing between the third, fourth, and fifth versions seem weak.[4]

Since Seiler's dissertation of 1932 there have been two significant studies of the date and composition of the *Defense against the Arians*. In a brief and trenchant note, A. H. M. Jones drew attention to a passage concerning Rufus, who wrote the *hypomnemata* of the commission sent to the Mareotis in 335: according to the manuscripts,

> the man who wrote them is Rufus, now a *speculator* in the office of the *Augustalis* (ἐν τῇ Αὐγουσταλιανῇ sc. τάξει). (83.4)

Opitz had emended the transmitted reading to 'in the province of Augustamnica' (ἐν τῇ Αὐγουσταμνικῇ) ον the grounds that there was no *praefectus Augustalis* until 382.[5] Jones defended the transmitted reading and showed that the first prefect of Egypt to be styled *praefectus Augustalis* was Eutolmius Tatianus, prefect from 367 to 370 (*Chr. min.* 1.295).[6] The title and rank of the prefect changed when the Egyptian provinces ceased to belong to the diocese of Oriens and formed instead a separate diocese of Aegyptus—an administrative change which occurred between January 370 and 11 February 371 (*CTh* 13.5.14, cf. 12.1.63).[7] The prefect thus added the functions of *vicarius* of the new diocese of Aegyptus to his existing duties as governor of the province of Egypt, and the more grandiose title of *praefectus Augustalis* marked his enhanced status. It follows that the statement that Rufus is 'now a *speculator* in the office of the *Augustalis*' was written no earlier than 370, whether by Athanasius himself or by an Alexandrian editor who published the *Defense* shortly after his death.

T. Orlandi has given an account of the genesis of the *Defense* which somewhat resembles that of Seiler, to whom he oddly does not refer. Orlandi argues that Athanasius prepared some of the material in the second part as early as 335 and that this was incorporated in the Alexandrian letter of 338 (3–19), but that the composition of the *Defense* as it survives began in 346, when Athanasius put together the documents relating to Ischyras and Arsenius (63–81). Thereafter, there was a 'strong development' after 351, with the introduction (1–2) being written c. 352/3, but the 'definitive redaction' or 'definitive form' belongs to 357/8, though the work also received some retouching after 367.[8] Orlandi's analysis, though acutely argued, is largely unconvincing. The 'enemies' of the opening sentence (1.1) cannot be Ursacius and Valens, as Orlandi assumed: on the contrary, as O. Bardenhewer crisply noted long ago, the overall argument of the first part makes sense only during the period between their *volte face* in 347 and the death of Constans in early 350.[9]

The nature of the case probably precludes strict proof. Nevertheless, the following hypothesis, which seeks to include what is valuable in earlier discussions, will explain both why Athanasius wrote the separate parts and why the *Defense against the Arians* has its present peculiar form. The work (it may be presumed) evolved in four stages:

(1) Athanasius prepared a brief account of his episcopal career to date for the Council of Alexandria in 338, with documents appended.
(2) In 341 he combined the narrative sketch and the appended documents into a documented résumé of his career almost identical to the present second part (59.1–88.2) and laid it before the Council of Rome.[10]
(3) Athanasius composed the first part (1–58) and a peroration (probably 88.3 and

90.1, 3) to defend himself at the Council of Antioch which met and deposed him in 349, shortly before the death of Constans (Sozomenus, *HE* 4.8.4),[11] and he included the already existing second part (59.1–88.2) to show that the charges brought against him had always been false (cf. 58.6).

(4) Athanasius subsequently retouched the work, especially at the end, on several different occasions, perhaps separated by many years, adding allusions to events after 353 (89, 90.2), and perhaps still tinkering with the text after 370 (83.4). He never, however, revised the work systematically, gave it the polish appropriate to a finished literary product,[12] or in any sense published it in his lifetime.

This hypothesis greatly enhances the value of the *Defense against the Arians* as historical evidence for the career of Athanasius: once its three main strata have been identified, the single work illuminates the proceedings of no fewer than three councils of bishops—at Alexandria in 338, at Rome in 341, and at Antioch in 349.[13]

A general observation will be apposite. Most of those works of Athanasius which relate to his career (except the *Encyclical Letter*) were not in any real sense 'published' by him: hence he was free to retouch them whenever the fancy took him, and the posthumous editor or editors who put together the collected edition which has survived in mediaeval manuscripts also had the opportunity to alter the text where they deemed it appropriate. Moreover, even some works which were written for wider circulation rather than for ephemeral use at a council of bishops (such as the *Defense of His Flight* and *On the Councils of Ariminum and Seleucia*) show signs of later additions or retouching.[14] Schwartz declared forthrightly that this was the case with most of Athanasius' works from the late 350s.[15] It has been unfortunate for the understanding of Athanasius that Opitz took it upon himself to espouse the diametrically opposed analysis whenever and wherever possible—and that he penned an unduly harsh, dismissive, and influential footnote attacking Seiler's fundamentally accurate assessment of the *Defense against the Arians*.[16]

Appendix 3

THE *DEFENSE BEFORE CONSTANTIUS*

The *Defense before Constantius* presents literary problems very similar to those of the *Defense against the Arians*. Since Athanasius describes events of 356 and 357 (25–35), it seems natural to regard the work as a unitary composition written in the summer of 357 to refute the charges in the imperial order for his arrest.[1] Yet the contents and tone of much of the work are difficult to reconcile with this assumption, and Archibald Robertson argued long ago that 'the main, or apologetic, part' (which he identified as chapters 1–26) was written before the final chapters (27–35): for the former he proposed the date of 356, so that it would be contemporaneous with Athanasius' *Letter to the Bishops of Egypt and Libya*.[2] That hypothesis does not go far enough. More recently, J.-M. Szymusiak analysed the *Defense* as follows:[3]

I. *Original* Defense *(written between mid-353 and mid-355)*

1   Preface

2–21   Refutation of four charges against Athanasius:

      2–5   that he fostered enmity between Constantius and Constans before 350

      6–13   that he corresponded with the usurper Magnentius in 350

      14–18   that he used the Great Church begun by Gregory before it had been dedicated[4]

      19–21   that he disobeyed an imperial summons to come to court in 353

II. *Continuation (added in 357)*

22–25ᵃ   Diogenes' attempt to dislodge Athanasius between August and December 355

25ᵇ–26 Syrianus' attempt to arrest him in February 356

27–31   Persecution in the name of Constantius, especially his attempts to capture Athanasius

32–35   Justification of Athanasius' flight

This analysis has the virtue of giving the original *Defense before Constantius* a real purpose: Athanasius writes as if he were delivering a real speech (3.1/2, 5.1, 8.1, 11.3, 18.6)

196

and as if Constantius would listen and react to the work (16.2: 'you smile and show that this is so by your smile'), and he could have sent the original version to the emperor in 354. Szymusiak grounded his analysis in the claim that the whole of the first part is composed carefully with 'un véritable souffle oratoire,' while the flattering protestations of loyalty and deference in the second part are suffused with biting irony.[5]

Szymusiak was undoubtedly correct to distinguish between the beginning and the end of the *Defense* as different in nature and purpose. But he did not draw the dividing-line between the two parts of the work in exactly the right place. It should be drawn between chapters 18 and 19. Chapter 18 concludes with an invitation to Constantius to visit Alexandria and a prayer for his well-being—both of which are common features of a formal peroration.[6] On grounds of both style and content, chapters 19–21 belong with the continuation, not with the original speech. However, chapter 7 refers to the suicide of Magnentius in August 353,[7] and chapter 13 contains a clear allusion to the exile in 357 of Egyptian bishops who supported Athanasius (cf. 28; *Hist. Ar.* 72.2–5). Hence the hypothesis which best explains the present form of the *Defense* is the following modification of Szymusiak's schema:

(1) Athanasius composed a speech comprising chapters 1–12 and 14–18 for presentation to Constantius before 23 May 353, when Montanus arrived from court to summon him to Italy (*Hist. ac.* 1.8; *Index* 25).

(2) In 357 he revised the existing draft superficially and added a continuation comprising chapters 13 and 19–35, which began in the same general vein and gradually became more hostile toward Constantius. (A document of 353 is missing from the end of chapter 19—possibly because Athanasius wrote the continuation outside Alexandria.) As with the *Defense against the Arians*, however, Athanasius probably never revised this composite work thoroughly for publication.

From this analysis of its genesis, it follows that the original *Defense before Constantius* is probably identical with the communication from Athanasius to the emperor which his envoys who set out from Alexandria on 19 May 353 must have taken with them (*Hist. ac.* 1.7; *Index* 25, cf. Sozomenus, *HE* 4.9.6). The original *Defense*, therefore, was presumably composed in the spring of 353. As for the continuation, Athanasius appears to be writing before he learned of the capitulation of Liberius in the summer of 357.[8]

A prosopographical detail confirms that Athanasius wrote the first part of the *Defense before Constantius* at an earlier date than the subsequent chapters. Chapter 10 describes Athanasius' public protestations of loyalty when envoys from Magnentius passed through Egypt in 350. Among the witnesses of his actions whom Athanasius invokes are the *comes* Asterius and Palladius, who subsequently became *magister palatii*, i.e., *magister officiorum* (10.3). The same pair of names recurs in chapter 22 as the men who brought to Alexandria a letter of Constantius written upon receipt of the news that Constans had been killed in late January or February 350. In this later passage Palladius is described in exactly the same words as before, but his companion, is 'Asterius, who became *dux* of Armenia'—an appointment which he presumably received after Athanasius wrote the earlier passage.[9]

Appendix 4

THE DATE OF

ON THE COUNCIL OF NICAEA

The work which is conventionally known as the *Epistula de decretis Nicaenae synodi* or, more briefly, as *De Decretis* has a far from compendious title in the Greek manuscripts of Athanasius: 'that the Council at Nicaea, having seen the villainy of the Eusebians, properly and piously propounded its decisions against the Arian heresy.' It is not easy to date precisely. In his introduction to the standard English translation of the work, Archibald Robertson contented himself with a date between 351 and the end of 355.[1] On the other hand, H.-G. Opitz, followed by the authors of recent patrological handbooks and surveys, deduced a date of 350/1 from the fact that Athanasius attacks the Arians for their readiness to use violence in the near future (2.2).[2] The argument derives from Schwartz's observation that 'the new persecution which started shortly after the Battle of Mursa (28 September 351) was already threatening.'[3] Recently H. C. Brennecke has proposed a date after 356, perhaps as late as c. 360, on a combination of historical and theological grounds: since Athanasius uses the term *homoousios* and defends the Nicene creed, which (so Brennecke holds) was 'never explicitly attacked' before 357, he can hardly be writing at an earlier date.[4] The inference depends upon a general interpretation of the theological developments of the 350s which is both implausible in itself and explicitly rejected elsewhere in this volume.[5] On the contrary, the text of *On the Council of Nicaea* fails to reflect the theological debates of the late 350s in any precisely identifiable way.[6] Moreover, even though Opitz was over-optimistic in deducing the date of 350/1, Schwartz was certainly correct in holding that the fact that Athanasius writes as if violence were threatening but had not yet been employed excludes a date after he was dispossessed of his see in February 356.

The date of 352/3 postulated in this book is deduced from the following considerations. Athanasius addressed *On the Council of Nicaea* to someone whom he neither names nor expressly describes, but who must surely be another bishop.[7] Athanasius discloses that he had provided a 'broader refutation' of the Arians in an earlier letter to the same addressee (5.7), and that he is writing now because the latter reported to him the question he had posed 'to those advocating (πρεσβεύοντας) the views of Arius, among whom were both some of the associates of Eusebius and very many of the brothers who share the opinions of the church' (1.1). Can the occasion to which Athanasius refers be identified?

The bishop to whom Athanasius was writing had asked him what happened at the Council of Nicaea (2.3). Athanasius had of course attended the council, but he spurned the opportunity to give a detailed account of the events of 325, on which he spends little space. Instead he defends the word *homoousios* and the phrase 'of the essence of the Father' against the charge of being unscriptural, and ridicules his theological adversaries for inconsistency. In 325, he observes, the Eusebians had accepted and subscribed to the terms which they now reject (3.2), and they object to the proper use of unscriptural terms although they themselves use unscriptural terms to advocate impiety (18.4). It is not necessary to see here any allusion to the Sirmian manifesto of 357, which first expressly prohibited the use of unscriptural terms in credal statements.[8] Nor is it necessary to see an allusion to Aetius in Athanasius' attribution to his opponents of the assertion that the Logos is 'a stranger to and in essence unlike the Father' (6.1), since the *Orations against the Arians* had used the self-same phrase long before 350 to characterise the Christology of Arius himself, of Eusebius of Nicomedia, and of Asterius (for example, 'the Logos is alien to and in everything unlike the essence and individuality of the Father' [1.5])[9]—and *On the Council of Nicaea* clearly draws on the earlier work.[10] Hence it has been argued that Athanasius' main theological target was the so-called long creed of 344, and that Aetius later chose to emphasise the term 'unlike' in his teaching precisely because *On the Council of Nicaea* had already attacked it.[11] It is also theoretically possible that Athanasius may have heard reports of Aetius' teaching before Aetius in any sense published them.

Athanasius appears to have written *On the Council of Nicaea* in Alexandria, since he quotes at length (and obviously not from memory) from the *Hypotyposeis* of Theognostus, from Dionysius of Alexandria against Sabellius (25), from Dionysius of Rome against the Sabellians (26), and from Origen's *De Principiis* (27.2/3). It is a reasonable hypothesis that he addressed the work to a prominent western bishop, but one with whom he had yet had no personal dealings. Hence the addressee may be identified without discomfort as Liberius, who is known to have written to Athanasius shortly after his consecration as bishop of Rome in May 352 (*CSEL* 65.155). One detail fits a bishop of Rome particularly well. Athanasius instructs the addressee in respectful terms on how to use the letter:

> You, however, dearly beloved, read it by yourself when you receive it, and if you happen to decide that it is good, read it also to the brothers present on that occasion, so that they too, learning these things, may realise the council's devotion to the truth and its precise intentions, and may condemn the audacity of the Arians who fight Christ and their vain excuses, which they have learned among themselves to invent for the sake of their own impious heresy. (32.5)

If Liberius' name has disappeared from the title of *On the Council of Nicaea*, it could be because in 357 he finally subscribed to the synodical letter of the Council of Sirmium of 351[12]—precisely the document which *On the Council of Nicaea* asked him to reject.

Appendix 5

NARRATIVE AND

CHRONOLOGY IN SOCRATES

Socrates begins the second book of his *Ecclesiastical History* by stating that he has re-written the first two books avoiding the chronological errors of Rufinus which he had earlier repeated (such as putting the Council of Tyre after the death of Constantine [cf. Rufinus, *HE* 10.17] and omitting Athanasius' exile in Gaul in 335–337). Socrates explains that he became aware of Rufinus' errors when he came across treatises by Athanasius and contemporary letters: hence the rewritten first two books, with their copious quotations instead of the bare narrative of the first edition (*HE* 2.1.1–5). The following brief analysis of the second book of the *Ecclesiastical History* notes the correct dates where they are known in order to show how unsatisfactory Socrates' account remains as a sequential narrative, despite the vast amount of excellent information it contains on particular individuals and episodes.[1]

2	After the death of Constantine, which Socrates correctly dates to 22 May 337 (1.40.3), the Eusebians cause disorder in the church by attempting to reintroduce Arianism.
3.1–4	Letter of Constantinus to the Christians of Alexandria (17 June 337, quoted from Athanasius, *Apol. c. Ar.* 87.1–4).
3.5–7	Athanasius returns to Alexandria (23 November 337), and plots are made against him. Socrates alludes to Athanasius' condemnation by a Council of Antioch and to his expulsion from his see (spring 339).
4	Acacius becomes bishop of Caesarea in place of Eusebius (who died in late May 339).
5	Constantinus dies (Socrates gives the correct consular date of 340).
6	Alexander of Constantinople dies and Paul is elected as his successor (late summer 337).
7	Paul is deposed, and Eusebius of Nicomedia replaces him (early autumn 337).

8	The 'Dedication Council' meets at Antioch in the consular year 341, which by inclusive counting Socrates reckons as the fifth year after the death of Constantine (5). Socrates has apparently conflated the council of January 341 (1–5) with the council of 338/9 which deposed Athanasius (6–7).
9	The career of Eusebius of Emesa summarised from the life by George of Laodicea, including his refusal to be named as Athanasius' successor in Alexandria (6–7).
10.1–20	The Council of Antioch appoints Gregory bishop of Alexandria (1) and issues credal documents (4–8 from Athanasius, *Syn.* 22.3–7; 10–18 from *Syn.* 23.2–10), which Gregory subscribes before going to Alexandria (19). Socrates continues to conflate the councils of 338/9 and 341 (cf. Athanasius, *Syn.* 22.2).
10.21–22	Roman territory is invaded by the Franci (21) and great earthquakes occur in the East, with Antioch shaken for a whole year (22). The Frankish invasion and the earthquake are dated to the fourth year of Constantius (340/1) by Jerome, *Chronicle* 235^{b,c} Helm, and to the consular year 341 in *Chr. min.* 1.236.
11	Gregory enters Alexandria, and Athanasius flees to Rome. The narrative partially conflates the entry of Gregory in March 339 with the attempted arrest of Athanasius in February 356: although the burning of the Church of Dionysius occurred in 339 (6), the *dux* Syrianus and his five thousand soldiers belong to 356 (1, cf. Athanasius, *Fug.* 24.3; *Hist. Ar.* 81.6). Moreover, the chapter ends with an apparent reference to the Roman council of summer 341 (7).
12–13	After Eusebius of Nicomedia dies, Paul returns to Constantinople, the Arians elect Macedonius, Hermogenes is killed when he tries to expel Paul, and finally Constantius comes from Antioch to do so. All these events belong to the winter of 341/2: Socrates gives the consular date of 342 for both the murder of Hermogenes and Constans' defeat of the Franci (13.4, cf. *Chr. min.* 1.236).
14	The Arians replace Gregory with George of Cappadocia. This chapter reveals a hopeless muddle: Gregory died in Alexandria on 26 June 345, well before George was first named bishop of the city in 349 (Sozomenus, *HE* 4.8.4).
15	Athanasius, Paul of Constantinople, Asclepas of Gaza, Marcellus of Ancyra, and Lucius of Adrianople, all in Rome, approach Julius; armed with letters from Julius, they reoccupy their sees (3), despite opposition from the supporters of George when Athanasius entered Alexandria (6). This return is sheer fantasy, but may ultimately be based on a confused recollection of the attempts of Lucius and Paul to resume their sees after the Council of Serdica.
16	The praetorian prefect Philippus expels Paul from Constantinople and restores Macedonius as bishop (late 344).

17.1–11	Athanasius goes to Rome, and Julius writes to the bishops who had met at Antioch. The charge of embezzlement (2) was made against Athanasius in 337/8. Socrates refers to the letter of the Egyptian bishops in early 338 (6, cf. Athanasius, *Apol. c. Ar.* 3–19), to the letter of a council of Antioch which appears to be the 'Dedication Council' (5, 10, cf. 15.4–5), and to Julius' long letter of 341 (7–9, cf. *Apol. c. Ar.* 21–35).
17.12	'Shortly afterward' Paul of Constantinople goes from Thessalonica to Italy (early winter 344/5).
18.1–6	The bishops Narcissus, Theodorus, Maris, and Marcus present a creed to Constans (3–6, from Athanasius, *Syn.* 25.2–5). The context in Athanasius indicates that this embassy occurred in 342.
18.7	The heresy of Photinus.
19	The 'long creed,' quoted from Athanasius, *Syn.* 26 (344).
20	The Council of Serdica (343), which Socrates misdates to the consular year 347 (4). Socrates states that there was a delay of eighteen months between the summoning and the meeting of the council (6): that might derive from Julius' letter of 341 (*Apol. c. Ar.* 29.2), which in fact refers to Athanasius waiting in Rome in 339/40.
21	Digression in defense of Eusebius of Caesarea against the charge of being an Arian.
22	Constans threatens to restore Athanasius and Paul by force. The letter from which Socrates quotes (5) belongs to early 345.
23	Constantius allows the restoration of Athanasius and the other exiled bishops. Socrates quotes seven letters from Athanasius (*Apol. c. Ar.* 51–56). Athanasius entered Alexandria on 21 October 346 (*Hist. ac.* 1.2; *Index* 18).
24	Athanasius returns to Alexandria via Jerusalem, and Ursacius and Valens enter into communion with him.
25	Rapid survey of political history from May 337 to June 350.
26	After the death of Constans in the consular year 350 (1), attacks on Athanasius resume; Paul is deposed and killed; Marcellus is expelled; Lucius dies in prison; and Athanasius flees to avoid being killed on Constantius' orders. Socrates again conflates events of different dates: the death of Lucius of Adrianople (6) belongs to the period immediately after the Council of Serdica, but the complaints about Athanasius' flight are those which he answered in 357 (9, cf. *Fug.* 1). The expulsion of Marcellus (6) is unhistorical, since he was not allowed to return to Ancyra in the 340s at all.
27	Macedonius becomes bishop of Constantinople in place of Paul (probably in 349).
28.1–15	The conduct of George in Alexandria, from Athanasius, *Fug.* 6.1–7.5 (describing events of 356).
28.16–20	Vetranio abdicates (25 December 350).

28.21	Constantius proclaims Gallus Caesar (15 March 351) and sends him to Syria.
28.22	As Gallus reaches Antioch, a cross appears in the sky (7 May 351). 28.23 Constantius sends his generals against Magnentius (summer 351).
29–30	A council at Sirmium deposes Photinus in the consular year 351. Socrates quotes from Athanasius both the creed of the Council of Sirmium (30.5–30, from *Syn.* 27.2–3) and the 'blasphemy' of 357 (30.31–41, from *Syn.* 28.2–12) without realising that the latter does not belong in 351. He also puts after the council the preliminary interrogation of Photinus by Basil of Ancyra, which occurred before it (30.43–45, cf. Epiphanius, *Pan.* 71.1.4–6).
31.1–4	Ossius of Corduba is forced to subscribe to the decisions of the Council of Sirmium (he submitted only in 357).
31.5	Constantius remains in Sirmium awaiting the outcome of the campaign against Magnentius.
32.1–10	Defeat and death of Magnentius, which Socrates dates c. 15 August 353 (8). The Battle of Mursa, which Socrates transfers from Pannonia to Gaul (2), occurred on 28 September 351.
32.11	Usurpation of Silvanus (355).
33	Gallus suppresses a Jewish rebellion (352).
34.1–5	Misdeeds and execution of Gallus in the consular year 354.
34.5	Julian is proclaimed Caesar (6 November 355).
34.6	Constantius visits Rome (357).
34.7–8	Julius dies, and Liberius becomes bishop of Rome (352).
35	The career of Aetius.
36	The Council of Milan (355).
37	The Council of Ariminum in 359 (cf. 39.5–7). Socrates prefaces his account of the council with a digression on how Eudoxius of Germanicia became bishop of Antioch (6–11). Although Socrates, by dating the death of Leontius 'about this time,' implicitly puts Eudoxius' election too in 359, his statement that Eudoxius was in Rome with Constantius when he received news of Leontius' death indicates that the correct date is 357. In his account of the council, Socrates quotes from Athanasius the 'dated creed' of 22 May 359 (18–24, from *Syn.* 8.3–7); a long passage of Athanasius himself (31–49, from *Syn.* 3.1–4.4); the letter of the Council of Ariminum to Constantius (54–74, from *Syn.* 10.1–12); and the emperor's reply to the council (78–87, from *Syn.* 55.2–7). He then narrates the exile of Liberius (355–357) as if it were a consequence of Liberius' refusal to accept the creed presented at Ariminum (90–94), and he concludes the long chapter with the creed of Nike (95–97: 10 October 359).
38.1	Introductory: earlier events in the East.

38.2	Acacius and Patrophilus install Cyril as bishop of Jerusalem (probably 348 or 349).[2]
38.3–42	Activities of Macedonius in Constantinople, especially his persecution of Novatianists, with details supplied by Auxanon (10).
39–40	The Council of Seleucia. Socrates records that it convened on 27 September 359 (39.7, cf. 5) and quotes a document presented by Acacius (40.8–17, cf. Epiphanius, *Pan.* 73.25).
41–42	The Council of Constantinople (January 360: 41.8–16 quote Athanasius, *Syn.* 30.2–10).
43.1–7[a]	Eustathius of Sebasteia. Socrates summarises the canons of the Council of Gangra (3–6), which he expressly dates after the Council of Constantinople: Sozomenus, *HE* 4.24.5, puts Gangra before Constantinople, correctly so it seems.[3]
43.7[b]–16	Eudoxius becomes bishop of Constantinople. Socrates records the consecration of the great church of Hagia Sophia on 15 February 360 (11).
44	Meletius becomes bishop of Antioch, but is soon replaced by Euzoius (5). Socrates refers to Constantius' journey to Antioch for the Persian war early in 360 (7).
45.1–8	The deposed Macedonius founds a sect.
45.9–17	Council of Antioch meets in the consular year 361 (10).
46	The two Apollinarii of Laodicea in Syria.
47	Constantius dies on 3 November 361.

Appendix 6

SOCRATES, SOZOMENUS, AND SABINUS

Socrates begins his *Ecclesiastical History* with the accession of Constantine in 306 (*HE* 1.2.1, 40.3), and he concludes it with the seventeenth consulate of Theodosius in 439 (*HE* 7.48.8): it seems highly probable that he completed the work in the latter year.[1]

Socrates was born in Constantinople shortly before 380 (*HE* 5.24.9, cf. 5.16.9), and he drew much oral information from the aged Novatianist priest Auxanon, who in his youth had attended the Council of Nicaea in 325 (*HE* 1.13.2, cf. 10.5).[2] Hence no doubt his full and excellent accounts of episodes in the career of Paul of Constantinople.[3] The classic treatment of F. Geppert identified Socrates' main written sources as (1) Rufinus' *Ecclesiastical History*, Eusebius' *Life of Constantine*, and Athanasius (all extant); (2) a brief chronicle compiled in Constantinople and lists of bishops, which together provided the chronological framework; and (3) two collections of documents which have not survived—the *Synodicus* of Athanasius and the *Synagoge* of Sabinus. Geppert also argued that Socrates used no fewer than fourteen subsidiary sources, of which four come into the reckoning for his account of the reign of Constantius—the lives of Eusebius of Caesarea by Acacius (*HE* 2.4) and of Eusebius of Emesa by George of Laodicea (*HE* 1.24.3; 2.9.1), Eutropius' *Breviarium*, and a lost series of brief imperial biographies also used in the *Origo Constantini Imperatoris* and much later by Zonaras.[4]

Geppert's analysis retains its general validity even after nearly a century, but some of his identifications of specific sources are mistaken. In particular, the history which Socrates ascribes to Rufinus (*HE* 2.1.1) was probably the lost Greek *Ecclesiastical History* of Gelasius of Caesarea, supplemented by a Greek translation of what Rufinus added to his Greek exemplar in his Latin adaptation and continuation of Gelasius down to 395.[5] The *Synodicus* of Athanasius probably never existed: it is mentioned only in a sentence of Socrates' *Ecclesiastical History* which appears to be an interpolation (*HE* 1.13.12), and everything which Socrates (and Sozomenus) were supposed to have taken from it may be derived instead from Sabinus' *Synagoge*, which, though lost, is well attested.[6] Moreover, there is no need to posit yet another 'Sammlung von Kaiserbiographien . . . deren Original für uns völlig verloren ist' in order to explain the similarities of the *Origo*, Socrates, and Zonaras: they are sporadic and mainly factual, and they do not show a consistent parallelism of phraseology.[7]

Sozomenus composed his *Ecclesiastical History* some years after Socrates. Sozomenus' preface refers to a recent journey of the emperor Theodosius across Bithynia to Heraclea Pontica in the heat of summer (*HE* pr. 13): this visit has usually been dated to 443, and the inference has usually been drawn that Sozomenus was writing in or shortly after that year.[8] Both premise and conclusion are vulnerable. C. Roueché has shown that Theodosius' visit to Heraclea Pontica need not belong to 443,[9] and Alan Cameron has noted that Sozomenus' praise of Pulcheria, particularly his statement that 'we shall find that she especially is responsible for the fact that new heresies are not victorious in our own day' (*HE* 9.1.9), implies that the last book at least was written in 450 after Pulcheria's return to power and favor in the last months of Theodosius' life.[10]

Sozomenus was a native of Bethelea near Gaza (*HE* 5.15.14), who settled in Constantinople apparently after 425 (cf. *HE* 8.27.7). A lawyer like Socrates (*HE* 2.3.10), he decided to outdo his predecessor by composing a more literary *Ecclesiastical History* covering the period from the third consulate of the Caesars Crispus and Constantinus in 324 to the seventeenth consulate of Theodosius in 439 (*HE* pr. 19). Socrates had deliberately renounced rhetorical ornament in order to write in a plain and unadorned style, which he held to be appropriate for a Christian historian (*HE* 1.1.3; 3.1.4; 6 pr.). Sozomenus employed Socrates as his main source and rewrote him in a more elevated style, more in keeping with the traditions of serious pagan historiography.[11] But, in addition to these systematic stylistic changes, Sozomenus often supplemented Socrates: he drew, for example, on his legal experience for an account of the legislation of Constantine which ranges beyond the laws included in the Theodosian Code (*HE* 1.8.13, 9.3).[12] Sozomenus sometimes also mined more fully the self-same authors whom Socrates followed or quoted (Gelasius/Rufinus, Eusebius' *Life of Constantine*, and Athanasius). But some of the most valuable sections of Sozomenus' *Ecclesiastical History* are entirely independent of Socrates and Socrates' sources: for example, Sozomenus drew on Persian *acta martyrum* for an account of the persecution of Shapur (*HE* 2.9–14); he provides two long excursuses on monks and holy men (*HE* 3.14–16; 6.28–34, with many similarities to Palladius' *Lausiac History* and the *Historia Monachorum in Aegypto*); and he used the lost history of Olympiodorus for the political narrative of events down to 425 which forms the structure of his unfinished ninth book.[13] Several passages also show knowledge of the violently anti-Christian history of Eunapius of Sardis.[14]

For the reign of Constantius, an important source for both Socrates and Sozomenus was the *Synagoge* of Sabinus of Heraclea. Unfortunately, Sozomenus never names Sabinus—or any of his principal sources.[15] Socrates, however, names Sabinus in some ten passages (*HE* 1.8.24–26; 1.9.28; 2.15.8–11; 2.17.10–11; 2.20.5; 2.39.8; 3.10.11; 3.25.18; 4.12.41; 4.22.1), which make it clear that Sabinus not only quoted (or omitted) conciliar documents, but also provided commentary. It is sometimes difficult, therefore, to tell whether Sozomenus' report of a document depends on the document itself as quoted by Sabinus or on Sabinus' digest of something which he did not quote.[16] P. Batiffol demonstrated Sozomenus' constant recourse to Sabinus:[17] the subsequent monograph by G. Schoo on the sources of Sozomenus unfortunately did not attempt to distinguish consistently between the passages where Sozomenus quotes or reports the contents of a document which he found in Sabinus and those where he merely reproduces Sabinus' narrative or his commentary on a document which he did not quote.[18]

For the most part, the narrative framework of Books Three and Four of Sozomenus' *Ecclesiastical History* faithfully follows Socrates and reproduces most of his grosser factual and chronological errors. Yet Sozomenus' account of the reign of Constantius has great intrinsic value because he has often supplemented Socrates. The following are some of the most important passages relating to ecclesiastical politics of the period 337–361 where Sozomenus demonstrates his independence of Socrates, usually by showing knowledge of documents not quoted by him or by supplying authentic details not found in his main source:[19]

Book Three

5.1–6.7   The 'Dedication Council.'[20] Sozomenus follows Socrates closely (*HE* 2.8.1–5), but adds three details: a claim that the creed was Lucian's; the names of eight bishops prominent at the council; and a note that Eusebius of Emesa voted with the rest. Sozomenus has presumably used Sabinus, who included the council's letter to Julius (Socrates, *HE* 2.17.10).

8.3   Brief summary of a letter sent by Julius of Rome to the eastern bishops: apparently not the letter of 341 quoted by Athanasius (*Apol. c. Ar.* 21–35), but an earlier one to which Athanasius refers, probably written in 339 (*Apol. c. Ar.* 20.1).

8.4–8   Summary of the letter of the 'Dedication Council' to Julius of Rome. Sozomenus clearly believed that this letter was written by a later council.

11.4–12.7   The Council of Serdica. Sozomenus shows detailed knowledge of three documents not quoted by Socrates: the synodical letters of both the eastern and the western bishops (*CSEL* 65. 48–67; 103–126: the latter also known from Athanasius, *Apol. c. Ar.* 42–47), and the letter of Ossius and Protogenes to Julius (*EOMIA* 1.644). He had probably already used the first of these documents to supply the charge on which Asclepas of Gaza had been deposed (8.1, cf. *CSEL* 65.55).

20.4,7–9   Leontius as bishop of Antioch (cf. Theodoretus, *HE* 1.22.1; 2.24.3).

22   Letter of the Council of Jerusalem, 346 (quoted from Athanasius, *Apol. c. Ar.* 57.2–6).

23–24   Letters of Ursacius and Valens to Julius and Athanasius (quoted from *Apol. c. Ar.* 58).

Book Four

3   Sozomenus shows knowledge of the *Passion of the Holy Notaries* (*BHG*³ 1028y). Although the *Passion* names Philippus as the prefect who executed Martyrius and Marcianus, Sozomenus leaves him anonymous.

5   Account of the cross which appeared over Jerusalem on 7 May 351, based on Cyril of Jerusalem's letter to Constantius (*BHG*³ 413 = *CPG* 3587).

6.2   The theological views of Photinus.

6.12   Excerpt from the 'dated creed': apparently not from Socrates, since the text of Sozomenus agrees with the corresponding section of the creed of Nike as quoted by Theodoretus (*HE* 2.21.3–7) against Socrates (*HE* 2.37.23–24) and Athanasius (*Syn.* 8.7). Like Socrates, Sozomenus misdates the creed to 351 (6.6), but he presumably took his brief quotation from Sabinus, whereas Socrates reproduces the whole document from Athanasius.

8.4   Report of the Council of Antioch which deposed Athanasius shortly before 350. Though not explicitly attested elsewhere, this council should be accepted as historical.[21]

9.6–9   Athanasius sends envoys to the court of Constantius in 353. Sozomenus' source is the original of the *Historia acephala* (1.7).

10.8–11   George in Alexandria (cf. *Hist. ac.* 2.2–6).[22]

11.4–10   Report of the interview between Constantius and Liberius after his arrest in 355: Sozomenus appears to be summarising the document quoted by Theodoretus (*HE* 2.16).

12.4–7   Report of the letter of a council held at Antioch by the newly elected Eudoxius to Ursacius, Valens, and Germinius (winter 357/8).

13.2–3   Letter of George of Laodicea (early 358).

14   Letter of Constantius to the church of Antioch (late 357).

16.14–20   Report of correspondence between Constantius and Basil of Ancyra.

17.1   Report of Constantius' letter to the Councils of Ariminum and Seleucia.

22   The Council of Seleucia. Sozomenus closely follows Socrates, but he adds some details omitted by him, such as the speech of Eleusius (22). Sozomenus refers to the *hypomnemata* of the council as if he had consulted them himself (28).

23   Negotiations at court after the Councils of Ariminum and Seleucia.

24–25   Report of the decisions of the Council of Constantinople which deposed Macedonius, Eleusius, and others. Sozomenus' report is considerably fuller than the parallel report in Socrates (*HE* 2.42–43.6).

28   Meletius as bishop of Antioch. Sozomenus again gives a much fuller account than Socrates (cf. Theodoretus, *HE* 2.31).

For most of the documents whose source is not extant, consultation of Sabinus is the most probable explanation of Sozomenus' knowledge.[23] However, it is sometimes not at all easy, especially in his narrative of events preceding the Councils of Ariminum and Seleucia, to be certain whether Sozomenus is paraphrasing a document (either at first or second-hand) or supplementing his sources by ratiocination and imaginative reconstruction.[24]

Appendix 7

DOCUMENTS IN THEODORETUS

Theodoretus wrote his *Ecclesiastical History* in the late 440s.[1] He thus wrote after Socrates, whose work he appears to have known and occasionally used,[2] but before Sozomenus, who was still working on his *Ecclesiastical History* in 450.[3] Theodoretus has a low reputation as a historian and has been denounced as 'without question by far the least significant in the series of Greek ecclesiastical historians.'[4] That is a mistaken estimate—of Theodoretus as a literary artist no less than of his value as a source of information. Theodoretus' interests were primarily dogmatic rather than historical, and he transformed the raw materials of his *Ecclesiastical History* to suit his own purposes more thoroughly than either Socrates or Sozomenus.[5]

Theodoretus consciously set out to supplement Gelasius and Socrates (*HE* 1.1.2), and some significant documents and other writings which he quotes or paraphrases have not survived independently.[6] He appears to have taken pains to differ from his predecessors as far as possible. For example, he completely omits Socrates' detailed and colorful accounts of how Paul of Constantinople was expelled from the imperial capital:[7] instead, he begins by alleging that popular support made it impossible to summon Paul to Serdica, then passes to his deposition, deportation to Cucusus, and death, illustrated by a brief quotation from Athanasius (*HE* 2.5, cf. *Fug.* 3.6).[8]

It is chronologically possible for Theodoretus to have read or consulted the *Ecclesiastical History* of Philostorgius, and it has been argued that he used it.[9] However, the fragmentary preservation of Philostorgius makes derivation difficult to prove, especially since it seems clear that Theodoretus drew directly on an important source of Philostorgius not used by Socrates—the lost ecclesiastical history written in the later 360s, whose unknown author has traditionally been styled 'the anonymous Arian historian,' but whose viewpoint was distinctively homoean.[10]

Theodoretus' individuality as a historian of the Christian church in the fourth century reveals itself in features such as his obvious and frequent interest in Antioch: for example, he preserves a long and extremely valuable quotation from Eustathius on the Council of Nicaea (*HE* 1.8.1–4 = Eustathius, frag. 32 Spanneut)[11] and a fuller account of the maltreatment of Christians in Antioch under Julian than can be found in other narrative sources (*HE* 3.10–19, cf. 22: an episode at Beroea not independently recorded). Adducing quotations in later Greek writers, L. Parmentier demonstrated that Theodoretus took much of his information about Antioch and the career of Eunomius from Theodore of Mopsuestia's lost work against Eunomius.[12]

The following passages of Book Two, which covers the reign of Constantius, either preserve information relevant to ecclesiastical politics which has no analogue in Rufinus and Socrates or which diverges from these earlier accounts of the same events:[13]

1.1	The length of Athanasius' sojourn in Trier (two years and three months).
7.1–8.52	The Council of Serdica, from 'ancient accounts.' Theodoretus and the version preserved in Cod. Ver. LX (58), fols. 81ʳ–88ʳ, alone preserve the credal statement omitted from the versions of the letter of the western bishops quoted by Athanasius (*Apol. c. Ar.* 44–49) and Hilary (*CSEL* 65.103–128).
8.54–10.2	The embassy of bishops escorted by Flavius Salia, the plot of Stephanus of Antioch, and his consequent disgrace and deposition. Theodoretus' account, which is much fuller than that given by Athanasius (*Hist. Ar.* 20), appears to reflect local knowledge or traditions.
14.13	Brief extract from a lost work of Athanasius consoling virgins who had suffered violence in Alexandria in 357 (*CPG* 2162).
16	'Dialogue of the emperor Constantius and Liberius, bishop of Rome' (1–27), and his exile (28/9). Sozomenus (*HE* 4.11.3–10) summarises this dialogue, which also survives in Syriac (Vatican Library, Syr. 145, fols. 65ᵛ–67ʳ). Theodoretus' account of Liberius' exile may also owe something to Athanasius (*Hist. Ar.* 35–40).
17	Liberius' return to Rome.
19–21	Letters of the Council of Ariminum to Constantius and of Constantius to the council, and the creed of Nike. The three documents quoted all stand in Athanasius (*Syn.* 10, 55, 30) and Socrates (*HE* 2.37–54–87, 41.8–16), who quotes them from Athanasius. But Theodoretus' text often diverges in linguistic details: it derives, therefore, from an independent Greek translation of the lost Latin originals (possibly by way of Sabinus).
23	Quotation of Athanasius, *Ep. ad Afros* 3–4.[14]
24–26.3	Leontius and Eudoxius as bishops of Antioch (24.2 quotes Athanasius, *Fug.* 26.3).
26.4–11	Council of Seleucia.[15]
27–28	Council of Constantinople, with quotation of its letter to George of Alexandria, presumably taken from Sabinus.
29	The career of Eunomius, mainly repeated from Theodoretus' earlier work *Haereticarum Fabularum Compendium* (4.3 [PG 83.417–422]).
30	The siege of Nisibis by the Persian king Shapur, largely quoted from Theodoretus' *Historia Religiosa* (1 [PG 82.1304/5]).

It is symptomatic of the narrative confusion which prevails in Theodoretus' account of the reign of Constantius, no less than in that of Socrates,[16] that he places Shapur's third siege of Nisibis at the end of the reign of Constantius after the Council of Constantinople, thus implying a date of 360 or 361 for an event which occurred a decade earlier.

Appendix 8

PAUL OF CONSTANTINOPLE

The career of Paul, who was bishop of Constantinople in the first half of the reign of Constantius, has often been discussed.[1] But the existing reconstructions of his career do not do full justice to the primary evidence, in particular to the account of Paul's career given by Athanasius in his *History of the Arians* (*Hist. Ar.* 7.1–6), and most of them base important deductions on the assumption that the Council of Serdica met in 342 rather than 343.[2] On the other hand, Athanasius' account of the career of Paul turns out to be far from straightforward when it is confronted with the excellent information that Socrates supplies. For the ecclesiastical historian knew much about events in Constantinople in the middle of the fourth century. His explicit chronology is as usual muddled,[3] but he narrates four separate episodes in the career of Paul with a wealth of circumstantial detail which allows each of them to be dated quite precisely from internal criteria.

PAUL'S ELECTION AND FIRST DEPOSITION

Alexander had been bishop of Byzantium and then Constantinople for twenty-three years. When he died, there were two candidates for the vacant see: Paul, who was a priest and comparatively young, and Macedonius, an elderly deacon, the candidate of the Arian party. The election was disputed, and the adherents of Paul ordained him bishop without waiting (as was required) for their choice to be ratified by the bishops of adjacent sees. This occurred while Constantius was absent from the city: when the emperor returned, he summoned a council of bishops which deposed Paul and installed Eusebius of Nicomedia as bishop of Constantinople, and then went to Antioch.

Thus Socrates (*HE* 2.6/7), whose account is rewritten and rhetorically embellished by Sozomenus (*HE* 3.3/4). Socrates puts the election of Paul after the deaths of both Eusebius of Caesarea in May 339 and the emperor Constantinus, and for the latter he correctly states the consular date of 340 (*HE* 2.4/5). The date of 340 or later thus implied for Paul's election is impossible, since the details which Socrates supplies show that Paul's first tenure of the see of Constantinople must belong to the summer and autumn of 337.[4]

Three separate arguments converge. First, Alexander was still alive in July 336, when the Council of Constantinople admitted Arius to communion and was about to compel Alexander to admit him to his church when Arius suddenly died (Athanasius, *De Morte Arii* 2.1/2; *Letter to the Bishops of Egypt and Libya* 19). On the other hand, Eusebius of Nicomedia was already bishop of Constantinople when Eusebius of Caesarea wrote his work *Against Marcellus* after the death of Constantine, presumably in late 337 or early 338 (1.4.20, cf. 2.4.29). Second, the movements of Constantius fit 337 perfectly. Constantius was in Antioch in the spring of 337 when Constantine fell mortally ill; he traveled to Constantinople (which he reached shortly after 22 May), spent some time in the Balkans, and then returned to Antioch for the winter of 337/8.[5] Third, Athanasius was present when Paul was accused prior to his deposition (*Hist. Ar.* 7.1). Now Athanasius was in Trier on 17 June 337 (*Apol. c. Ar.* 87.4–7) and entered Alexandria on 23 November (*Index* 10), after an audience with Constantius at Viminacium (*Apol. ad Const.* 5.2). Hence, if Alexander was still alive in 336, then Athanasius can have been in Constantinople to witness an accusation of Paul only in the late summer or early autumn of 337.[6]

Three facts have often been held to prove that Paul became bishop before 337, or even that he was already bishop in 331/2.[7] First, the presence of Athanasius when Paul was accused (*Hist. Ar.* 7.1); second, Athanasius' statement that Paul was exiled by Constantine (*Hist. Ar.* 7.3); third, Paul's subscription to the deposition of Athanasius at the Council of Tyre in 335.[8] But Athanasius passed through Constantinople as he returned from exile in 337, and the correct reading in the relevant passage is 'by Constantius,' not 'by Constantine.' As for Paul's presence at the Council of Tyre, the explicit evidence says nothing whatever about his rank or status in 335: he presumably attended as the delegate of Alexander while still a priest and subscribed to the conciliar document in this capacity.[9] After all, Alexander was ninety-eight when he died two years later (Socrates, *HE* 2.6.2).

Paul, therefore, replaced Alexander in the summer of 337 (say c. July). But attempts to remove him began immediately after the contested election, and a council deposed him from office in the autumn (say c. September). He was exiled to Pontus (*Hist. Ar.* 7.3), whence he returned when the see fell vacant again through the death of his successor.

PAUL'S RETURN IN 341/2

Eusebius of Nicomedia died late in 341, before he received (or at least before he answered) the letter which Julius had written in the name of the Council of Rome in the summer of that year (Socrates, *HE* 2.12.1: the letter is that quoted in Athanasius, *Apol. c. Ar.* 21–35). The Christians of Constantinople thereupon brought Paul into his church, while the Arians elected Macedonius bishop with the help of the leading Arian bishops. Rioting ensued. When Constantius in Antioch heard the news, he instructed the general Hermogenes to expel Paul. Paul's adherents resisted with force, and when Hermogenes persisted in attempting to use soldiers to remove Paul from his church, a mob burned the house where Hermogenes was staying and lynched him. Constantius himself then came post-haste from Syria to Constantinople to expel Paul, fined the city by reducing the amount of free bread distributed daily from 80,000 to 40,000 *modii*, and returned to Antioch, leaving Macedonius as bishop.

So Socrates, giving a consular date of 342 (*HE* 2.12/3, amplified by Sozomenus, *HE*

3.7). The mission of Hermogenes (styled merely *comes*) and his lynching in the streets of Constantinople are noted in the *Historia acephala* (1.4). Libanius confirms Constantius' hasty visit to Constantinople during the winter (*Orat.* 59.96/7), while Jerome puts the death of Hermogenes in the fifth year of Constantius, which corresponds to 341/2 (*Chronicle* 235ᶠ Helm), and the so-called *Consularia Constantinopolitana* have the entry 'tractus Hermogenes' under the consular year 342 (*Chr. min.* 1.236).[10] Paul, therefore, was expelled from Constantinople in the early months of 342. He betook himself (it seems) directly to the western imperial court at Trier (*CSEL* 65.67.2/3), where Constans was soon persuaded to champion his cause—and that of Athanasius.[11]

PAUL'S EXPULSION BY PHILIPPUS

Although the western bishops at Serdica in 343 refrained from uttering his name, it is clear that Paul was among the exiled bishops whom they reinstated.[12] But Constantius was very slow to restore the bishops deposed from eastern sees who were in exile in the West, and Paul made a premature attempt to return to his see. Socrates again gives a detailed account (*HE* 2.16, repeated and rewritten by Sozomenus, *HE* 3.9), but again he sets an authentic episode in a false context, for not only does he place it before the Council of Serdica rather than after, but he also imagines that Paul had been restored by Julius (Socrates, *HE* 2.15.3). Again, however, there is no cause to doubt Socrates' accuracy about events in Constantinople, and he furnishes details which establish the correct date.

While Constantius was in Antioch (Socrates writes), he heard with displeasure that Paul had resumed possession of his see. Accordingly, he wrote to Philippus, the praetorian prefect, ordering him to expel Paul and restore Macedonius. Philippus, aware of the practical dangers which he might face when he enforced the emperor's command, kept his instructions secret and summoned Paul to him in the baths of Zeuxippus as if to do him honor. But when Paul presented himself, Philippus produced the emperor's order, locked all the entrances to the baths except one, took Paul quickly to the imperial palace, bundled him aboard a ship, and sent him to Thessalonica.

Since 'the bishop patiently endured the condemnation without trial' and was allowed to travel freely in Illyricum, but was expressly forbidden to set foot in the East (Socrates, *HE* 2.16.5/6), Paul was clearly deported from the territory ruled by Constantius and sent to Thessalonica because that was the nearest large port in the territory of Constans. The date cannot be earlier than July 344, since Flavius Domitius Leontius was the praetorian prefect of Constantius until at least 6 July 344 (*CTh* 13.4.3, cf. *ILS* 1234). In fact, the episode probably belongs to the autumn of 344—and hence constitutes the earliest attestation of Flavius Philippus as praetorian prefect.[13] Paul soon left Thessalonica and went to Italy (Socrates, *HE* 2.17.30). Not long thereafter, in the spring of 345, he was with Athanasius at the court of Constans when the emperor wrote to Constantius demanding that he restore the two exiled bishops forthwith (*HE* 2.22.5).[14]

PAUL'S IMPRISONMENT AND DEATH

Athanasius describes the circumstances of Paul's death in some detail (*Hist. Ar.* 7.3–6). After his final deposition, Paul was imprisoned at Cucusus in Cappadocia, where he was starved, then suffocated. The instigator of Paul's death, according to Athanasius, was the prefect Philippus, whom divine justice punished with ignominious dismissal from office and death before a year had passed. Since Philippus was still the praetorian prefect of Constantius in 351 and went to Magnentius as an envoy from Constantius shortly before the Battle of Mursa (Zosimus 2.46–48), his death must have occurred in the late summer of 351. Paul, therefore, was put to death in the autumn of 350. Now Socrates (*HE* 2.26.6, whence Sozomenus, *HE* 4.2.2) dates Paul's exile as well as his death to 350, making it a consequence of the revolt of Magnentius in that year (*HE* 2.26.1). Moreover, the *Historia acephala* (1.3) implies, and the *Passion of the Holy Notaries* (*BHG*³ 1028y)[15] explicitly states, that the main charge on which Paul was deposed was treasonable correspondence with Magnentius. It seems reasonable, therefore, to deduce that Paul was deposed in the summer of 350 and killed almost as soon as he reached Cucusus.[16]

This reconstruction, however, has an insecure foundation. There is no reason to doubt that Magnentius, who wrote to Athanasius in 350 (*Apol. ad Const.* 6–12), also wrote to Paul, and that Constantius' officials thereupon ordered Paul's death in exile. But would our sources have been capable of distinguishing between Paul's death in 350 and a slightly earlier deposition and exile? To do so would require a degree of precision which was probably beyond their abilities. What Athanasius says about Paul's exiles should be construed to imply that he was deposed and exiled before 350 (*Hist. Ar.* 7.3). Since the passage is not only contorted but in need of emendation, it requires presentation with an *apparatus criticus* and the readings argued below to be correct:

καὶ τὸ μὲν πρῶτον εἰς τὸν Πόντον ἐξωρίσθη παρὰ
2   Κωνσταντίου, τὸ δὲ δεύτερον παρὰ Κωνστάντιον δεθεὶς
ἁλύσεσι σιδηραῖς εἰς Σίγγαρα τῆς Μεσοποταμίας ἐξωρίσθη,
4   εἶτα ἐκεῖθεν εἰς τὴν Ἔμισαν μετηνέχθη, καὶ τὸ τέταρτον
εἰς Κούκουσον τῆς Καππαδοκίας περὶ τὰ ἔρημα τοῦ Ταύρου,
6   ἔνθα καί, ὡς οἱ συνόντες ἀπήγγειλαν, ἀποπνιγεὶς παρ᾿αὐτῶν
ἐτελεύτησε.

1 παρὰ REF   ὑπὸ BKPO
2 Κωνσταντίου Migne, per merum errorem ut videtur
    Κωνσταντίνου mss. et ceteri editores
    Κωνστάντιον conieci   Κωνσταντίου mss. et editores omnes

The first clause and its readings should be considered separately from the rest of the sentence. The evidence that Paul's first tenure of the see of Constantinople belongs after the death of Constantine is strong, and it is impossible to suppose Athanasius mistaken about the identity of the emperor who exiled him: therefore, the transmitted reference to Constantine must be emended into a reference to Constantius.[17] The choice between ὑπό (which Opitz prints) and παρά is easy: παρά with the genitive of the agent represents Athanasius' normal usage,[18] while the former is a corruption which substitutes the more common and stylistically more acceptable preposition.

The second and third clauses are extremely slippery. Paul was indeed exiled from Constantinople four times. Yet Athanasius cannot refer to either the second or the third expulsion, since both in 342, after the lynching of Hermogenes, and again in 344, after his deportation by Philippus, Paul went west to the territory of Constans—a fact which Athanasius has carefully suppressed. It follows that the last three places which Athanasius names must all be places to which Paul was sent after his fourth expulsion from Constantinople. But why was he sent to Singara in Mesopotamia, then from there to Emesa before his final banishment to Cucusus? It might seem plausible in itself to claim that he was taken to Singara 'as a convict sent to do forced labor in fortifications on the Persian front.'[19] But, if that were so, why was Paul transferred from Singara to Emesa? The obvious and natural explanation is that after his condemnation by a council of bishops, Paul was sent to the emperor, who happened to be at Singara,[20] and kept with the court as it traveled to Emesa, where the emperor then decided that he should be exiled to Cucusus. Hence the emendation proposed here from 'by Constantius,' which in this context would constitute a lame and pointless repetition, to 'to Constantius.' Athanasius' use of the genitive and then the accusative of the same proper name with the same preposition makes an effective and subtle rhetorical contrast: when he uses παρά followed by an accusative designating a person with a verb of motion, he is normally referring to journeys to the imperial court (*Apol. c. Ar.* 4.5, 21.1, 32.1; *Hist. Ar.* 81.5; *Syn.* 13.7).[21] The process of textual corruption presumably began with a careless change of case from παρὰ Κωνστάντιον to παρὰ Κωνσταντίου: the first occurrence of Constantius' name was then deliberately altered to restore some rhetorical contrast to a passage which had lost its point through the preceding change of case.

Athanasius may also let slip an allusion to the council which deposed Paul between 346 and 350 in the two sentences which precede his description of Paul's exiles (*Hist. Ar.* 7.1/2):

καὶ γὰρ ὁ κατηγορήσας αὐτοῦ Μακεδόνιος ὁ νῦν ἐπίσκοπος ἀντ' αὐτοῦ γενόμενος παρόντων ἡμῶν κατὰ τὴν κατηγορίαν κεκοινώκηκεν αὐτῷ καὶ πρεσβύτερος ἦν ὑπ' αὐτὸν τὸν Παῦλον. καὶ ὅμως, ἐπειδὴ Εὐσέβιος ἐπωφθαλμία θέλων ἁρπάσαι τὴν ἐπισκοπὴν τῆς πόλεως (οὕτω γὰρ καὶ ἀπὸ Βηρύτου εἰς τὴν Νικομήδειαν μετῆλθεν), ἔμεινεν ἡ πρόφασις κατὰ Παύλου, καὶ οὐκ ἠμέλησαν τῆς ἐπιβουλῆς, ἀλλ' ἔμειναν διαβάλλοντες.

When did Macedonius accuse Paul? All scholars who have so far discussed the passage in print assume that Athanasius refers to the occasion when Paul was deposed and replaced by Eusebius of Nicomedia. But Athanasius appears rather to say: 'Macedonius, the one who accused him and who is now the present bishop in his place, when we were present, communicated with him on the occasion of the accusation and was a priest under Paul.' That is to say, Macedonius accepted ordination as a priest from Paul (he was only a deacon when Alexander died) and supported him in 337 when Athanasius was in Constantinople. If this is what Athanasius is really saying, then he refers to two accusations, not one, and since the first belongs to 337, when Paul was condemned despite Macedonius' support, the second must be the occasion when Paul was condemned, then exiled for the last time, on a charge brought by Macedonius.

Can the date of Paul's final deposition be discovered? The year may in fact be indirectly attested. The *Historia acephala* contains an inserted passage relating to the exile of Paul (1.2–6), which makes the following statements:

(1) in the consular year 349 Theodorus, Narcissus, and George came to Constantinople to urge Paul to enter into communion with them;
(2) when he repulsed them, they plotted against him in association with Eusebius of Nicomedia;
(3) by means of a charge relating to his alleged dealings with Constans and Magnentius, they expelled him from Constantinople in order to install an Arian successor;
(4) the populace continued to support Paul and killed the *comes* Hermogenes when he tried to eject Paul's successor;

(5) as a result his enemies were able to exile Paul to Armenia;

(6) Theodorus and his allies wished to make Eudoxius, the bishop of Germanicia, the new bishop of Constantinople.

The passage as a whole is horribly confused and records in apparent chronological order events whose stated or implied dates are, respectively, (1) 349, (2) 337, (3) 350, (4) 342, (5) 349 or 350, and (6) 359/60. But each item which can be checked has some verifiable basis in fact: hence it is legitimate to infer from (1), albeit tentatively, that Theodorus of Heraclea, Narcissus of Neronias, and George, who was still a priest, took the lead in having Paul tried, condemned, and deposed by a council of bishops hostile to him in 349.

Paul was arrested by Philippus. Two passages of Socrates provide the proof. In the first, Socrates states that 'those who took him away strangled him at Cucusus' (*HE* 2.26.6), while the second notes that Theodosius brought his body back to Constantinople from Ancyra and adds that 'Philippus the prefect of the emperors had sent [Paul] into exile because of Macedonius and caused [him] to be strangled at Cucusus in Armenia' (*HE* 5.9.1).

CHRONOLOGICAL SUMMARY OF THE CAREER OF PAUL

If the conclusions argued above are correct, then the career of Paul must be reconstructed as follows:

337   elected bishop of Constantinople c. July, deposed c. September, and exiled to Pontus;

342   attempts to regain his see, is expelled from Constantinople c. February, and goes to Trier;

343   reinstated by the western bishops at the Council of Serdica;

344   attempts to regain his see in the autumn and is deported to Thessalonica;

345   at the court of Constans with Athanasius (spring);

346   allowed to resume possession of his see;

349   deposed again (spring) and taken to the court of Constantius, then sent to Cucusus (late summer or autumn);

350   killed in prison (autumn).

Appendix 9

IMPERIAL RESIDENCES
AND JOURNEYS, 337–361

The three sons of Constantine conferred in Pannonia in the late summer of 337 (Julian, *Orat.* 1, 19a), and it is a reasonable assumption that all three were together when they were jointly proclaimed Augusti on 9 September (*Chr. min.* 1.235). An earlier work plotted the known and probable movements of these three emperors from their proclamation as Caesars (1 March 317, 8 November 324, and 25 December 333 respectively) as far as the autumn of 337.[1] This appendix, which recapitulates, emends, and expands a preliminary study of 'Imperial Chronology, A.D. 337–350,'[2] uses the same format to plot their movements between 9 September 337 and their deaths, which occurred in 340, 361, and 350 respectively, and it extends the treatment to the Caesar Gallus and the emperor Julian down to December 361.[3]

CONSTANTINUS

Principal residence

329–340 Trier

Attested movements

337, c. Sept.	Confers with Constantius and Constans in Pannonia	Julian, *Orat.* 1, 19a, cf. Libanius *Orat.* 59.75 (suppressing the existence of Constantinus)
?338	German campaign	*CIL* 3.12483 = *ILS* 724 + add. (3, p. clxxii) (Troesmis: 337/340)[4]
339, Jan. 8	?At Trier	*CTh* 12.1.27 (to Celsinus, proconsul of Africa)[5]
340, late winter	Invades the territory of Constans and is killed near Aquileia	Jerome, *Chronicle* 235ª; *Chr. min.* 1.236; *Epitome* 41.21; Socrates, *HE* 2.5; Zonaras 13.5[6]

CONSTANTIUS

Principal residences

337–350	Antioch for the winter, with summers on campaign in Mesopotamia (Libanius, *Orat.* 18.206/7)[7]
351–359	Sirmium and Milan
360–361	Antioch

Attested movements

337, ?July	At Viminacium	Athanasius, *Apol. ad Const.* 5.2[8]
?Aug./Sept.	Campaign against the Sarmatae	*CIL* 3.12483[9]
c. Sept.	Confers with Constantinus and Constans in Pannonia	Julian, *Orat.* 1, 19a, cf. Libanius, *Orat.* 59.75[10]
?Sept.	Returns to Constantinople	Socrates, *HE* 2.7
?Nov.	Returns to Antioch for the winter	Socrates, *HE* 2.7, cf. Libanius, *Orat.* 59.75, 77
338, spring	At Caesarea in Cappadocia	Athanasius, *Apol. ad Const.* 5.2[11]
	Restores Arsaces to the throne of Armenia	Julian, *Orat.* 1, 20d–21a, cf. Libanius, *Orat.* 59.76–80[12]
Oct. 11	At Antioch	*CTh* 12.1.23
Oct. 28	At Emesa	*CTh* 12.1.25
Dec. 27	At Antioch	*CTh* 2.6.4
339, c. Jan.	At Antioch	Athanasius, *Ep. enc.* 2.1; *Hist. Ar.* 10.1
339 or 340	At Hierapolis	*P. Abinn.* 1.8–10[13]
340, summer	Invades Persian territory	*Itinerarium Alexandri*, pr. 1, cf. 4[14]
340, Aug. 12	At Edessa	*CTh* 12.1.30[5] (the place of issue is transmitted as *Bessae*)
Sept. 9	At Antioch	*CTh* 6.4.5/6[15]
341, Jan. 6	Attends the 'Dedication Council' at Antioch	Athanasius, *Syn.* 25.1; Philostorgius p. 212.19–22 Bidez
Feb. 12	At Antioch	*CTh* 5.13.1/2
341/2	Winters in Antioch	Socrates, *HE* 2.13.5, cf. Jerome, *Chronicle* 235[f]; *Chr. min.* 1.236
342, early	Visits Constantinople to expel the bishop Paul and returns at once to Antioch	Libanius, *Orat.* 59.94–97; Socrates, *HE* 2.13.7, cf. Jerome, *Chronicle* 235[f]; *Chr. min.* 1.236
342, March 31–May 11	In Antioch	*CTh* 3.12.1; 12.1.33/4 (April 5, 8); 11.36.6

343, Feb. 18	At Antioch	*CTh* 9.21.5
June 9–July 4	In Hierapolis	*CTh* 8.1.1[5] (319 mss.); 12.1.35 (June 27); 15.8.1[16]
summer/ autumn	Wins a victory over the Persians	Athanasius, *Hist. Ar.* 16.2, cf. Festus, *Brev.* 27[17]
Oct./Nov.	?Visits Constantinople[18]	
344, c. April	At Antioch	Theodoretus, *HE* 2.8.56, 9.9–10, cf. Athanasius, *Hist. Ar.* 20.5
?344, summer	Defeats the Persians near Singara	Julian, *Orat.* 1, 26a; Libanius, *Orat.* 59.88, 99–120; Jerome, *Chronicle* 236[1]; *Chr. min.* 1.236 (both giving the date as 348), cf. Festus, *Brev.* 27[19]
345	At Nisibis	*CTh* 11.7.5, cf. Ephraem, *Carmina Nisibena* 13.4–6, 14/5[20]
summer	At Edessa	Athanasius, *Apol. c. Ar.* 51.6
346, March 21	At Antioch	*CTh* 10.14.1[5] (315 mss.)
c. Sept.	At Antioch	Athanasius, *Apol. ad Const.* 5.2; *Hist. Ar.* 44.5, *Hist. ac.* 1.2; *Index* 17; Jerome, *Chronicle* 236[e]
347, March 8	At Ancyra	*CTh* 11.36.8
?347, spring	Themistius delivers his first imperial panegyric before Constantius at Ancyra	Themistius, *Orat.* 1[21]
May 11	?At Hierapolis	*CTh* 5.6.1[22]
?348, summer	Engages the Persians in battle near Singara[23]	Festus, *Brev.* 27
349, April 1	At Antioch	*CTh* 12.1.39
349, summer	At Singara, then Emesa	Athanasius, *Hist. ar.* 7.3[24]
Oct. 3	?At Constantinople	*CTh* 12.2.1 + 15.1.6[25]
350, spring	At Edessa	Philostorgius, *HE* 3.22[26]
350, summer	?In Antioch while Shapur besieges Nisibis	Theodoretus, *HE* 2.30.1, 9/10, 31.1[27]
	?Visits Nisibis after the siege	Zonaras 13.7 (p. 195.4–7 Dindorf)
autumn	Sets out westward from Antioch	Philostorgius, p. 215.22–24 Bidez
	Travels via Heraclea to Serdica	Zonaras 13.7 (pp. 195.19–196.2 Dindorf)
Dec. 25	Engineers the abdication of Vetranio at Naissus	Jerome, *Chronicle* 238[e] (place and year); *Chr. min.* 1.238 (day: year

		wrongly given as 351); Zosimus 2.44.3/4[28]
351, March 15	Proclaims Gallus Caesar at Sirmium	Chr. min. 1.238
351, summer and autumn	In Sirmium before and during the campaign against Magnentius	Sulpicius Severus, Chron. 2.38.5–7; Socrates, HE 2.28.23; Zosimus 2.45.3, 48.3[29]
?Oct.	Present at the Council of Sirmium which deposed Photinus	Socrates, HE 2.28.23, 29.1
352, Feb. 26	At Sirmium	CJ 6.22.5
May 12	At Sirmium	CTh 3.5.1[S] (319 mss.)
summer	?Campaign against the Sarmatae[30]	
?Sept.	Enters Italy	Chr. min. 1.67 (Naeratius Cerealis becomes praefectus urbi on Sept. 27)
Nov. 3	At Milan	CTh 15.14.5
353, spring–summer	In Milan	Hist. ac. 1.7, cf. Index 25; CTh 11.1.6 + 12.1.42 (May 22: year emended from 354)[31] 16.8.7[S] (July 3: 357 mss.)
	Visits Albingaunum	ILS 735
Sept. 6	At Lugdunum	CTh 9.38.2[S] (354 mss.)
353, c. Oct.–354, spring	Winters in Arles	Ammianus 14.5.1; CTh 8.7.2S (Nov. 3: 326 mss.); Ammianus 14.10.1[32]
354, spring	At Valentia	Ammianus 14.10.1/2
	Crosses the Rhine at Rauracum	Ammianus 14.10.6
354, autumn–355, spring	Winters in Milan	Ammianus 14.10.16; CTh 11.34.2 (Jan. 1); CJ 6.22.6 (Feb. 18)[33]
355, c. June	Conducts expedition into Raetia	Ammianus 15.4.1
	Goes to winter quarters in Milan	Ammianus 15.4.13, cf. Sulpicius Severus, Chron. 2.39.3, 8 (Council of Milan)
355, July 6–356, July 5	In Milan	CTh 14.3.2; CTh 12.1.43 (July 17); 1.5.5 (July 18); 6.29.1 (July 22); 2.1.2 (July 25); 12.12.1 (Aug. 1); 9.34.6 (Oct. 31); 16.10.6 (356, Feb. 19); 9.42.2 (March 8);

		11.16.8^S (April 1: 357 mss.); 11.16.7 (April 2); 6.4.8–10 (April 11); 6.29.2^S (April 17: 357 mss.); 13.10.3^S (April 29: 357 mss.); 9.17.4^S = CJ 9.19.4^S (June 13: 357 mss.); CTh 8.5.8^S (June 24: 357 mss.); 1.2.7 (July 5)
355, Nov. 6	Proclaims Julian Caesar at Milan	Ammianus 15.8.17; Chr. min. 1.238; CIL 1², p. 277; Socrates, HE 2.34.5
Dec. 1	Escorts Julian out of the city, then returns to Milan	Ammianus 15.8.18
356, summer autumn	Campaign against the Alamanni on the Upper Rhine	Ammianus 16.12.15/6
July 25	At Messadensis	CTh 11.30.25^S (355 mss.)
Sept. 2	At Dinumma	CTh 11.7.8^S (355 mss.)[34]
356, Nov. 10–357, March 19	In Milan	CTh 16.2.13^S (357 mss.); 9.16.5^S (Dec. 4: 356 or 357); 8.5.9^S, 16.2.14^S (Dec. 6: 357 mss.); 8.7.7^S (Dec. 27: year implied to be 357); 12.12.2 (Jan. 15); 9.17.4 (Jan. 15: 'id.Iun.' mss.);[35] 9.16.4 (Jan. 25); 15.1.1^S (Feb. 2: 320 mss.); 10.20.2^S (358 mss.)
357, April 28	Enters Rome	Chr. min. 1.239
April 28–May 29	In Rome	Ammianus 16.10.20 (length of stay); CTh 8.1.5 (May 6); 10.1.2^S (May 17: 319 mss.)
June 7 or 10	At Helvillum	CTh 1.5.6 + 7[36]
July 5	At Ariminum	CTh 9.16.6^S (358 mss.)
July 21	At Ravenna	CTh 12.1.40^S (353 mss.)
	Passes through Tridentum on his way to the Danube	Ammianus 16.10.20
	Visits Pannonia and Moesia	Zosimus 3.2.2; Julian, Ep. ad Ath. 279^d
357, Oct.–358, March 3	Winters in Sirmium	Ammianus 16.10.21; 17.12.1; CTh 8.5.10 (Oct. 27: transmitted year either 357 or 358);[37] 1.15.3^S (Dec. 3: 353 mss.);[38] 7.4.3, 11.30.27 (Dec. 18); 2.21.2^S (Dec. 18: 360 mss.); 9.42.4 (357, Jan. 4); CJ 3.26.8

358, April	Invades the territory of the Sarmatae Limigantes	Ammianus 17.12.4–6
	Returns in triumph to Sirmium	Ammianus 17.13.33
June 21–23	In Sirmium	CTh 12.1.44 + 45 (June 21); 8.13.4, 11.36.13 (June 23)
June 27	At Mursa	CTh 12.1.46
358, c. Oct.– 359, c. March	Winters in Sirmium	Ammianus 18.4.1; 19.11.1; CTh 2.21.1 (Dec. 19)
359, spring	Begins a campaign against the Sarmatae	Ammianus 19.11.2
	In the province of Valeria	Ammianus 19.11.4
	Defeats the Limigantes near Acimincum	Ammianus 19.11.5–16
	Returns to Sirmium	Ammianus 19.11.17
359, May 22	At Sirmium	CTh 6.4.14 + 15; Athanasius, Syn. 8.3; Socrates, HE 2.37.18
May 28	At Sirmium	CTh 1.7.1
June 18	At Singidunum	CTh 11.30.28
?	?At Adrianople	Athanasius, Syn. 55.2/3 (implying intent to visit)
359, autumn	Goes to Constantinople and winters there	Ammianus 19.11.17; 20.8.1; Socrates, HE 2.41.1; Sozomenus, HE 4.23.3, cf. Chr. min. 1.239 (implying Constantius' presence in the city before Dec. 11)
359, Dec.– 360, March	In Constantinople	Sozomenus, HE 4.23.4–7 (late Dec.–Jan. 1); Hilary, Ad Const. 2.2 (CSEL 65.198.9/10, cf. Jerome, De vir. ill. 100; CTh 4.13.4[s]; 11.36.10[s] (Jan. 18: 356 and 354 mss.);[39] 11.24.1 (Feb. 4); 14.1.1[s] (Feb. 24: 357 mss.); 7.4.5[s] (March 14: 359 mss.)
360, ?March	At Caesarea in Cappadocia when he receives news that Julian has been proclaimed Augustus	Ammianus 20.9.1
	Travels via Melitene, Lacotena, and Samosata to Edessa	Ammianus 20.11.4[40]
360, after Sept. 21	Leaves Edessa	Ammianus 20.11.4

	Visits Amida	Ammianus 20.11.4/5
	Besieges Bezabde	Ammianus 20.11.6–31
Dec. 17	At Hierapolis	CTh 7.4.6ˢ (May 17 mss.)
360, late Dec.– 361, c. March	Winters in Antioch	Ammianus 20.11.32; CTh 16.2.16 (Feb. 14); Socrates, HE 2.45.10
361, May 3	At Gephyra	CTh 1.6.1, 28.1; 6.4.12, 13; 7.8.1; 11.1.7, 15.1, 23.1; 12.1.48; 13.1.3; 15.1.7 (all extracts from the same law)
May 29	At Doliche	CTh 7.4.4ˢ (358 mss.: place of issue transmitted as Doridae)
	Crosses the Euphrates at Capersana, goes to Edessa, and later returns to Hierapolis (or possibly Nicopolis)	Ammianus 21.7.7, 13.8[41]
autumn	Returns briefly to Antioch	Ammianus 21.15.1/2[42]
Oct.	At Hippocephalus	Ammianus 21.15.2
	Falls ill at Tarsus	Ammianus 21.15.2
Nov. 3	Dies at Mopsucrenae in Cilicia	Jerome, Chronicle 242ᵇ; Ammianus 21.15.3 (date emended from Oct. 5); Chr. min. 1.240; Socrates, HE 2.47.4; 3.1.1[43]

CONSTANS

Principal residences

337–340	?Naissus (Zonaras 13.5)
340–350	Trier, Milan, and Sirmium[44]

Attested movements

337, c. Sept.	Confers with Constantinus and Constantius in Pannonia	Julian, Orat. 1, 19a, cf. Libanius, Orat. 59.75
Dec. 6	At Thessalonica	CTh 11.1.4; 11.7.7ˢ (353 mss.)[45]
probably 338	Campaign against the Sarmatae	CIL 3.12483[46]
338, June 12	At Viminacium	CTh 10.10.4
July 27	At Sirmium	CTh 15.1.5; CJ 10.48.7
?339, April 6	At Savaria	CTh 10.10.6ˢ (342 mss.)
340, Jan. 19– Feb. 2	At Naissus	CTh 12.1.29; 10.10.5
	In Dacia when he hears of Constantinus' invasion	Zonaras 13.5

of his territory

April 9	At Aquileia	*CTh* 2.6.5; 10.15.3
June 25	At Milan	*CTh* 9.17.1
?340	?Visits Rome	*Passio Artemii* 9 = Philostorgius, *HE* 3.1ᵃ[47]
341, June 24	At Lauriacum	*CTh* 8.2.1 = 12.1.31
late 341	Campaign against the Franci in Gaul	Jerome, *Chronicle* 235ᵇ; *Chr. min.* 1.236
342	Victory over the Franci and treaty with them	Libanius, *Orat.* 59.127–136; Jerome, *Chronicle* 235ᵉ; *Chr. min.* 1.236; Socrates, *HE* 2.13.4[48]
summer	In Trier	Socrates, *HE* 2.18
autumn	Interviews Athanasius in Milan	Athanasius, *Apol. ad Const.* 4.3
Dec. 4	At Milan	*CTh* 9.7.3
343, Jan. 25	At Bononia	*CTh* 11.16.5, cf. *CJ* 3.26.6
	Crosses to Britain in winter	Firmicus Maternus, *De err. prof. rel.* 28.6; Libanius, *Orat.* 59.137–140; Ammianus 20.1.1
343, spring	Soon returns from Britain to Gaul	Libanius, *Orat.* 59.139, 141
June 30	At Trier	*CTh* 12.1.36
summer	Interviews Athanasius in Trier	Athanasius, *Apol. ad Const.* 4.4, cf. 3.7
344, autumn	In Pannonia	Libanius, *Orat.* 59.133[49]
345, early	Receives an embassy from Constantius at Poetovio	Athanasius, *Apol. ad Const.* 3.3
April 7	At Aquileia at Easter, where he interviews Athanasius	Athanasius, *Apol. ad Const.* 15.4, cf. 3.7; *Index* 17[50]
May 15	At Trier	*CTh* 10.10.7
June 9 or July 11	At Cologne	*CTh* 3.5.7
?autumn	Interviews Athanasius in Trier	Athanasius, *Apol. ad Const.* 4.5, cf. 3.7[51]
?346, March 5	At Sirmium	*CTh* 10.10.8ˢ (353 mss.)
346, May 23	At Caesena	*CTh* 12.1.38[52]
348, June 17	At Milan	*CTh* 10.14.2
349, May 27	At Sirmium	*CTh* 7.1.2 + 8.7.3[53]
350, shortly after Jan. 18	Killed at Helena in Gaul	Eutropius, *Brev.* 10.9.4.; Jerome, *Chronicle* 237ᶜ; *Chr. min.* 1.237;

Epitome 41.23; Zosimus 2.42.5

GALLUS

Principal residence

351–354	Antioch (*Chr. min.* 1.238)

Attested movements

351, March 15	Proclaimed Caesar at Sirmium	*Chr. min.* 1.238 (day); *Passio Artemii* 12 = Philostorgius, *HE* 3.26[a]
May 7	Reaches Antioch	Socrates, *HE* 2.28.22[54]
	?Campaign in Mesopotamia	Philostorgius, *HE* 3.28
352, summer	Suppresses a Jewish rebellion in Galilee	Jerome, *Chronicle* 238[155]
353, late summer –354, spring	At Antioch	Ammianus 14.1.4–9, 7.1–4[56]
354, c. March	Visits Hierapolis	Ammianus 14.7.5
April–Aug.	At Antioch	Ammianus 14.7.9–17
c. Sept. 1	Leaves Antioch	Ammianus 14.11.12
Sept. 14–30	?At Nicomedia	*P. Laur.* 169 (consular date of 354 restored)[57]
	Stripped of his imperial rank at Poetovio	Ammianus 14.11.19/20
Oct.	Tried and executed near Pola	Ammianus 14.11.20–23

JULIAN

Principal residences

355/6, winter	Vienne
356/7, winter	Sens
358, Jan.–360	Paris
360/1, winter	Vienne

Attested movements[58]

355, Nov. 6	Proclaimed Caesar at Milan	Ammianus 15.8.7; *CIL* 1², p. 277; *Chr. min.* 1.238; Socrates, *HE* 2.34.5
Nov. 6–30	At Milan	Ammianus 15.8.18
Dec. 1	Leaves Milan	Ammianus 15.8.18
	Travels via Turin to Vienne	Ammianus 15.8.18–21
355, Dec.–	At Vienne	Ammianus 16.1.1, 2.1

356, spring		
356, April/May	?Present at the Council of Baeterrae	Hilary, *Ad Const.* 2 (*CSEL* 65.198.5–15)[59]
356, June 24	Reaches Autun	Ammianus 16.2.2
	Passes through Auxerre	Ammianus 16.2.5
	Advances via Troyes, Rheims, Decem Pagi, Brotomagus	Ammianus 16.2.6–8
356, c. Aug.	Recaptures Cologne	Ammianus 16.3.1/2, cf. Julian, *Ep. ad Ath.* 279b[60]
	Visits Trier	Ammianus 16.3.3
356/7	Winters at Sens	Ammianus 16.3.3, 7.1, 11.1[61]
357, spring	Goes to Rheims	Ammianus 16.11.1
	Marches toward Strasbourg and wins a victory over the Alamanni	Ammianus 16.11.8–12.67[62]
	Returns to Tres Tabernae	Ammianus 17.1.1
	Goes to Mainz	Ammianus 17.1.2
	Conducts raid across the Rhine	Ammianus 17.1.2/3
357, Dec.– 358, Jan.	For 54 days besieges barbarians who had fortified a town on the Meuse	Ammianus 17.2.2/3
358, Jan.–July	Winters in Paris	Ammianus 17.2.4, 8.1
July–autumn	Campaigns against the Salian Franci in Toxandria	Ammianus 17.8.3–10.10
359, Jan. 1	In winter-quarters at Paris	Ammianus 18.1.1
	Strengthens the Rhine frontier from Castra Herculis to Bingen	Ammianus 18.2.4
	Crosses the Rhine from Mainz and conducts a raid into German territory	Ammianus 18.2.7–19
360, Jan. 1	In winter-quarters at Paris	Ammianus 20.1.1
?Feb.	Proclaimed Augustus at Paris	Julian, *Ep. ad Ath.* 283a–285a; Ammianus 20.4.4–22; Zosimus 3.9.1–3[63]
summer	Crosses the Rhine at Tricesima and attacks the Franci Attuarii	Ammianus 20.10.1/2
autumn	Marches up the left bank of the Rhine to Rauracum, then via Besançon to Vienne	Ammianus 20.10.3

360, Nov. 6– 361, c. March	Winters at Vienne	Ammianus 20.10.3; 21.1 (Nov. 6); 21.2.5 (Jan. 6), 3.1
361, spring	Attacks Germans, crosses the Rhine, and goes to Rauracum	Ammianus 21.3.3–4.8, 8.1
	Leaves Rauracum, advances up the Rhine, then down the Danube	Ammianus 21.8.1–10.2
mid-July	via Sirmium as far as the Pass of Succi[64]	
	Returns to Naissus	Ammianus 21.10.5
	At Naissus	Ammianus 21.12.1; Zosimus 3.11.2
	After receiving news of the death of Constantius, leaves Naissus and travels via Philippopolis and Heraclea/ Perinthus to Constantinople	Ammianus 21.12.3; 22.2
Dec. 11	Enters Constantinople	Ammianus 22.2.4; *Chr. min.* 1.240; Socrates, *HE* 3.1.2

Appendix 10

CREEDS AND COUNCILS,

337–361

Socrates spoke of a labyrinth of creeds in the reign of Constantius (*HE* 2.41.17), and J. N. D. Kelly entitled the relevant chapter of his study of early Christian creeds 'The Age of Synodal Creeds.'[1] The list below states the date and place of the councils at which the surviving creeds were promulgated. Each entry states or discusses the following:

(1) the number of the document in A. Hahn and G. L. Hahn, *Bibliothek der Symbole und Glaubensregeln der alten Kirche*[3] (Breslau, 1897), 183–209, followed by its number in M. Geerard, *Clavis Patrum Graecorum* 4 (Turnhout, 1980);
(2) the source or best edition of the text which is printed by the Hahns;
(3) where relevant, the conventional name or designation of the creed;
(4) the nature of the document and the date and place of the council at which it was promulgated or adopted.

Hahn and Hahn 153 (*CPG* 8556)
Athanasius, *Syn.* 22.3–7, whence Socrates, *HE* 2.10.4–8
The 'first creed' of the 'Dedication Council' (Antioch, January 341): not in fact a formal creed at all, but a quotation from the letter which the council sent to Julius, bishop of Rome.[2]

Hahn and Hahn 154 (*CPG* 8557)
Athanasius, *Syn.* 23.2–10, whence Socrates, *HE* 2.10.10–18 (Latin version in Hilary, *Syn.* 31–33)
The 'second creed' of the 'Dedication Council': a credal statement which formed part of the council's synodical letter to eastern bishops.

Hahn and Hahn 155 (*CPG* 8558)
Athanasius, *Syn.* 24.2–5
The 'third creed' of the 'Dedication Council.' Athanasius states specifically that Theophronius, the bishop of Tyana, 'put forward this creed in the presence of all, to which all also subscribed, receiving the fellow's creed' (*Syn.* 24.1). It seems unlikely that

the council itself in any sense adopted Theophronius' creed: it merely accepted it as proof of his personal orthodoxy.[3]

Hahn and Hahn 156 (*CPG* 8559)
Athanasius, *Syn.* 25.2–5, whence Socrates, *HE* 2.18.3–6
Conventionally, but misleadingly, styled the 'fourth creed' of the 'Dedication Council,' this creed was adopted by a different and later Council of Antioch in the summer of 342.

Hahn and Hahn 157 *(CPG* 8561*)*
Theodoretus, *HE* 2.8.39–52
The so-called homoousian creed of Serdica, which is omitted from the version of the synodical letter of the western bishops at Serdica quoted by Athanasius (*Apol. c. Ar.* 44–48) and Hilary (*CSEL* 65.103–128), but included in the Latin retroversion of the letter in Cod. Ver. LX (58), fols. 81ʳ–88ʳ (*EOMIA* 1.645–653).[4]

Hahn and Hahn 158 (*CPG* 8573)
CSEL 65.69–73[5]
The creed which the eastern bishops at Serdica in late 343 appended to the synodical letter they wrote before their departure (*CSEL* 65.48–67).

Hahn and Hahn 159 (*CPG* 8575)
Athanasius, *Syn.* 26.I–X, whence Socrates, *HE* 2.30.5–30
The 'long creed,' or '*ecthesis macrostichos*,' adopted by the so-called third Council of Antioch in 344.

Hahn and Hahn 160 *(CPG* 8577*)*
Athanasius, *Syn.* 27.2–3, whence Socrates, *HE* 2.30.5–30 (Latin version in Hilary, *Syn.* 37)
The creed, with anathemas, of the Council of Sirmium in 351.

Hahn and Hahn 161 (*CPG* 8578)
Hilary, *Syn.* 11 (Greek version in Athanasius, *Syn.* 28.2–12, whence Socrates, *HE* 2.30.31–41)
The theological manifesto drawn up at Sirmium in 357 and denounced by Hilary as 'the blasphemy of Sirmium.'

Hahn and Hahn 162 (*CPG* 8579)
Epiphanius, *Pan.* 73.10.1–11.10
The anathemas from the letter written to the bishops of Phoenice and elsewhere by a council which met at Ancyra shortly before Easter 358.

Hahn and Hahn 163 (*CPG* 8581)
Athanasius, *Syn.* 8.4–7, whence Socrates, *HE* 2.37.19–24
A creed drawn up by a small gathering of bishops in the presence of Constantius at Sirmium on 22 May 359, often styled the 'dated creed.'

Hahn and Hahn 164 (*CPG* 8588)
Theodoretus, *HE* 2.21.3–7[6]
The creed signed by a delegation of western bishops from the Council of Ariminum at Nike in Thrace on 10 October 359.

Hahn and Hahn 165 (*CPG* 8589)
Athanasius, *Syn.* 29.2–9. (There is a fuller text with minor variants in Epiphanius, *Pan.* 73.25, and Socrates, *HE* 2.40.8–17.)
A statement including a creed which Acacius presented to the Council of Seleucia on 28 September 359.

Hahn and Hahn 166
Jerome, *Dialogus contra Luciferianos* 17 (*PL* 23.179)
Jerome makes his orthodox protagonist quote an *infidelitas* written in the name of unity in the consular year 359: this is a deliberately selective quotation in a literary work, not a document quoted entire in the manner of Hilary or Athanasius.[7] Since the quotation contains the assertion that the Son is *similem genitori suo patri secundum scripturas,* Jerome presumably refers to the version of the creed adopted at Nike on 10 October 359.

Hahn and Hahn 167 (*CPG* 8591)
Athanasius, *Syn.* 30.2–10, whence Socrates, *HE* 2.41.8–16
The 'homoean creed' proclaimed as the official creed of the Roman Empire by the Council of Constantinople in January 360.

The Councils of Sirmium already caused trouble to the ecclesiastical historians of the fifth century, who sometimes confused them most horribly: Socrates, for example, attributes the 'blasphemy of Sirmium,' which belongs to 357 (Hahn and Hahn 161), to the council of 351 (*HE* 2.30.3, 31–41). Three Councils of Sirmium are in fact extremely problematical in different ways: one probably needs to be eliminated from the historical record altogether, while two others were small or informal gatherings rather than properly convened councils of bishops.

First, the 'first Council of Sirmium' in 347 or 348.[8] The only evidence for this council is a narrative fragment deriving from Hilary of Poitiers which notes the reconciliation of Ursacius and Valens with the western bishops as a result of their petition to Julius in 347 (*CSEL* 65.145), then continues:

> verum inter haec Sirmium convenitur. Fotinus haereticus deprehensus, olim reus pronuntiatus et a communione iam pridem unitatis abscisus, ne tum quidem per factionem populi potuit ammoveri. * * * (*CSEL* 65.146.5–8)[9]

The date and place of three condemnations of Photinus are well attested—those at Antioch in 344, at Milan in early 345, and at Sirmium in 351.[10] Photinus was also condemned in 347, by a council which met in Rome (*CSEL* 65.142.17–25). The alleged Council of Sirmium in 347 or 348 is problematical on general historical grounds: at that date, when Constans was still alive and hence ruler of Pannonia, a council held at Sirmium cannot be a council of eastern bishops (as has often been assumed),[11] and it is hard to see why western bishops determined to depose Photinus would gather in Sirmium itself, where he had strong local support. It seems safest, therefore, to assume that Hilary in fact refers to the Council of Sirmium in 351—and perhaps to posit a lacuna before the passage quoted as well as after, so that *inter haec* need not refer back to events of the mid-340s.

Second, the so-called third Council of Sirmium in 357. It has often been assumed that this was a large council attended by the emperor which promulgated a creed to which bishops were expected to subscribe.[12] But the 'blasphemy,' according to Hilary, was written by Ossius and Potamius, and the text as he quotes it states that it was drawn up in the presence of the bishops Ursacius, Valens, and Germinius—and no others (*Syn.* 3, 11 [*PL* 10.482/3, 487]). Although Athanasius sneers that the 'blasphemy' was written by the same men who had drawn up the creed of 351 (*Syn.* 28.1), his manuscripts and Socrates must be in error when they add the words 'and the rest' after the names of Valens, Ursacius, and Germinius (*Syn.* 28.2; *HE* 2.30.31). Socrates, dutifully followed in error by Sozomenus (*HE* 4.6.11/2, 12.6/7), confuses the Council of Sirmium in 351 with the small gathering of 357.

It is possible that other bishops were in Sirmium at the time and that they constituted themselves as a small council, but the reaction which the 'blasphemy' provoked makes it clear that few (if any) bishops from Asia Minor or the East were present. Moreover, it is hard to see either why most western bishops would wish to attend or what the advertised agenda can have been. Neither Hilary nor the bishops who met at Ancyra in the spring of 358 refer to the gathering at Sirmium in 357 as a council. On the contrary, when the bishops at Ancyra speak of 'the Council at Sirmium' (Epiphanius, *Pan.* 73.2.10), they mean the council of 351: their reference would be ambiguous if the meeting of 357 had been another formally constituted 'Council of Sirmium.' Furthermore, the 'blasphemy' itself 'does not conform to any of the usual creed patterns.'[13] It was not a creed at all in the usual sense, but a theological manifesto or 'position paper.'

Third, the 'fourth Council of Sirmium' in 358, which is sometimes alleged to have renewed earlier semi-Arian creeds including that of the 'Dedication Council' of 341 or to have adopted a moderate creed.[14] Only two items of explicit evidence have ever been adduced. A letter of George of Laodicea written in the summer of 359 states that in the preceding year bishops went from the East to Sirmium and refuted the evil of the 'blasphemy' of 357 (Epiphanius, *Pan.* 73.14.8). According to the traditional view, George refers to 'the council of the homoiousians at Sirmium in 358' described by Sozomenus (*HE* 4.15).[15] In this passage, however, Sozomenus seems to be describing not a formal council, but rather the political activities of a small number of eastern bishops at court (he names Basil, Eustathius, and Eleusius). Moreover, the fact that he connects these activities (*HE* 4.15.2/3) closely with the presence at court of Liberius, who had recently, he alleges, been summoned from Beroea (15.1) and who was subsequently allowed to return to Rome (15.4–6), suggests that he is indulging in imaginative reconstruction rather than drawing on documents which he found in Sabinus of Heraclea.[16] For there can be little doubt that Liberius returned to Rome in the summer of 357—a full year before the events Sozomenus is describing.[17]

In sum, the only formal and well-attested Council of Sirmium during the reign of Constantius is the council of 351 which condemned Athanasius, Marcellus, and Photinus and promulgated the creed (Hahn and Hahn 160) which was subsequently presented to the Councils of Arles and Milan.[18]

Appendix 11

EDITIONS OF THE
HISTORIA ACEPHALA

A. Martin, *Sources chrétiennes* 317 (1985), 305/6, gives a concordance of the divisions of the text of the *Historia acephala* in all editions including her own. For the convenience of readers of this book, tabulated below is a concordance of the reference-systems of the most widely accessible and quoted modern editions:

(1) A. Martin, *Sources chrétiennes* 317 (1985), 138–168;
(2) P. Batiffol, 'Historia acephala Arianorum, édition diplomatique d'après le ms. Veronensis LX,' *Mélanges de littérature et d'histoire religieuses offerts à l'occasion du jubilé episcopal de Mgr. de Cabrières, évêque de Montpellier* 1 (Paris, 1899), 100–108; H. Fromen, *Athanasii historia acephala* (Diss. Münster, 1914), 69–85 (the section divisions in Robertson, *Select Writings* [1892], 496–499, correspond with Batiffol's except for the omission of a separate 13bis);
(3) H.-G. Opitz, *EOMIA* 1.2.4 (1939), 663–671.

MARTIN	BATIFFOL	OPITZ
1.1–6	1–2	1–2
1.7–8	3	3
1.9	4	4
1.10–2.1	5	5
2.2–4	6	6, lines 1–28
2.5–7	7	6, line 28–section 7 (end)
2.8–10	8	8
3.1	9	9, lines 1–6
3.2–4	10	9, line 7–section 10 (end)
3.5–6	11	11
4.1–2	12	12, lines 1–14
4.3–4	13	12, lines 14–32

MARTIN	BATIFFOL	OPITZ
4.5–6	13bis	13–14
4.7	14	15
5.1–3	15	16
5.4–7	16	17–18, line 2
5.8–10	17	18, lines 2–28
5.11–13	18	19
5.14	19	20

NOTES

I. INTRODUCTION

1. *Decline and Fall*, chap. 21: the character-sketch paraphrased here can be found in the edition by J. B. Bury (London, 1909), 2.383–385.

2. S. Maffei, *Osservazioni letterarie che possono servir di continuazione al Giornal de' letterati d'Italia* 3 (Verona, 1738), 60–63. Gibbon makes no reference either to J. D. Mansi's discussion of the new evidence in a dissertation on the chronology of Athanasius' career included in his *Sacrorum Conciliorum nova et amplissima Collectio* 3 (Florence, 1759), 87–124.

3. A. J. A. Symons, *The Quest for Corvo: An Experiment in Biography* (London, 1934); H. Trevor-Roper, *A Hidden Life: The Enigma of Sir Edmund Backhouse* (London, 1976), published in the United States and in a second, revised English edition under the title *Hermit of Peking: The Hidden Life of Sir Edmund Backhouse* (London, 1979). Fergus Millar suggests a comparison also with B. Wasserstein, *The Secret Lives of Trebitsch Lincoln* (New Haven and London, 1988)—who invokes the same two models (7).

4. 'Zur Geschichte des Athanasius,' *Nachrichten der königlichen Gesellschaft der Wissenschaften zu Göttingen,* Philologisch-historische Klasse 1904.333–401; 1905.164–187, 257–299; 1908.354–359, 365–374; 1911.367–426, 469–522. For ninteenth- and twentieth-century opinions of Athanasius, see the recent survey by D. W.-H. Arnold, *The Early Episcopal Career of Athanasius of Alexandria* (Notre Dame/London, 1991), 14–23.

5. For example, Schwartz makes a serious and easily avoidable mistake over the meaning of a Syriac word while excoriating an earlier scholar for his ignorance of the language (*Ges. Schr.* 3 [1959], 2 n. 2, 9/10, 257 n. 2, cf. *JTS*, N.S. 37 [1986], 588/9).

6. Schwartz, *Ges. Schr.* 3 (1959), 1, 72, cf. 101 n. 1. Even more revealing is Schwartz's analysis of the *Festal Letters* as 'a conglomerate of homiletic trivialities and whole-sale biblical quotations' delivered in a tone of unsurpassable arrogance: 'predigt der Hierarch der konstantinischen Reichskirche von oben herab wie aus der Wolke;

---

unter den schweren Falten der Patriarchenmantels zeichnet sich keine menschliche Gestalt ab' (188/9).

7. Schwartz, *Ges. Schr.* 3 (1959), 181–195 (originally published in 1908 and 1911); *Kaiser Constantin und die christliche Kirche*[2] (Leipzig, 1936), 126–160.

8. On the importance of Opitz's work, see the brief but perceptive appreciation by W. Schneemelcher, 'Die Epistula encyclica des Athanasius,' *Aufsätze* (1974), 290–337, at 293–295; on his deficiencies as an editor, the harsh, but not entirely unjustified, assessment by F. Scheidweiler, 'Zur neuen Ausgabe des Athanasius,' *BZ* 47 (1954), 73–94.

9. Klein, *Constantius* (1977), xiii–xiv. The first part of the book is devoted to disproving the allegations that Constantius was 'Arian' (16–67), politically dependent, and vacillating in religious matters (68–105) or despotic (105–156). Unfortunately, Klein's use of the term 'Arianism' blurs the vital distinction between homoeans and anomoeans (Chapters XV, XVI).

10. Robertson, *Select Writings* (1892), xi–xci.

11. N. H. Baynes, 'Athanasiana,' 11 (1925), 58–69: pages 61–65 only are reprinted as 'An Athanasian Forgery?' in his *Byzantine Studies and Other Essays* (London, 1955), 282–287.

12. P. Peeters, 'Comment Saint Athanase s'enfuit de Tyr en 335,' *Bulletin de l'Académie Royale de Belgique,* Classe des Lettres[5] 30 (1944), 131–177, reprinted in his *Recherches d'histoire et de philologie orientales* 2 (*Subsidia Hagiographica* 27 [Brussels, 1951]), 53–90; 'L'épilogue du synode de Tyr en 335 (dans les Lettres Festales de saint Athanase),' *Analecta Bollandiana* 63 (1945), 131–144.

13. Schwartz's *Gesammelte Schriften* 3: *Zur Geschichte des Athanasius* (Berlin, 1959) appeared nearly twenty years after his death in 1940. The editors (W. Eltester and H.-D. Altendorf) omitted the second paper completely in accordance with Schwartz's wishes, and reprinted only a small part of the fifth: the second, entitled 'Konstantins Aufstieg zur Alleinherrschaft,' contains nothing of direct relevance to Athanasius, while the fifth comprises a vitriolic attack on Adolf Harnack for denying the authenticity of 'Das antiochenische Synodalschreiben von 325' (*Urkunde* 18), which Schwartz published in 1905.

14. Excellent general guidance is provided by M. Simonetti, 'Alcune considerazioni sul contributo di Atanasio alla lotta contro gli Ariani,' *Studi e materiali di storia delle religioni* 38 (1967), 513–535, and M. Tetz, 'Athanasius von Alexandrien,' *TRE* 4 (1979), 331–349. I have tried to acknowledge fully what I owe to others, but have decided to make no reference to unpublished dissertations which I have consulted, such as L. Bayer, *Untersuchungen zu Konstantin und Athanasius* (Diss. Tübingen, 1954), or R. A. Riall, *Athanasius Bishop of Alexandria: The Politics of Spirituality* (Diss. Cincinnati, 1987).

15. For critical reaction to *Constantine* (1981) and *New Empire* (1982), see especially the review-article by Averil Cameron, 'Constantinus Christianus,' *JRS* 73 (1983), 184–190, with her subsequent observations in *History as Text: The Writing of Ancient History* (London, 1989), 86/7, 206–208; the long and detailed review by F. Kolb, *Gnomon* 60 (1988), 45–50; and the attempted refutation of the hypothesis that Constantine attended the Council of Arles by K. M. Girardet, 'Konstantin d. Gr. und das Reichskonzil von Arles (314): Historisches Problem und methodologische Aspekte,' *Oecumenica et Patristica. Festschrift für Wilhelm*

Schneemelcher zum 75. Gerburtstag (Geneva, 1989), 151–174. I have defended and tried to buttress central aspects of my interpretation in 'The Conversion of Constantine,' *Classical Views,* N.S. 4 (1985), 371–391; 'The Constantinian Reformation,' *The Crake Lectures 1984* (Sackville, 1986), 38–57; 'Christians and Pagans in the Reign of Constantius,' *L'Église et l'empire au IVᵉ* siècle (*Entretiens sur l'antiquité classique* 34 [Vandoeuvres 1989]), 301–337; 'Panegyric, History, and Hagiography in Eusebius' *Life of Constantine,' The Making of Orthodoxy: Essays in Honour of Henry Chadwick* (Cambridge, 1989), 94–123; 'The Constantinian Settlement,' *Eusebius, Christianity, and Judaism* (Detroit, 1992), 635–657.

16. A. Martin, with M. Albert, *Histoire 'acéphale' et Index syriaque des Lettres festales d'Athanase d'Alexandrie (Sources chrétiennes* 317, 1985), reviewed at length in *JTS,* N.S. 37 (1986), 576–589. For Maffei's *editio princeps,* see his *Osservazioni letterarie* 3 (1738), 60–83.

17. E. A. Lowe, *Codices Latini Antiquiores* 4 (Oxford, 1937), No. 510. For a detailed list of the contents of the manuscript, see F. Maassen, *Geschichte der Quellen und der Literatur des canonischen Rechts im Abendland* 1 (Graz, 1870), 546–551; *EOMIA* 1.625/6; W. Telfer, 'The Codex Verona LX (58),' *HTR* 36 (1943), 169–246, at 178–184; A. Martin, *Sources chrétiennes* 317 (1985), 11–19.

18. C. H. Turner, 'The Verona MSS of canons: The Theodosian MS and its connexion with St. Cyril,' *Guardian,* 11 December 1895: 1121; 'Eduard Schwartz and the *Acta Conciliorum Oecumenicorum,' JTS* 30 (1929), 113–120, at 115/6; Schwartz, *Ges. Schr.* 3 (1959), 30–72, reprinted from *Nach. Göttingen,* Phil.-hist. Kl. 1904.357–391; W. Telfer, *HTR* 36 (1943), 169–246; A. Martin, *Sources chrétiennes* 317 (1985), 11–67.

19. *Sources chrétiennes* 317 (1985), 69–121 (the historical value of the *Historia acephala* and the *Festal Index,* and the Latinity of the former), 138–168 (text and translation), 171–213 (commentary). All references to the *Historia acephala* will be given according to the chapters and sections of Martin's edition: since her numeration differs from that of earlier editors, a concordance is given in App. 11.

20. G. R. Sievers, 'Athanasii vita acephala: Ein Beitrag zur Geschichte des Athanasius,' *Zeitschrift für die historische Theologie* 37 (1868), 89–163.

21. On all aspects of the transmission of the *Festal Letters* and the *Index,* see now Camplani, *Lettere* (1989), with the review in *JTS,* N.S. 41 (1990), 258–264.

22. All translations from the *Festal Letters* and *Festal Index* are, unless it is stated otherwise, taken from J. Payne Smith, in Robertson, *Select Writings* (1892), 503–553. On the calendaric aspects of the *Index,* see E. Schwartz, *Christliche und jüdische Ostertafeln (Abhandlungen der königlichen Gesellschaft der Wissenschaften zu Göttingen,* Philologisch-historische Klasse, N.F. 8.6, 1905).

23. For example, *Index* 2: 'In this year he went through the Thebais.' There has been some disagreement about what calendaric period 'this year' designates in the *Index:* Gwatkin, *Arianism²* (1900), 107–109, argued that the *Index* always employs Egyptian years; F. Loofs, 'Die chronologischen Angaben des sogenannten "Vorberichts" zu den Festbriefen des Athanasius,' *Sitzungsberichte der königlichen preussischen Akademie der Wissenschaften zu Berlin* 1908.1013–1022, that it always means the relevant consular year; Schwartz, *Ges. Schr.* 3 (1959), 2–14, 327–334, that the year intended is sometimes the Egyptian, sometimes the consular. Given the nature of the *Index* as an introduction to a corpus of *Festal Letters,* reckoning from one Eas-

ter to the next is *a priori* most probable. Eusebius had used almost the same variable for the 'years of persecution' in his *Martyrs of Palestine* (*Constantine* [1981], 149–154, 355–357).

24. Camplani, *Lettere* (1989), 32–34, 73–79.

25. On which, see App. 1.

26. *P. Lond.* 1913, 1914, cf. Chapter III, at nn. 43–45.

27. All of the seven works listed below are included in W. Bright, *Historical Writings of St. Athanasius* (Oxford, 1881). Schwartz, *Ges. Schr.* 3 (1959), 85, 285 n. 2, 311, denounced the use of this title for what he characterised as pamphlets and 'sehr deutliche Beispiele der antiken Publizistik'—and he issued a dire warning against the dates which Bright appends in the margins of his edition (for example, the letter of the Council of Alexandria in 338 is dated to '339–340' [13]). For a recent general introduction to these works (unfortunately not always accurate in detail), see B. H. Warmington, 'Did Athanasius Write History?' *The Inheritance of Historiography, 350–900*, ed. C. Holdsworth and T. P. Wiseman (Exeter, 1986), 7–16; on the problem of defining their literary genre, Schneemelcher, *Aufsätze* (1974), 280–297.

28. On the textual history of Athanasius' works, see esp. H.-G. Opitz, *Untersuchungen zur überlieferung der Schriften des Athanasius* (Berlin/Leipzig, 1935); M. Tetz, 'Les écrits "dogmatiques" d'Athanase: Rapport sur les travaux relatifs à l'édition des oeuvres d'Athanase, tome I,' *Politique et théologie* (1974), 181–188.

29. Opitz 169–177 *(Ep. enc.)*, cf. Chapter V. On the importance of Opitz's critical text of this work, see Schneemelcher, *Aufsätze* (1974), 318–324.

30. Opitz 87–168 *(Apol. c. Ar.)*, cf. App. 2. The title *Apologia secunda* is both inauthentic and seriously misleading: it derives from the editorial decision after Athanasius' death which placed it immediately after the *Defense of His Flight* in the corpus of his polemical writings—an order faithfully preserved in the extant manuscripts of Athanasius.

31. Opitz 1–45 *(Decr.)*, cf. App. 4.

32. Opitz 279–300 *(Apol. ad Const.)*, cf. App. 3. I have used Opitz's edition throughout, even though only pages 279/80 have been published, as being superior to the edition by J. Szymusiak, *Sources chrétiennes* 56 (1958), 88–132 (reprinted with few changes other than revised pagination as *Sources chrétiennes* 56bis [1987], 86–174). Szymusiak did not regard it as one of his duties as editor to take account of Opitz's unpublished edition, to which he nowhere refers.

33. There is no modern critical edition of the work (*CPG* 2092): all references will be given to the chapter divisions in Montfaucon's text as reprinted in *PG* 25.537–593.

34. Opitz 68–86 *(Fug.)*, cf. Chapter XIV.

35. Opitz 183–230 *(Hist. Ar.)*, cf. Chapter XIV.

36. Opitz 231–278 *(Syn.)*, cf. Chapter XIV.

37. See Chapter XIII n. 9. Lucifer is most recently and most competently edited by G. F. Diercks, *CCL* 8 (1978), with a long and helpful introduction. On the historical value of his pamphlets, see still G. Krüger, *Lucifer Bischof von Caralis und das Schisma der Luciferianer* (Leipzig, 1886), esp. 25.

38. Brennecke, *Hilarius* (1984), 199–371. For criticism of his basic thesis that the Nicene creed played no part in the debates at the Councils of Arles (353/4), Milan (355), or Baeterrae (356), see J. Doignon, 'Hilaire de Poitiers "Kirchenpolitiker"? À propos d'un ouvrage récent,' *RHE* 80 (1985), 441–454.

39. Edited by A. Feder, *CSEL* (1916), 41–193. For a conspectus of the documents and their dates, together with an argument for dating the original composition of the work to the winter of 357/8, see 'The Capitulation of Liberius and Hilary of Poitiers,' *Phoenix* 46 (1992), 256–265.

40. Gregory of Nazianzus, *Orat.* 21 (*PG* 35.1081–1128), recently edited and translated into French by J. Mossay, *Grégoire de Nazianze: Discours 20–23* (*Sources chrétiennes* 270, 1980), 110–192.

41. Rufinus, *HE* 10, pr.

42. *CPG* 3521, cf. F. Winkelmann, *Untersuchungen zur Kirchengeschichte des Gelasios von Kaisareia* (*Sitzungsberichte der Deutschen Akademie der Wissenschaften*, Klasse für Sprachen, Literatur und Kunst 1965, Abh.3 [1966]); 'Die Quellen der Historia Ecclesiastica des Gelasius von Cyzicus (nach 475),' *Byzantinoslavica* 27 (1966), 104–130; 'Charakter und Bedeutung der Kirchengeschichte des Gelasios von Kaisareia,' *Polychordia: Festschrift F. Dölger* (*Byzantinische Forschungen* 1, 1966), 346–385; 'Vita Metrophanis et Alexandri *BHG* 1279,' *Analecta Bollandiana* 100 (1982), 147–184. The exact scope of Gelasius' lost history is uncertain. Winkelmann, *Untersuchungen* (1966), 106–108, took it beyond the death of Athanasius to the mid-370s, while P. Nautin, *Dictionnaire de géographie et d'histoire ecclésiastiques* 20 (1984), 300, extended it as far as the death of Theodosius. On the other hand, J. Schamp, 'Gélase ou Rufin: Un fait nouveau: Sur des fragments oubliés de Gélase de Césarée (*CPG*, No. 3521),' *Byzantion* 57 (1987), 360–390, argues from Photius, *Bibliotheca* 15, 88, that Gelasius of Caesarea (like Gelasius of Cyzicus) concentrated on the Council of Nicaea and did not go beyond the death of Arius.

43. On these, see F. Thelamon, *Païens et chrétiens au IVe siècle: L'apport de l'"Histoire ecclésiastique" de Rufin d'Aquilée* (Paris, 1981), 37–122.

44. On 'legends in Rufinus,' see Gwatkin, *Arianism*[2] (1900), 97–102.

45. Chapters II, III.

46. Socrates, *HE* 2.1.2, cf. Apps. 5, 6.

47. Socrates, *HE* 1.10.

48. App. 8.

49. App. 5 n. 1.

50. Socrates, *HE* 3.3 = Julian, *Ep.* 60 Bidez.

51. App. 7.

52. App. 6.

53. Sozomenus, *HE* 2.25, cf. Chapter III; *HE* 4.8.4, cf. Chapter XI.

54. On the value of Philostorgius' account of Athanasius, see the contrasting assessments of W. G. Rusch, 'À la recherche de l'Athanase historique,' *Politique et théologie* (1974), 161–177; D. W.-H. Arnold, *Early Career* (1991), 25–62.

55. See the classic edition by J. Bidez (*GCS* 21, 1913), revised with substantial addenda by F. Winkelmann (Berlin, 1972: third edition 1981).

56. *BHG*[3] 170–171c = *CPG* 8082, now edited by B. Kotter, *Die Schriften des Johannes von Damaskos 5* (*Patristische Texte und Studien* 29 [Berlin], 1988), 202–245. The attribution to John was argued by F. J. Dölger in 1951 in an unpublished study which Kotter acknowledges and quotes (ib. 185/6).

57. P. Batiffol, 'Un historiographe anonyme arien du IVe siècle,' *Römische Quartalschrift* 9 (1895), 57–97.

58. J. Bidez, *Philostorgius Kirchengeschichte* (1913), 202–241, Anhang VII: 'Fragmente eines Arianischen Historiographen.'

59. Gwatkin, *Arianism*[2] (1900), 219–224; Brennecke, *Homöer* (1988), 92–95, 114–157.

60. Ammianus 15.7.7–10; 22.11.9–11.

61. *Chron.* 2.36–45, cf. Chapter XVI.

62. *BHG*[3] 183–186; Auctarium 186[c-f]; *BHL* 728–733; *BHO* 112–117. The principal Greek lives were edited by Montfaucon and reprinted by Migne, namely, Photius, *Bibliotheca* 258 (*PG* 25.ccxi–ccxxiii), the pre-metaphrastic life (*PG* 25.clxxxv–ccxi), and the reworking by Symeon the Metaphrast (*PG* 25.ccxxiii–ccxlvi).

63. Respectively, *Synodicon vetus* 42 (edited, translated, and annotated by J. Duffy and J. Parker, *Corpus Fontium Historiae Byzantinae* [Washington, 1979]), and Photius, *Homily* 16.7, p. 159 Laourda, cf. C. Mango, *The Homilies of Photius, Patriarch of Constantinople* (Cambridge, Mass., 1958), 238, 271 n. 33.

64. On the relation of Athanasius' theology to his career, see W. Schneemelcher, 'Athanasius von Alexandrien als Theologe und als Politiker,' *ZNW* 43 (1950–1951), 242–255, reprinted in his *Aufsätze* (1974), 274–289.

The present work assumes that the *Life of Antony* (*BHG*[3] 140 = *CPG* 2101) is not by Athanasius: for recent discussion of its authorship, see 'Angel of Light or Mystic Initiate? The Problem of the *Life of Antony,*' *JTS*, N.S. 37 (1986), 353–367; L. Abramowski, 'Vertritt die syrische Fassung die ursprüngliche Gestalt der Vita Antonii? Eine Auseinandersetzung mit der These Draguets,' *Mélanges A. Guillaumont* (*Cahiers d'orientalisme* 20 [Geneva, 1988]), 47–56; A. Louth, 'St. Athanasius and the Greek *Life of Antony,*' *JTS*, N.S. 39 (1988), 504–509; R. Lorenz, 'Die griechische Vita Antonii des Athanasius und ihre syrische Fassung,' *ZKG* 100 (1989) 77–84; S. Rubenson, *The Letters of St. Antony: Origenist Theology, Monastic Tradition, and the Making of a Saint* (Lund, 1990), 126–144, with the review in *JTS*, N.S. 42 (1991), 723–732. None of these writers discusses the earliest reference to the *Life*, which occurs in a letter of Serapion of Thmuis in 362/3: ἐξ ὑμῶν ἀββᾶ Ἀντώνιος δι' ἀκρότατον βίον γενόμενος οὗ καὶ ὁ βίος ἔγγραπτος παρ' ὑμῖν διασώζεται (*Ep. ad monachos* 13 [*PG* 40.940]). That is surely an odd way for Serapion to refer to the *Life* if he believed that it had been written by Athanasius in Alexandria.

II. BISHOP ALEXANDER

1. The earliest explicit rule on the subject is Canon 11 of the council held at Neocaesarea between 314 and 325 (*EOMIA* 1.132–135), cf. J. Gaudemet, *L'Église dans l'empire romain aux IV*[e] *et V*[e] *siècles* (Paris, 1957), 124–127.

2. O. von Lemm, 'Koptische Fragmente zur Patriarchengeschichte Alexandriens,' *Mémoires de l'Académie Impériale des Sciences de St.-Pétersbourg*[7] 36, No. 11 (1888), 20, frag. P.5 (text), 36 (translation and discussion).

3. *Epistula Ammonis* 13—claiming that Pachomius defended his election. A. Martin, 'Athanase et les Mélitiens (325–335),' *Politique et théologie* (1974), 31–61, at 42/3, argues that the election was irregular.

4. See the texts edited by W. Telfer, 'St. Peter of Alexandria and Arius,' *Analecta Bollandiana* 67 (1949), 117–130, at 126; P. Devos, 'Une passion grecque inédite de S. Pierre d'Alexandrie et sa traduction par Anastase le Bibliothécaire,' *Analecta*

Bollandiana 83 (1965), 157–187, at 167, 180: they are translated and discussed by
T. Vivian, *St. Peter of Alexandria: Bishop and Martyr* (Philadelphia, 1988), 64–84.

5. Rufinus, *HE* 10.15; Socrates, *HE* 1.15; Sozomenus, *HE* 2.17.5–31; Gelasius of
Cyzicus, *HE* 3.13.10–14 (and later lives of Athanasius and Constantine). The im-
mediate or indirect source of all the extant writers is Gelasius of Caesarea (frag. 27
in the numeration of F. Winkelmann, 'Charakter und Bedeutung der
Kirchengeschichte des Gelasios von Kaisareia,' *Polychordia: Festschrift F. Dölger*
[*Byzantinische Forschungen* 1, 1966], 346–385).

6. Socrates, *HE* 4.13.4. G. Bardy, *Saint Athanase (296–373)³* (Paris, 1925), 1 n. 2,
states that Athanasius was succeeded as bishop in 373 by his brother Peter: that
appears to be a confusion with the attested fact that Peter, who is not known to be
related to Athanasius, was succeeded by his brother Timothy (*Hist. ac.* 5.14;
Sozomenus, *HE* 7.7.3).

7. Gregory of Nazianzus, *Orat.* 21.6. As time went by, Athanasius' cultural attain-
ments were inevitably enhanced and exaggerated: whereas Rufinus agrees with
Gregory in making Alexander provide the young Athanasius with instruction from
a *notarius* and a *grammaticus,* both singular (*HE* 10.15), and Socrates paraphrases
the same passage as stating that Alexander gave him an education (*HE* 1.15.3),
Sozomenus speaks of Athanasius attending plural *grammatici* and rhetors (*HE*
2.17.10).

8. Gwatkin, *Arianism²* (1900), 72–74.

9. G. C. Stead, 'Rhetorical Method in Athanasius,' *Vig. Chr.* 30 (1976), 121–137.

10. *C. Gent.* 10.36/7 Thomson; *De Incarn.* 2.16–18, 43.34–38, cf. Plato, *Rep.* 327a;
Tim. 30a; *Pol.* 273d.

11. For Homer, Gwatkin, *Arianism²* (1900), 73, admitted that he could find 'only a few
stock phrases': of his two examples one comes from the fourth *Oration against the
Arians* (CPG 2230), while the other is the phrase ἀθάνατον κακόν (*Hist. Ar.* 68.2),
which need not be 'a quotation' of *Odyssey* 12.118. Athanasius names Homer
once, as the inventor of epic poetry (*C. Gent.* 18.26), but he could well have known
that without ever reading a single line of either the *Iliad* or the *Odyssey.* For
Aristotle, Gwatkin appealed to J. H. Newman, *Select Treatises of S. Athanasius,
Archbishop of Alexandria, in Controversy with the Arians* 2 (Oxford, 1844), 501.
But Newman had observed merely that certain phrases in the same fourth *Oration
against the Arians* 'remind the reader of Aristotle rather than S. Athanasius.'

12. Chapters VII, XIII.

13. For discussion of Athanasius as an orator, see R. W. Smith, *The Art of Rhetoric in
Alexandria: Its Theory and Practice in the Ancient World* (The Hague, 1974), 100–
104; G. A. Kennedy, *Greek Rhetoric under Christian Emperors* (Princeton, 1983),
208–212. Kennedy's assessment is unfortunately based largely on the *Life of
Antony,* whose Athanasian authorship is here rejected (Chapter I n. 64), but he nevertheless reaches the reasonable conclusion that Athanasius 'adopts [the] techniques of invention, but not the arrangement and style' of classical rhetoric (255).

14. For Tertullian, see J.-C. Fredouille, *Tertullien et la conversion de la culture antique*
(Paris, 1972); T. D. Barnes, *Tertullian: A Historical and Literary Study²* (Oxford,
1985), esp. 187–232. Basil and Gregory had studied with Himerius and
Proaeresius in Athens and with Libanius in Antioch (Gregory of Nazianzus, *Orat.*
43.14–20; Socrates, *HE* 4.26.6)—and it shows in their writings: G. L. Kustas,

'Saint Basil and the Rhetorical Tradition,' *Basil of Caesarea: Christian, Humanist, Ascetic*, ed. P. J. Fedwick (Toronto, 1981), 221–279; R. R. Reuther, *Gregory of Nazianzus: Rhetor and Philosopher* (Oxford, 1969), esp. 55–128; G. A. Kennedy, *Greek Rhetoric* (1983), 214–239.

15. Respectively, *PG* 40.925–941 (*CPG* 2487); Theodoretus, *HE* 4.22.1–35 (paraphrased in Chapter XX).

16. *Constantine* (1981), 82–84, 196/7. Significantly, Athanasius receives no mention whatever in the excellent and sensitive article by A. Spira, 'The Impact of Christianity on Ancient Rhetoric,' *Studia Patristica* 18.2 (1989), 137–153.

17. *De Incarn.* 56/7. There is no compelling reason to identify the bishop of Alexandria with the Athanasius whose autograph letter to the holy man Paphnutius survives (*P. Lond.* 1929), as argued by H. I. Bell, *Jews and Christians in Egypt* (London, 1924), 115–118.

18. W. Schneemelcher, 'Der Schriftgebrauch in den "Apologien" des Athanasius,' *Text, Wort, Glaube: Studien zur Überlieferung, Interpretation und Autorisierung biblischer Texte Kurt Aland gewidmet*, ed. M. Brecht (*Arbeiten zur Kirchengeschichte* 50 [Berlin and New York, 1980]), 209–219.

19. R. W. Thomson, *Athanasius*, Contra Gentes *and* De Incarnatione (Oxford, 1971), xvii, sums the matter up very well: 'He was unphilosophic and repetitive in argument, but had a profound grasp of scriptural exegesis.'

20. *De Incarn.* 55.1–12.

21. E. P. Meijering, *Orthodoxy and Platonism in Athanasius: Synthesis or Antithesis²* (Leiden, 1974); J. M. Rist, 'Basil's "Neoplatonism": Its Background and Nature,' *Basil of Caesarea: Christian, Humanist, Ascetic*, ed. P. J. Fedwick (Toronto, 1981), 137–220, at 173–178.

22. *Constantine* (1981), 178–186.

23. R. W. Thomson, *Athanasius* (1972), xxii.

24. *C. Gent.* 1.13–15.

25. M. Slusser, 'Athanasius, *Contra Gentes* and *De Incarnatione*: Place and Date of Composition,' *JTS* N.S. 37 (1986), 114–117. He argues principally from *C. Gent.* 23.10–18 and *De Incarn.* 51.6–10, contrasting them with the knowledge of the West shown in the *Letter to the Bishops of Egypt and Libya* 8; *Apol. ad Const.* 3; *Hist. Ar.* 28.

26. *Constantine* (1981), 206/7.

27. C. Kannengiesser, 'La date de l'Apologie d'Athanase *Contre les paiens* et *Sur l'Incarnation du Verbe*,' *Rech. sci. rel.* 58 (1970), 383–428. However, H. Nordberg, 'A Reconsideration of the Date of St. Athanasius' *Contra Gentes* and *De Incarnatione*,' *Studia Patristica* 3 (*Texte und Untersuchungen* 78, 1961), 262–266; *Athanasius' Tractates Contra Gentes–De Incarnatione: An Attempt at Redating* (Societas Scientiarum Fennica: *Commentationes Humanarum Litterarum* 28.3 [Helsinki, 1961]), argued for the impossibly late date of 362/3. On the other hand, A. Stülcken, *Athanasiana: Litterar- und dogmengeschichtliche Untersuchungen* (*Texte und Untersuchugen* 19.4, 1899), 1–23, argued for a date of c. 323, but conceded in a footnote that 'selbst 327 wäre nicht ausgeschlossen' (5 n. 1).

28. Respectively, E. P. Meijering, *Athanasius: De Incarnatione Verbi* (Amsterdam, 1989), 11–20; W. A. Bienert, 'Zur Logos-Christologie des Athanasius von Alexandrien in *contra Gentes* und *de Incarnatione*,' *Studia*

Patristica 21 (1989), 402–419, at 407–412.

29. T. Kehrhahn, *De sancti Athanasii quae fertur Contra Gentes oratione* (Diss. Berlin, 1913), 9–11, 20–23, 34/5, 37–43, 44–50 (also arguing that the work uses Eusebius, *Praep. Evang.* 7.10), 56/7, 62–65. Kehrhahn drew the unconvincing conclusion that a work which copied Eusebius could not be by Athanasius (71/2). More recently, M.-J. Rondeau, 'Une nouvelle preuve de l'influence littéraire d'Eusèbe de Césarée sur Athanase: L'interprétation des Psaumes,' *Rech. sci. rel.* 56 (1968), 385–434, argued that Athanasius also used Eusebius' *Commentary on the Psalms* in his own exegesis of the Psalms. But the Athanasian authorship of the texts upon which she relied has been disproved by G. Dorival, 'Athanase ou pseudo-Athanase?' *Rivista di storia e letteratura religiosa* 16 (1980), 80–89. Significantly, the word θεοφάνεια occurs in four passages alleged to derive from Athanasius' *Commentary on the Psalms* (*PG* 27.80, 220, 229, 529), cf. below, n. 31. For the date of the *Theophany*, which Eusebius is often wrongly supposed to have written after 330, see *Constantine* (1981), 186–188.

30. As argued most recently by E. P. Meijering, *Athanasius* (1989), 11–20.

31. See R. W. Thomson, *Athanasius* (1971), 5, 23, 25, 67, 69, 71, 85, 111, 133, 171, 267. A small but telling indication of Athanasius' indebtedness to Eusebius is the occurrence of the word θεοφάνεια in *De Incarn.* 8.3. The concept is central to Eusebius' interpretation of the course of human history, but virtually unique to him among Christian theologians: see P. W. L. Walker, *Holy City, Holy Places? Christian Attitudes to Jerusalem and the Holy Land in the Fourth Century* (Oxford, 1990), 87. In Athanasius it occurs elsewhere only at *Orat. c. Ar.* 1.63 (*PG* 26.144), cf. Müller, *Lexicon* (1952), 650.

32. E. Mühlenberg, 'Verité et bonté de Dieu: Une interprétation de *De incarnatione,* chapitre VI, en perspective historique,' *Politique et théologie* (1974), 215–230, at 227–230; W. A. Bienert, *Studia Patristica* 21 (1989), 409/10.

33. A date between 328 and 335 was deduced from a comparison with the early *Festal Letters* by A. L. Pettersen, 'A Reconsideration of the Date of the *Contra Gentes–De Incarnatione* of Athanasius of Alexandria,' *Studia Patristica* 17.3 (1982), 1030–1040, cf. Camplani, *Lettere* (1989), 239–244.

34. A. Pettersen, '"To Flee or Not to Flee": An Assessment of Athanasius' *De Fuga Sua,*' *Persecution and Toleration* (*Studies in Church History* 21, 1984), 29–42, at 40–42.

35. M. Krause, 'Das christliche Alexandrien und seine Beziehungen zum koptischen Ägypten,' *Alexandrien: Kulturbegegnungen dreier Jahrtausende im Schmelztiegel einer mediterranen Grossstadt,* ed. N. Hinske (*Aegyptiaca Treverensia* 1 [Mainz, 1981]), 53–62, at 55: 'der einzige Bischof Alexandriens, der auch koptisch sprechen konnte.'

36. For example, L. T. Lefort, 'S. Athanase: Sur la virginité,' *Le Muséon* 42 (1929), 197–275, published what he claimed to be the original Coptic of a letter or treatise on virginity (*CPG* 2147). For proof that it was composed in Greek, see M. Aubineau, 'Les écrits de Saint Athanase sur la virginité,' *Revue d'ascétique et de mystique* 31 (1955), 140–173, reprinted in his *Recherches patristiques* (Amsterdam, 1974), 163–196.

37. L. T. Lefort, 'St. Athanase, écrivain copte,' *Le Muséon* 46 (1933), 1–33; C. D. G. Müller, 'Athanasios I. von Alexandrien als koptischer Schriftsteller,' *Kyrios:*

Vierteljahresschrift für Kirchen- und Geistesgeschichte Europas, N.F. 14 (1974), 195–204.

38. P. Peeters, *Orient et Byzance: Le tréfonds oriental de l'hagiographie grecque* (*Subsidia Hagiographica* 21 [Brussels, 1950]), 29–32.

39. T. Orlandi, 'The Future of Studies in Coptic Biblical and Ecclesiastical Literature,' *The Future of Coptic Studies,* ed. R. McL. Wilson (Leiden, 1978), 143–163, at 153, cf. 151.

40. G. Bardy, *La question des langues dans l'église ancienne* 1 (Paris, 1948), 131. Bardy argued that the fact that Athanasius quotes the letter which Constantius wrote to him in 350 in two slightly different versions of the same Latin original (*Apol. ad Const.* 23; *Hist. Ar.* 24) implies that he made the Greek translation himself on each occasion. He presumably also translated the letter of Ursacius and Valens to Julius, which he obtained from Paulinus of Trier (*Hist. Ar.* 26.2/3, cf. *Apol. c. Ar.* 58.1–4). For discussion of Athanasius' knowledge of Latin Christian writers, see J. L. North, 'Did Athanasius (letter 49, to Dracontius) know and correct Cyprian (letter 5, Hartel)?' *Studia Patristica* 17.3 (1982), 1024–1029. On the different question of what Latin Christian texts might have been available to Athanasius in Greek, see E. Dekkers, 'Les traductions grecques des écrits patristiques latins,' *Sacris Erudiri* 5 (1953), 193–233, esp. 197.

41. Seeck, *Geschichte* 4 (1911), 332, 503/4.

42. W. H. C. Frend, 'Athanasius as an Egyptian Christian Leader in the Fourth Century,' *New College Bulletin* 8 (1974), 20–37, reprinted his *Religion Popular and Unpopular in the Early Christian Centuries* (London, 1976), No. XVI. However, Frend presents Athanasius as coming from 'an Alexandrian middle-class background' (21 n. 1) with appeal to Sozomenus, *HE* 2.17.10 (on which, see above, n. 7).

43. *CSEL* 65.154.19; Socrates, *HE* 1.8.13; Sozomenus, *HE* 1.17.7.

44. *Constantine* (1981), 215–219.

45. On the origins of the Melitian schism, see briefly *Constantine* (1981), 201/2; for full discussion and bibliography, T. Vivian, *St. Peter* (1988), 15–50. The earliest stages of the quarrel between Peter and Melitius are documented by two contemporary letters, one of four bishops to Melitius, the other of Peter to his congregation, preserved in Cod. Ver. LX (58), fols. 113^v–116^r, and most readily accessible in *EOMIA* 1.634–636. Athanasius indirectly implies that the schism began in 306 (*Letter to the Bishops of Egypt and Libya* 22).

46. Epiphanius, *Pan.* 68.1.4–3.4; Sozomenus, *HE* 1.15.2.

47. *P. Lond.* 1913–1922, published by H. I. Bell (with W. E. Crum), *Jews and Christians in Egypt* (London, 1924), 38–99. Another document from the same dossier was subsequently published by W. E. Crum, 'Some Further Melitian Documents,' *JEA* 13 (1927), 19–26.

48. A plan of Alexandria is given by C. Andresen, '"Siegreiche Kirche" im Aufstieg des Christentums: Untersuchungen zu Eusebius von Caesarea und Dionysios von Alexandrien,' *Aufstieg und Niedergang der römischen Welt* 2.23.1 (Berlin and New York, 1979), 387–459, facing p. 440.

49. Epiphanius, *Pan.* 69.1.2, 2.2–7, cf. Socrates, *HE* 5.22.43–46.

50. Debate about Arius himself and his views has been lively in recent years: among major contributions, note A. M. Ritter, 'Arianismus,' *TRE* 3 (1978), 692–719; 'Arius,' *Gestalten der Kirchengeschichte,* ed. M. Greschat 1 (Stuttgart, 1984), 215–

223; R. Lorenz, *Arius judaizans? Untersuchungen zur dogmengeschichtlichen Einordnung des Arius* (Göttingen, 1979), with the review by R. Williams, *JTS*, N.S. 34 (1983), 293–296; R. Lorenz, 'Die Christusseele im Arianischen Streit: Nebst einigen Bemerkungen zur Quellenkritik des Arius und zur Glaubwürdigkeit des Athanasius,' *ZKG* 94 (1983), 1–51; R. C. Gregg and D. E. Groh, *Early Arianism— A View of Salvation* (Philadelphia, 1981); J. T. Lienhard, 'Recent Studies in Arianism,' *Religious Studies Review* 8 (1982), 330–337; R. Williams, 'The Logic of Arianism,' *JTS*, N.S. 34 (1983), 56–81; *Arius: Heresy and Tradition* (London, 1987), with the review by R. C. Gregg, *JTS*, N.S. 40 (1989), 247–254; the collective volume *Arianism* (1985); Hanson, *Search* (1988), 3–128.

Williams advances the historically attractive interpretation that Arius was 'a committed theological conservative' with a distinctly Alexandrian stamp (175) who attempted to bring Christian theology into the 'post-Plotinian and post-Porphyrian world' (230). But both Plotinus and Porphyry taught in Rome, and that interpretation of Arius may well over-estimate the diffusion of their ideas in the East in the early decades of the fourth century, on which see J. M. Rist, *Basil of Caesarea* (1981), 165–179.

On the reconstruction of Arius' lost *Thalia*, see now K. Metzler and F. Simon, *Ariana et Athanasiana: Studien zur Überlieferung und zu philologischen Problemen der Werke des Athanasius von Alexandrien* (*Abhandlungen der Rheinisch-Westfälischen Akademie der Wissenschaften* 83 [Oplanden, 1991]), 11–45.

51. Eusebius, *C. Marc.* 1.3.18; *Eccl. Theol.*, passim.

52. See the trenchant remarks of G. Gentz, *RAC* 1 (1950), 647; Hanson, *Search* (1988), xvii/xviii.

53. Epiphanius, *Pan.* 69.3.3. Some sources allege that Arius had been ordained deacon by the schismatic Melitius (*EOMIA* 1.635/6; Sozomenus, *HE* 1.15.2). But the early Melitian Arius was an accidental homonym, exploited for polemical purposes: see R. Williams, 'Arius and the Melitian Schism,' *JTS*, N.S. 37 (1986), 35–52; A. Martin, 'Les relations entre Arius et Mélitios dans la tradition Alexandrine,' *JTS*, N.S. 40 (1989), 401–413.

54. *Urkunde* 6—where it must be suspected that the three concluding names (those of the Libyan bishops Secundus and Theonas, and Pistus) are later additions to the original document. Both the order of events and the absolute chronology of the controversy before late 324 are uncertain. Both the order and the absolute dates for the documents included by H.-G. Opitz in his *Urkunden* (1934) which he had argued in the article 'Die Zeitfolge des arianischen Streites von den Anfängen bis zum Jahre 328,' *ZNW* 33 (1934), 131–159, have largely been accepted in recent scholarship, as in *Constantine* (1981), 202–206, 374–376. For some significant revisions to Opitz's dates, and in turn objections to the revised dates, see R. Williams, *Arius* (1987), 48–66; U. Loose, 'Zur Chronologie des arianischen Streites,' *ZKG* 101 (1990), 88–92.

55. *Urkunde* 4b.11.

56. *Urkunde* 1. Also preserved in whole or in part are letters from Eusebius of Nicomedia to Arius (*Urkunde* 2) and to Paulinus of Tyre (8), from Eusebius of Caesarea to Euphration of Balaneae and to Alexander of Alexandria defending Arius' central thesis (3, 7), fragments of a letter by Paulinus (9), and an attempt by George, the future bishop of Laodicea, to mediate between Alexander and Arius (12, 13).

57. Sozomenus, *HE* 1.15.11, 10, whence *Urkunden* 10, 5. Opitz dated these two councils to c. 320 and c. 321/2 respectively: in favor of regarding the Palestinian one as the earlier (against Sozomenus), see R. Williams, *Arius* (1987), 50–60. However, it seems unlikely that the Bithynian council occurred three years after the Palestinian, as he posits (58).

58. *Urkunden* 14, 16. The latter is known only from an allusion in a letter by Liberius written in 353/4 (*CSEL* 65.91.24–28).

59. *Urkunde* 14.3–8, 57/8; Epiphanius, *Pan.* 69.3.2. Arius' return may be the occasion of Alexander's circular to all bishops (*Urkunde* 15).

60. *Urkunden* 4b, 14. The first letter is sometimes identified from its opening words as *Henos somatos*, and the second sometimes similarly from its opening words as *He philarchia*.

61. M. Aubineau, 'La tunique sans couture du Christ: Exégèse patristique de Jean 19, 23–24,' *Kyriakon: Festschrift Johannes Quasten* 1 (Münster, 1970), 100–127, esp. 107–109, reprinted in his *Recherches patristiques* (1974), 351–378, at 358–360; A. Pettersen, *Studia Patristica* 17.3 (1982), 1030–1040.

62. G. C. Stead, 'Athanasius' Earliest Written Work,' *JTS*, N.S. 39 (1988), 76–91.

63. G. C. Stead, *JTS*, N.S. 39 (1988), 83–86.

64. G. C. Stead, *JTS*, N.S. 39 (1988), 82–84.

65. Eusebius, *VC* 1.51.1, cf. *Constantine* (1981), 376 n. 154.

66. Eusebius, *VC* 2.63–73. The envoy, identified as Ossius by Socrates, *HE* 1.7.1, is argued to be the *notarius* Marianus by B. H. Warmington, 'The Sources of Some Constantinian Documents in Eusebius' *Church History* and *Life of Constantine*,' *Studia Patristica* 18.1 (1985), 93–98, at 95/6.

67. John Chrysostom, *De beato Philogonio* (*PG* 47.747–756), cf. Theodoretus, *HE* 1.7.10.

68. On this council, see now Hanson, *Search* (1988), 146–151. It was unknown to modern scholarship until Eduard Schwartz published *Urkunde* 18 in 1905 (*Ges. Schr.* 3 [1959], 134–155). On its creed, see esp. L. Abramowski, 'Die Synode von Antiochien 324/25 und ihr Symbol,' *ZKG* 86 (1975), 356–366.

69. *Urkunde* 20.

70. On the Council of Nicaea, whose proceedings can be reconstructed only in the barest outline, see *Constantine* (1981), 215–219; C. Luibhéid, *The Council of Nicaea* (Galway, 1982), 67–124.

71. *Urkunde* 23.6–10, cf. A. Martin, *Politique et théologie* (1974), 33–38.

72. *Urkunden* 31.2, 27, 28; Philostorgius, *HE* 1.10.

73. For other evidence and proof of the date, see 'Emperor and Bishops, A.D. 324–344: Some Problems,' *AJAH* 3 (1978), 53–75, at 59/60. These arguments are ignored in the restatement of a case for dating the fall of Eustathius to 330/1 by R. P. C. Hanson, 'The Fate of Eustathius of Antioch,' *ZKG* 95 (1984), 171–179; *Search* (1988), 208–211.

74. Theodoretus, *HE* 1.22.1, cf. Eusebius, *VC* 3.59–62.

75. The principal evidence for this council comprises *Urkunden* 29–32; Eusebius, *VC* 3.23; Athanasius, *Apol. c. Ar.* 59.3; Philostorgius, *HE* 2.7, 7ᵃ. For the reconstruction of events assumed here, see *AJAH* 3 (1978), 60/1; *Constantine* (1981), 229; *New Empire* (1982), 77. The council is sometimes misleadingly called 'the second Council of Nicaea,' as recently by Hanson, *Search* (1988), 174–178. Its existence is

still denied by some scholars: for example, C. Luibhéid, 'The Alleged Second Session of the Council of Nicaea,' *JEH* 34 (1983), 165–174; A. Martin, 'Le fil d'Arius,' *BHE* 84 (1989), 297–320. The latter argues that Arius was in exile continuously from 325 to 335 and dates *Urkunde* 29 to 334, *Urkunden* 32 and 31 to 335.

76. Epiphanius, *Pan.* 68.7.2, 69.11.4. Both passages are unfortunately misunderstood by D. W.-H. Arnold, *The Early Episcopal Career of Athanasius of Alexandria* (Notre Dame/London, 1991), 29, 31, who fails to recognise either reference to the imperial court.

77. Sozomenus, *HE* 2.17.4, 25.6. Sozomenus also quotes Apollinaris of Laodicea (*HE* 2.17.2/3 = frag. 168 Lietzmann), who confirms that Athanasius was absent from Alexandria when Alexander died. The account of his election which Athanasius himself penned in 338 (*Apol. c. Ar.* 6.5/6) is predictably tendentious: see L. W. Barnard, 'Two Notes on Athanasius,' *Orientalia Christiana Periodica* 41 (1975), 344–356, reprinted in his *Studies in Church History and Patristics* (ΑΝΑΛΕΚΤΑ ΒΛΑΤΑΔΩΝ 26 [Thessaloniki, 1978]), 329–340.

III. ATHANASIUS AND CONSTANTINE

1. Philostorgius, *HE* 2.11. The nature of episcopal elections in Alexandria has been a matter of some contention: see the successive discussions by K. Müller, 'Kleine Beiträge zur alten Kirchengeschichte 16: Die älteste Bischofswahl und -weihe in Rom und Alexandrien,' *ZNW* 28 (1929), 274–296; W. Telfer, 'Episcopal Succession in Egypt,' *JEH* 3 (1952), 1–13; E. W. Kemp, 'Bishops and Presbyters at Alexandria,' *JEH* 6 (1955), 125–142; J. Lécuyer, 'Le problème des consécrations épiscopales dans l'Église d'Alexandrie,' *BHE* 65 (1964), 241–267; 'La succession des évêques d'Alexandrie aux premiers siècles,' *BHE* 70 (1969), 81–98; Girardet, *Kaisergericht* (1975), 52–57; D. W.-H. Arnold, *The Early Episcopal Career of Athanasius of Alexandria* (Notre Dame and London, 1991), 38–62. Philostorgius quoted what purports to be Constantine's reply to the city (*HE* 2.11[a]). G. Fernandez Hernandez, 'La elección episcopal de Atanasio de Alejandría según Filostorgio,' *Gerión* 3 (1985), 211–229, argues that the emperor allowed an election which he knew to be uncanonical because he feared that the Melitian schism might produce social unrest and thus endanger the supply of Egyptian grain to his new capital on the Bosporus.

2. Epiphanius, *Pan.* 68.6. The date is deduced from the fact that Constantine was in the West continuously from the spring of 328 to the spring of 330 (*New Empire* [1982], 77/8). What follows is based on *Constantine* (1981), 231–240; for recent discussion and bibliography, see D. W.-H. Arnold, *Early Career* (1991), 103–173.

3. This visit, whose implied date is 329/30, appears to find an echo in monastic sources: see P. Rousseau, *Pachomius: The Making of a Community in Fourth-Century Egypt* (Berkeley, 1985), 161/2. Many of the dates for the 330s in the *Index* are one year too early (*New Empire* [1982], 152 n. 30). Observe also that the *Index* was not originally composed for the extant collection of *Festal Letters,* and that the extant *Festal Letter* 3 was written for Easter 352, not for Easter 330 (App. 1).

4. Socrates, *HE* 1.13.4/5 (not at all precisely dateable), cf. Philostorgius, *HE* 1.9[a]. Philumenus was believed to have interceded with Constantine on behalf of Donatus in 315 (Optatus 1.26, cf. Augustine, *Brev. Coll.* 3.20.38).

5. *Urkunde* 34. The document was taken to Alexandria by the *magistriani* Syncletius

and Gaudentius while Paterius was governor of Egypt (*Urkunde* 34.43). On the situation in Libya at this period, see D. W.-H. Arnold, *Early Career* (1991), 118–126.

6. For the Council of Caesarea, see P. *Lond.* 1913; *CSEL* 65.54.1/2 (dating it to the year before the Council of Tyre); *Index* 6; Theodoretus, *HE* 1.28.2; Sozomenus, *HE* 2.25.1, 17. On the necessity of identifying it with 'the court of the *censor*' (*Apol. c. Ar.* 65.4), see 'Emperor and Bishops, A.D. 324–344: Some Problems,' *AJAH* 3 (1978), 53–75, at 61/2.

7. P. *Lond.* 1913.

8. Eusebius, *VC* 4.41.3/4 (Constantine's letter to the council); Athanasius, *Apol. c. Ar.* 72.1/2. The emperor makes it clear that Dionysius was to be an observer at the council, not a member of it, still less to preside.

9. J.-M. Sansterre, 'Eusèbe de Césarée et la naissance de la théorie "Césaropapiste,"' *Byzantion* 42 (1972), 131–195, 532–594, at 563–565, arguing from the letter of Dionysius partly quoted by Athanasius, *Apol. c. Ar.* 81.

10. Sozomenus, *HE* 2.25.2–6 (from the *acta* of the council), cf. *CSEL* 65.53/4.

11. Sozomenus, *HE* 2.25.12. Sozomenus also repeats from Gelasius of Caesarea the fictitious story that Athanasius was accused of sexual impropriety (cf. Rufinus, *HE* 10.18), but notes that 'it is not included in the *acta*' (*HE* 2.25.8–11).

12. Eusebius, *VC* 4.43–45; Athanasius, *Apol. c. Ar.* 84; Sozomenus, *HE* 2.27.1.

13. *Index* 8; Epiphanius, *Pan.* 68.9.4, cf. P. Peeters, 'L'épilogue du synode de Tyr en 335 (dans les Lettres festales de Saint Athanase),' *Analecta Bollandiana* 63 (1945), 131–144; T. D. Barnes, *JTS*, N.S. 37 (1986), 586–589.

14. Sozomenus, *HE* 2.25.15–19.

15. As assumed in *Constantine* (1981), 239, 400 n. 44.

16. P. *Lond.* 1914, cf. below, at n. 43.

17. For full arguments in favor of the reconstruction adopted here, see P. Peeters, 'Comment Saint Athanase s'enfuit de Tyr en 335,' *Bulletin de l'Académie Royale de Belgique, Classe des Lettres*[5] 30 (1944), 131–177, reprinted in his *Recherches d'histoire et de philologie orientales* 2 (*Subsidia Hagiographica* 27 [Brussels, 1951]), 53–90). His conclusions, adopted with slight modifications in *Constantine* (1981), 239/40, have recently been challenged by H. A. Drake, 'Athanasius' First Exile,' *Greek, Roman, and Byzantine Studies* 27 (1986), 193–204, who puts Athanasius' first interview with Constantine on 30 October and his second on 6 November.

18. *Index* 8; Epiphanius, *Pan.* 68.9.5/6.

19. As the Caesar Constantinus asserted in 337 (*Apol. c. Ar.* 87.4).

20. As is supposed by Girardet, *Kaisergericht* (1975), 68–73, 104/5, 155/6.

21. Eusebius, *VC* 4.27.2.

22. On the meaning of the phrase οἱ περὶ τὸν δεῖνα in ancient Greek of all periods, see S. Radt, 'Noch einmal Aischylos, Niobe Fr. 162 N.[2] (278 M),' *ZPE* 38 (1980), 47–58; 'Οἱ (αἱ, etc.) περὶ + acc. nominis proprii bei Strabo,' *ZPE* 71 (1988), 35–40; 'Addendum,' *ZPE* 74 (1988), 108. In normal Greek usage of the period, such a phrase often designates the individual named alone (as in Socrates, *HE* 2.22.4, 23.2): see E. Schwyzer and A. Debrunner, *Griechische Grammatik* 2[3] (Munich, 1966), 504; N. Turner, *A Grammar of New Testament Greek* 3 (Edinburgh, 1963), 16. Although Müller detects this usage in Athanasius too (*Lexicon* [1952], 1169/70: 'non raro hac formula sola persona ut dux factionis significatur'), I am

not convinced that Athanasius ever uses it to designate a single individual: hence I have consistently taken οἱ περὶ Εὐσέβιον (or some other name) in Athanasius to mean 'Eusebius and his supporters.'

23. Sozomenus, *HE* 2.31.

24. App. 2.

25. Opitz on 139.15; T. D. Barnes, *AJAH* 3 (1978), 61.

26. The eastern bishops at Serdica in 343 complained that Athanasius had had Ischyras confined in military custody (*CSEL* 65.51.19).

27. Thus the synodical letter of the Council of Alexandria in 338, written by Athanasius himself (*Apol. c. Ar.* 11/2), thus the western bishops at Serdica in 343 (*CSEL* 65.115.6–116.1).

28. On the 'odd man out' Colluthus, see R. Williams, *Arius: Heresy and Tradition* (London, 1987), 45–47.

29. Chapter IV.

30. *CSEL* 65.76 No. 34; Socrates, *HE* 2.20.23, cf. Feder, *Studien* II (1910), 79–81.

31. The precise date of the list is uncertain: Opitz on 149.19 dated it to 325/6, whereas A. Martin, 'Athanase et les Mélitiens (325–335),' *Politique et théologie* (1974), 31–61, at 37, suggests November 327. Although Martin denies its existence, the Council of Nicomedia, which discussed the Melitian schism in December 327 or January 328 (Chapter II, at n. 75) provides an appropriate context for Alexander's reception of such a list.

32. Gelasius of Cyzicus, *HE* 3.18. The two versions are conveniently printed in parallel by G. Loeschke, 'Das Syntagma des Gelasius Cyzicenus,' *Rheinisches Museum*, N.F. 60 (1905), 594–613; 61 (1906), 34–77, at 34–36.

33. L. Parmentier, *Theodorets Kirchengeschichte* (*GCS* 19, 1911), lxii/lxiii; Schwartz, *Ges. Schr.* 3 (1959), 258 n. 1; Opitz on 164.12: 'Gelasius . . . der den Brief in seiner phantastischen Art erweitert.' For a recent statement of the case, see C. T. H. R. Ehrhardt, 'Constantinian Documents in Gelasius of Cyzicus, Ecclesiastical History,' *Jahrbuch für Antike und Christentum* 23 (1980), 48–57. His argument rests upon the explicit (and mistaken) assumption that 'there were hundreds of copies of the authentic text in the eastern provinces' (55 n. 47).

34. G. Loeschke, *Rheinisches Museum*, N.F. 61 (1906), 38/9.

35. As Opitz 165.7.

36. Constantine was born at Naissus (Firmicus Maternus, *Math.* 1.10.13; *Origo Constantini Imperatoris* 2), but Julian, *Misopogon* 18, 348d, appears to indicate that his ancestors came from Dacia Ripensis: see R. Syme, 'The Ancestry of Constantine,' *Bonner Historia-Augusta-Colloquium 1971* (1974), 237–253, reprinted in his *Historia Augusta Papers* (Oxford, 1983), 63–79.

37. *CJ* 1.40.4.

38. *New Empire* (1982), 79 n. 136.

39. Socrates, *HE* 2.23.15–32, quotes Julius' letter to the Alexandrian church in 346 (*Apol. c. Ar.* 52/3) with an extra paragraph in the middle (*HE* 2.23.22–26ª). Opitz on 133.19ff. assumed that the extra material must be a later addition: 'der Brief ist aus Athan(asius) bei Sokr(ates) II.23, 15–32 mit einigen Erweiterungen erhalten.' More charitably, Montfaucon opined that modesty led Athanasius to omit a passage which praised him strongly (*PG* 25.345 n. 23).

40. Gelasius, *HE* 3.18.4–8.

41. N. H. Baynes, 'Athanasiania,' *JEA* 11 (1925), 58–69, at 63 = *Byzantine Studies and Other Essays* (London, 1955), 285: 'no Athanasian forgery, but Athanasian suppression of embarrassing veracity.'

42. *P. Lond.* 1914, published by H. I. Bell, *Jews and Christians in Egypt* (London, 1924), 53–71. For important textual and historical observations, see also K. Holl, 'Die Bedeutung der neuveröffentlichten melitianischen Urkunden für die Kirchengeschichte,' *Sitzungsberichte der preussischen Akademie der Wissenschaften zu Berlin*, Philosophisch-historische Klasse 1925.18–31, reprinted in his *Gesammelte Aufsätze zur Kirchengeschichte* 2 (Tübingen, 1927), 283–297. An unsuccessful attempt to impugn the inferences drawn by Bell and Holl has recently been made by D. W.-H. Arnold, 'Sir Harold Idris Bell and Athanasius: A Reconsideration of *London Papyrus 1914*,' *Studia Patristica* 21 (1989), 377–383; *Early Career* (1991), esp. 62–89, 175–186.

43. K. Holl, *Sb. Berlin*, Phil.-hist. Kl. 1925.21–24; H. Hauben, 'On the Melitians in P. London VI (P. Jews) 1914: The Problem of Papas Heraiscus,' *Proceedings of the Sixteenth International Congress of Papyrology* (*American Studies in Papyrology* 23 [Chico, 1981]), 447–456.

44. On the 'behavior of Athanasius' and the importance of *P. Lond.* 1914, see now Hanson, *Search* (1988), 239–262.

IV. A JOURNEY TO CAPPADOCIA

1. *New Empire* (1982), 85–87; below, App. 9.
2. For discussion of the dynastic murders of 337 and their political context, see J. W. Leedom, 'Constantius II: Three Revisions,' *Byzantion* 48 (1978), 132–135; R. Klein, 'Die Kämpfe um die Nachfolge nach dem Tode Constantins des Grossen,' *Byzantinische Forschungen* 6 (1979), 101–150; C. Piétri, 'La politique de Constance II: Un premier "césaropapisme" ou l'*imitatio Constantini?*' *L'Église et l'empire au IVe siècle* (*Entretiens sur l'antiquité classique* 34 [Vandoeuvres, 1989]), 113–172, at 116–127. Klein unfortunately starts from the assumption that the three sons of Constantine met at Viminacium in June 338 (101).
3. *New Empire* (1982), 198–200.
4. J. P. C. Kent, *RIC* 8 (1981), 32/3. On *CTh* 12.1.37, see App. 9 n. 5.
5. App. 9.
6. *Constantine* (1981), 250.
7. Julian, *Caes.* 329 cd; *CIL* 3.12483, cf. App. 9 n. 4.
8. *CSEL* 65.54.25–55.5. Since the letter was originally written in Greek, I take the plural *aliqui* and its oblique cases to reflect an original τινές, etc., and translate accordingly.
9. For what follows, see Socrates, *HE* 2.6–7, with App. 8.
10. Quoted and discussed in App. 8.
11. Theodoretus, *HE* 2.3.8.
12. For proof that the year must be 337, not 338, see Schwartz, *Ges. Schr.* 3 (1959), 269/70; W. Schneemelcher, 'Die Epistula encyclica des Athanasius,' *Aufsätze* (1974), 290–337, at 312/3; A. Martin, *Sources chrétiennes* 317 (Paris, 1985), 81–89; C. Piétri, *L'Église et l'empire au IVe siècle* (1989), 120/1.
13. Observe that the *History of the Arians* states that the council wrote to Constantinus and Constans denouncing Athanasius (9.1), whereas the Council of

Alexandria in 338 speaks of a letter 'to the emperors,' that is, to all three imperial brothers (*Apol. c. Ar.* 3.5–7).

14. So, recently, L. W. Barnard, 'Two Notes on Athanasius,' *Orientalia Christiana Periodica* 41 (1975), 344–356, reprinted in his *Studies in Church History and Patristics* (ΑΝΑΛΕΚΤΑ ΒΛΑΤΑΔΩΝ 26 [Thessaloniki, 1978]), 341–353; B. H. Warmington, 'Did Athanasius Write History?' *The Inheritance of Historiography, 350–900,* ed. C. Holdsworth and T. P. Wiseman (Exeter, 1986), 7–16, esp. 7, 12. Schwartz, *Ges. Schr.* 3 (1959), 279–290 (originally published in 1911) correctly and carefully distinguished between the two councils held at Antioch in the winters of 337/8 and 338/9 respectively. Nevertheless, several subsequent treatments conflate them—and Schneemelcher, *Aufsätze* (1974), 297–313, 329–330, reaches the surprising conclusion that in 339 Athanasius was not deposed by a council of bishops, but merely dismissed by the emperor.

15. Emending the genitive ἐπισκόπων (Opitz 92.18) to the nominative ἐπίσκοποι.

16. Chapter III.

17. So, recently, W. H. C. Frend, *The Rise of Christianity* (Philadelphia, 1984), 527.

18. At Opitz 98.22 I read οὐδέν for οὐδενί.

19. Listed by Opitz on 89.1ff.

20. Opitz on 89.1ff.: 'das Schreiben ist dem Stil nach von Athanasius verfasst.'

21. πυκτία τῶν θείων γραφῶν: G. W. H. Lampe, *A Patristic Greek Lexicon* (Oxford, 1961), 1207, cites this passage for the meaning 'book/volume (opp. papyrus roll).'

22. Eusebius, *VC* 4.36, cf. G. A. Robbins, '"Fifty Copies of the Sacred Writings" (*VC* 4:36): Entire Bibles or Gospel Books?' *Studia Patristica* 19 (1989), 91–98.

23. *Constantine* (1981), 124/5.

24. A. Rahlfs, 'Alter und Heimat der vatikanischen Bibelhandschrift,' *Nachrichten der königlichen Gesellschaft der Wissenschaften zu Göttingen,* Philologisch-historische Klasse 1899.72–79; T. Zahn, 'Athanasius und der Bibelkanon,' *Festschrift der Universität Erlangen für Prinzregent Luitpold* (Leipzig, 1901), 1–36; J. N. Birdsall, *Cambridge History of the Bible* 1 (Cambridge, 1970), 359/60, cf. J. Ruwet, 'Le canon alexandrin des Écritures: S. Athanase,' *Biblica* 33 (1952), 1–29. The Alexandrian origin of the Codex Vaticanus, already a very strong probability, was rendered certain by P. Bodmer XIV, published in 1961: see the bibliography and brief discussion in B. M. Metzger, *Manuscripts of the Greek Bible* (New York and Oxford, 1981), 68, 74.

25. Athanasius says that the letter was sent 'to all [bishops] and to Julius, the bishop of Rome' (*Apol. c. Ar.* 20.1), but that must surely be an exaggeration.

26. C. Piétri, 'La question d'Athanase vue de Rome (338–360),' *Politique et théologie* (1974), 93–126, at 95–100.

27. Schwartz, *Ges. Schr.* 3 (1959), 278/9, deduced that Secundus had consecrated Pistus bishop of the Mareotis. But the verb καθίστημι and the cognate noun κατάστασις are used with equal frequency of the consecration of bishops and the ordination of priests.

28. Schwartz, *Ges. Schr.* 3 (1959), 284/5.

29. Above, at n. 12.

30. Chapter X.

31. For example, by Seeck, *Regesten* (1919), 186; N. H. Baynes, 'Athanasiania,' *JEA* 11 (1925), 58–69, at 65–69, on the assumption that Athanasius returned to Alex-

andria in November 338. For an attempt to squeeze the interview in Cappadocia into the autumn of 337, see C. Piétri, *L'Église et l'empire au IVe siécle* (1989), 124, 174/5.

32. App. 9.

33. Julian, *Orat.* 1, 20d–21a, cf. P. Peeters, 'L'intervention politique de Constance II dans la Grande Arménie, en 338,' *Bulletin de l'Académie Royale de Belgique, Classe des Lettres*⁵ 17 (1931), 10–47, reprinted in his *Recherches d'histoire et de philologie orientales* 1 (*Subsidia Hagiographica* 27 [Brussels, 1951]), 222–250. Peeters dated Constantius' intervention in Armenia late in the year because he placed Shapur's first siege of Nisibis in 338, with appeal to E. Stein, *Geschichte des spätrömischen Reiches* 1 (Vienna, 1928), 212, and to N. H. Baynes, *JEA* 11 (1925), 66–69. But Athanasius' journey to Caesarea must belong to the spring of 338, not the autumn: the siege, therefore, should belong to 337, as argued by Baynes, ib. 66, and in 'Constantine and the Christians of Persia,' *JRS* 75 (1985), 126–136 at 133.

34. *CSEL* 65.55.26–56.7.

35. As argued by Schwartz, *Ges. Schr.* 3 (1959), 291/2.

36. Respectively, V. Peri, 'La cronologia delle lettere festali di Sant' Atanasio e la Quaresima,' *Aevum* 35 (1961), 28–86, esp. 48–50; M. Albert, 'La 10e lettre festale d'Athanase d'Alexandrie (traduction et interprétation),' *Parole de l'Orient* 6–7 (1975–1976), 69–90.

37. See now the facsimile edition with German translation by Lorenz, *Osterfestbrief* (1986), 38–65.

38. App. 1.

39. In the three passages quoted here, I have changed Jessie Payne Smith's translation fairly freely in the light of the German version of Lorenz, *Osterfestbrief* (1986), 39–65.

40. On the theological and polemical content of the letter, see further Lorenz, *Osterfestbrief* (1986), 68–89; Camplani, *Lettere* (1989), 245–256.

41. On the date of the letter, see further App. 1, at nn. 47–51.

42. *Index* 10; *Vita Antonii* 69–71. M. Tetz, 'Athanasius und die Vita Antonii: Literarische und theologische Relationen,' *ZNW* 73 (1982), 1–30, at 23/4, argues that Antony visited Alexandria in 337 before Athanasius returned from Trier and that the 'we' in *Vita Antonii* 71 reflects the fact that this account of Antony's visit to Alexandria was originally written by Serapion of Thmuis.

43. Gregory of Nazianzus, *Orat.* 21.28. For Philagrius' second term as prefect, see now *P. Oxy.* 3793, 3794, 3820, with the comments of J. R. Rea, *Oxyrhynchus Papyri* 55 (London, 1988), 62–67, 221–224, corrected in certain particulars by W. H. C. Frend, 'Dioscorus of Oxyrhynchus and His Correspondence (P. Oxy. LV 3820),' *ZPE* 79 (1989), 248–250.

44. Socrates, *HE* 2.8.6: ὅτι μὴ γνώμῃ κοινοῦ συνεδρίου τῶν ἐπισκόπων τὴν τάξιν τῆς ἱεροσύνης ἀνέλαβεν. The fact that Socrates confuses the council of the winter of 338/9 with the 'Dedication Council' of 341 in no way impairs the value of his testimony (App. 5).

45. For the various surviving versions of the synodical letter and canons of this earlier council, see *CPG* 8535, 8536; on the date, Schwartz, *Ges. Schr.* 3 (1959), 216–222; T. D. Barnes, 'Emperor and Bishops, A.D. 324–344: Some Problems,' *AJAH* 3 (1978), 53–75, at 59/60.

46. Socrates, *HE* 2.9, expressly basing himself on the lost biography of Eusebius by George of Laodicea—which also reported that Eusebius used to accompany Constantius on military campaigns. On the theology of Eusebius, see Hanson, *Search* (1988), 387–396; M. F. Wiles, 'The Theology of Eusebius of Emesa,' *Studia Patristica* 19 (1989), 267–280.

47. Socrates, *HE* 2.10.1, cf. *CSEL* 65.55.5/6: 'sancto et integro sacerdote'—an admittedly partisan, but nevertheless specific and emphatic, description.

V. ATHANASIUS IN ROME

1. For a modern example of the commonplace, compare Newman to Bishop Ullathorne on 28 January 1870 with reference to the Vatican Council: 'What have we done to be treated, as the faithful never were treated before?' (*Letters and Diaries of John Henry Newman*, ed. S. Dessain and T. Gornall 25 [Oxford, 1973], 18).

2. For a more detailed analysis, see Schneemelcher, 'Die Epistula encyclica des Athanasius,' *Aufsätze* (1974), 290–337.

3. Opitz on 173.14ff. rightly rejects the common view that the Friday in *Ep. enc.* 4.4 is Good Friday (13 April).

4. Socrates, *HE* 2.11.6. The burning of the church is also mentioned by Julius in his letter of 341 (*Apol. c. Ar.* 30.3). On the different churches of Alexandria, see A. Martin, 'Les premiers siècles du Christianisme à Alexandrie: Essai de topographie religieuse (IIIᵉ–IVᵉ siècles),' *REAug* 30 (1984), 211–235.

5. *CSEL* 65.55.5–7.

6. Chapter IV.

7. *CSEL* 65.55.

8. So Schwartz, *Ges. Schr.* 3 (1959), 291/2.

9. W. Eltester, 'Die Kirchen Antiochias im IV. Jahrhundert,' *ZNW* 36 (1937), 251–286, at 245–256; W. Schneemelcher, 'Die Kirchweihsynode von Antiochien 341,' *Bonner Festgabe Johannes Straub zum 65. Geburtstag am 18. October 1977 dargebracht von Kollegen und Schülern* (Bonn, 1977), 319–346.

10. I take γράμματα as reflecting an original *litterae* in the sense of 'a (single) letter,' and I have replaced Julius' 'we' with the first-person singular. For other Latinisms in the Greek translation of Julius' letter quoted by Athanasius, see F. E. Brightman, 'Six Notes,' *JTS*, 29 (1928), 158–165, at 159.

11. Opitz on 108.31 made the correct deduction, though inevitably, given the date at which he was writing, he assumed that the 'Dedication Council' met in the second half of 341.

12. Rather than in hiding before he left Egypt, as is supposed by W. Schneemelcher, *Bonner Festgabe* (1977), 322.

13. Chapter VII, at n. 19.

14. App. 9, cf. *New Empire* (1982), 198–200.

15. The date is inferred from Paulinus, *Vita Ambrosii* 3/4, cf. 'Imperial Chronology, A.D. 337–350,' *Phoenix* 34 (1980), 160–166, at 161 n. 5.

16. *CTh* 11.12.1: 'publicus ac noster inimicus.'

17. For a critical text and discussion, see now J.-P. Callu, 'La préface à l'*Itinéraire d'Alexandre*,' *De Tertullien aux Mozarabes: Mélanges offerts à J. Fontaine* 1 (Paris, 1992), 429–443.

18. H. A. Cahn, '*Abolitio nominis* de Constantin II,' *Mélanges de numismatique offerts*

à P. Bastien (Wetteren, 1987), 201/2. Constantinus' name is found erased on inscriptions at Smyrna in Asia (*CIL* 3.474, 477, 7198), at Celeia in Noricum (*CIL* 3.5207), at Brescia in Italy (*CIL* 5.8030), and at Avita Bibba in Africa (*CIL* 8.12272). Cahn plausibly suggests that the gold and silver coinage of Constantinus was withdrawn from circulation and melted down (202).

19. Libanius, *Orat.* 59, esp. 34, 43 (where the orator speaks of the two sons and their father), 75 (the conference of 337). On the date of the speech, see App. 9, n. 19.

20. Chapter IV, at nn. 18–23.

21. In the dialogue of 355 reported by Theodoretus, Constantius complains to Liberius that Athanasius, 'not satisfied with the ruin of the older of my brothers, did not cease from inciting the blessed Constans to hatred against me' (*HE* 2.16.21).

22. The form of the names must be regarded as quite uncertain: Opitz 283.20, 21, printed Ἀβουήριον and Σπειράντιον, but one important manuscript offers Ἀβουτήριον. Neither man earns an entry in *PLRE* 1.

23. *PLRE* 1.316. Accordingly, I have translated σου in 4.5 as 'the emperor's,' since it must refer to Constantius. It seems impossible to reproduce in translation the word-play on the form of Eutropia's name unanimously given by the manuscripts (Εὔτροπος = 'morally good').

24. Jerome, *Epp.* 127.5. However, there are serious chronological difficulties involved in accepting Jerome's precise statement that Athanasius told Marcella about Antony and Pachomius: on the standard reconstruction of her family connections, Marcella's mother Albina was the daughter of a man born in 303 (see *PLRE* 1.32, 542/3, with 'Two Senators under Constantine,' *JRS* 65 [1975], 40–49). Hence Marcella herself, who died in 410/1, cannot have been born before c. 340.

25. Chapter VI.

26. *PG* 26.12–468 (from Montfaucon). The fourth *Oration* (*PG* 26.468–525) has long been recognised to be from another hand (*CPG* 2230), but Athanasius' authorship of the third is also denied by C. Kannengiesser, 'Le mystère pascal du Christ selon Athanase d'Alexandrie,' *Rech. sci. rel.* 63 (1975), 407–442; *Athanase* (1983), 310–368, who attributes it to Apollinaris of Laodicea. In favor of the transmitted attribution, see the review by G. C. Stead, *JTS*, N.S. 36 (1985), 227–229; D. Schmitz, 'Schimpfwörter in Athanasius' Reden gegen die Arianer,' *Roma Renascens: Beiträge zur Spätantike und Rezeptionsgeschichte Ilona Opelt gewidmet,* ed. M. Wissemann (Frankfurt, Bern, New York, and Paris, 1988), 308–320 (showing that the first three *Orations* all use precisely the same techniques of polemical defamation).

As for the process of composition, C. Kannengiesser, 'Athanasius of Alexandria: Three Orations against the Arians: A Reappraisal,' *Studia Patristica* 17.3 (1982), 981–995; *Athanase* (1983), esp. 369–374, detects a 'genèse graduelle' of the first two *Orations* in the course of the 340s. On the other hand, there are good reasons for thinking that Athanasius wrote the first two *Orations* c. 340, then composed the homily on Matthew 11.27 (*PG* 25.207–220; *CPG* 2099) as part of a projected third *Oration,* which he completed along slightly different lines only some time later: see V. Hugger, 'Des hl. Athanasius Traktat in Mt. 11, 27,' *Zeitschrift für die katholische Theologie* 42 (1918), 437–441; M. Tetz, *TRE* 4 (1978), 339, 345. Hugger shows that, while Chapter 6 of the homily is spurious, the rest overlaps with the third *Oration,* in which Tetz detects allusions to the teaching of Photinus, who first attained prominence c. 344 (3.1, 3.30).

27. Kannengiesser, *Athanase* (1983), 19–111.

28. Observe, however, that the word τριάς is used only once (1.58) outside two passages each of which repeats it several times (1.17/8, 3.15): see J. Wolinski, 'L'emploi de τριάς dans les "Traités contre les Ariens" d'Athanase d'Alexandrie,' *Studia Patristica* 21 (1989), 448–455.

29. Chapter XVI.

30. W. Bright, *The Orations of St. Athanasius against the Arians* (Oxford, 1873), lxviii–lxxiv; A. Stegmann, 'Zur Datierung der "drei Reden des hl. Athanasius gegen die Arianer" (Migne, Patrol. Graec. XXVI, 9–468),' *Theologische Quartalschrift* 96 (1914), 423–450; 98 (1916), 227–231.

31. Chapter XIV. The term occurs only once in the *Orations*, in a quasi-credal context: the Son 'θεός ἐστιν ἀληθινός, ἀληθινοῦ πατρὸς ὁμοούσιος ὑπάρχων' (1.9).

32. On the quotations of the *Thalia*, see esp. R. D. Williams, 'The Quest of the Historical *Thalia*,' *Arianism* (1985), 1–35; S. G. Hall, 'The *Thalia* of Arius in Athanasius' Accounts,' ib. 37–58. On the letter of Alexander (*Urkunde* 4b), see Chapter II, at nn. 60–64.

33. Kannengiesser, *Athanase* (1983), 151–181, cf. G. Bardy, *Recherches sur Saint Lucien d'Antioche et son école* (Paris, 1936), 341–347; Hanson, *Search* (1988), 32–41.

34. *Constantine* (1981), 241.

VI. JULIUS AND MARCELLUS

1. *EOMIA* 1.30, 50, 51, cf. Hanson, *Search* (1988), 217.

2. Julius praises his role at the council most warmly (*Apol. c. Ar.* 23.3, 32.2). No work is transmitted under the name of Marcellus except for the quotations in Eusebius (*CPG* 2800) and his letter to Julius (*CPG* 2801), but modern scholars have made a strong case for regarding him as the author of several works attributed to other writers of the fourth century: of these, the *De sancta ecclesia*, which is transmitted under the name of Anthimus, bishop of Nicomedia early in the century (*CPG* 2802), was probably written c. 340 in the West: see A. H. B. Logan, 'Marcellus of Ancyra and anti-Arian Polemic,' *Studia Patristica* 19 (1989), 189–197.

3. Sozomenus, *HE* 2.33.3.

4. Eusebius, *Contra Marcellum* 1.1.3, 1.4.1–65, 2.4.29.

5. Eusebius, *Contra Marcellum* 2.4.29; *CSEL* 65.50.18–51.15; Sozomenus, *HE* 2.33.1/2, cf. 'Emperor and Bishops, A.D. 324–344: Some Problems,' *AJAH* 3 (1978), 53–75, at 64/5; *Constantine* (1981), 240–242.

6. *CSEL* 65.55.

7. *Constantine* (1981), 263–265.

8. Chapter IV, at nn. 44–45.

9. Marcellus had been in Rome for one year and three months before he submitted a written statement of his theological views to Julius (Epiphanius, *Pan.* 72.2.3).

10. Sozomenus, *HE* 3.8.3, cf. Socrates, *HE* 2.15.3.

11. The number of bishops present is given by Hilary, *Syn.* 28 (*PL* 10.502); Sozomenus, *HE* 4.22.22. On all aspects of the 'Dedication Council,' see the magisterial study of W. Schneemelcher, 'Die Kirchweihsynode von Antiochien 341,' *Bonner Festgabe Johannes Straub zum 65. Geburtstag am 18. October 1977*

dargebracht von Kollegen und Schülern (Bonn, 1977), 319–346. It is unfortunately neglected by Hanson, *Search* (1988), 270–293, who follows earlier writers (such as Simonetti, *Crisi* [1975], 146–160) in making Julius' letter (*Apol. c. Ar.* 21–35) precede the 'Dedication Council,' to which it is in fact a riposte.

12. The day is known only from a Syriac chronicle written in 724 (ed. E. W. Brooks, CSCO, Scriptores Syri[3] 4 [1903], 130.21–24, with Latin translation by J. B. Chabot [Versio 102.3–5]), but it derives from a source written in the 360s (Philostorgius, Anhang VII, p. 212 Bidez, cf. Chapter I, at nn. 57–59) and deserves to be accepted: see W. Eltester, 'Die Kirchen Antiochias im IV. Jahrhundert,' *ZNW* 36 (1937), 251–286, at 254–256.

13. J. T. Lienhard, 'Acacius of Caesarea's *Contra Marcellum*: Its Place in Theology and Controversy,' *Studia Patristica* 19 (1989), 183–188. Only a long fragment survives, quoted by Epiphanius, *Pan.* 72.6–10 (*CPG* 3512). On Acacius' career, see J.-M. Leroux, 'Acace, évêque de Césarée de Palestine (341–365),' *Studia Patristica* 8 (*Texte und Untersuchungen* 93, 1966), 82–85.

14. W. Schneemelcher, *Bonner Festgabe* (1977), 331–339.

15. Kelly, *Creeds*[3] (1972), 263/4.

16. On the nature and theological motivation of this creed (which are disputed), see Kelly, *Creeds*[3] (1972), 268–271; W. Schneemelcher, *Bonner Festgabe* (Bonn, 1977), 340–346.

17. Marcellus frag. 96 Klostermann = Eusebius, *Contra Marcellum* 1.4.33/4.

18. Kelly, *Creeds*[3] (1972), 266. Observe Hilary, *Syn.* 28 (*PL* 10.502): 'exposuerunt qui adfuerunt episcopi nonaginta septem, cum in suspicionem venisset unus ex episcopis quod prava sentiret.'

19. See now M. Tetz, 'Die Kirchweihsynode von Antiochien (341) und Marcellus von Ancyra: Zu der Glaubenserklärung des Theophronius von Tyana und ihren Folgen,' *Oecumenica et Patristica: Festschrift für Wilhelm Schneemelcher zum 75. Geburtstag* (Geneva, 1989), 199–218. This article proposes an important and convincing emendation in *Syn.* 24.5 (Opitz 250.19–21).

20. Sozomenus, *HE* 3.8.4–8. Schwartz, *Ges. Schr.* 3 (1959), 297–300, conveniently prints together the summary of Sozomenus and the quotations and allusions in Julius' letter: for comment, see Girardet, *Kaisergericht* (1975), 157–162.

21. It is implausibly argued by L. W. Barnard, 'Pope Julius, Marcellus of Ancyra and the Council of Serdica: A Reconsideration,' *Revue de théologie ancienne et médiévale* 38 (1971), 69–79, reprinted in his *Studies in Church History and Patristics* (ΑΝΑΛΕΚΤΑ ΒΛΑΤΑΔΩΝ 26 [Thessaloniki, 1978]), 341–353, that Julius was more conciliatory than the council, which compelled him to take a hard line.

22. Bishops of, respectively, Caesarea in Cappadocia, Antioch, Neronias, Constantinople, Chalcedon, Mopsuestia, and Heraclea. The fact that Dianius' name comes first may indicate that he had presided over the council: according to the *Synodicon vetus* 42, he was accompanied by the sophist Asterius.

23. H. J. Sieben, *Die Konzilsidee der Alten Kirche* (Paderborn, 1979), 31–34. Julius' letter has often been discussed for its relevance to the claims of the Roman see to primacy, as recently by P.-P. Joannou, *Die Ostkirche und die Cathedra Petri im 4. Jahrhundert* (*Päpste und Papsttum* 3 [Stuttgart, 1972]), 36–70; W. de Vries, 'Die Ostkirche und die Cathedra Petri im IV. Jahrhundert,' *Orientalia Christiana*

Periodica 40 (1974), 114–144, at 121–129; Girardet, *Kaisergericht* (1975), 87–105; Piétri, *Roma* (1976), 189–207; V. Twomey, *Apostolikos Thronos: The Primacy of Rome as Reflected in the Church History of Eusebius and the Historico-apologetical Writings of Saint Athanasius the Great* (Münster, 1982), 398–425.

24. Opitz on 103.24 correctly compares 35.3 and notes that Julius implicitly appeals to the fifth Nicene canon—which provides only that a provincial council of bishops may review the cases of excommunicated clergy and laity, but says nothing whatever about deposed bishops. A more pertinent precedent would have been the readmission of Eusebius, Theognis, and Arius by the Council of Nicomedia in 327/8 (*Urkunden* 29–32). But Athanasius studiously avoided any explicit mention of that council (Chapter III, at n. 25).

25. Reiterated in his recapitulation of the whole case (31.1).

26. For Athanasius' use of the same collection of documents in 338 and in his *Defense against the Arians*, see Chapter III, at n. 31; Chapter IV, at n. 19.

27. Opitz on 109.1 aptly cites the *Itinerarium Antonini* 147.1–154.5 Wesseling (p. 21 Cuntz), which confirms the figure exactly. Like so much in Julius' letter, this complaint comes from the mind of Athanasius, who makes the same polemical point in reference to the appointments of eastern bishops to western sees in the 350s (*Letter to the Bishops of Egypt and Libya* 7; *Hist. Ar.* 74.5).

28. Epiphanius, *Pan.* 72.2.1/2, cf. M. Tetz, 'Zum altrömischen Bekenntnis: Ein Beitrag des Marcellus von Ancyra,' *ZNW* 75 (1984), 107–127.

29. Kelly, *Creeds*[3] (1972), 102–111.

30. Opitz on 113.1ff. aptly comments: 'Der Urheber dieser Argumentation kann nur Athanasius sein.'

31. For the identifications in the text, see Opitz on 111.11, citing *CSEL* 65.55/6; *Fug.* 3.3; *Hist. Ar.* 5.1/2; Socrates, *HE* 1.24.3; 2.15.2.

32. Chapters VII, VIII, X.

33. Epiphanius, *Pan.* 72.2.3.

VII. THE INTERVENTION OF CONSTANS

1. Chapter X. Lucifer of Caralis depicts Constantius as saying that he allowed the return of Athanasius at the insistence of Constans precisely because 'timui ne inter nos bella fuissent orta' (*De Athanasio* 1.29.28).

2. Chapter XIII.

3. App. 3. The later additions to the first eighteen chapters comprise a reference to the death of Magnentius (7.3[b]) and a general description of disorder in the church everywhere which includes an allusion to the exile of Egyptian bishops in 357 (13, cf. 28.1).

4. The passage is translated and discussed above in Chapter IV, at nn. 28–29.

5. Chapter II.

6. The procedures and techniques of argumentation taught by Greek rhetors in the Roman Empire are well described by D. A. Russell, *Greek Declamation* (Cambridge, 1983), esp. 40–73.

7. Quintilian states the norm in lapidary fashion: 'ordine ipso narrationem sequitur confirmatio' (*Inst. Orat.* 4.3.1). For *narratio* as a standard element in speeches, see *Rhetorica ad Herennium* 1.12–16; Cicero, *De Inventione* 1.27–30; *Orator* 122; Quintilian, *Inst. Orat.* 4.2, with K. Barwick, 'Die Gliederung der narratio in der

rhetorischen Theorie und ihre Bedeutung für die Geschichte des antiken Romans,' *Hermes* 63 (1928), 261–287.

8. The manuscripts have Κρισπῖνος ὁ τῆς Παταβων: the form is paralleled by the *civitas Patavi* found in late antique maps: see K. Miller, *Itineraria Romana: Römische Reisewege an der Hand der Tabula Peutingeriana* (Berlin, 1916), 259.

9. All manuscripts and editors read Διονύσιος ὁ ἐν Ληίδι, and the bishop's see is normally identified as the small north Italian town of Laus Pompeia: so C. H. Turner, *EOMIA* 1.557; Opitz on 281.14. But it is linguistically implausible to identify a 'Leis' (where the emphatic vowel is represented by the Greek *eta*) with the modern Lodi: all attested ancient forms of the name of the town exhibit the o-vowel which survives in the modern name (K. Miller, *Itineraria* [1916], 204). Feder, *Studien* II (1910), 43, saw that the Dionysius in Athanasius should be identical with the *dionisius ab Acaia de Elida* who subscribed the synodical letter of the western bishops at Serdica in 343 (*CSEL* 65.138 No. 48). Hence the name of the see ought to be emended from Ληίδι to ᾽Ηλίδι. The bishop of Elis presumably had business at the imperial court: it is doubtless relevant that he had been deposed before the Council of Serdica, apparently by western bishops (*CSEL* 65.61.12/3: quem ipsi exposuerunt).

10. The Serdican subscriptions identify his see as Capua (*CSEL* 65.134 No. 14).

11. Feder, *Studien* I (1909), 157/8. Both Fortunatianus and Vincentius were to be persuaded (or compelled) to renounce communion with Athanasius in 357 (*Apol. ad Const.* 27.3, cf. Jerome, *De vir. ill.* 97).

12. See, respectively, R. Aigrain, 'St. Maximin de Trèves,' *Bulletin de la Société des Antiquaires de l'Ouest* 4 (1916–1918, publ. 1919), 69–93; J.-C. Picard, *Le souvenir des évêques* (*Bibliothèque des écoles françaises d'Athènes et de Rome* 268 [Rome, 1988]), 35, 41–44. Protasius appears to have died in 346 or 347; Aigrain argued that Maximinus was consecrated bishop of Trier on 13 August 329 and died on 12 September 346.

13. After Eugenius' death the emperors Constantius and Julian restored the statue of him in the forum of Trajan at Rome which 'ante sub divo Constante vitae et fidelissimae devotionis gratia meruit': since the inscription from the base of the statue records that after a career in the palatine service Eugenius was designated ordinary consul (*ILS* 1244), it is usually inferred that he must have died no later than 349 (so *PLRE* 1.292). But Athanasius assumes that Eugenius was still alive in 353: it may be suspected, therefore, that he was in fact designated consul for 355 as a reward for loyalty to the house of Constantine and perhaps for service rendered to Constantius during the usurpation of Magnentius.

14. Libanius, *Orat.* 14.10/11.

15. *PLRE* 1.886. The principal narrative evidence for his career comes from Zosimus 2.48.5, *Passio Artemii* 12 = Philostorgius, *HE* 3.12ᵃ, and Ammianus 14.1.10 (in office in summer 353), 7.9 (his death). Thalassius was one of the *comites* of Constantius who wrote to Athanasius urging him to return to Alexandria in 345/6 (*Hist. Ar.* 22.1).

16. Socrates, *HE* 2.22.5, cf. Chapter X.

17. Opitz 281.26 rightly prints Montfaucon's emendation <τετάρ>τῳ ἐνιαυτῷ (*PG* 25.600): it is hard to see how the transmitted τῷ ἐνιαυτῷ can be defended.

18. In his second edition of the speech, J.-M. Szymusiak correctly marks a break be-

tween paragraphs here (*Sources chrétiennes* 56bis [1987], 94).

19. As asserted by Girardet, *Kaisergericht* (1975), 108, with appeal to Schwartz, *Ges. Schr.* 3 (1959), 326; Opitz on 281.22ff.

20. Socrates, *HE* 2.12.1.

21. Socrates, *HE* 2.12.2–13.7, cf. App. 8.

22. Apps. 5, 9.

23. *CSEL* 65.67.1–7. Since the *clades* must be the large number of deaths in Constantinople after Paul's return in 341/2, *ut* in 67.4 presumably renders a Greek word which stated cause rather than result, and I have translated accordingly.

24. Socrates, *HE* 2.18.1/2.

25. Socrates, *HE* 2.18.3–6.

26. App. 9.

27. Kelly, *Creeds*[3] (1972), 271–273.

28. Constans is attested in Milan on 4 December 342 (*CTh* 9.7.3).

29. App. 9.

30. *CTh* 11.16.5; Firmicus Maternus, *De err. prof. rel.* 28.6; Libanius, *Orat.* 59.137–140; Ammianus 20.1.1.

31. *CTh* 12.1.36.

32. *CTh* 10.10.8[s]; 12.1.38, cf. App. 9.

VIII. THE COUNCIL OF SERDICA

1. Chapter VII.

2. Socrates, *HE* 2.20.6. The explicit evidence for the date of the Council of Serdica is either erroneous or ambiguous. Socrates, *HE* 2.20.4 (followed by Sozomenus, *HE* 3.12.7) alleges that it took place in the eleventh year after the death of Constantine in the consular year 347—which is impossible. The *Festal Index* points to either 342 or 343 (15), while a historical fragment in Cod. Ver. LX (58), fol. 71[v], has the notice: 'congregata est synodus consolatu Constantini et Constantini aput Serdicam.' Schwartz, *Ges. Schr.* 3 (1959), 11, 55/6, 325–334, argued that the correct date is 342 and emended the date accordingly to 'consolatu Constantii III et Constantis II,' while H.-G. Opitz subsequently printed this emendation in his edition of the fragment in *EOMIA* 1.637. But the notice could relate to the summoning of a council by Constans rather than to the gathering of the bishops at Serdica: see Simonetti, *Crisi* (1975), 167 n. 12.

   For varied and converging arguments in favor of 343 (the date assumed throughout the present work), see H. Hess, *The Canons of the Council of Serdica, A.D. 343: A Landmark in the Early Development of Canon Law* (Oxford, 1958), 140–144; Piétri, *Roma* (1976), 212/3 n. 3; T. D. Barnes, 'Emperor and Bishops, A.D. 324–344: Some Problems,' *AJAH* 3 (1978), 53–76, at 67–69; L. W. Barnard, 'The Council of Serdica: Some Problems Reassessed,' *Annuarium Historiae Conciliorum* 12 (1980), 1–25. However, Schwartz's date of 342 continues to find advocates: see, recently, M. Richard, 'Le comput paschal par octaétéris,' *Le Muséon* 87 (1974), 307–339, at 318–327; Brennecke, *Hilarius* (1984), 25–29; T. G. Elliott, 'The Date of the Council of Serdica,' *Ancient History Bulletin* 2 (1988), 65–72. There seems to be no ancient evidence that the council met in the sweltering heat of late summer, as asserted by L. W. Barnard, o.c. 18 ('perhaps in late August').

3. *CSEL* 65.128.4–16.

4. For the forms 'Ossius' and 'Serdica' (rather than 'Osius' and 'Sardica'), see *EOMIA* 1.532/3.
5. Athanasius is customarily believed, as by K. Baus, in *History of the Church*, ed. H. Jedin and J. Dolan, trans. A. Biggs 2 (New York, 1980), 37, 82.
6. L. W. Barnard, 'The Site of the Council of Serdica,' *Studia Patristica* 17.1 (1982), 9–13, reprinted together with the first part of the article cited in n. 2 as 'The Council of Serdica—Two Questions,' *Ancient Bulgaria*, ed. A. G. Poulter 2 (Nottingham, 1983), 215–231.
7. *CSEL* 65.119.5–120.6. On the four extant texts of this western synodical letter of the Council of Serdica, see below n. 30. In the present chapter references are normally given to Feder's base text in *CSEL* 65.103–126 (the version from Hilary).
8. *CSEL* 65.58.14–19; *Index* 15, cf. H. Hess, *Canons* (1958), 17/8.
9. *CSEL* 65.121.1–9; *Hist. Ar.* 15.4.
10. The eastern bishops reckoned their own number at eighty (*CSEL* 65.58.26). That is clearly a rounded figure: Sabinus of Heraclea gave the exact number as seventy-six (Socrates, *HE* 2.20.5, repeated without the name of the source by Sozomenus, *HE* 3.12.7), which appears to be confirmed by the surviving list of signatories, even though it actually contains only seventy-three names (*CSEL* 65.74–78, cf. Feder, *Studien* II [1910], 70–93).
11. Feder, *Studien* II (1910), 18–62, cf. H. Hess, *Canons* (1958), 9. The lists of signatories to the western synodical letter and to the Serdican canons preserved in collections of canon law contain, respectively, sixty-one and fifty-nine names (*CSEL* 65.132–139; *EOMIA* 1.545–559).
12. *CSEL* 65.48.12–16. On Eutychius and Fortunatus, see Feder, *Studien* II (1910), 113–115. Desiderius seems to be otherwise unknown.
13. *CSEL* 65.60.16/7, 109.7–112.2, 140.4–7. In 60.17 the primary manuscript has *de hanc* with a line of deletion drawn through the two words. Feder prints *de hinc* as the start of a new sentence, but the whole passage will run far better if one reads: 'immensa autem confluxerat ad Sardicam multitudo sceleratorum omnium ac perditorum adventantium de Constantinopoli, de Alexandria, de [h]Anc<yra> . . .'
14. *CSEL* 65.58.26–59.27.
15. *CSEL* 65.58.23–25; *Hist. Ar.* 16.1.
16. *CSEL* 65.60.1–15.
17. *CSEL* 65.59.25: 'per plurimos dies.'
18. *CSEL* 65.48–78.
19. *CSEL* 65.58.8–13, 61.9–12, 66.6/7. The letter names one of the four councils in question as the Council of Constantinople in 336, which Cyriacus of Naissus also attended (51.15–19), and one of the other three should be the Council of Tyre in 335: the remaining two will be councils which condemned Marcellus after his return in 337, but the council which condemned Paul can only be the Council of Constantinople which replaced him with Eusebius of Nicomedia in the autumn of 337 (Chapter IV, at nn. 8–10).
20. *CSEL* 65.61.12–22.
21. *CSEL* 65.61.23–30.
22. *CSEL* 65.57.20–22, cf. App. 8.
23. *CSEL* 65.57.18–20: 'adhuc cum esset episcopus Athanasius, Asclepam depositum sua sententia ipse damnavit.' If the text is sound, that must mean that Athanasius

accepted the deposition of Asclepas when he became bishop of Alexandria. There is perhaps a possibility that the original Greek of the eastern synodical letter had 'when Athanasius was [not yet] bishop'—and referred to an action taken by him as a delegate or envoy of Alexander. The fact that Asclepas was deposed 'ante decem et septem annos' (56.19) implies that he was condemned by the Council of Antioch in 327 presided over by Eusebius of Caesarea, which tried and deposed Eustathius of Antioch: see *AJAH* 3 (1978), 59/60.

24. *CSEL* 65.66.16–30.
25. *CSEL* 65.63.23–64.5. A later passage names the excommunicated allies of the exiles as Julius, Ossius, Protogenes, Gaudentius, and Maximinus (65.31–66.5).
26. *CSEL* 65.69–73, cf. *Syn.* 25/6.
27. Kelly, *Creeds*³ (1972), 275–277.
28. *CSEL* 65.72.4–73.5, cf. Athanasius, *Syn.* 25.5ᵇ, 26.II. My translation deliberately conflates the various versions.
29. Kelly, *Creeds*³ (1972), 276.
30. *CSEL* 65.103.5–104.4. The letter survives in three other versions: (1) Cod. Ver. LX (58), fols. 81ʳ–88ʳ, which is edited separately in *EOMIA* 1.645–653, appears to be a retroversion from Greek rather than the original Latin: see E. Schwartz, 'Der griechische Text der Kanones von Serdika,' *ZNW* 30 (1931), 1–35; I. Gelzer, 'Das Rundschreiben der Synode von Serdica,' *ZNW* 40 (1941), 1–24; (2) Athanasius, *Apol. c. Ar.* 44–49, contains a list of signatories which adds the names of more than two hundred bishops who subscribed their names after 343; (3) Theodoretus, *HE* 2.8.1–54, like (1), contains a significant passage not in the other two versions (see below, at nn. 35–41).
31. *CSEL* 65.104.9–113.7.
32. *CSEL* 65.113.8–125.3.
33. *CSEL* 65.125.4–126.3.
34. Athanasius, *Apol. c. Ar.* 42–50, quotes a Greek version of the Latin text printed in *CSEL* 65.103–126, followed by a list of two hundred and eighty-three subscriptions, including the priests Archidamus and Philoxenus, who subscribed on behalf of Julius of Rome in second place after Ossius who presided (not in the Latin subscriptions preserved from Hilary [*CSEL* 65.132–139]). The same work claims that more than three hundred bishops subscribed (*Apol. c. Ar.* 1.2).
35. For a critical text, see now M. Tetz, 'Ante omnia de sancta fide et de integritate veritatis: Glaubensfragen auf der Synode von Serdica,' *ZNW* 76 (1985), 243–269, at 252–254. The theological statement is preserved only in the versions of the letter in Theodoretus, *HE* 2.8.1–52, and Cod. Ver. LX (58), fols. 81ʳ–88ʳ (*EOMIA* 1.645–653).
36. Kelly, *Creeds*³ (1972), 277. On its theological content, see also F. Loofs, *Das Glaubensbekenntnis der Homousianer von Sardica* (*Abhandlungen der königlichen preussischen Akademie der Wissenschaften zu Berlin*, Philosophisch-historische Klasse 1909, Abhandlung 1), 11–39; M. Tetz, *ZNW* 76 (1985), 255–266.
37. Kelly, *Creeds*³ (1972), 278.
38. As S. G. Hall, 'The Creed of Serdica,' *Studia Patristica* 19 (1989), 173–182.
39. M. Tetz, *ZNW* 76 (1985), 266–269.
40. *Tomus ad Antiochenos* 5.1.
41. *EOMIA* 1.644, reedited by M. Tetz, *ZNW* 76 (1985), 247/8.

42. *CSEL* 65.107.8: 'Athanasium et Marcellum, Asclepium, et alios'; 122.5–8: 'carissimos quidem fratres et coepiscopos nostros Athanasium Alexandriae et Marcellum Ancyro-Galatiae et Asclepium Gazae et eos qui cum ipsis erant ministrantes deo innocentes et puros pronuntiavimus.'

43. *CSEL* 65.134 No. 19, cf. Feder, *Studien* II (1910), 32/3.

44. *CSEL* 65.55.10/1: 'Paulo Constantinopolitanae civitatis quondam episcopo.'

45. As is often assumed: for example, A. Lippold, 'Paulus 29,' *RE*, Supp. 10 (1965), 510–520; Hanson, *Search* (1988), 293–306.

46. Chapter VII, at nn. 20–23.

47. Socrates, *HE* 2.20.12. Photius in the ninth century knew from hagiographical sources that Paul was at Serdica as well as vindicated by the council, and he plausibly states that Ossius on his return to Spain held a council at Corduba to confirm the decisions of the Council of Serdica (*Bibliotheca* 257, 476 a 20/1; 258, 481 b 40/1; *Homily* 16.6/7, pp. 158/9 Laourda, cf. C. Mango, *The Homilies of Photius, Patriarch of Constantinople* [Cambridge, Mass., 1958], 238, 271 n. 33). The even later *Synodicon vetus* 43–50 also correctly states that the cases of Paul and Athanasius were linked in the 340s.

48. *CSEL* 65.126–131.

49. The letters of Athanasius to the clergy of Alexandria and to the churches of the Mareotis (*EOMIA* 1.654–656, 659) and of the council to the churches of the Mareotis (*EOMIA* 1.657/8) refer to the reading of letters from the addressees at sessions of the council.

50. *Apol. c. Ar.* 37–41, with Opitz's important textual note on 118.19ff.

51. *EOMIA* 1.657/8.

52. *Chr. min.* 1.63 (Rome); *Index* 15 (Alexandria).

53. The Paschal cycle in Cod. Ver. LX (58), fols. 79ᵛ–80ᵛ, published in E. Schwartz, *Christliche und jüdische Ostertafeln* (*Abhandlungen der königlichen Gesellschaft der Wissenschaften zu Göttingen*, Philologisch-historische Klasse, N.F. 8.6, 1905), 122/3; *EOMIA* 1.641–643 includes a list of the dates at which a Jewish community, probably in Asia Minor or Syria, observed Passover from 328 to 343—a further proof, were one needed, that the council met later than the spring of 343, cf. T. C. G. Thornton, 'Problematical Passovers: Difficulties for Diaspora Jews and Early Christians in Determining Passover Dates during the First Three Centuries A.D.,' *Studia Patristica* 20 (1989), 402–408, at 405 n. 14.

54. F. Maassen, *Geschichte der Quellen und der Literatur des canonischen Rechts im Abendland* 1 (Graz, 1870), 50–65, 420–721; H. Hess, *Canons* (1958), 151–158.

55. C. Munier, *Concilia Africae A. 345–A. 525* (CCL 149, 1974), 6: 'nam et memini concilii Sardicensis similiter statutum.'

56. H. Hess, *Canons* (1958), 49–67.

57. For the various versions of the text, see *CPG* 8553, 8554; on the date and nature of the council, 'The Date of the Council of Gangra,' *JTS*, N.S. 40 (1989), 121–124.

58. See H. Hess, *Canons* (1958), 138, Table B. (For obvious practical reasons I have followed the numbering of the canons used by Hess, who gives a concordance to other systems in his *Canons* [1958], 137, Table A.)

59. H. Hess, *Canons* (1958), 71–136, devotes a separate chapter to each of these topics, which consider in order the following canons: (i) 1, 2, 3a, 14, 15, 16, 18–21; (ii) 5, 6, 13; (iii) 3c, 4, 7, 17; (iv) 8, 10b, 9, 10a, 11, 12. On the complicated third canon

and ecclesiastical appeals, see also Girardet, 'Appellatio: Ein Kapitel kirchlicher Rechtsgeschichte in den Kanones des vierten Jahrhunderts,' *Historia* 23 (1974), 98–127; *Kaisergericht* (1975), 120–132; H. C. Brennecke, 'Rom und der dritte Kanon von Serdika (342),' *Zeitschrift der Savigny Stiftung für Rechtsgeschichte, Kanonistische Abteilung* 69 (1983), 15–45.

60. *EOMIA* 1.530/1. Also Canon 20 (ib. 526–529).
61. Canons 3c, 4, 7, cf. H. Hess, *Canons* (1958), 109–127.
62. Canons 8–12, cf. H. Hess, *Canons* (1958), 128–136.
63. For the evidence and bibliography, see now J. L. Maier, *Le dossier du Donatisme* 1 (*Texte und Untersuchungen* 134, 1987), 198–254.
64. W. H. C. Frend, *The Donatist Church* (Oxford, 1952), 177–187.
65. *CSEL* 65.129.15–130.3; *Apol. c. Ar.* 39.1; *EOMIA* 1.657.
66. *CSEL* 65.181–184 (probably not complete). This document, traditionally known as Hilary's *Liber I ad Constantium*, was first correctly identified by A. Wilmart, 'L'*Ad Constantium liber primus* de S. Hilaire de Poitiers et les *Fragments historiques*,' *Revue bénédictine* 24 (1907), 149–179, 291–317, cf. Feder, *Studien* I (1910), 133–151.
67. *CSEL* 65.181.13–182.2.

IX. ATHANASIUS AND THE MARTYRS OF ADRIANOPOLE

1. Chapter X.
2. Chapter IV.
3. On this pair of names, see below, n. 8.
4. Müller, *Lexicon* (1952), 1507, glosses ὑπέμνησαν here as 'scripta scil(icet) priora redintegrare.'
5. Ammianus 31.6.2; *Not. Dig.*, Oriens 11.32, cf. A. H. M. Jones, *Later Roman Empire* (Oxford, 1964), 834–836.
6. App. 9. The hypothesis that Constantius was in Constantinople at the time of the Council of Serdica was advanced by Klein, *Constantius* (1977), 74 n. 179, though he dated the council to 342/3.
7. *CSEL* 65.55.21–24, 134 No. 19; Socrates, *HE* 2.20.23, cf. Feder, *Studien* II (1910), 32/3.
8. *CSEL* 65.137 Nos. 41, 42. Also *Apol. c. Ar.* 48.2 Nos. 54, 61. The evidence relating to the name and see of both Arius and Asterius is not altogether straightforward. (1) The Hilarian version of the western synodical letter of 343 has 'Ario scilicet ex Palestina <ac> Stefano de Arabia' (*CSEL* 65.121.1/2), where the other three versions, including that quoted by Athanasius, have Macarius of Palestine and Asterius of Arabia. (In *Apol. c. Ar.* 46.3, Opitz prints the name Arius against the consensus of the manuscripts, which unanimously offer Macarius.) (2) Athanasius, *Hist. Ar.* 18.3, states that Arius' see was Petra (ἀπὸ Πέτρων τῆς Παλαιστίνης). (3) One of the bishops who attended the Council of Alexandria in 362 was Asterius, 'the bishop of Petra in Arabia' (*Tomus ad Antiochenos* 10.1: Πέτρων τῆς ᾿Αραβίας). There are two possible solutions to the apparent conflict of evidence. Feder, *Studien* II (1910), 39/40, damned Πέτρων in *Apol. c. Ar.* 18.3 as an intrusive and mistaken gloss: he held that Asterius was bishop of Petra in 343 and returned to his see under Julian. The alternative is to accept the manuscript reading in *Apol. c. Ar.* 18.3 and to deduce that Arius was bishop of Petra (which belonged

to the province of Palaestina until 357/8, then to Palaestina Tertia), that the Asterius of 343 held some other see, possibly Bostra, and that the Asterius of 362 was the successor of Arius.

9. *EOMIA* 1.658 Nos. 10, 16.
10. *Apol. c. Ar.* 46.3 = *CSEL* 65.120/1.
11. *CSEL* 65.135 No. 25. Athanasius, *Apol. c. Ar.* 48.2 No. 31, has Diodorus' name but not his see.
12. *CSEL* 65.120.3–6.
13. *CSEL* 65.110 = *Apol. c. Ar.* 43.2, cf. Feder, *Studien* II (1910), 121. Opitz 120.22 obelises ἀπέθανεν and asserts that *decessit* in the original Latin of the letter preserved by Hilary means 'entzog er sich durch die Flucht,' which Theodoretus, *HE* 2.8.13, correctly renders ἀνέστη, which in turn becomes *surrexit* in the Latin retroversion in Cod. Ver. LX (58), fols. 81ᵛ–88ᵛ.
14. Canon 17, cf. Feder, *Studien* II (1910), 55/6.
15. So Opitz on 70.10.
16. *PLRE* 1.268: otherwise totally unknown.
17. Also Socrates, *HE* 2.20.9.
18. So Opitz on 192.9: 'Athan(asius) wird 346 auf seiner Reise nach Antiochien dort vorbeigekommen sein.'
19. Chapter X.
20. Socrates, *HE* 2.16.
21. App. 5.
22. *CTh* 13.4.3.
23. *CTh* 11.22.1, cf. 'Praetorian Prefects, 337–361,' *ZPE* 94 (1992), 249–260, at 254.
24. Chapter X.

X. RETURN TO ALEXANDRIA

1. Theodoretus, *HE* 2.8.54–10.2.
2. *PLRE* 1.796; *Consuls* (1987), 230/1. Theodoretus may, however, have conflated the embassy of the winter of 343/4 with a later one (below, at nn. 12–15).
3. Athanasius dates this creed three years later than the creed taken to Trier in 342, that is, two years later on inclusive reckoning (*Syn.* 25.1, 26.1, cf. Chapter VII, at nn. 23–27).
4. Kelly, *Creeds*³ (1972), 279, cf. Brennecke, *Hilarius* (1984), 53–56.
5. On the theology of Photinus, see M. Simonetti, *Studi sull'Arianesimo* (Rome, 1965), 135–159; L. A. Speller, 'New Light on the Photinians: The Evidence of Ambrosiaster,' *JTS*, N.S. 34 (1983), 88–113. He appears to have become bishop of Sirmium shortly after the Council of Serdica, when the attested *Euterius a Pannoniis* was presumably bishop of the city (*CSEL* 65.137 No. 40, cf. Feder, *Studien* II [Vienna, 1910], 39).
6. Chapter IX, cf. App. 8.
7. Chapter VII, at nn. 15–16.
8. App. 9. The date of the council is deduced from Liberius' statement in his letter to Constantius, apparently in the winter of 353/4, that it occurred *ante annos octo* (*CSEL* 65.91.19)—though 'VIII' should perhaps be emended to 'VIIII' to allow for inclusive reckoning.
9. *CSEL* 65.146.8–18.

10. *CSEL* 65.91.15–23 (Liberius in 353/4); 142.17–19 (from Hilary's connecting narrative); 144.4–14 = *Apol. c. Ar.* 58.3/4 (the *libellus* submitted by Ursacius and Valens to Julius in 347).

11. Chapter VII, at nn. 31–32.

12. Socrates, *HE* 2.22.5.

13. As it was by E. Schwartz, 'Zur Kirchengeschichte des vierten Jahrhunderts,' *ZNW* 34 (1935), 129–213, at 139 n. 1, reprinted in his *Gesammelte Schriften* 4 (Berlin, 1960), 1–110, at 13 n. 1; Opitz on 193.14. Girardet, *Kaisergericht* (1975), 145, accepts 'den sachlichen Kern dieser Mitteilungen,' but denies that Socrates' actual quotation can be authentic. Most recently, Hanson, *Search* (1988), 307/8, rejects the letter on two grounds: first, that Constans was not so irresponsible as to 'plunge the Empire into civil war . . . for the sake of a few bishops'; second, that Athanasius' silence 'tells against authenticity.'

14. Rufinus, *HE* 10.20 (986.20–23): 'scribit ad fratrem pro certo se comperisse, quod sacerdos dei summi Athanasius iniuste fugas et exilia pateretur. hunc recte faceret si absque ulla molestia loco suo restitueret; si id nollet, sibi curae futurum, ut ipse id impleret regni eius intima penetrans et poenas dignissimas de auctoribus sceleris sumens.'

15. Philostorgius, *HE* 3.12; Theodoretus, *HE* 2.8.53–55.

16. Theodoretus, *HE* 2.8.53: 'the letter contained not only exhortation and advice, but also a threat suitable to a pious emperor.'

17. Sozomenus, *HE* 3.20.1.

18. Philostorgius, *HE* 3.12: 'Athanasius has come to me and proved that the bishopric at Alexandria belongs to him: let him recover it through you, since he will [otherwise] recover it by the force of my arms.'

19. *CTh* 10.10.7, cf. *PLRE* 1.310/1.

20. On these men, see briefly 'Christians and Pagans in the Reign of Constantius,' *L'Église et l'empire au IVe siècle* (*Entretiens sur l'antiquité classique* 34 [Vandoeuvres, 1989]), 301–337, at 313. Polemius and Datianus were ordinary consuls in 338 and 358, while Taurus and Florentius held the fasces together in 361. For Thalassius, see above, at n. 7; Chapter VII, at nn. 15–16; XIII, at n. 2.

21. *Consuls* (1987), 226/7. The only strictly contemporary attestation of this imperial consulate from the territory of Constans is a pair of gold multiples from the mint of Siscia which depict Constantius and Constans in consular robes with an attendant holding a palm branch between them (*RIC* 8.356, Siscia Nos. 105, 106, cf. 341/2). At Rome and in Italy the dating formula *post consulatum Amanti et Albini* persisted until at least September—and there is no contemporary document from the last three months of the year.

22. Girardet, *Kaisergericht* (1975), 150, puts the summons to the court of Constans in summer 345 and Athanasius' visit to Rome early in 346. That seems too early.

23. Socrates, *HE* 2.23.15–32, offers a fuller text: it seems that Athanasius has omitted part of the letter out of modesty (Chapter III n. 39).

24. The former was the route taken by Germanicus and Lucius Verus; for the routes of pilgrims in the fourth century, see E. D. Hunt, *Holy Land Pilgrimage in the Later Roman Empire* (Oxford, 1982), 52 (map). Observe also that, after his deportation by Philippus, Socrates states that Paul of Constantinople went from Thessalonica to Italy by way of Corinth (*HE* 2.17.12). Athanasius' later correspondence with

Epictetus, the bishop of Corinth, may reflect an acquaintance made in 346 (Chapter XVII, at n. 74), but his visit to Adrianople should be assigned to 344 (Chapter IX).

25. Sozomenus, *HE* 3.20.4.
26. Sozomenus, *HE* 6.24.7.
27. Gregory of Nazianzus, *Orat.* 21.29—comparing the event to Christ's entry into Jerusalem, cf. A. K. Bowman, *Egypt after the Pharaohs, 332 B.C.–A.D. 642* (Berkeley, 1986), 217. It should be noted that Gregory appears to conflate the return of 346 with those of 337 and 362 (27–29).
28. On the career of Marcellus after 345, see M. Tetz, 'Zur Theologie des Markell von Ancyra. III,' *ZKG* 83 (1972), 145–194; 'Markellianer und Athanasius,' *ZNW* 64 (1975), 75–121. The Council of Sirmium which is alleged to have condemned Marcellus in 347 or 348 is unhistorical (App. 10).
29. *CSEL* 65.147.10–22 (a narrative fragment of Hilary).
30. Socrates, *HE* 2.23.42; Sozomenus, *HE* 3.24.3. A return to Ancyra in 344 or 345 is postulated by Hanson, *Search* (1988), 219/20, with appeal to E. Schwartz, *ZNW* 34 (1935), 142; V. C. De Clercq, *Ossius of Cordova: A Contribution to the History of the Constantinian Period* (Washington, 1954), 417/8.
31. Chapter XVII.
32. Epiphanius, *Pan.* 72.11, cf. M. Tetz, *ZNW* 67 (1973), 75–121.
33. Epiphanius, *Pan.* 72.1.1, cf. *EOMIA* 1.30, 50, 51 (the list of bishops who attended the Council of Ancyra in 314).
34. To the period after the Council of Serdica belong the majority of the works, for which modern scholarship has established Marcellus' authorship—the *Sermo maior de fide*, the *Expositio fidei*, the *Contra Theopaschitas/Epistula ad Liberium*, and the *De Incarnatione et contra Arianos* (*CPG* 2803–2806): see F. Scheidweiler, 'Wer ist der Verfasser des sog. Sermo Maior de Fide?' *BZ* 47 (1954), 333–357; M. Tetz, 'Zur Theologie des Markell von Ancyra,' *ZKG* 75 (1964), 217–270; 79 (1968), 3–42; 83 (1972), 145–194; J. T. Lienhard, 'Marcellus of Ancyra in Modern Research,' *Theological Studies* 43 (1982), 486–503; 'Basil of Caesarea, Marcellus of Ancyra, and "Sabellius,"' *Church History* 58 (1989), 157–167.
35. Canon 1.
36. Basil, *Ep.* 69.2.
37. Epiphanius, *Pan.* 72.4.4.

XI. THE CONDEMNATION OF 349 AND ITS CONTEXT

1. The letters which Athanasius wrote for the Easters of 341 and 342 survive in the Syriac corpus of the *Festal Letters* (13, 3), which also contains notifications of the date of the Easters of 345 and 346 written in 344 and 345 respectively (17, 18). The absence of other festal letters for the period of Athanasius' second exile by no means proves that he wrote none (App. 1).
2. *EOMIA* 1.654, 657, 659.
3. *Apol. c. Ar.* 37–41; *EOMIA* 1.657/8.
4. *EOMIA* 1.654–656, 659–662.
5. Chapters VII, IX; App. 8.
6. One pair of names, consecutive in the document to which they subscribed (*Apol. c. Ar.* 78.7 Nos. 5, 6), belongs to joint bishops of a single see—

Ammonianus and Tyrannus of Antinoopolis (*Festal Letter* 19.10).

7. *Letter to Serapion* (in the collection of *Festal Letters*), cf. App. 1, at nn. 47–51.

8. *CSEL* 65.76/7 Nos. 34, 41, 42, 52, 53, 58: for their known careers, see Feder, *Studien* II (1910), 79–86. To judge from his name, Ammonius, whose see is not specified (No. 66), should also be an Egyptian: he could be the Melitian bishop of Diospolis Superior, cf. Camplani, *Lettere* (1989), 296/7.

9. L. T. Lefort, *CSCO* 151 = *Scriptores Coptici* 20 (Louvain, 1955), 28.30–29.14, 33.32–34.16, 39.28–36, 41–45 (French translation).

10. Ptolemaeus of Thmuis and Apollonius of Oxyrhynchus (*Syn.* 12.3; Epiphanius, *Pan.* 73.26.6, cf. *Libellus precum* 100 [*CSEL* 35. 36]).

11. Camplani, *Lettere* (1989), 262–282.

12. P. J. Sijpestein and K. A. Worp, *Zwei Landlisten aus dem Hermupolites* (*P. Landlisten*) (*Studia Amstelodamensia* 7 [Zutphen, 1978]): on the date, R. A. Bagnall, 'The Date of the Hermopolite Land Registers: A Review Article,' *Bulletin of the American Society of Papyrologists* 16 (1979), 159–168; W. van Gucht, 'Some Egyptian Bishops and the Date of P. Landlisten,' *Atti del XVII Congresso internazionale di papirologia* (Naples, 1984), 1135–1140.

13. A. K. Bowman, 'Landholding in the Hermopolite Nome in the Fourth Century A.D.,' *JRS* 75 (1985), 137–163.

14. P. J. Sijpestein and K. A. Worp, *Landlisten* (1978), G 298, 305, 512; F 147, 510, 519, 731; Anh. 50, cf. W. van Gucht, *Atti* (1984), 1135–1140; T. D. Barnes, *JTS*, N.S. 42 (1991), 729. The appointment of Arion as bishop of Antinoopolis in place of Ammonius and Tyrannus is approved by Athanasius in *Festal Letter* 19.10: he added his name to the synodical letter of the western bishops at Serdica after Athanasius returned to Alexandria (*Apol. c. Ar.* 49.3 No. 195: Opitz on 129 duly noted the other evidence). Priests appear at G 552; F 771, 809, 818; and one entry relates to church propety (G 534).

15. H. I. Bell, V. Martin, E. G. Turner, and D. van Berchem, *The Abinnaeus Archive: Papers of a Roman Officer in the Reign of Constantius II* (Oxford, 1962), cf. T. D. Barnes, 'The Career of Abinnaeus,' *Phoenix* 39 (1985), 368–374. A further papyrus from the archive, not included in that collection, refers to 'the priest of the village': see *Sammelbuch* 11380, published by R. Rémondon, 'Un papyrus inédit des archives d'Abinnaeus (P. Berlin inv. 11624),' *Journal of Juristic Papyrology* 18 (1974), 33–37. On the other hand, *P. Abinn.* 65 = *P. Geneva* 60 does not belong to the archive: see H. Cadell, '*P. Genève* 60, *B.G.U.* II 456 et le problème du bois en Égypte,' *Chronique d'Égypte* 51 (1976), 331–348.

16. *P. Abinn.* 1, 44. On the chronology of Abinnaeus' movements, see *Phoenix* 39 (1985), 369/70. Valacius is attested as *dux* in 340 and perhaps in 339: *P. Oxy.* 3793, with J. R. Rea, *Oxyrhynchus Papyri* 55 (London, 1988), 63/4, 224 (commentary on *P. Oxy.* 3820.14). He may well, therefore, have arrived in Egypt in 338 with Philagrius and Arsacius (Chapter IV, at n. 43).

17. *P. Abinn.* 2. The draft petition of 340 or 341 (which has corrections and variants in Abinnaeus' own hand) and this letter from Valacius are the only documents in the archive to be written in Latin.

18. *P. Abinn.* 58, 59.

19. *Vita Antonii* 86; *Hist. Ar.* 14.4.

20. *P. Abinn.* 47, 55.

NOTES TO PAGES 96–99

21. As suggested in *Phoenix* 39 (1985), 373/4, on the basis of a petition to Abinnaeus dated 11 February 351 by one who describes himself as 'a deacon of the catholic church' (*P. Abinn.* 55).

22. Chapter III, at n. 3.

23. Sozomenus, *HE* 2.31; *Index* 11. The *Life of Antony* 69–71 records the visit, but includes no reference to Athanasius.

24. *Vita Antonii* 91: Antony received new from Athanasius the pallium which he bequeathed him.

25. *Sancti Pachomii Vita Prima* 120 (ed. F. Halkin, *Sanci Pachomii Vitae Graecae* [*Subsidia Hagiographica* 19, 1932], 77/8).

26. *PG* 25.524–533 = Opitz 303–308, cf. M. Tetz, 'Zur Biographie des Athanasius von Alexandrien,' *ZKG* 90 (1979), 304–338, at 325–329.

27. *CSEL* 65.142.17–19: 'igitur ad tollendum ex episcopatu Fotinum, qui ante biennium iam in Mediolanensi synodo erat haereticus damnatus, ex plurimis provinciis congregantur sacerdotes.'

28. *CSEL* 65.142.20–145.4. Ursacius and Valens composed and submitted their letter to Julius in Rome itself (*CSEL* 65.143.4–6, 145.6/7; *Hist. Ar.* 26.1, 29.2, 44.5). Against the traditional view that the council of 347 met in Sirmium or Milan, see App. 10. Bishops of Rome made it a principle not to attend councils of bishops held in other cities: M. Wojtowytsch, *Papsttum und Konzile von den Anfängen bis zu Leo I (440–461): Studien zur Entstehung der Überordnung des Papstes über Konzile* (*Päpste und Papsttum* 17 [Stuttgart, 1981]).

29. *CSEL* 65.145.5–16.

30. The other evidence is entirely consistent with the hypothesis that Paulinus became bishop of Trier in 347: see Chapter VII n. 12.

31. Socrates, *HE* 2.26.6, 5.9.1.

32. On the interpretation of this difficult passage, see App. 8.

33. Eugenius of Nicaea attended the Council of Antioch which deposed Athanasius in 349 (Sozomenus, *HE* 4.8.4), while Cecropius was translated from Laodicea in Phrygia to replace Amphion, who is attested as bishop of Nicomedia in 343 (*CSEL* 65.48.12–15), allegedly as a reward for intrigues against the orthodox (*Letter to the Bishops of Egypt and Libya* 7; *Hist. Ar.* 74.5). He attended the Council of Sirmium in 351 (*CSEL* 65.170.6) and died in the earthquake of 24 August 358 (Sozomenus, *HE* 4.16.5).

34. Sozomenus, *HE* 4.8.3/4, with a reference back to 3.20.1 (Chapter X n. 17).

35. Sozomenus, *HE* 4.7.3–8.2. Hence the council has often been dated to 351 or later: Hanson, *Search* (1988), 325, 338 (351 or possibly 352); A. Martin, *Sources chrétiennes* 317 (Paris, 1985), 184 n. 59 (351 or 352); Brennecke, *Hilarius* (1984), 117–121 (352); K. M. Girardet, 'Constance II, Athanase, et l'Édit d'Arles (353): À propos de la politique religieuse de l'empereur Constance II,' *Politique et théologie* (1974), 63–91, at 67, 82 (probably 352); C. Piétri, 'La question d'Athanase vue de Rome (338–360),' *Politique et théologie* (1974), 93–126, at 119; *Roma* (1976), 237 (355); Opitz on 68 (356 at the earliest).

36. App. 6.

37. See Kopecek, *Neo-Arianism* (1979), 103, 133 (dating the council to 347 or 348). Also in favor of a date before 350, see Seeck, *Geschichte* 4 (1911), 135; Klein, *Constantius* (1977), 81/2.

38. App. 2.
39. Chapter III.
40. The manuscripts of the *Defense against the Arians* omit the second letter, but have a scribal note to the effect that it was virtually identical with the preceding letter. The first letter, however, contains a passage (40.3) which Opitz on 118.19ff. plausibly identified as a stray fragment of the second.
41. Chapter 89, which refers to events of 357, must be a later addition (App. 2).

XII. THE USURPATION OF MAGNENTIUS

1. Victor, *Caes.* 41.23/4. For Victor's homophobia, cf. *Caes.* 28.6/7. The *Epitome de Caesaribus* has a substantially similar indictment, but adds that Constans was 'nulla a barbaris formidine' (41.24)—an aspersion emphatically contradicted by Ammianus 30.7.5. Eutropius is more favorable, allowing an initial period when Constans' rule was just and energetic before he slipped into *gravia vitia* (*Brev.* 10.9.3).
2. *Chr. min.* 1.237; Jerome, *Chronicle* 237ᶜ.
3. The most precise evidence is provided by a scholiast on Julian, *Orat.* 3, 95c: see J. Bidez, 'Amiens, ville natale de l'empereur Magnence,' *Revue des études anciennes* 27 (1925), 312–318.
4. For the numerous sources, which supply complementary details, see *PLRE* 1.220.
5. *Chr. min.* 1.69. For a full discussion of the career of Titianus (consul in 337), see Chastagnol, *Fastes* (1962), 107–111.
6. *RIC* 8.325/6 Aquileia 122 appears to celebrate his arrival in Aquileia near the beginning of March, cf. A. Jeločnik, 'Les multiples d'or de Magnence découverts à Émona,' *Revue numismatique*⁶ 9 (1967), 209–235, at 215/6. (The article is reprinted in its original language in *Arheološki Vestnik* 19 [1968], 201–220.)
7. For the numerous partial accounts of the 'usurpation,' see *PLRE* 1.954. Constantina was the widow of Hannibalianus, who had been killed in 337 (*Origo Constantini Imperatoris* 35; Ammianus 14.1.2). Her role in the proclamation of Vetranio is recorded in *Chr. min.* 1.237; Philostorgius, *HE* 3.22. That she resided in Rome in the 340s is inferred from the fact that she built the basilica of St. Agnes and a monastery in the city and was buried by the Via Nomentana (*PLRE* 1.222).
8. *PLRE* 1.624. For Nepotianus' coinage, see *RIC* 8.261 Rome 166/7, 265/6 Rome 198–203; J. and D. Gricourt, 'Le pronunciamiento de Népotien et ses répercussions sur l'organisation et le fonctionnement des hôtels monétaires de Rome, d'Arles, et d'Aquilée,' *Mélanges de numismatique offerts à Pierre Bastien* (Wetteren, 1987), 217–231.
9. For the complicated negotiations of 350, see the table in J. Šašel, 'The Struggle between Magnentius and Constantius II for Italy and Illyricum,' *Živa antika* 21 (1971), 205–216, at 209.
10. Zonaras 13.8. On the date (which is controverted), see P. Bastien, *Le monnayage de Magnence (350–353)*² (Wettern, 1983), 15/6; 'Décence, Poemenius: Problèmes de chronologie,' *Quaderni ticinesi: Numismatica e antichità classiche* 12 (1983), 177–189. D. Gricourt, *Mélanges de numismatique offerts à Pierre Bastien* (Wetteren, 1987), 221, argues for June. The fact that Decentius became consul only in 352, not 351, creates a presumption that he was proclaimed Caesar in 351 rather than 350 (*Consuls* [1987], 239). But Gaiso, who shared the consulate of 351 with

Magnentius, had killed Constans for him (*Epit. de Caes.* 41.23; Zosimus 2.42.5)—and may already have been designated consul for 351 before Decentius was proclaimed Caesar.

11. Zosimus 4.43.1; John of Antioch, frag. 187, cf. *PLRE* 1.488/9. Justina later became the second wife of Valentinian: for the hypothesis that her father, Justus, was the son of Vettius Justus, consul in 328, and a daughter of the Caesar Crispus, see *New Empire* (1982), 44, 103.

    Socrates, *HE* 4.31.11–13, reports that Justus governed Picenum 'in the time of Constantius' and was executed by Constantius because of a dream in which his daughter gave birth to an emperor. *PLRE* 1.490 puts his governorship of Aemilia and Picenum between 352 and 361, but a date before 350 is preferable: Justus was presumably put to death in 352 or 353 for consenting to his daughter's marriage to the defeated usurper, cf. J. Rougé, 'Justine, la belle Sicilienne,' *Latomus* 33 (1974), 676–679.

12. *ILS* 742 (a milestone between Pavia and Turin). The mint of Arles advertised *Vict(oria) Aug(usti) Lib(ertas) Rom(ana)* / *Romanor(um)* / *Rom(ani) orb(is)* (*RIC* 8.213/4 Arles 131/2, 158/9).

13. *RIC* 8.261 Rome 168, 266/7 Rome 207/8, cf. W. Kellner, *Libertas und Christogramm: Motivgeschichtliche Untersuchungen zur Münzprägung des Kaisers Magnentius (350–353)* (Diss. Freiburg, publ. Karlsruhe, 1968), 15–56.

14. *RIC* 8.157 Trier 260.

15. *Constantine* (1981), 75, 209.

16. J. Ziegler, *Zur religiösen Haltung der Gegenkaiser im 4. Jh. n. Chr.* (*Frankfurter Althistorische Studien* 4 [Opladen, 1970]), 53–69.

17. Eusebius, *VC* 2.45.1. In favor of accepting Eusebius' clear statement that Constantine prohibited sacrifice (which is usually discounted), see *Constantine* (1981), 210/1; 'Constantine's Prohibition of Pagan Sacrifice,' *American Journal of Philology* 105 (1984), 69–72; 'Christians and Pagans in the Reign of Constantius.' *L'Église et l'empire au IVᵉ siècle* (*Entretiens sur l'antiquité classique* 34 [Vandoeuvres, 1989]), 301–337, at 322–325, 330.

18. *CTh* 16.10.1.

19. Firmicus Maternus, *De err. prof. rel.* 28.6.

20. H. Broise and J. Scheid, *Recherches archéologiques à la Magliana: Le balneum des frères arvales* (*Roma antica* 1, 1987), 275–277.

21. *CTh* 16.10.5, cf. J. Ziegler, *Zur religiösen Haltung* (1970), 67/8.

22. P. Salama, 'L'empereur Magnence et les provinces africaines,' *Mélanges de numismatique offerts à Pierre Bastien* (Wetteren, 1987), 203–216.

23. Athanasius does not name Magnentius in connection with Paul's death: for the hypothesis that he was executed, though not deposed and exiled, for treasonable correspondence with Magnentius, see App. 8.

24. *Apol. c. Ar.* 49.1 Nos. 85, 112. Opitz on 127 declared that the *acta* of the Council of Cologne in 346 (C. Munier, *Concilia Galliae A. 314–A. 506* [CCL 148, 1963], 27–29) were 'unzweifelbar echt': in fact, the *acta* are a forgery of the eighth century, but the forger appears to have used a genuine list of the names of Gallic bishops from the 340s: see H. C. Brennecke, 'Synodum congregavit contra Euphratam nefandissimum episcopum: Zur angeblichen Kölner Synode gegen Euphrates,' *ZKG* 90 (1979), 176–200. The names in the heading of the letter (27) include

Maximinus of Trier—who is otherwise first attested as bishop in 347 (Chapter XI, at nn. 29–30).

25. For ταῦτά ποτε (Opitz 285.16), read ταῦτα; πότε.

26. As argued in Chapter XI.

27. Athanasius quotes a different Greek translation of the same Latin original in *Hist. Ar.* 24.

28. App. 9.

29. Seeck, *Geschichte* 4 (1911), 103, 429/30.

30. On Julius Constantius, see *New Empire* (1982), 108.

31. Socrates, *HE* 3.1, and Sozomenus, *HE* 5.2.9, allege that he was spared because he was ill and expected to die. Julian's mother was Basilina, the daughter of Julianus, the former praetorian prefect of Licinius (Libanius, *Orat.* 18.8/9): she died a few months after her son was born (Julian, *Misopogon* 22, 352b).

32. Julian, *Ep. ad Ath.* 271c–272a. The role of George is deduced from the fact that he allowed the young Julian to borrow and transcribe books from his library (*Ep.* 107, 378c). It is not relevant here whether the six years run from 342 to 348 or from 344 to 350.

33. *Chr. min.* 1.238; Philostorgius, *HE* 3.26ᵃ.

34. See the careful discussion of J. Šašel, *Živa antika* 21 (1971), 210–216. The fullest extant account is in Zosimus 2.45–53, which Seeck, *Geschichte* 4 (1911), 435, derived from a panegyric of Constantius: on problems in it, see N. H. Baynes, 'A Note of Interrogation,' *Byzantion* 2 (1925), 149–151; F. Paschoud, *Zosime: Histoire nouvelle* 1 (Paris, 1971), xlii, 120/1, 253–261.

35. *RIC* 8.372 Siscia 318/9. J. P. C. Kent dates the issue to September 351 and argues that Magnentius held the city for a month before the Battle of Mursa (ib. 345).

36. *Chr. min.* 1.237. On the high casualties, see Eutropius, *Brev.* 10.12.1; Jerome, *Chronicle* 238ᵈ; *Epit. de Caes.* 42.2.

37. App. 9, at n. 30.

38. *AE* 1982.383 (an epitaph dated by the consuls Decentius and Paulus). A hoard at Emona appears to reflect the flight of Magnentius' officials: A. Jeločnik, *Revue numismatique⁶* 9 (1967), 226–231.

39. The governor of Aemilia and Picenum transferred his loyalty rapidly: see G. Camodeca, 'Per la redazione dei fasti delle provincie italiche: Fl. Romulus, consularis Flaminiae et Piceni nel 352(-3),' *ZPE* 28 (1978), 151–158. He reinterprets *AE* 1975.358 = 1978.290 (near Urbs Salvia) and reedits *AE* 1951.17 (Alba Fucens).

40. *Chr. min.* 1.69, cf. Chastagnol, *Fastes* (1962), 135–139.

41. *RIC* 8.188/9 Lyons 153–176, cf. W. Kellner, *Libertas und Christogramm* (1968), 63–80.

42. *RIC* 8.164/5 Trier 328–337; Ammianus 15.6.4, cf. J. P. C. Kent, 'The Revolt of Trier against Magnentius,' *Numismatic Chronicle⁵* 19 (1959), 105–108; P. Bastien, *Quaderni ticinesi* 12 (1983), 187–189.

43. *Chr. min.* 1.238; Eutropius, *Brev.* 10.12.2, cf. Seeck, *Geschichte* 4 (1911), 439. Athanasius, *Apol. ad Const.* 7.3, diverges from the narrative sources which record the death of Magnentius by making him hang (not stab) himself.

44. *CTh* 9.38.2, cf. *CJ* 12.1.5.

45. Ammianus 14.5.1, cf. 'Structure and Chronology in Ammianus, Book 14,' *HSCP*

92 (1989), 413–422, at 419.

46. App. 9.

47. Matthews, *Ammianus* (1989), 34/5, 406–408.

48. Especially Thalassius, the praetorian prefect, and the *quaestor* Montius (Philostorgius, *HE* 3.26[a]).

49. Ammianus 14.11.6–34.

50. Ammianus 15.5.1–34, 8.19.

51. Matthews, *Ammianus* (1989), 81–93.

52. For Athanasius' attacks on Constantius, see Chapter XIV; for Hilary's, Chapter XVI, at nn. 54–57. The abuse which Lucifer heaped on the emperor is catalogued at length in W. Tietze, *Lucifer von Calaris und die Kirchenpolitik des Constantius* (Diss. Tübingen, 1976): in *De non parcendo in deum delinquentibus* alone, Constantius is compared to Saul, Holofernes, Antiochus IV, Herod, Judas Iscariot, and the Jewish high priests who tried Jesus. K. M. Girardet, 'Kaiser Konstantius II als "Episcopus Episcoporum" und das Herrscherbild des kirchlichen Widerstandes (Osius von Corduba und Lucifer von Caralis),' *Historia* 26 (1977), 95–128, aptly observes that the heated abuse of Constantius does not prove that his treatment of the Christian church differed from that of his father.

53. Jerome, *De vir. ill.* 112, states that Cyril composed the work *in adulescentia*.

54. F. M. Young, *From Nicaea to Chalcedon* (London, 1983), 125. On Cyril's career and theology, see esp. E. J. Yarnold, *TRE* 8 (1981), 261–266; R. C. Gregg, 'Cyril of Jerusalem and the Arians,' *Arianism* (1985), 85–109.

55. Hanson, *Search* (1988), 402–413.

56. Jerome, *De vir. ill.* 112: 'saepe pulsus ecclesia et receptus ad extremum, sub Theodosio principe octo annos inconcussum episcopatum tenuit.' The *Chronicle* gives the following succession of bishops of Jerusalem: Cyril, Eutychius, Cyril again, Irenaeus, Cyril for the third time, Hilarius, Cyril for the fourth time (237[a]). Epiphanius, *Pan.* 66.20.3, shows Hilarius in possession of the see in 376.

57. Theodoretus, *HE* 2.25.6.

58. Jerome, *Chronicle* 237[a].

59. Cyril's letter (*BHG*[3] 413 = *CPG* 3587) is best edited by E. Bihain, 'L'épître de Cyrille de Jérusalem à Constance sur la vision de la croix (BHG[3] 413),' *Byzantion* 43 (1973), 264–296. The letter gives the nones of May as the day (4.17); that the year was 351 (not 350) is strongly implied by Socrates, *HE* 2.28.22, cf. *Chr. min.* 1.237/8.

60. *RIC* 8.416 Thessalonica 146; C. Brenot, 'Sirmium d'août à octobre 351: La reprise des émissions de billon d'après le trésor de Kosmaj,' *Mélanges de numismatique offerts à Pierre Bastien* (Wetteren, 1987), 233–239 No. 1 (Sirmium, probably minted shortly before the Battle of Mursa).

61. Sulpicius Severus, *Chron.* 2.38.5–8.

XIII. SIRMIUM, ARLES, AND MILAN

1. Socrates, *HE* 2.28.23, 29.1, whence Sozomenus, *HE* 4.6.4. Socrates states that the bishops who attended included not only Marcus of Arethusa, George of Alexandria, Basil of Ancyra, Pancratius of Pelusium, Hypatianus of Heraclea, and the apparently inseparable Ursacius and Valens, but also Ossius—which must reflect some confusion with his visit to Sirmium in 357. A fuller list is preserved in the fragments

deriving from Hilary (*CSEL* 65.170.3–8, cf. Feder, *Studien* II [1910], 101–103): it includes Narcissus, Theodorus, Eudoxius, Cecropius, Macedonius, and Acacius, but not Pancratius or Hypatianus.

2. Epiphanius, *Pan.* 71.1.5–8. However, Zosimus 2.48.5 states that Thalassius was still with Constantius shortly before the Battle of Mursa. On the wider significance of Epiphanius' list of witnesses, see 'Christians and Pagans in the Reign of Constantius,' *L'Église et l'empire au IVe siècle* (*Entretiens sur l'antiquité classique* 34 [Vandoeuvres, 1989]), 301–337, at 314/5.

3. As asserted by Seeck, *Regesten* (1919), 198; *PLRE* 1.879: 'the committee which tried Photinus.' On the impossibility of such a 'trial,' see Chapter XVIII.

4. Socrates, *HE* 2.29.4, cf. *Hist. Ar.* 74.5.

5. Hilary, *Syn.* 38; Athanasius, *Syn.* 27, cf. Kelly, *Creeds*³ (1972), 281/2.

6. Sulpicius Severus, *Chron.* 2.37.5: 'igitur Arriani astuto consilio miscent innoxium criminosis, damnationemque Photini et Marcelli et Athanasii eadem sententia comprehendunt.'

7. Chapter XII.

8. Below, at nn. 21–25.

9. The essential arguments are set out by K. M. Girardet, 'Constance II, Athanase, et l'Édit d'Arles (353): À propos de la politique religieuse de l'empereur Constance II,' *Politique et théologie* (1974), 63–91. Unfortunately, he spoils a compelling case by identifying the *sententiae Orientalium* to which Constantius required assent in 355 (Liberius, *Ep. ad Eusebium* 1.1.2 [*CCL* 9.121.7–9]) with the synodical letter of a council which he supposes to have met in Antioch in 347/8 (73–83). The counter-arguments which Brennecke, *Hilarius* (1984), 184–192, marshals against Girardet are not valid against the modified form of his thesis adopted here. The direct evidence (*Fug.* 4.2; *Hist. Ar.* 31.3–6; Liberius, *Ep. ad Eusebium* 1.1.2; Sulpicius Severus, *Chron.* 2.39) makes it clear that there was an imperial edict requiring all bishops to accept the decisions of a council of eastern bishops which contained both a condemnation of Athanasius and a creed, and that imperial officials carried the relevant document through the provinces for signature by individual bishops upon pain of exile. Moreover, Lucifer of Caralis not only refers to the edict condemning Athanasius, but also protests constantly that Constantius is both persecuting Athanasius and championing heresy: see esp. *De Athanasio* 1.10.58–64 Diercks, 2.30.15–51; *De non conveniendo cum haereticis* 6, 9.60–63, 12; *De non parcendo in deum delinquentibus* 9.22–24, 35.40–42; *Moriundum esse pro dei filio* 2.27–37, 9.14–24, 12.41–52.

10. *CSEL* 65.155.7–9; *Chr. min.* 1.76.

11. A contemporary source gives the day as 21 May (*Chr. min.* 1.76): in favor of 17 May, see L. Duchesne, *Le Liber Pontificalis* 1 (Paris, 1883), ccl.

12. Chapters IV, VI.

13. *CSEL* 65.155.5–22.

14. *CSEL* 65.90.13–21 = *CCL* 8.312.42–55.

15. *CSEL* 65.90.18/9 = *CCL* 8.312.52/3. On this Roman council of late 352, see E. Caspar, *Geschichte des Papsttums* 1 (Tübingen, 1930), 169–171; Piétri, *Roma* (1976), 238–241.

16. *CSEL* 65.167.4–7: 'inter haec [since these are the opening words of the extract, their reference is unclear] . . . multi ex Italia coepiscopi convenerunt, qui mecum

religiosissimum imperatorem Constantium fuerant deprecati, ut iuberet, sicut ipsi placuerat dudum, concilium ad Aquileiam congregari.'

17. App. 4.

18. Athanasius' argument assumes that these quotations from third-century writers are genuine: L. Abramowski, 'Dionys von Rom (†268) und Dionys von Alexandrien (†264/5) in den arianischen Streitigkeiten des 4. Jahrhunderts,' *ZKG* 93 (1982), 240–272, contends that they come from a pseudonymous work composed c. 340.

19. The nine documents quoted in *Dec.* 33–42 are also edited by Opitz as *Urkunden* 22, 4a, 4b, 23, 25, 33, 34, 27, 28 respectively.

20. See esp. F. Dinsen, *Homoousios: Die Geschichte des Begriffs bis zum Konzil von Konstantinopel (381)* (Diss. Kiel, 1976), 115–153; G. C. Stead, 'Homousios (ὁμοούσιος),' *RAC* 16 (1992), 364–433. Both these scholars adopt the conventional date of 350/1 for *On the Council of Nicaea*.

21. Sozomenus, *HE* 4.9.6.

22. The *Defense* refers to an individual accuser (ὁ κατήγορος) at 3.1, 5.1, 7.1, 17.2, 17.6, 19.6, though plural slanderers also appear (3.4, 3.8). The fictive setting is clearest in remarks such as 'I wish that he [the accuser], whoever he is, could have been here' (8.1) and 'since they have dared to speak against me before you' (12.1).

23. Gwatkin, *Arianism*[2] (1900), 72, claimed that Athanasius modeled the speech on Demosthenes' classic apologia for his career, the *De Corona*, appealing to the list of borrowings given by E. Fialon, *Saint Athanase: Étude littéraire* (Paris, 1877), 286/7 —a scholar who presents Athanasius as 'formé par l'étude des grands écrivains de Grèce' and 'le dernier des Attiques' (284–297). But the passages which Fialon quotes (in French translation) fail to prove either derivation from or knowledge of Demosthenes, and elsewhere Fialon notes that Athanasius' use of documents in the *Defense before Constantius* differs from that of his presumed model (145). The truth is the exact opposite: like all of Athanasius' other works, the *Defense before Constantius* lacks the formal polish which would be expected of one who had received a traditional rhetorical training: it exhibits what J. Quasten, *Patrology* 3 (Utrecht, Antwerp, and Westminster, Md., 1960), 23, denounced as Athanasius' principal faults as a writer—'a certain negligence in form and a lack of order in the arrangement of his material that cause prolixity and frequent repetition.'

24. Socrates, *HE* 2.26.3.

25. See the passages translated and discussed in Chapters IV, VII, and XII.

26. M. Meslin, *Les Ariens d'Occident, 335–430* (*Patristica Sorbonensia* 8 [Paris, 1967]), 29–44.

27. Lucifer, *De non conveniendo cum haereticis* 7.18 (CCL 8.175); CSEL 65.46.1–4; Sulpicius Severus, *Chr.* 2.40.4, 45.7.

28. On Epictetus' career, see Meslin, *Ariens* (1967), 37–39. In 355 he was present during the interview between Constantius and Liberius in Milan (Theodoretus, *HE* 2.16; Sozomenus, *HE* 4.11) and helped to consecrate Felix as Liberius' successor (*Hist. Ar.* 75. 3; Jerome, *De vir. ill.* 98). The *Libellus precum* which the Luciferian priests Marcellinus and Faustinus submitted to Theodosius in Constantinople in 383/4 (*CSEL* 35.8–44, reedited by M. Simonetti, *CCL* 69 [1967], 361–392), alleges that he interfered in the church of Naples when Maximus was exiled and that he maltreated Rufinianus—whose identity is not stated (25/6). Epictetus is last heard of as an

ambassador sent by Constantius to Julian in 360 (Julian, *Ep. ad Ath.* 15, 286c).

29. Hilary, *Contra Auxentium* 8 (*PL* 10.614), cf. Meslin, *Ariens* (1967), 41–44.

30. *Libellus precum* 62–65, cf. Meslin, *Ariens* (1967), 36/7.

31. *Clavis Patrum Latinorum²* (1961), Nos. 541–544, cf. *PLS* 1.202–216. On all aspects of his life and writings, see the thorough discussion by A. Montes Moreira, *Potamius de Lisbonne et la controverse arienne* (Louvain, 1969), 39–323.

32. *Libellus precum* 32.

33. *CSEL* 65.155.24–156.1.

34. Hilary, *Syn.* 3, 11 (*PL* 10.482/3, 487).

35. Phoebadius of Agen, *Contra Arianos* 5 (*PL* 20.16 = *CCL* 64.27). Centuries later Alcuin quoted from an otherwise unknown letter of Athanasius to Potamius which poses a number of theological questions (*PL* 101.113, cf. J. Madoz, 'Potamio de Lisboa,' *Revista Española de Teología* 7 [1947], 79–109, at 86): in favor of the authenticity of the quotation, see A. Wilmart, 'Le *De Lazaro* de Potamius,' *JTS* 19 (1918), 289–304, at 289 n. 1; A. Montes Moreira, *Potamius* (1969), 159–167.

36. On the Council of Arles, see Brennecke, *Hilarius* (1984), 133–147 (with earlier bibliography).

37. There is no direct evidence: Brennecke, *Hilarius* (1984), 137.

38. Sulpicius Severus, *Chron.* 2.39.1–3, 37.7, cf. H. Crouzel, 'Un "résistant" toulousain à la politique pro-arienne de l'empereur Constance II: L'évêque Rhodanius,' *BHE* 77 (1976), 173–190. For earlier references to the deposition of Paulinus by the council, see *CSEL* 65.102.9–13.

39. *CSEL* 65.166.15–167.16: respectively, Vincentius of Capua and Marcellus, who was also a bishop in Camapania.

40. Sulpicius Severus, *Chron.* 2.37.7.

41. Liberius, *Ep. ad Eusebium* 1.1.2 (*CCL* 9.121.7–9).

42. *CSEL* 65.89.13–16.

43. *CSEL* 65.89–93 = *CCL* 8.311–316 (two versions with many minor variants). On Liberius' actions after the Council of Arles, see the recent discussion by Brennecke, *Hilarius* (1984), 147–164—who has some difficulty in excluding theological issues altogether.

44. Three letters are preserved from Liberius to Eusebius before the Council of Milan (*CCL* 9.121–123), and one from Lucifer, Pancratius, and Hilarius (*CCL* 9.120): on the murky question of Eusebius' precise role in 355, see Brennecke, *Hilarius* (1984), 172–185; L. A. Speller, 'A Note on Eusebius of Vercellae and the Council of Milan,' *JTS*, N.S. 36 (1985), 157–165.

45. For full discussion and bibliography, see Brennecke, *Hilarius* (1984), 164–184. However, his denial that the Nicene creed was ever mentioned during the proceedings is unconvincing: see J. Doignon, 'Hilaire de Poitiers "Kirchenpolitiker"? À propos d'un ouvrage récent,' *RHE* 80 (1985), 441–454.

46. Socrates, *HE* 2.36.1. Magnified further into 'plusieurs centaines d'Occidentaux' by Piétri, *Roma* (1976), 294.

47. The letter and the subscriptions were published by Cardinal Baronius in his *Annales Ecclesiastici*, anno 355, paras. 6, 22, from a manuscript 'in Archivo Ecclesiae Vercellensis.' The manuscript is now lost, but there is no reason to doubt the authenticity of either the letter or the subscriptions: see Brennecke, *Hilarius* (1984), 165/6. The letter has recently been reedited by V. Bulhart, *CCL* 9.119; the

most accessible text of the subscriptions is C. Baronius, *Annales Ecclesiastici* 4 (Antwerp, 1865), 537.

48. Predictably, Socrates, *HE* 2.36, mentions only Athanasius. The charges of 335 still appear to have formed part of the indictment of Athanasius: *CCL* 9.119.4; Theodoretus, *HE* 2.15.2.

49. Sulpicius Severus, *Chron.* 2.39.3–6.

50. Jerome, *Chronicle* 239^i; Sulpicius Severus, *Chron.* 2.39.4.

51. *CSEL* 65.186.19–187.19.

52. Brennecke, *Hilarius* (1984), 178–184.

53. Chapter V; above, at nn. 17–19.

54. Hilary, *Syn.* 91 (*PL* 10.545): 'regeneratus pridem et in episcopatu aliquantisper manens, fidem Nicaenam numquam nisi exulaturus audivi.' On the interpretation of Hilary's words, see further Chapter XV n. 50.

55. Ammianus 15.7.6–10.

56. Theodoretus, *HE* 2.16, cf. Sozomenus, *HE* 4.11, who states that Ursacius and Valens were there too. For discussion of the document, see V. Monachino, 'Il Primato nella controversia Ariana: Saggi storici intorno al Papato,' *Miscellanea Historiae Pontificiae* 21 (1959), 17–89; J. Herrmann, 'Ein Streitgespräch mit Verfahrensrechtlichen Argumenten zwischen Kaiser Konstantius und Bischof Liberius,' *Festschrift für Hans Liermann zum 70. Geburtstag* (*Erlangener Forschungen*, Reihe A: Geisteswissenschaften 16 [1964]), 77–86; R. Klein, 'Zur Glaubwürdigkeit historischer Aussagen des Bischofs Athanasius von Alexandria über die Religionspolitik des Kaisers Constantius II,' *Studia Patristica* 17.3 (1982), 996–1017, at 996–1002.

57. Jerome, *De vir. ill.* 98. Athanasius' taunt that Felix was consecrated 'in the palace' (*Hist. Ar.* 75.3) should not be taken literally.

58. *Quae gesta sunt inter Liberium et Felicem* 2 (*CSEL* 35.1).

59. *Quae gesta sunt* 3; Philostorgius, *HE* 4.3; Theodoretus, *HE* 2.17.7; Sozomenus, *HE* 4.11.12. Observe, however, that the date of *CTh* 16.2.14, issued at Milan and addressed 'Felici episcopo,' must be emended from 6 December 357 to 6 December 356 (Seeck, *Regesten* [1919], 202).

60. Theodoretus, *HE* 2.17.3; Sozomenus, *HE* 4.11.11. These clear statements must be preferred to the accusation of Arianism leveled by Rufinus, *HE* 10.23; Socrates, *HE* 2.37.

61. T. Mommsen, 'Die römischen Bischöfe Liberius und Felix II.' *Deutsche Zeitschrift für Geschichtswissenschaft,* N.F. 1 (1896–1897), 167–179, reprinted in his *Gesammelte Schriften* 6 (Berlin, 1910), 570–581. Felix died on 21 November 365 (*Quae gesta sunt* 4), but the *Liber Pontificalis* 28 (p. 211 Duchesne) states that Constantius executed him as a martyr.

62. Ammianus 27.3.12/3. The account in *Quae gesta sunt* 8–12 gives a still higher total: the supporters of Damasus killed one hundred and sixty men and women in church.

63. George returned on 26 November 361 and was lynched four weeks later (*Hist. ac.* 2.6, cf. Chapter XVII, at n. 18.

64. The Greek of the relative clause (ἐξεπλήττοντο οὓς ἔτι γρύζειν εἰκὸς ὑπὸ ὀδόντα) is extremely obscure, but must reflect an original Latin containing the phrase *mussitare sub dente* or something closely similar. I have adopted (with some misgiv-

ings) the traditional interpretation of Montfaucon (*PG* 25.634), followed by M. Atkinson and A. Robertson (*Select Writings* [1892], 250).

65. On missionary activity under Constantius, see W. H. C. Frend, 'The Church in the Reign of Constantius II (337–361): Mission, Monasticism, Worship,' *L'Église et l'empire au IVe siècle* (*Entretiens sur l'antiquité classique* 34 [Vandoeuvres, 1989]), 73–111.

66. *CTh* 12.12.2^s: Mommsen, ad loc., emends the text to avoid the absurdity of making Constantius forbid ambassadors to spend a year in Alexandria itself.

67. E. Littmann, *Deutsche Axum-Expedition* 4 (Berlin, 1913), Nos. 4 (= *OGIS* 200), 6, 7 (the same text in Greek, Sabaitic, and Ethiopic), 10, 11, cf. E. Littmann, *Deutsche Axum-Expedition* 1 (Berlin, 1913), 48. On Constantius' letter and the inscriptions, see esp. A. Dihle, *Umstrittene Daten: Untersuchungen zum Auftreten der Griechen am Roten Meer* (*Wissenschaftliche Abhandlungen der Arbeitsgemeinschaft für Forschung des Landes Nordrhein-Westfalen* 32 [Cologne and Opladen, 1964]), 51–56, 65–67; 'L'ambassade de Théophile l'Indien ré-examiné,' *L'Arabie préislamique et son environnement historique et culturel*, ed. T. Fahd (Strasbourg, 1989), 461–468.

XIV. APOLOGIA, POLEMIC, AND THEOLOGY

1. *Historia Lausiaca* 63, cf. M. Tetz, 'Zur Biographie des Athanasius von Alexandrien,' *ZKG* 90 (1979), 304–338, at 316–319. Rufinus knows the story, but places it immediately after the Council of Tyre in 335 (*HE* 10.19).

2. Robertson, *Select Writings* (1892), lvii, justly observed that 'the history of Athanasius during this period is the history of his writings.'

3. For Antony and Athanasius, see Chapter III, at n. 23; Chapter IV, at n. 42; Chapter XI, at n. 24.

4. *Epistula Ammonis* 2, 5, 13, 31; *Sancti Pachomii Vita Graeca Prima* 120, 137/8, cf. P. Rousseau, *Pachomius: The Making of a Community in Fourth-Century Egypt* (Berkeley, 1985), 72, 161/2, 189/90; J. E. Goehring, *The Letter of Ammon and Pachomian Monasticism* (*Patristische Texte und Studien* 27 [Berlin and New York]), 190, 201–205, 234–236, 282–285.

5. For comment, see A. Martin, *Sources chrétiennes* 317 (1985), 297, with J. Dummer, 'Fl. Artemius dux Aegypti,' *Archiv für Papyrusforschung* 21 (1971), 121–144.

6. Apart from the *Festal Letters* (App. 1), no systematic collection or ancient edition was ever made of Athanasius' letters: hence, as is also the case with the emperor Julian, the manuscript attestation of different letters and groups of letters varies widely (*CPG* 2094/5, 2097/8, 2100, 2103/4, 2106–2112). Among the letters transmitted under Athanasius' name, which are either interpolated or fictitious, are two letters to Lucifer of Caralis (*CPG* 2232, now edited by G. F. Diercks, *CCL* 8 [1978], 306–310): for proof that they are ancient forgeries, see L. Saltet, 'Fraudes littéraires des schismatiques Lucifériens aux IVe et Ve siècles,' *BHE* 1906.300–326, at 305–315.

7. The *Index* states that Athanasius wrote no *Festal Letter* for any Easter from 357 to 361 (29–33). But a fragment of *Letter* XXIX, written for Easter 357, is preserved by Severus of Antioch: edited and translated by J. Lebon, *CSCO* 101 (1933), 294; 102 (1933), 216/7.

8. Opitz 181/2. This letter is dated 340 by Kannengiesser, *Athanase* (1983), 375–397.
9. *PG* 26.1185–1188 (*CPG* 2108). The ancient Latin version of this letter preserved with the works of Lucifer of Cagliari is now edited by G. F. Diercks, *CCL* 8.316/7.
10. The fragments, previously published as *CIG* 8607; H. E. White and W. E. Crum, *The Monastery of Epiphanius at Thebes* 2 (New York, 1927), 124 No. 585, were reedited by G. de Jerphanion, 'La vraie teneur d'un texte de saint Athanase rétablie par l'épigraphie: L'Epistula ad Monachos,' *Rech. sci. rel.* 20 (1930), 529–544—with important consequences for the textual history of the complete Greek and Latin versions.
11. Chapters XV, XVI.
12. Athanasius twice refers to his presence 'in these parts' without specifying where he is (5, 7): for discussion, see Robertson, *Select Writings* (1892), li/lii, 222.
13. Chapter XII.
14. It need not be assumed, however, that the extant version was ever in any sense published in Athanasius' lifetime (App. 3).
15. The reference to the capitulation of Ossius (5.3)—which Athanasius may have added before he ever circulated the work.
16. Opitz on 68.
17. Socrates, *HE* 2.37.7–9. Socrates states that Eudoxius learned of the actual death of Leontius in Rome: in that case, however, he would surely have arrived in Antioch too late to secure election as Leontius' successor.
18. Chapter XV, at nn. 1–8.
19. On Athanasius' possible knowledge of Cyprian, see J. L. North, 'Did Athanasius (Letter 49, to Dracontius) Know and Correct Cyprian (Letter 5, Hartel)?' *Studia Patristica* 17.3 (1982), 1024–1029.
20. Chapter II, at nn. 45–47.
21. On the argument of the work, and its underlying assumptions, see M. Tetz, *ZKG* 90 (1979), 320–325; A. Pettersen, '"To Flee or Not to Flee": An Assessment of Athanasius' *De Fuga Sua*,' *Persecution and Toleration* (*Studies in Church History* 21, 1984), 29–42; O. Nicholson, 'Flight from Persecution as Imitation of Christ: Lactantius' Divine Institutes IV.18, 1–2,' *JTS*, N.S. 40 (1989), 48–65.
22. Robertson, *Select Writings* (1892), lvii.
23. But the letter to the monks which precedes it in the manuscripts (Opitz 181/2) is not to be regarded as an introductory letter to it (Opitz on 181.1).
24. Opitz on 183.
25. The traditional date of 358 (Opitz on 183, 206.11, 210.16, 216.13) depends on dating the capitulation of Liberius to 358 instead of 357.
26. On which, see respectively 'Synesius in Constantinople,' *GRBS* 27 (1986), 93–112; Averil Cameron, *Procopius and the Sixth Century* (Berkeley, 1985), 49–66.
27. Opitz 178–180. In favor of a date c. 340, see Kannengiesser, *Athanase* (1983), 380–397. Athanasius embroidered the story in his *Letter to the Bishops of Egypt and Libya* (18/9), cf. A. Martin, 'Le fil d'Arius,' *BHE* 84 (1989), 297–333, at 320–333.
28. For the year and context, see *Constantine* (1981), 242. An early martyrology may attest the day as 6 June (*Patrologia Orientalis* 10.17).
29. In 5.2 another nine exiled bishops are named, cf. Chapter VI.
30. On the normal, coarse meaning of the verb γαμεῖν at this period, see Alan Cameron, 'Strato and Rufinus,' *Classical Quarterly*, N.S. 32 (1982), 162–173, at

163/4. Müller, *Lexicon* (1952), 212, is mistaken to gloss it as 'in matrimonium duco.' In *Ep. ad Dracontium* 9.2 (*PG* 26.533 = Opitz 307.19) it also refers to copulation, not marriage.

31. In fact, to Arsaces, the thoroughly respectable Christian king of Armenia (Ammianus 20.11.13).

32. In 8.1 the phrase ταῦτα συνορῶντες refers back to the events of the reign of Constantine described in 1–6: the whole of Paul's episcopal career is later than the recall of exiled bishops in June 337 (App. 8).

33. Most conspicuously, Constantius' alleged dictum 'Let what I wish be a rule of the church' (33.7) has often been treated as an accurate and impartial definition of the relationship between the emperor and the church: see T. Mommsen, 'Die römischen Bischöfe Liberius und Felix II.' *Deutsche Zeitschrift für Geschichtswissenschaft*, N.F. 1 (1896–1897), 167–179, reprinted in his *Gesammelte Schriften* 6 (Berlin, 1910), 570–581; K. M. Setton, *Christian Attitude towards the Emperor in the Fourth Century* (New York, 1941), 86/7; H. Berkhof, *Kirche und Kaiser: Eine Untersuchung der Entstehung der byzantinischen und der theoktatischen Staatsauffassung im vierten Jahrhundert* (Zürich, 1947), 79 ('Das ist Staatskirche, ohne Vorbehalt oder Verschleierung'); S. L. Greenslade, *Church and State from Constantine to Theodosius* (London, 1954), 25; K. Aland, 'Kaiser und Kirche von Konstantin bis Byzanz,' *Kirchengeschichtliche Entwürfe* (Gütersloh, 1960), 257–279; W. Schneemelcher, *Kirche und Staat im 4. Jahrhundert* (*Bonner Akademische Reden* 37 [Bonn, 1970]), 18; K. Baus, *History of the Church,* ed. H. Jedin and H. Dolan, trans. A. Biggs 2 (New York, 1980), 82/3.

34. Chapter IX.

35. Socrates, *HE* 2.22.5, translated in Chapter X, at n. 12.

36. Chapter X.

37. Chapter XII. Significantly, the *History of the Arians* names Magnentius as a legitimate emperor, together with Vetranio and Gallus (74.4), and it calls Constantinus 'blessed' (50.2).

38. For the apparently double diminutive neuter formation Κοστύλλιον, see R. Kühner and F. Blass, *Ausführliche Grammatik der griechischen Sprache* 1.2³ (Hanover and Leipzig, 1892), 277, 280. Opitz on 234.4 takes it to be masculine, not neuter.

39. Chapter XV, at n. 21.

40. W. Bright, *Historical Writings of St. Athanasius* (Oxford, 1881), lxxvii: 'It is not, and does not pretend to be, a textual reproduction of what they said or wrote, but a representation *ad invidiam* of what is assumed to have been in their minds.'

41. As Klein, *Constantius* (1977), 16–159.

42. Chapter XVI.

43. *CTh* 16.2.12, cf. Chapter XVIII, at nn. 31–38.

44. Chapter IV, at n. 44.

45. Hanson, *Search* (1988), 639–875.

46. For bibliography and discussion, see A. Heron, 'Zur Theologie der "Tropici" in den Serapionbriefen des Athanasius: Amos 4, 13 als Pneumatologische Belegstelle,' *Kyrios: Vierteljahresschrift für Kirchen- und Geistesgeschichte Osteuropas*, N.F. 14 (1974), 3–24.

47. The set of *Letters to Serapion* (CPG 2094) has not been edited since Montfaucon, whose text is reprinted in *PG* 26.529–648, but there are two modern translations

with helpful notes and substantial introductions: J. Lebon, *Sources chrétiennes* 15 (Paris, 1947); C. R. B. Shapland, *The Letters of Saint Athanasius concerning the Holy Spirit* (London, 1951). I follow the consensus of scholarship in treating the second and third letters as a single letter wrongly divided in transmission.

48. Opitz on 231, 258.21, holds the work to be a unitary composition of the winter of 361/2. But at that date it would have been pointless for Athanasius to write as he does—ignoring almost all the events of the intervening two years.

49. On nos. (2) to (8), see briefly App. 10.

50. In 38.1, 4, Acacius and Eudoxius are invoked as Athanasius' main adversaries.

XV. NEW THEOLOGICAL CONTROVERSIES

1. The principal source for the career of Aetius is Philostorgius, *HE* 3.15–17, 27: for other sources and full discussion, see Kopecek, *Neo-Arianism* (1979), 61–132; R. A. Kaster, *Guardians of Language: The Grammarian and Society in Late Antiquity* (Berkeley, 1988), 5/6, 376; Hanson, *Search* (1988), 598–603.

2. Sozomenus, *HE* 3.15.8, also notes his standing with Gallus (and summarises his career briefly).

3. Gregory of Nyssa, *Contra Eunomium* 1.48/9 (pp. 38/9 Jaeger); Theodoretus, *HE* 2.27.8. Epiphanius, *Pan.* 76.1.1, 8, alleges that it was George who ordained Aetius deacon.

4. Sozomenus, *HE* 4.13.3 (letter of George of Laodicea).

5. Philostorgius, *HE* 4.8.

6. On the *Syntagmation* and Aetius' subsequent exile, see L. R. Wickham, 'The *Syntagmation* of Aetius the Anomoean,' *JTS*, N.S. 19 (1968), 532–569.

7. Julian, *Ep.* 46; Philostorgius, *HE* 9.4; Sozomenus, *HE* 5.5.9.

8. On his career, see Hanson, *Search* (1988), 611–617. R. P. Vaggione, 'Some Neglected Fragments of Theodore of Mopsuestia's *Contra Eunomium*,' *JTS*, N.S. 31 (1980), 403–470, publishes and discusses Syriac fragments of the lost *Contra Eunomium* of Theodore of Mopsuestia.

9. Philostorgius, *HE* 5.3; Sozomenus, *HE* 4.25.6, cf. Kopecek, *Neo-Arianism* (1979), 299–360.

10. For these two works, see the exemplary edition and reconstruction by R. P. Vaggione, *Eunomius: The Extant Works* (Oxford, 1987), 34–127, who also provides a careful discussion of their date and context (5–9, 82–89).

11. Gregory of Nyssa, *Contra Eunomium* 2.604 (p. 402.28 Jaeger); Gregory of Nazianzus, *Orat.* 29.21, cf. 27.2.

12. As noted by Jerome, *Dialogus contra Luciferianos* 11 (*PL* 23.174).

13. E. Vandenbussche, 'La part de la dialectique dans la théologie d'Eunomius "le technologue,"' *RHE* 40 (1944–1945), 47–72; J. Daniélou, 'Eunome l'Arien et l'exégèse néo-platonicienne du Cratyle,' *Revue des études grecques* 69 (1956), 412–432. The latter argues that with his 'Neoplatonic system' and 'mystical Aristotelianism' Eunomius 'est l'hiérophante d'une gnose, d'une doctrine secrète' (431).

14. L. R. Wickham, *JTS*, N.S. 19 (1968), 558–561; J. M. Rist, 'Basil's "Neoplatonism": Its Background and Nature,' *Basil of Caesarea: Christian, Humanist, Ascetic,* ed. P. J. Fedwick (Toronto, 1981), 137–220, at 185–188.

15. By M. Albertz, 'Zur Geschichte der jung-arianischen Kirchengemeinschaft,'

Theologische Studien und Kritiken 82 (1909), 205–278.

16. On the concept 'Neunizänismus,' see H. C. Brennecke, 'Erwägungen zu den Anfängen des Neunizänismus,' *Oecumenica et Patristica: Festschrift für Wilhelm Schneemelcher zum 75. Geburtstag* (Geneva, 1989), 241–258. The English equivalent seems not to have established itself in patristic scholarship—and neither 'Neo-Nicene' nor 'Neo-Arian' gains admittance to the second edition of the *Oxford English Dictionary* (1989).

17. As Athanasius gleefully emphasised in his *De Morte Arii* (Chapter XIV, at nn. 27–28).

18. *Constantine* (1981), 241/2, 264/5.

19. So, recently, R. P. Vaggione, *Eunomius* (1987), xiii: 'Eunomius represents the second generation of Arian thinkers . . . which attempted to carry on the theological work of Arius and Eusebius of Nicomedia.' The discussion in Hanson, *Search* (1988), 603–611, 617–636, though adopting the term 'Neo-Arian,' presents Aetius as obsessed with metaphysics and Eunomius as 'an individualist, philosophically eclectic theologian' who purveyed his own 'peculiar brand of rationalist Unitarianism.' For a more sympathetic and accurate assessment of Eunomius, see M. F. Wiles, 'Eunomius: Hair-splitting Dialectician or Defender of the Accessibility of Salvation?' *The Making of Orthodoxy: Essays in Honour of Henry Chadwick*, ed. R. Williams (Cambridge, 1989), 157–172.

20. Chapter XIII, at nn. 55–58.

21. Theodoretus, *HE* 2.17; *Quae gesta sunt inter Liberium et Felicem episcopos* 3 (*CSEL* 35.2.3–8); *Liber Pontificalis* 37.6 (p. 208 Duchesne), cf. 'The Capitulation of Liberius and Hilary of Poitiers,' *Phoenix* 46 (1992), 256–265.

22. *CSEL* 65.155/6, 168–170. Jerome, *De vir. ill.* 97, states that Fortunatianus was instrumental in persuading Liberius to accept heresy.

23. On the 'fall of Ossius,' see the lengthy and embarrassed discussion in V. C. De Clercq, *Ossius of Corduba: A Contribution to the History of the Constantinian Period* (Washington, 1954), 459–525.

24. Hilary, *Syn.* 11 (*PL* 10.487–489); Athanasius, *Syn.* 28.

25. Phoebadius of Agen, *Contra Arianos* 3 (*PL* 20.15 = *CCL* 64.25).

26. I have omitted the words *et quod dicitur homoeousion* ('or the term *homoiousios*') from my translation, because I suspect that they did not stand in the original document of 357, but were added in 358 (see below, n. 32). Although they occur in Athanasius' version (*Syn.* 28.6: ἢ τὸ λεγόμενον ὁμοιούσιον), and Hilary comments on them (*Syn.* 10, 79, 81), they are reported to be missing in several of his manuscripts (*PL* 10.488 n. [j]).

27. See App. 10. It is also impossible on chronological grounds to identify it as the document which Liberius subscribed (as argued by Brennecke, *Hilarius* [1984], 265–297).

28. Socrates, *HE* 2.37.7–9; Philostorgius, *HE* 4.4; Theodoretus, *HE* 2.25.1; Sozomenus, *HE* 4.12.3–5. Sozomenus implies that Eudoxius had been at court since 355 (*HE* 4.11.3).

29. Sozomenus, *HE* 4.12.5–7. Those present included Acacius of Caesarea and Uranius of Tyre.

30. Sozomenus, *HE* 4.13.1–3.

31. Gwatkin, *Arianism*[2] (1900), 164/5.

32. Epiphanius, *Pan.* 73.2–11, cf. Hilary, *Syn.* 13–28. On this important document, see the classic study by J. Gummerus, *Die homöusianische Partei bis zum Tode des Konstantius* (Leipzig, 1900), 66–89; more recently, J. T. Lienhard, 'The Epistle of the Synod of Ancyra, 358: A Reconsideration,' *Arianism* (1985), 349–357. It is somewhat surprising that this letter avoids the technical term *homoiousios*—if it was already current. It must be suspected, therefore, that the word was coined after the Council of Ancyra, precisely to sum up its theological standpoint in an easily remembered slogan, and hence that it did not stand in the original text of the Sirmian manifesto of 357 (above, n. 26).

33. Sozomenus, *HE* 4.13.4–6, cf. Philostorgius, *HE* 4.8; Theodoretus, *HE* 2.25.3/4. For contemporary, but less precise, references to the embassy, see Hilary, *Syn.* 78, 91; Marius Victorinus, *Adv. Arium* 1.28.24–29 (below, n. 56).

34. Sozomenus, *HE* 4.14.

35. Sozomenus, *HE* 4.16.1–13, cf. Philostorgius, *HE* 4.8–11.

36. On the 'Council of Sirmium of 358' accepted by many scholars, see App. 10.

37. Philostorgius, *HE* 4.8.

38. Chapter XVI.

39. Hilary, *Syn.* 8 (*PL* 10.485); Socrates, *HE* 2.39.1–7; Sozomenus, *HE* 4.16.14–22.

40. *PL* 20.13–30, reedited with new chapter-divisions by R. Demeulenaere, *CCL* 64 (1985), 23–54. On Phoebadius' work as an immediate, almost instinctive reaction to the Sirmian manifesto, see still Gwatkin, *Arianism*² (1900), 162–164.

41. So, most recently, D. H. Williams, 'A Reassessment of the Early Career and Exile of Hilary and Poitiers,' *JEH* 42 (1991), 202–217, at 213/4.

42. *Contra Arianos* 28.3 (23): 'quid si diversa nunc sentit . . . ?' V. C. De Clercq, *Ossius of Corduba* (1954), 525–530, concluded that Ossius died during the winter of 357/ᵖ. But Athanasius in Alexandria appears to have heard of his death before the end of 357 (Chapter XIV, at n. 25).

43. Hilary, *In Const.* 2, 11. For this interpretation (and against the hypothesis that the charges against Hilary were primarily or exclusively political), see 'Hilary of Poitiers on his Exile,' *Vig. Chr.* 46 (1992), 129–140.

44. Only fragments survive, from a later edition of c. 366 (superbly edited by A. Feder in *CSEL* 65 [1916]).

45. Hilary, *Syn.* 1–5, 8. P. Gläser, *Phoebadius von Agen* (Diss. Augsburg, 1978), 21–25, argues that Phoebadius presided over the council.

46. Unfortunately, there is as yet no modern critical edition: *faute de mieux,* therefore, references are given to Coustant's edition of 1693 reprinted in *PL* 10.478–546.

47. *Apologetica responsa* 2 (*PL* 10.545). These marginal notes indicate the intransigence of Lucifer: two not included in Coustant's edition reprinted by Migne are published by P. Smulders, 'Two Pasages of Hilary's "Apologetica Responsa" Rediscovered,' *Bijdragen: Tijdschrift voor Philosophie en Theologie* 39 (1978), 234–243 = *Texte und Textkritik: Eine Aufsatzsammlung,* ed. J. Dummer (*Texte und Untersuchungen* 133 [Berlin, 1987]), 539–547.

48. *Syn.* 63.

49. *Syn.* 77–92.

50. *Syn.* 91: 'fidem Nicaenam numquam nisi exsulaturus audivi.' This need not mean that Hilary was totally unacquainted with or had 'never heard of' the Nicene creed, as is assumed by many: for example, H. Lietzmann, *RE* 8 (1913), 1601; Kelly,

Creeds[3] (1972), 258; G. C. Stead, '"Homoousios" dans la pensée de saint Athanase,' *Politique et théologie* (1974), 231–253, at 239 ('je n'entendis rien au sujet de la foi de Nicée'); Brennecke, *Hilarius* (1984), 217; D. H. Williams, *JEH* 42 (1991), 203, 207, 214. The context is tendentious, and Hilary may mean only that he had never heard the creed of 325 recited aloud.

51. Chapter XVI.

52. The work survives in two recensions, which were reedited without examination of the manuscripts by V. Bulhart, *CCL* 69 (1967), 221–247. The revised recension, which sets out to remove possible theological ambiguities, seems to come from Gregory's own hand: see M. Simonetti, 'La doppia redazione del "De Fide" di Gregorio di Elvira,' *Forma Futuri: Studi in onore del Cardinale Michele Pellegrino* (Turin, 1975), 1022–1040. For proof of Gregory's use of Phoebadius and Hilary, see B. Marx, 'Zwei Zeugen für die Herkunft der Fragmente I und II des sog. Opus historicum s. Hilarii: Ein Beitrag zur Lösung des Fragmentenproblems,' *Theologische Quartalschrift* 88 (1906), 390–406, at 391/2.

53. The traditional date is 360 or even 361: A. Wilmart, *La tradition des opuscules de Foebadius, Gregorius Illiberitanus, Faustinus* (*Sitzungsberichte der kaiserlichen Akademie der Wissenschaften in Wien,* Philosophisch-historische Klasse 159, Abhandlung 1, 1908), 1; M. Simonetti, *Patrologia* 3 (Rome, 1978), 80. But the work is dated c. 358 by G. Bardy, 'L'occident et les documents de la controverse arienne,' *Rev. sci. rel.* 20 (1940), 28–63, at 30, 55; J. Doignon, *Handbuch der lateinischen Literatur der Antike 5* (Munich, 1989), 491–493.

54. On his career and writings, see now G. Madec and P. L. Schmidt, *Handbuch der lateinischen Literatur der Antike 5* (Munich, 1989), 342–355.

55. On the chronology of Victorinus' works, see P. Hadot, *Marius Victorinus: Recherches sur sa vie et ses œuvres* (Paris, 1971), 263–272. Unfortunately, he rests too much on the assumptions that there was a Council of Sirmium in 358 and that Liberius returned to Rome in 358 bringing with him the letter of Basil to which the *Adversus Arium* 1.28 refers.

56. *Adv. Arium* 1.28.22–42, esp. 24–29: 'et toto tempore postea, usquequo imperator Romae fuit, praesens audisti multa contraria, conviva exsistens istorum hominum quos nunc anathematizas, iratus vel quod sine te fidem scripserunt, an coactus a magistris legatus venisti in defensionem proditionis.' Victorinus' allusions to Constantius' visit to Rome, the Sirmian manifesto, and Basil's journey to court in 358 permit two important deductions: first, Basil accompanied Constantius to Rome; and second, Ursacius and Valens were also with the emperor. The French translation by P. Hadot, *Sources chrétiennes* 68 (Paris, 1960), 269, takes *conviva* as meaning no more than 'being in communion with,' but there seems to be no clear parallel for this attenuated metaphorical sense (*Thesaurus Linguae Latinae* 4.879/80), and the immediate context strongly supports the literal interpretation of the word.

57. Note the explicit equation of homoeousians with acknowledged heretics in *Adv. Arium* 1.45.1–23: 'discedant ergo Patripassiani . . . discedant Marcelli et Photini discipuli . . . discedant et Basilii et ὁμοιούσιοι.'

XVI. THE HOMOEAN CREED

1. The traditional term is rejected by E. D. Hunt, 'Did Constantius II Have "Court

Bishops"?' *Studia Patristica* 19 (1989), 86–90. Similarly, Klein, *Constantius* (1977), 86–89, argues that Constantius was not influenced by Ursacius and Valens. But it is clear that normally bishops were in attendance wherever the imperial court happened to be: when Constantius visited Rome in 357, his entourage included Ursacius, Valens, Basil of Ancyra, and Eudoxius of Germanicia (Chapter XV, at nn. 28, 56).

2. Whence Socrates, *HE* 2.37.18–24, who notes that the original was in Latin. For the role of Marcus and the names of the bishops present, see Epiphanius, *Pan.* 73.22.5–8 (letter of George of Laodicea written in 359); *CSEL* 65.163.10–26 (letter of Germinius written in 366). The list of names in Epiphanius diverges from the bishops named in Germinius' letter in two particulars: Germinius' own name has been corrupted to Germanus, and it has Hypatianus, but omits Pancratius. It is not clear whether that is an error: it is possible that Hypatianus, who is attested as bishop of Heraclea in 364 (Sozomenus, *HE* 6.7.1), was present as well as Pancratius.

3. Kelly, *Creeds*³ (1972), 290/1.

4. It was alleged at Seleucia that Acacius had used the phrase ὅμοιος κατὰ πάντα to describe the relationship of Father and Son in his published writings (Socrates, *HE* 2.40.33). It does not appear to occur in the exiguous fragments of his writings that survive (*CPG* 3510–3512).

5. Epiphanius, *Pan.* 73.22.6/7 (George of Laodicea).

6. Sozomenus, *HE* 4.17.1. On George's allegedly very profitable business activities, see Epiphanius, *Pan.* 76.1.4–7, with A. K. Bowman, *Egypt after the Pharaohs, 332 B.C.–A.D. 642* (Berkeley, 1986), 221.

7. *CSEL* 65.93/4.

8. Sulpicius Severus, *Chron.* 2.41.1, cf. App. 10. On the Council of Ariminum, see esp. Y.-M. Duval, 'La "manoeuvre frauduleuse" de Rimini: À la recherche du *Liber adversus Ursacium et Valentem,*' *Hilaire et son temps* (Paris, 1969), 51–103; Brennecke, *Homöer* (1988), 23–40; Hanson, *Search* (1988), 371–380. An official record of the council was certainly kept: Socrates specifically notes the presence of shorthand writers at the parallel Council of Seleucia (*HE* 2.39.8). These *acta* must be the source of the conciliar documents preserved by Hilary: Auxentius of Milan sent to the emperor Valentinian a copy of 'ea quae gesta sunt in concilio Ariminensi' (quoted by Hilary, *Contra Auxentium* 15 [*PL* 10.618]). It is not clear whether Sulpicius Severus drew directly on the *acta* or knew them only through Hilary's work. Modern discussion has centered on the question of how much use Jerome made of the *acta* in his *Dialogus Luciferiani et Orthodoxi*: P. Batiffol, 'Les sources de l'*Altercatio Luciferiani et Orthodoxi* de St. Jérôme,' *Miscellanea Geronimiana* (Rome, 1920), 97–114; Y.-M. Duval, 'Saint Jérôme devant la baptême des hérétiques: D'autres sources de l'*Altercatio Luciferiani et Orthodoxi*,' *REAug* 14 (1968), 145–180.

9. Sulpicius Severus, *Chron.* 2.41.2–6, with the creed and condemnation edited by Y.-M. Duval, 'Une traduction latine inédite du symbole de Nicée et une condemnation d'Arius à Rimini: Nouveaux fragments historiques d'Hilaire ou pièces des actes du concile?' *Revue bénédictine* 82 (1972), 7–25, at 10–12, cf. H. Silvestre, 'À propos d'une récente édition de la "Damnatio Arii" de Rimini,' *RHE* 68 (1973), 102–104. The latter was edited by Coustant as part of Hilary's lost historical work, whence *PL* 10.698/9, but excluded by A. L. Feder from *CSEL* 65 (1916) because of

its different manuscript attestation: for proof that both documents derive ultimately from Hilary, see Y.-M. Duval, *Revue bénédictine* 82 (1972), 7–25. The
number of four hundred bishops present is confirmed by Athanasius, *Syn.* 8.1,
whence Sozomenus, *HE* 4.17.2. Philostorgius, *HE* 4.8, has three hundred.

10. *CSEL* 65.96/7, partly quoted by Athanasius, *Syn.* 11.1–3. For Gaius, see Feder,
    Studien II (1910), 115 No. 32.

11. *CSEL* 65.78–85. A Greek version is preserved, with substantial differences from
    the original, in Athanasius, *Syn.* 10; Socrates, *HE* 2.37.54–74; Theodoretus, *HE*
    2.19.1–13; Sozomenus, *HE* 4.18.

12. Sulpicius Severus, *Chron.* 2.41.1, 43.3. The letter of Constantius quoted by
    Athanasius, *Syn.* 55.2, states the number of envoys as twenty (instead of the pre-
    scribed ten), cf. below, n. 18.

13. Sulpicius Severus, *Chron.* 2.41.5. This hostile account implies that it was a pagan
    shrine and asserts that it had been deliberately left vacant ('aedem tum de industria
    vacantem orationis loco capiunt').

14. *CSEL* 65.87/8.

15. As Sulpicius Severus complained: 'ex parte nostrorum leguntur homines
    adulescentes, parum docti et parum cauti; ab Arrianis autem missi senes, callidi et
    ingenio valentes, veterno perfidiae imbuti' (*Chron.* 2.41.7). All ten names of the
    members of this delegation are known: they include Ursacius, Valens, Germinius,
    Gaius, and Epictetus (*CSEL* 65.174.5–7, 87.5/6, cf. Feder, *Studien* II [1910], 103/4).

16. App. 9.

17. Athanasius, *Syn.* 55.2/3, whence Socrates, *HE* 2.37.78–81 (letter of Constantius to
    the bishops at Ariminum); *CSEL* 65.85.11–18. In his letter Constantius hypocriti-
    cally apologises for being unable to see the envoys because he was compelled to
    march against barbarians—so that his soul was not in a pure enough state to deal
    with matters concerning the law of God. Athanasius also preserves the reply of the
    bishops from Ariminum, in which they plead to be allowed to return home to their
    leaderless churches before harsh winter weather commences (*Syn.* 55.4–7, whence
    Socrates, *HE* 2.37.83–87: Theodoretus, *HE* 2.20, has a slightly different Greek ver-
    sion of the same Latin original).

18. *CSEL* 65.85.20–86.23. The heading of the document contains fourteen names:
    apart from Restitutus all appear to be otherwise unknown: see Feder, *Studien* II
    (1910), 106.

19. For a comparison of the two documents, see Kelly, *Creeds*[3] (1972), 291/2.

20. Socrates, *HE* 2.37.96; Sozomenus, *HE* 4.19.8.

21. See, recently, Brennecke, *Homöer* (1988), 40–56. Socrates, *HE* 2.39/40, who ex-
    plicitly acknowledges Sabinus of Heraclea as his source, provides the principal nar-
    rative source on which the following account of the council is based: in principle,
    references are given only where other sources furnish supplementary details.

22. The total given by Socrates, *HE* 2.39.5, is confirmed by Athanasius, *Syn.* 12.1
    (where the text states the date on which the bishops assembled as 14 September),
    but Theodoretus has a total of one hundred and fifty (*HE* 2.26.9).

23. On the career of Cyril, see Chapter XII, at nn. 53–58; on that of Eustathius, 'The
    Date of the Council of Gangra,' *JTS*, N.S. 40 (1989), 121–124, arguing that the
    Council of Gangra which condemned him should be dated c. 355 and identified as
    a provincial synod of Paphlagonian bishops—which lacked the jurisdiction to de-

pose a bishop whose see (Sebasteia) belonged to the province of Armenia.

24. The list of bishops who subscribed the document which Acacius presented to the council contained forty-three names, though some have been lost in transmission (Epiphanius, *Pan.* 73.26, with the comments of K. Holl, ad loc.). Socrates, *HE* 2.39.16, states that the supporters of George, Uranius, and Eudoxius numbered only thirty-two. Hilary of Poitiers has a different division of parties from that of Socrates: according to him, there were one hundred and five homoeousians, while nineteen bishops held the view that the proper term to characterise the relationship of Father and Son was '*anomoeousion,* id est dissimilis essentiae,' and only the Egyptian bishops (with the exception of George) defended the *homoousion* (*In Const.* 12). The last assertion is one-sided and misleading, since several Egyptian bishops attended and supported Acacius, including Pancratius of Pelusium; the Melitian Ptolemaeus, who had replaced Serapion as bishop of Thmuis; and Apollonius, the Melitian bishop of Oxyrhynchus (Athanasius, *Syn.* 12.3; Epiphanius, *Pan.* 73.26).

25. For the full text and subscriptions, see Epiphanius, *Pan.* 73.25/6. Incomplete versions are quoted in Athanasius, *Syn.* 29.2–9; Socrates, *HE* 2.40.8–17 (from Sabinus). For an analysis of its theology, see J. Gummerus, *Die homöusianische Partei bis zum Tode des Konstantius* (Leipzig, 1900), 142–152.

26. Sozomenus, *HE* 4.22.22, quotes a part of his argument omitted by Socrates, again supplementing his main source from Sabinus.

27. Athanasius, *Syn.* 12.5, confirms all eighteen names given by Socrates, *HE* 2.40.43–45.

28. Sozomenus, *HE* 4.23.1.

29. Socrates, *HE* 2.41.1–4; Sozomenus, *HE* 4.23.1.

30. Sulpicius Severus, *Chron.* 2.43.1–44.8, naming Phoebadius of Agen and Servatius of Tongres as leaders of the opposition to Constantius' demands. On the extremely obscure question of exactly what constituted the alleged *fraus,* see Y.-M. Duval, *Hilaire et son temps* (1969), 84–103.

31. Sulpicius Severus, *Chron.* 2.44.1, makes the prefect Taurus say that the bishops are in their seventh month of confinement in Ariminum—which implies that the final capitulation did not occur until January 360.

32. Sulpicius Severus, *Chron.* 2.45.1; Theodoretus, *HE* 2.27.7–12; Sozomenus, *HE* 4.23.1–7.

33. *CSEL* 65.174.3–175.4. The heading contains eighteen names, on which see Feder, *Studien* II (1910), 104–106. The absence of Basil of Ancyra, Eustathius of Sebasteia, and Eleusius of Cyzicus, who are known to have been among the ten envoys of the majority (Theodoretus, *HE* 2.27.3–6), implies that the letter was written by the supporters of Acacius.

34. Sozomenus, *HE* 4.23.8.

35. The *Paschal Chronicle* (543/4 Bonn) states that seventy-two bishops were present when Eudoxius was enthroned on 27 January 360 and names more than fifty of them (unfortunately without their sees). For accounts of the council, see Socrates, *HE* 2.41.5/6; Philostorgius, *HE* 4.12; Sozomenus, *HE* 4.24.1.

36. The creed is transmitted independently of Athanasius by Socrates, *HE* 2.41.8–17; Theodoretus, *HE* 2.21.3–7. For brief comment on the document as a whole, see Kelly, *Creeds*[3] (1972), 293–295.

37. For the names of the bishops deposed and details of the charges against them, which are not relevant here, see Socrates, *HE* 2.42/3; Sozomenus, *HE* 4.24/5 (with some discrepancies).

38. Theodoretus, *HE* 2.28, preserves a letter of the council to George of Alexandria 'in condemnation of his deacon Aetius on account of his unlawful blasphemy.'

39. Hilary, *In Const.* 26, reports that the African bishops had set their names to a formal condemnation of the blasphemy of Ursacius and Valens.

40. Hilary, *In Const.* 15.10–12.

41. Sozomenus, *HE* 4.26.1.

42. For complementary accounts of the situation in the church of Antioch in 360, see Socrates, *HE* 2.44; Theodoretus, *HE* 2.31; Sozomenus, *HE* 4.28; for other evidence and full discussion, Brennecke, *Homöer* (1988), 66–81.

43. John Chrysostom, *In Meletium* (*PG* 50.515–520).

44. Rufinus, *HE* 10.25.

45. See the excellent survey by K. Schäferdiek, 'Germanenmission,' *RAC* 10 (1978), 492–548.

46. *Syn.* 28–63 (*PL* 10.501–523). Hilary describes the council of 341 as a gathering of saints (*Syn.* 32). Similarly, he salutes the eastern bishops in general and Basil of Ancyra, Eustathius of Sebasteia, and Eleusius of Cyzicus by name as *sanctissimi viri* (80, 90).

47. Sulpicius Severus, *Chron.* 2.42.2.

48. Sulpicius Severus, *Chron.* 2.42.3–5, gives him an implausibly prominent role.

49. Sulpicius Severus, *Chron.* 2.45.3.

50. Edited by A. L. Feder, *CSEL* 65.197–205. The earliest and best manuscript, of the sixth century (Vatican, Archivo di San Pietro D 182), states that Hilary presented the work to the emperor in Constantinople ('quem et Constantinopoli ipse tradidit'), perhaps echoing Jerome's description of the work as 'ad Constantium libellus quem viventi ei Constantinopoli porrexerat' (*De. vir. ill.* 100). The text fully bears out these statements, but there has been some uncertainty over the precise date. Feder, *Studien* III (1912), 12–14, argued for December 359. However, the fact that Hilary calls the dated creed of 22 May 359 *proximi anni fides* (5.2, cf. 3.3) implies that he is writing in January 360.

51. Compare *Syn.* 78, where Hilary presents Constantius as being deceived by bishops with erroneous views.

52. *Ad Const.* 1–3. The context clearly indicates that it is unwise to take what Hilary says here about his condemnation and exile in 356 *au pied de la lettre*.

53. *Ad Const.* 10, 6.1, 8.1, 11, 7.1.

54. *Ad Const.* 8.1.

55. *In Const.*, esp. 1/2, 5–11, 27. Hilary predictably compares Constantius to Herod and Antiochus (6): on his vocabulary of abuse, see I. Opelt, 'Hilarius von Poitiers als Polemiker,' *Vig. Chr.* 27 (1973), 203–217.

56. Chapter XIV.

57. On the unity of the work, see *JTS*, N.S. 39 (1988), 610, criticising the complicated theory of composition in stages spread over almost two years advanced in the recent edition by A. Rocher, *Sources chrétiennes* 334 (Paris, 1987), 29–38.

XVII. THE ELDER STATESMAN

1. Chapter XIV.
2. Kelly, *Creeds*³ (1972), 254–283.
3. *CSEL* 65.198.5–15.
4. Chapter XV, at n. 43.
5. For discussion, see J. F. Drinkwater, 'The "Pagan Underground," Constantius II's "Secret Service," and the Survival and the Usurpation of Julian the Apostate,' *Studies in Latin Literature and Roman History*, ed. C. Deroux 3 (*Collection Latomus* 180 [Brussels, 1983]), 348–387.
6. Ammianus 21.2.4/5.
7. Chapter XVI.
8. Brennecke, *Hilarius* (1984), 360–367.
9. Despite Sulpicius Severus, *Vita Martini* 6.7: 'cum sancto Hilario comperisset regis paenitentia potestatem indultam fuisse redeundi . . .' ; *Chron.* 2.45.4: 'redire ad Gallias iubetur absque exilii indulgentia.' For discussion, see Y.-M. Duval, 'Vrais et faux problèmes concernant le retour d'exil d'Hilaire de Poitiers et son action en Italie en 360–363,' *Athenaeum*, N.S. 48 (1970), 251–275.
10. *CSEL* 65.43–46. Authorship of the letter is claimed for Phoebadius of Agen by P. Gläser, *Phoebadius von Agen* (Diss. Augsburg, 1978), 74–80.
11. Sulpicius Severus 2.45.5.
12. Brennecke, *Homöer* (1988), 87 n. 1, holds that Julian was probably also present, but his known movements in 360 tell against this attractive hypothesis (App. 9).
13. For the usual inference, see J. Bidez and F. Cumont, *Iuliani Imperatoris Epistulae et Leges* (Paris, 1922), 51.
14. On the career of Modestus, consul in 372, see *PLRE* 1.605–608. What is reported about his religious attitudes makes it clear that he was a time-server: under Julian he claimed to have been a secret pagan before 362 (Libanius, *Ep.* 804, cf. 791), but later he adopted the creed of his master Valens (Gregory of Nazianzus, *Orat.* 43.48; Sozomenus, *HE* 6.18.3).
15. As Gregory of Nazianzus complained (*Orat.* 4.84/5). Rufinus, *HE* 10.33 (994.21–25), goes so far as to state that Julian used neither violence nor torture.
16. On Julian's religious policies, see esp. J. Bidez, 'L'évolution de la politique de l'empereur Julien en matière religieuse,' *Bulletin de l'Académie Royale de Belgique, Classe des Lettres* 7 (1914), 406–461; J. Vogt, *Kaiser Julian und das Judentum: Studien zum Weltanschauungskampf der Spätantike* (*Morgenland* 30 [Leipzig, 1939]); G. W. Bowersock, *Julian the Apostate* (Cambridge, Mass., 1978), 79–93.
17. *Constantine* (1981), 39, 148–163.
18. Julian, *Ep.* 60, 378c–380d: preserved in Socrates, *HE* 3.3.
19. Rufinus, *HE* 10.28, states that Eusebius, not Athanasius, convened the council.
20. Philostorgius p. 230.14–22 Bidez, cf. *Tomus ad Antiochenos* 3.1.
21. Rufinus, *HE* 10.28; Socrates, *HE* 3.5; Theodoretus, *HE* 3.4; Sozomenus, *HE* 5.12.1/2.
22. M. Tetz, 'Ein enzyklisches Schreiben der Synode von Alexandrien (362),' *ZNW* 79 (1988), 262–281. Tetz provides a critical edition (271–273) of the letter (*PG* 28.81–84; *CPG* 2241), which Montfaucon had pronounced spurious in his edition of Athanasius published in 1698 (2.28–30). Since Montfaucon's condemnation was universally accepted, the letter is not employed in earlier scholarly accounts of

the council, such as C. B. Armstrong, 'The Synod of Alexandria and the Schism at Antioch in A.D. 362,' *JTS* 22 (1921), 206–221, 347–355; J.-M. Leroux, 'Athanase et la seconde phase de la crise arienne (345–373),' *Politique et théologie* (1974), 145–156, at 151–154; Hanson, *Search* (1988), 639–653.

23. *PG* 25.796–809, reedited by Opitz 320–329, whose chapter and section divisions are here employed.

24. Hence the un-Athanasian vocabulary which led Montfaucon to deny his authorship: M. Tetz, *ZNW* 79 (1988), 266–270, shows that the language of the letter is no obstacle to joint authorship—and that the content fits the historical context of 362.

25. The phrase ὁμοούσιος τριάς appears to be a new coinage in 362, but it was soon repeated by Serapion of Thmuis, *Ep. ad monachos* 11 (*PG* 40.936), cf. M. Tetz, *ZNW* 79 (1988), 276/7.

26. *Epistula Catholica,* edited by M. Tetz, *ZNW* 79 (1988), 271–273.

27. Rufinus, *HE* 10.30 (992.11–13).

28. *Tomus* 9.1/2.

29. For a thorough analysis of the whole document, see M. Tetz, 'Über nikäische Orthodoxie: Der sog. Tomus ad Antiochenos des Athanasios von Alexandrien,' *ZNW* 66 (1975), 194–222. On *Tomus* 7, where some scholars have detected allusions to the teaching of Apollinaris of Laodicea, see also A. L. Pettersen, 'The Arian Context of Athanasius of Alexandria's *Tomus ad Antiochenos* VII,' *JEH* 41 (1990), 183–198.

30. *Tomus* 1.1–3.

31. *Tomus* 3.1–4.1, 6.1–4. The last requirement appears to reflect current theological debates in Antioch, cf. M. Tetz, *ZNW* 66 (1975), 201/2, 204–206.

32. *Tomus* 5.1–3, cf. Chapter VIII, at nn. 36–40. It is relevant that the theological statement forms part of the western synodical letter as quoted by Theodoretus, *HE* 2.8.1–54—who explicitly states that what he quotes was brought to Antioch.

33. As the concluding section emphasises (*Tomus* 8.2–9.1).

34. *Tomus* 2.1–3, 9.1/2.

35. *Tomus* 9.3–10.4.

36. *Tomus* 11.1/2; Epiphanius, *Pan.* 77.2.1, cf. M. Tetz, *ZNW* 66 (1975), 218–221. The final line of the text presents a serious problem. It reads: ἐρρῶσθαι ὑμᾶς εὔχομαι ἐγὼ Καρτέριος, ἐστὶ δὲ πόλεως Συρίας. The last four words are an editorial addition, and Opitz on 329.16 argued that Carterius was an error for Cymatius (as in the manuscripts of *Hist. Ar.* 5.2), whose declaration has been lost in transmission. Tetz argues that the text is complete, but that Carterius is an error for Asterius (221/2).

37. Rufinus, *HE* 10.31 (993.6–994.5). For a brief sketch of Lucifer's life after 361, see G. F. Diercks, *CCL* 8 (1978), xxvii–xxxv.

38. Rufinus, *HE* 10.31 (993.16–18), cf. Socrates, *HE* 3.25.18 (the bishops who attended the Council of Antioch in 363).

39. Basil, *Ep.* 69.1, cf. Rufinus, *HE* 10.31 (993.18). Basil's letter goes on to ask Athanasius to condemn Marcellus (69.2), which he also declined to do, cf. M. Tetz, 'Markellianer und Athanasius,' *ZNW* 64 (1973), 75–121. After Athanasius' death, his exiled successor Peter accused Meletius of being an Arian in the presence of Damasus in Rome (Basil, *Ep.* 266.2).

40. Rufinus, *HE* 10.31 (994.5–10).
41. *Ep. ad Rufinianum* (*PG* 26.1180/1). Councils were also held in Asia Minor by the supporters of Macedonius, the former bishop of Constantinople, and Eustathius of Sebasteia (Basil, *Ep.* 251.4; Socrates, *HE* 3.10.4).
42. Gregory of Nazianzus, *Orat.* 4.86, with the scholiast, implies that Pythiodorus also stirred up anti-Christian riots.
43. Julian, *Ep.* 110, 398c–399a.
44. Julian, *Ep.* 111, 432c–435d.
45. Rufinus, *HE* 10.35; Socrates, *HE* 3.14.1; Sozomenus, *HE* 5.15.3.
46. There is a picturesque story of how Athanasius outwitted the soldiers pursuing him up the Nile by turning downstream, sailing boldly past their boat, and finding safety again in Alexandria: Rufinus, *HE* 10.35; Socrates, *HE* 3.14.1–6; Theodoretus, *HE* 3.9.3/4; *Vita Athanasii* (*BHG*³ 185) 26 (*PG* 25.ccviii); Photius, *Bibliotheca* 258, p. 484a25–b5; Simeon Metaphrastes, *Vita Athanasii* (*BHG*³ 183) 15 (*PG* 25.ccxliii). The final detail implies that incident, if it is historical, belongs to Athanasius' flight from the agents of Constantius in the late 350s—as Sozomenus saw (*HE* 4.10.4). But its obvious folk-lore motifs suggest that the story may be a 'Wanderanecdote' without any basis in reality: for discussion, see M. Tetz, 'Zur Biographie des Athanasius von Alexandrien,' *ZKG* 90 (1979), 304–338, at 310–316.
47. For two recent (and independent) accounts of Athanasius' dealings with Jovian, see Brennecke, *Homöer* (1988), 169–173; L. W. Barnard, 'Athanasius and the Emperor Jovian,' *Studia Patristica* 21 (1989), 384–389. Jovian himself should not be regarded as a nonentity: see G. Wirth, 'Jovian: Kaiser und Karikatur,' *Vivarium. Festschrift Theodor Klauser zum 90. Geburtstag (Jahrbuch für Antike und Christentum, Ergänzungsband* 11 [Münster, 1984]), 353–384.
48. On the text of *Index* 35, see M. Albert, *Sources chrétiennes* 317 (Paris, 1985), 265. Jovian is attested in Edessa on 27 September (*CTh* 7.4.9⁵), but he had arrived in Antioch by 22 October (*CTh* 10.19.2). Sozomenus, *HE* 6.5, states that Athanasius reached the emperor in Antioch.
49. *PG* 26.813, reedited by Opitz 330. The letter is rejected as spurious by E. Schwartz, 'Zur Kirchengeschichte des vierten Jahrhunderts,' *ZNW* 34 (1935), 129–213, at 166 n. 3 = *Gesammelte Schriften* 4 (Berlin, 1960), 1–110, at 50 n. 2; Opitz on 330.1ff.; Brennecke, *Homöer* (1988), 171 n. 82. The grounds alleged are inconclusive, and the letter was known to Rufinus, *HE* 11.1 (1002.10/1): 'honorificis et officiosissimis litteris Athanasium requirit.'
50. Socrates, *HE* 3.25.4.
51. Socrates, *HE* 3.25.10–17. Brennecke, *Homöer* (1988), 175/6, has demonstrated that the name of Acacius of Caesarea among the signatories of the letter must be an error: this Acacius was presumably the obscure bishop of some other see.
52. Basil, *Ep.* 89.2, later reminded Meletius that he had failed to take up an offer from Athanasius while he was in Antioch in 363/4 to enter into communion with him—but he neglects to disclose either the precise circumstances or the terms of the abortive offer.
53. *PG* 26.813–820 = Opitz 330–333, quoted by Theodoretus, *HE* 4.3.
54. *CSCO* 150.70.19–71.9 (text); 151.27.20–28.6 (French translation), cf. Camplani, *Lettere* (1989), 103–105.

55. *PG* 26.820–824 = Opitz 334–336, cf. Sozomenus, *HE* 6.5.2–4.

56. Socrates, *HE* 3.4.2, 4.1.14; *Hist. ac.* 4.7.

57. Eutropius, *Brev.* 10.18.2; Ammianus 26.1.5; Socrates, *HE* 3.36.5, 4.1.1.

58. Ammianus 26.1.7, 2.1/2, 4.3; *Chr. min.* 1.240.

59. Socrates, *HE* 4.16, 18; Sozomenus, *HE* 6.14, 18, cf. Rufinus, *HE* 11.5; Theodoretus, *HE* 4.17.1–4 (who have only the latter story).

60. Gwatkin, *Arianism*² (1900), 276/7; Brennecke, *Homöer* (1988), 224–242. The growth of legend can be seen in Gregory of Nazianzus: a single priest burnt at sea in *Orat.* 25.10 becomes a vague plural in a later speech which alleges that the persecution under Valens was worse than that under Maximinus at the start of the century (43.46, cf. 5).

61. On Valens' policy, which has often been misunderstood, see the acute and convincing analysis by Brennecke, *Homöer* (1988), 181–242.

62. See now P. Rousseau, *Basil of Caesarea* (Berkeley, forthcoming). Bishops who condemned the council of 360 were removed—like Eleusius of Cyzicus (Socrates, *HE* 4.6).

63. Sozomenus, *HE* 6.7. Sozomenus' account must be preferred to that of Socrates, *HE* 4.2, who has the Hellespontine bishops ask permission to hold a council from Valens alone after his return to Constantinople: Socrates has confused the request for permission to hold a council with the report of its decisions, which was made to Valens at Heraclea on his return from Pannonia (Sozomenus, *HE* 6.7.8).

64. Socrates, *HE* 4.12; Sozomenus, *HE* 6.10.3–12.5 (with complementary details in each author). Sozomenus, *HE* 6.12.3, implies that the Council of Antioch in Caria met in the early spring of 365.

65. The argument is Athanasius' own: it recalls his use of Constantius' letter of 353 summoning him to court in his *Defense before Constantius* (Chapter XIII).

66. Socrates, *HE* 4.13.4; Sozomenus, *HE* 6.12.12, describe his hiding place as 'his ancestral tomb.'

67. Ammianus 26.6–10 provides the fullest account: on it, see Matthews, *Ammianus* (1989), 191–203.

68. App. 2.

69. For these two churches, see A. Martin, 'Les premiers siècles du Christianisme à Alexandrie: Essai de topographie religieuse (IIIᵉ–IVᵉ siècles),' *REAug* 30 (1984), 211–235, at 215, 217/8.

70. Basil, *Epp.* 66, 67, 69, 80, 82. Another letter (61) refers to Athanasius' condemnation of a governor of Libya who was a compatriot of Basil. The episode is otherwise unknown, and the man is absent from *PLRE* 1: for an attempt at identification (unconvincing), see S. G. Hall, 'Le fonctionnaire impérial excommunié par Athanase vers 371: Essai d'identification,' *Politique et théologie* (1974), 157–159.

71. P. Rousseau, *Basil* (1993), chap. 8.

72. J.-M. Leroux, *Politique et théologie* (1974), 145–156, argues that he had been out of touch ever since his return to Alexandria in 346.

73. *PG* 26.1029–1048 = Opitz 309–319, cf. now C. Kannengiesser, '(Ps.-) Athanasius, *Ad Afros* Examined,' *Festschrift L. Abramowski* (Tübingen, forthcoming).

74. Chapter X. On the letter (*PG* 26.1049–1069, reedited by G. Ludwig, *Athanasii Epistula ad Epictetum* [Diss. Jena, 1911]), which appears to have been written around the year 370, see É. D. Moutsoulas, 'La lettre

d'Athanase d'Alexandrie à Epictète,' *Politique et théologie* (1974), 313–333.

XVIII. THE EMPEROR AND THE CHURCH

1. Cross-references to the actions of emperors and to church councils discussed in Chapters II–XVII are not given in what follows: the relevant passages can easily be located through the table of contents and the indices.

2. Matthews, *Ammianus* (1989), gives the best, fullest, and most recent exposition of this evaluation of the historian. For some reservations, see 'Ammianus Marcellinus and His World,' *CP* 88 (1993), 55–70.

3. See, briefly, 'Literary Convention, Nostalgia, and Reality in Ammianus Marcellinus,' *Reading the Past in Late Antiquity*, ed. G. W. Clarke (Rushcutters Bay, 1990), 59–92, at 75–82.

4. Ammianus 15.7.6–10, esp. 7: 'Athanasium episcopum eo tempore apud Alexandriam ultra professionem altius se efferentem scitarique conatum externa, ut prodidere rumores assidui, coetus in unum quaesitus eiusdem loci multorum—synodus ut appellant—removit a sacramento quod obtinebat.

5. E. D. Hunt, 'Christians and Christianity in Ammianus Marcellinus,' *Classical Quarterly*, N.S. 35 (1985), 186–200.

6. *PLRE* 1.694.

7. 'Christians and Pagans in the Reign of Constantius.' *L'Église et l'empire au IVe siècle* (*Entretiens sur l'antiquité classique* 34, 1989), 303–337, at 313–321. On Constantius' appointments in the West in the 350s, see R. O. Edbrooke, 'The Visit of Constantius II to Rome in 357 and Its Effect on the Pagan Roman Senatorial Aristocracy,' *American Journal of Philology* 97 (1976), 40–61.

8. Constans appointed the following western pagans as ordinary consuls: L. Aradius Valerius Proculus (340), M. Maecius Furius Baburius Caecilianus Placidus (343), Vulcacius Rufinus (347), and Aconius Catullinus (349). Ulpius Limenius, consul in 349 and *praefectus praetorio et urbis* from 347 to 349, Hermogenes, who held the latter office in 349/50 (*Chr. min.* 1.68/9), and Anatolius, who served Constans as praetorian prefect of Illyricum c. 344, appear to be easterners who decided to go to the West for the sake of their careers, perhaps because they were pagans: see A. Chastagnol, 'Remarques sur les sénateurs orientaux au IVe siècle,' *Acta Antiqua* 24 (1976), 341–356, at 348; 'La carrière sénatoriale du Bas-Empire (depuis Dioclétien),' *Epigrafia e ordine senatorio* 1 (*Tituli* 4, 1982, pub. 1984), 167–194, at 181; T. D. Barnes, *L'Église et l'empire au IVe siècle* (1989), 320 n. 93. On the career of Q. Flavius Maesius Egnatius Lollianus, consul in 355, see *PLRE* 1.512–514, with 'Two Senators under Constantine,' *JRS* 65 (1975), 40–49, at 40.

9. R. von Haehling, *Die Religionszugehörigkeit der hohen Amtsträger des Römischen Reiches seit Constantins I. Alleinherrschaft bis zum Ende der Theodosianischen Dynastie* (Bonn, 1978), 61–63.

10. Vogler, *Constance* (1979), 144.

11. Despite his title, R. Staats, 'Das Kaiserreich 1871–1918 und die Kirchengeschichtsschreibung,' *ZKG* 92 (1981), 69–96, has nothing to say on the important topic of how the political and cultural background affected historians of the Christian church. One contrast seems especially significant. Although Jacob Burckhardt uses the term 'Reichskirche' in the second edition of his classic book about Constantine and his age, published in Germany in 1880 (*Zeit Constantins*

des Grossen[2] [Leipzig, 1880], 264 = ed. B. Wyss [Bern, 1950], 449: 'Constantin wollte eine Reichskirche, und zwar aus politischen Gründen'), the sentence which contains it is absent from the corresponding passage of the first edition, which was published in Switzerland shortly after the failed revolutions of 1848 ([Basle, 1853], 412).

Even in the second edition, however, it should be noted that Burckhardt immediately went on to observe that the church of the fourth century was able to challenge the political power of the emperors. Edward Gibbon's view had been similar: 'the distinction of the spiritual and temporal powers, which had never been imposed on the free spirit of Greece and Rome, was introduced and confirmed by the legal establishment of Christianity,' and as a result 'a secret conflict between the civil and ecclesiastical jurisdictions embarrassed the operations of the Roman government' (*Decline and Fall*, chap. 20 [2.333/4 Bury]).

12. For example, K. Aland, 'Kaiser und Kirche von Konstantin bis Byzanz,' *Kirchengeschichtliche Entwürfe* (Gütersloh, 1960), 257–279, reprinted in G. Ruhbach, ed., *Die Kirche angesichts der konstantinischen Wende* (*Wege der Forschung* 306 [Darmstadt, 1976]), 43–73; W. Schneemelcher, *Kirche und Staat im 4. Jahrhundert* (*Bonner Akademische Reden* 37 [Bonn, 1970]), 11, 13, 17, 19, also reprinted in *Die Kirche* (1976), 122–148; Girardet, *Kaisergericht* (1975), 1: 'Eine der Folgen der "Konstaninischen Wende" ist die "kaiserliche Synodalgewalt."' In a later essay, however, Schneemelcher argues that it is wrong to speak of a 'Staatskirche' before 380 ('Das konstantinische Zeitalter: Kritisch-historische Bemerkungen zu einem modernen Schlagwort,' *Kleronomia* 6 [1974], 37–60).

13. For an influential statement of this view, see O. Seeck, *Geschichte des Untergangs der antiken Welt* 3[2] (Stuttgart, 1921), 415: 'Hatte er sich anfangs dem Konzil ganz fernhalten wollen, so schien es ihm jetzt nach den Ereignissen von Antiochia für das Gelingen seines Friedenswerkes durchaus erforderlich, dass er persönlich das Präsidium führte.'

14. So, recently, W. H. C. Frend, *The Rise of Christianity* (Philadelphia, 1984), 527.

15. E. Schwartz, *Kaiser Constantin und die christliche Kirche*[2] (Leipzig, 1936), 127: 'die Form der Verhandlung war keine andere als die eines vom Kaiser abgehaltenen Schiedsgerichts.' Similarly, Girardet, *Kaisergericht* (1975), 67/8, on the Council of Tyre in 335: 'der iudex in diesem Prozess ist Konstantin, die Bischöfe sind seine consiliarii.' More recently, Girardet has applied the same analysis to the Council of Rome in 313, to which Constantine referred the appeal of the Donatists: 'er konstituierte das kaiserliche *consilium* als *concilium,* die Bischofsversammlung von Rome Ende September/Anfang October 313 als die erste Reichssynode' ('Das Reichskonzil von Rom (313)—Urteil, Einspruch, Folgen,' *Historia* 41 [1992], 104–116, at 106).

16. Kelly, *Creeds*[3] (1972), 212. A footnote adds that Schwartz 'consistently exaggerated the degree of the Church's absorption in Constantine's "Reich."'

17. J. Gaudemet, *La formation du droit seculier et du droit de l'église au IV*[e] *et V*[e] *siècles* (Paris, 1957), 179–181. However, for a subtle argument which finds signs of incipient Caesaropapism toward the end of Constantius' reign, see C. Piétri, 'La politique de Constance II: Un premier "césaropapisme" ou l'*imitatio Constatini?*' *L'Église et l'empire au IV*[e] *siècle* (*Entretiens sur l'antiquité classique* 34 [Vandoeuvres, 1989]), 113–172.

18. For German doubts about the aptness of the term, see K. Baus, *Handbuch der Kirchengeschichte* 2.1 (Freiburg, Basle, and Vienna, 1973), 91–93 (= 89/90 in the English translation by A. Biggs [New York, 1980]). Significantly, the volume itself has the title 'Die Reichskirche nach Konstantin dem Grossen.'

19. Eusebius, *VC* 3.10–12.

20. Eusebius, *VC* 4.42, cf. B. H. Warmington, 'The Sources of Some Constantinian Documents in Eusebius' *Church History* and *Life of Constantine*,' *Studia Patristica* 18.1 (1985), 93–98.

21. C. J. Hefele and H. Leclercq, *Histoire des conciles* 1.1 (Paris, 1907); H. Marot, 'Conciles anténicéens et conciles oecuméniques,' *Le concile et les conciles* (Chevetogne, 1960), 19–43. For an assessment of the impact of Constantine on conciliar practise, see W. de Vries, 'Die Struktur der Kirche gemäss dem ersten Konzil von Nikaia und seiner Zeit,' *Wegzeichen: Festgabe zum 60. Geburtstag von Prof. Dr. Hermenegild M. Biedermann OSA* (Würzburg, 1971), 55–81. He concludes that 'die bisher verfolgte, aber freie Kirche, wird langsam zur "Reichskirche."'

22. *Constantine* (1981), 212–214, 378 n. 35.

23. The term 'ecumenical council' is first attested in 338: Eusebius, *VC* 3.6.1; Athanasius, *Apol. c. Ar.* 7.2. H. Chadwick, 'The Origin of the Title "Oecumenical Council,"' *JTS*, N.S. 23 (1972), 132–135, argues that the term was used in 325 itself and 'had some association in the first instance with the church's plea for exemption from tax'—and he draws the inference that the decisions of the Council of Nicaea were so widely accepted because it had succeeded in 'obtaining important fiscal relief.'

24. J. Gaudemet, *Formation du droit* (1957), 144, citing Augustine, *De baptismo* 2.3.4 (*CSEL* 51.178).

25. The letters of Basil of Caesarea appear to indicate how the system of twice-yearly provincial councils worked in practise: a council met each year in June at Phargamous (*Ep. 95*), while one on 7 September in Caesarea celebrated the martyr Eupsychius (*Epp.* 100, 142).

26. See *EOMIA* 2.50–53, 153, 172/3, 312–315. For the accidental nature of the earliest collections of canon law, see E. Schwartz, 'Die Kanonessammlungen der alten Reichskirche,' *Zeitschrift der Savigny Stiftung für Rechtsgeschichte*, Kanonistische Abteilung 25 (1936), 1–114, reprinted in his *Gesammelte Schriften* 4 (Berlin, 1960), 159–275. His conclusions may need partial modification if the Council of Gangra met c. 355, as argued in 'The Date of the Council of Gangra,' *JTS*, N.S. 40 (1989), 121–124.

27. Optatus, App. 5, p. 203.23–25 Ziwsa (314); Rufinus, *HE* 10.5 = Gelasius of Cyzicus, *HE* 2.27.10 (325)—from Gelasius of Caesarea.

28. Eusebius, *VC* 4.27.2.

29. F. Millar, *The Emperor in the Roman World* (London, 1977), esp. chaps. 7–9.

30. As does Girardet, *Kaisergericht* (1975), 60–62.

31. As stated by Girardet, *Kaisergericht* (1975), 63–65, 67.

32. Eusebius, *HE* 7.30.19/20, cf. F. Millar, 'Paul of Samosata, Zenobia, and Aurelian: The Church, Local Culture, and Political Allegiance in Third-Century Syria,' *JRS* 61 (1971), 1–17.

33. Despite Girardet, *Kaisergericht* (1975), 66–75.

34. *CTh* 1.27.1 (?318); *Const. Sirm.* 1 (333), cf. *Constantine* (1981), 51, 312 nn. 78–82. For the modern bibliography on this contentious topic, see now S. Elm, 'An Alleged Book-Theft in Fourth-Century Egypt: *P. Lips.* 43,' *Studia Patristica* 18.2 (1989), 209–217. *P. Lips.* 43 provides an example of episcopal jurisdiction in a case concerning the theft of some books. The name of the bishop is Plusianus: since the editor of the papyrus (U. Wilcken) dates the papyrus to the fourth century and gives its provenance as 'Hermupolis(?),' there is a chance that he may be none other than Plusianus, the bishop of Lycopolis, who was alleged to have burned the house of Arsenius on Athanasius' orders (Sozomenus, *HE* 2.25.12, cf. Camplani, *Lettere* [1989], 303).

35. Sozomenus, *HE* 1.9.6; *CJ* 1.13.1 (316); *CTh* 4.7.1 = *CJ* 1.13.2 (321).

36. J. F. Matthews, 'Gesandtschaft,' *RAC* 10 (1978), 653–685, esp. 679.

37. *CTh* 11.39.8 (381).

38. *CTh* 16.2.12 (my own deliberately free translation). The subscription reads: 'data epistula viiii kal(endas) Octob(res), acc(epta) non(is) Octob(ribus) Arbitione et Lolliano cons(ulibu)s.' Seeck, *Regesten* (1919), 11, construed the phrase *data epistula* as a reference to a letter of the praetorian prefect forwarding the emperor's instructions.

39. The execution of Priscillian is not an exception, since he was not a validly ordained bishop: see K. M. Girardet, 'Trier 385: Der Prozess gegen die Priszillianer,' *Chiron* 4 (1974), 577–608, and (briefly) 'Religion and Society in the Reign of Theodosius,' *Grace, Politics, and Desire: Essays on Augustine* (Calgary, 1990), 157–175, at 163.

40. Chapter XII n. 53; Chapter XIV; Chapter XVI, at nn. 54–57.

41. K. F. Hagel, *Kirche und Kaisertum in Lehre und Leben des Athanasius* (Diss. Tübingen, pub. Leipzig, 1933), 15–77, esp. 47–58. See also L. W. Barnard, 'Athanasius and the Roman State,' *Studies in Church History and Patristics* (ΑΝΑΛΕΚΤΑ ΒΛΑΤΑΔΩΝ 26 [Thessaloniki, 1978]), 312–328, reprinted from *Latomus* 36 (1977), 422–437: this article includes material already published in 'Athanase et les empereurs Constantin et Constance,' *Politique et théologie* (1974), 127–143.

42. J. Gaudemet, *Formation du droit* (1957), 181/2.

43. R. Klein, 'Zur Glaubwürdigkeit historischer Aussagen des Bischofs Athanasius von Alexandria über die Religionspolitik des Kaisers Constantius II,' *Studia Patristica* 17.3 (1982), 996–1017, at 1002–1010, argues that this is yet another invented quotation and that the sentiments are those of Athanasius rather than Ossius. It would not much affect the point at issue here if he were correct, but Athanasius claims to have read the letter (*Hist. Ar.* 43.4).

44. Optatus 3.3 (p. 73.20 Ziwsa).

XIX. BISHOPS AND SOCIETY

1. See esp. B. Biondi, *Il diritto romano cristiano* (Milan, 1952–1954); J. Gaudemet, *L'Église dans l'empire romain (IVᵉ–Vᵉ siècles)* (Paris, 1958); A. H. M. Jones, *The Later Roman Empire* (Oxford, 1964), 873–1024 (three long chapters on the church, religion and morals, and education and culture); and the succinct and perceptive survey by H. Chadwick, *The Role of the Christian Bishop in Ancient Society* (Centre for Hermeneutical Studies, Berkeley: Colloquy 35, 1980), 1–14, with the response by P. Brown (ib. 15–22). Further, for a brief analysis of the transforma-

tion of political power in the fourth century, see G. W. Bowersock, 'From Emperor to Bishop: The Self-Conscious Transformation of Political Power in the Fourth Century A.D.' *CP* 81 (1986), 298–307.

2. Among the vast amount of recent writing on these subjects, see esp. A. Martin, 'L'Église et la khora égyptienne au IVᵉ siècle,' *REAug* 25 (1979), 3–25; 'Aux origines de l'église copte: L'implantation et le développement du Christianisme en Égypte (Iᵉ–IVᵉ siècles),' *Revue des études anciennes* 83 (1981), 35–56; R. S. Bagnall, 'Religious Conversion and Onomastic Change,' *Bulletin of the American Society of Papyrologists* 19 (1982), 105–124; E. Wipszycka, 'La chiesa nell'Egitto del IV secolo: Le strutture ecclesiastiche,' *Miscellanea Historiae Ecclesiasticae* 6 (1983), 182–201; P. Rousseau, *Pachomius: The Making of a Community in Fourth-Century Egypt* (Berkeley, 1985); E. Wipszycka, 'La valeur de l'onomastique pour l'histoire de la Christianisation de l'Égypte: À propos d'une étude de R. S. Bagnall,' *ZPE* 62 (1986), 173–181; R. S. Bagnall, 'Conversion and Onomastics: A Reply,' *ZPE* 69 (1987), 243–256; D. J. Kyrtatas, *The Social Structure of Early Christian Communities* (London, 1987), 147–179; E. Wipszycka, 'La christianisation de l'Égypte aux IVᵉ–VIᵉ siècles: Aspects sociaux et ethniques,' *Aegyptus* 68 (1988), 117–165; S. Rubenson, *The Letters of St. Antony: Origenist Theology, Monastic Tradition, and the Making of a Saint* (Lund, 1990), 89–125. Also the collective volume, *The Roots of Egyptian Christianity,* ed. B. A. Pearson and J. E. Goehring (Philadelphia, 1986).

3. E. Wipszycka, *Les ressources et les activités économiques des églises en Égypte du 4ᵉ au 8ᵉ siècle* (Brussels, 1972).

4. M. J. Hollerich, 'The Alexandrian Bishops and the Grain Trade: Ecclesiastical Commerce in Late Roman Egypt,' *Journal of the Economic and Social History of the Orient* 25 (1982), 187–207.

5. N. H. Baynes, 'Alexandria and Constantinople: A Study in Ecclesiastical Diplomacy,' *JEA* 12 (1926), 145–156, reprinted in his *Byzantine Studies and Other Essays* (London, 1955), 97–115.

6. W. H. C. Frend, 'Athanasius as an Egyptian Christian Leader in the Fourth Century,' *New College Bulletin* 8 (1974), 20–37, reprinted as *Religion Popular and Unpopular in the Early Christian Centuries* (London, 1976), No. XVI.

7. F. Vittinghoff, 'Staat, Kirche, und Dynastie beim Tode Konstantins,' *L'Église et l'empire au IVᵉ siècle* (*Entretiens sur l'antiquité classique* 34 [Vandoeuvres, 1989]), 1–28; K. L. Noethlichs, 'Kirche, Recht, und Gesellschaft in der Jahrhundertmitte,' ib. 251–294.

8. For this interpretation, see *Constantine* (1981), 208–260; 'The Constantinian Reformation,' *The Crake Lectures 1984* (Sackville, 1986), 39–58; 'Christians and Pagans in the Reign of Constantius,' *L'Église et l'empire au IVᵉ siècle* (*Entretiens sur l'antiquité classique* 34 [Vandoeuvres, 1989]), 301–337; 'The Constantinian Settlement,' *Eusebius, Judaism, and Christianity* (Detroit, 1992), 635–657.

9. Chapter XVII, at nn. 13–17.

10. Theodoretus, *HE* 1.11.3, 4.4.2.

11. What follows is a revised version of 'The Career of Athanasius,' *Studia Patristica* 21 (1989), 390–405, at 393–395.

12. Eusebius, *HE* 10.7.2.

13. Eusebius, *VC* 2.46.3.

14. C. Piétri, 'Constantin en 324: Propagande et théologie impériales d'après les documents de la Vita Constantini,' *Crise et redressement dans les provinces européennes de l'empire romain (milieu du IIIᵉ au milieu de IVᵉ siècle ap. J. C.),* ed. E. Frézouls (Strasbourg, 1983), 63–90, at 71 n. 33, argues that Constantine sent this letter only to the metropolitan bishop of each province.

15. Canon 6, cf. H. Chadwick, 'Faith and Order at the Council of Nicaea: A Note on the Background of the Sixth Canon,' *HTR* 53 (1960), 171–195.

16. For the inference, based on Sozomenus, *HE* 3.9.5, which restricts it to Alexandria, see J. Karayannopulos, *Das Finanzwesen des frühbyzantinischen Staates* (*Südosteuropäische Arbeiten* [Munich 1958]), 216/7.

17. Presumably analogous to the *vestis militaris,* on which see J. Karayannopulos, *Finanzwesen* (1958), 112–117; J.-M. Carrié, 'L'Égypte au IVᵉ siècle: Fiscalité, économie, société,' *Proceedings of the Sixteenth International Congress of Papyrology* (*American Studies in Papyrology* 23 [Chico, 1981]), 431–446, at 434/5.

18. See now the recent volume edited by M. Beard and J. North, *Pagan Priests: Religion and Power in the Ancient World* (London, 1990): the first chapter, by M. Beard, rightly stresses the religious role of the Senate in the Roman republic, which far outstripped that of the priestly colleges or the individual priests, who were all of senatorial rank (19–48).

19. Canons 2–4, 55, 56, cf. *Constantine* (1981), 54, 314 n. 108.

20. *ILS* 705 (between 333 and 335).

21. C. Lepelley, *Les cités de l'Afrique romaine au Bas-Empire* 1 (Paris, 1979), 362–369.

22. For the systemic importance of patronage in the Greco-Roman world, see T. Johnson and C. Dandeker, 'Patronage: Relation and System,' *Patronage in Ancient Society,* ed. A. Wallace-Hadrill (London, 1989), 219–242.

23. P. Brown, 'The Rise and Function of the Holy Man in Late Antiquity,' *JRS* 61 (1971), 80–101; 'Town, Village, and Holy Man: The Case of Syria,' *Assimilation et résistance à la culture gréco-romaine dans le monde ancien,* ed. D. M. Pippidi (Bucharest, 1976), 213–220, both reprinted in his *Society and the Holy in Late Antiquity* (Berkeley, 1982), 103–165.

XX. EPILOGUE

1. On 2 May (*Index* 45): the *Historia acephala* 5.14 has 'VIII pachom mensis' (= 3 May), which should perhaps be emended to 'VII.'

2. Rufinus, *HE* 11.3; Socrates, *HE* 4.20.2–22.3; Theodoretus, *HE* 4.20; Sozomenus, *HE* 6.19.2–6.

3. Chapter XIII, at n. 62.

4. Theodoretus, *HE* 4.21.14, says that he is quoting a letter: it seems probable, therefore, that Peter in 373 wrote a letter analogous in form, scope, and aim to his predecessor's *Encyclical Letter* of 339 (Chapter V).

5. Theodoretus, *HE* 4.22.1–35. The extract concludes with the statement that certain orthodox clerics in Antioch have been exiled to Neocaesarea in Pontus—where they have perhaps died from the severity of the climate (36).

6. Socrates, *HE* 4.24.3–18, 22.6; Sozomenus, *HE* 6.20.1.

7. Rufinus, *HE* 11.2 (explicitly dated after the death of Athanasius). Tatianus is first

attested as *comes sacrarum largitionum* on 16 February 374 (*CTh* 10.20.8) and continued in office until 380. *PLRE* 1.876/7 argues that Rufinus is mistaken and that Tatianus 'conducted Valens' persecution of the Homoousians' in 368/9 as prefect. However, the Barbarus Scaligeri, which is in origin an Alexandrian document, makes Tatianus prefect again after the death of Athanasius (*Chr. min.* 1.296)—which presumably reflects the fact that he was again in Egypt after 373.

8. Socrates, *HE* 4.37.

9. *CTh* 16.1.2.

10. *CTh* 16.1.3 (30 July 381).

11. For a recent succinct account of Theodosius' 'legislation against heretics, pagans, and Jews,' see J. H. W. G. Liebeschuetz, *Barbarians and Bishops: Army, Church, and State in the Age of Arcadius and Chrysostom* (Oxford, 1990), 146–153.

APPENDIX 1. THE *FESTAL LETTERS*

1. On the *Festal Letters* of earlier bishops of Alexandria, see Camplani, *Lettere* (1989), 19–24.

2. Lorenz, *Osterfestbrief* (1986): see the brief assessment in *JTS*, N.S. 39 (1988), 249/50.

3. On the importance of Camplani's work, see *JTS*, N.S. 41 (1990), 258–264.

4. *JTS*, N.S. 37 (1986), 583/4.

5. Recently edited by W. Wanda-Comus, *Cosmas Indicopleustes: Topographie chrétienne* 3 (*Sources chrétiennes* 197, 1973), 241–253; P. Joannou, *Discipline générale antique* (*IVᵉ–IXᵉ s.*) 2: *Les canons des pères grecs* (*Fonti* 9 [Grottaferrata, 1963]), 71–76. Vaticanus graecus 1650 preserves Athanasius' list of the canon from the letter with interpolated line-lengths for each book: G. Mercati, 'Per l'"Apocritico" di Macario Magnete: Una tavola dei capi dei libri I, II, e III,' *Nuove note di letteratura biblica e cristiana* (*Studi e Testi* 95 [Vatican, 1941]), 49–84, at 56/7, 78–80.

6. For fuller details, see Camplani, *Lettere* (1989), 31–66; for a conspectus of editions down to 1974, *CPG* 2102.

7. W. Cureton, *The Festal Letters of Athanasius* (London, 1848).

8. A. Mai, *Nova Patrum Bibliotheca* 6 (Rome, 1853), 1–149.

9. H. Burgess, *The Festal Letters of S. Athanasius* (Oxford, 1854), 146–141.

10. For two conspicuous examples, see V. Peri, 'La cronologia delle lettere festali de Sant' Atanasio e la Quaresima,' *Aevum* 35 (1961), 28–86, esp. 48–50; M. Albert, 'La 10ᵉ lettre festale d'Athanase d'Alexandrie (traduction et interprétation),' *Parole de l'Orient* 6–7 (1975–1976), 69–90.

11. Robertson, *Select Writings* (1892), 503–553. The Syriac fragments of *Letters* XXVII, XXIX, and XLIV in Severus of Antioch's *Liber contra impium grammaticum* are edited and translated into French by J. Lebon, *CSCO* 101 (1933), 293–295; 102 (1933), 216/7. (Both volumes are also styled *CSCO, Scriptores Syri⁴* 6.)

12. Echoing without further arguments the verdict of W. Wright, *Catalogue of the Syriac Manuscripts in the British Museum* 2 (London, 1871), 406 No. dcccii: 'written in a peculiar, rather cursive hand of about the viiiᵗʰ cent.'

13. Camplani, *Lettere* (1989), 32–34.

14. Camplani, *Lettere* (1989), 73–79, cf. *JTS*, N.S. 41 (1990), 259.

15. L. T. Lefort, *S. Athanase: Lettres festales et pastorales en Copte* (*CSCO* 150 = *Scriptores Coptici* 19, 1955), 1–72 (text); (*CSCO* 151 = *Scriptores Coptici* 20, 1955), 1–55 (translation). Earlier editions are listed at *CSCO* 150 (1955), v.

16. R. G. Coquin and E. Luccesi, 'Un complément au corps copte des lettres festales d'Athanase,' *Orientalia Lovaniensia Periodica* 13 (1982), 137–142; R. G. Coquin, 'Les lettres festales d'Athanase (CPG 2101): Un nouveau complément: Le manuscrit IFAO, Copte 25 (Planche X),' ib. 15 (1984), 133–158.

17. Camplani, *Lettere* (1989), 34–40, 53–66.

18. Camplani, *Lettere* (1989), 68–72.

19. M. Pieper, 'Zwei Blätter aus dem Osterbrief des Athanasius vom Jahre 364 (Pap. Berol. 11948),' *ZNW* 37 (1938), 73–76, cf. Camplani, *Lettere* (1989), 40. The leaves were in Berlin in 1938, but now appear to be lost.

20. A. Laminski, *Der heilige Geist als Geist Christi und Geist der Gläubigen* (Leipzig, 1969), 114/5; M. Tetz, *TRE* 4 (1979), 341/2; Camplani, *Lettere* (1989), 101–103.

21. Camplani, *Lettere* (1989), 103–105.

22. Thus the *Index* states that Athanasius wrote no letter for Easter 341 or 342, but the Syriac corpus includes letters for both these years (*Letters* XIII, XIV).

23. A. Jülicher, *Göttingischer Gelehrte Anzeigen* 1913.706–708 (in a review of O. Bardenhewer, *Geschichte der altkirchlichen Literatur* 3 [Freiburg im Breisgau, 1912]); E. Schwartz, 'Zur Kirchengeschichte des vierten Jahrhunderts,' *ZNW* 34 (1935), 129–213, reprinted in his *Gesammelte Schriften* 4 (Berlin, 1960), 1–110. Their principal conclusions were accepted by L. Duchesne, *Origines du culte chrétien*[5] (Paris, 1920), 255/6; K. Holl, 'Die Schriften des Epiphanius gegen die Bilderverehrung,' *Sitzungsberichte der preussischen Akademie der Wissenschaften zu Berlin* 1916.828–868, reprinted in his *Gesammelte Aufsätze zur Kirchengeschichte* 2 (Tübingen, 1927), 351–387; O. Casel, 'Art und Sinn der ältesten christlichen Osterfeier,' *Jahrbuch für Liturgiewissenschaft* 14 (1938), 1–78.

24. F. L. Cross, *The Study of Athanasius* (Oxford, 1945), 16/7.

25. L. T. Lefort, 'Les lettres festales de s. Athanase,' *Bulletin de l'Académie Royale de Belgique,* Classe des Lettres[5] 39 (1953), 643–651. He attempted to evade the liturgical argument by postulating that the letters which mention a six-day fast were written after Lent had already begun (649).

26. J. Quasten, *Patrology* 3 (Utrecht, Antwerp, and Westminster, Md., 1960), 53: 'This new discovery proves Schwartz's chronology impossible.' That assessment was widely accepted: see V. Peri, *Aevum* 35 (1961), 28–62; C. Kannengiesser, 'Le témoignage des *Lettres festales* de Saint Athanase sur la date de l'*Apologie contre les païens, sur l'Incarnation du Verbe,*' *Rech. sci. rel.* 52 (1964), 91–100; P. Merendino, *Pachale Sacramentum: Eine Untersuchung über die Osterkatechese des hl. Athanasius von Alexandrien in ihrer Beziehung zu den frühchristlichen exegetisch-theologischen Überlieferungen* (*Liturgiewissenschaftliche Quellen und Forschungen* 42 [Münster, 1965]), vi; B. Altaner and A. Stuiber, *Patrologie*[7] (Freiburg, Basle, and Vienna, 1966), 277; T. D. Barnes, *Constantine* (1981), 233, 386. Observe, however, the doubts expressed by M. Tetz, *TRE* 4 (1979), 344.

27. G. Garitte, 'Les citations arméniennes des lettres festales d'Athanase,' *Handes Amsorya* 75 (1961), 425–440, Nos. 6, 5, cf. E. Schwartz, *ZNW* 34 (1935), 132–135.

28. L. T. Lefort, 'À propos des Festales de s. Athanase,' *Le Muséon* 67 (1954), 43–50,

stigmatising the unwelcome evidence as 'les données pseudo-chronologiques de Timothée.'

29. Lorenz, *Osterfestbrief* (1986), 20–28.
30. As argued by Camplani, *Lettere* (1989), 159.
31. Lorenz, *Osterfestbrief* (1986), 31–35.
32. C. J. Hefele, 'Die neu aufgefundenen Osterbriefe des h. Athanasius,' *Theologische Quartalschrift* 35 (1853), 146–167, at 150, cf. 162–167. Hefele was reviewing F. Larsow's annotated German translation, *Die fest-briefe des heiligen Athanasius, bischofs von Alexandria* (Leipzig, 1852).
33. C. J. Hefele, *A History of the Councils of the Church,* trans. H. N. Oxenham 2 (Edinburgh, 1876), 88 n. 1 = C. J. Hefele and H. Leclercq, *Histoire des conciles* 1.2 (Paris, 1907), 739 n. 4. The sentence also appears in W. Glück, 'Die Bistümer Noricums, besonders das lorchische, zur Zeit der römischen Herrschaft,' *Sitzungsberichte der kaiserlichen Akademie der Wissenschaften in Wien, Philosophisch-historischen Classe* 17 (1855), 60–150, at 64 n. 2: 'Dieser Vorbericht gehörte ursprünglich zu einer anderen nicht mehr vorhandenen Sammlung der Festbriefe des h. Athanasius und ward von einem späteren Abschreiber mit der obigen verbunden.'
34. Robertson, *Select Writings* (1892), 501 n. 6^a, 504 n. 17^b, 527 n. 1. For a tabulated comparison of what the *Index* and the headings to each letter state about the consuls of each year and the prefects of Egypt, see A. Martin, *Sources chrétiennes* 317 (1985), 313–319.
35. V. Peri, *Aevum* 35 (1961), 42/3. The March new moon appeared in Alexandria in the early morning of 15 March in 340, about midnight during the night of 9/10 March in 346: see H. H. Goldstine, *New and Full Moons, 1001 B.C. to A.D. 1651* (Philadelphia, 1973), 112/3. Hence the erroneous calculation must belong to 346 and cannot have been made for Easter 340; cf. A. Martin, *Sources chrétiennes* 317 (1985), 310/1).
36. Camplani, *Lettere* (1989), 115–129, 190–193.
37. For a similar list keyed to years rather than to the transmitted numbers of the letters, see Camplani, *Lettere* (1989), 195/6.
38. The dates of Easter at Alexandria between 328 and 373 are conveniently tabulated in Robertson, *Select Writings* (1892), 502. The underlying computation is not altogether clear: there are three deviations (in 333, 346, and 349) from the Alexandrian cycle assumed by E. Schwartz, *Christliche und jüdische Ostertafeln* (*Abhandlungen der königlichen Gesellschaft der Wissenschaften zu Göttingen,* Philologisch-historische Klasse, N.F. 8.6, 1905), 46–49, who asserts that in these years Athanasius changed the date to please Rome (26, 28).
39. E. Schwartz, *ZNW* 34 (1935), 133.
40. E. Schwartz, *ZNW* 34 (1935), 131/2, cf. *Ges. Schr.* 3 (1959), 270–272.
41. Robertson, *Select Writings* (1892), 527.
42. Chapter IV.
43. S. Sakkos, '῾Η Λθ´ ἑορταστικὴ ἐπιστολὴ τοῦ Μ. Ἀθανασίου,' *Τόμος ἑόρτιος χιλιοστῆς ἑξακοσιοστῆς ἐπετείου Μεγάλου Ἀθανασίου (373–1973)* (Thessaloniki, 1974), 129–196, at 129/30.
44. E. Schwartz, *ZNW* 34 (1935), 134. Camplani, *Lettere* (1989), 170/1, argues in favor of retaining the transmitted date.

45. It is not known why the Coptic version numbers XL, XLI, XLII, and XLIII as 41, 42, 43, and 44 respectively (R. G. Coquin, *Orientalia Lovaniensia Periodica* 15 [1984], 144–152, 154/5; *CSCO* 150.67.5–8 = 151.48.11–14).

46. Observe, however, that Kannengiesser, *Athanase* (1983), 398–403, argues that the letter 'date de Pâques 340.'

47. E. Schwartz, *ZNW* 34 (1935), 131/2; Lorenz, *Osterfestbrief* (1986), 28–30, cf. L. Duchesne, *Origines*⁵ (1920), 255/6. Duchesne himself had deduced from the *Letter to Serapion* that the Christians of Egypt were still fasting only for the week preceding Easter as late as 341.

48. V. Peri, *Aevum* 35 (1961), 53–70.

49. Camplani, *Lettere* (1989), 160–168.

50. Lorenz, *Osterfestbrief* (1986), 29, styles it an 'Exilsbrief.'

51. Chapter IV.

APPENDIX 2. THE COMPOSITION OF THE *DEFENSE AGAINST THE ARIANS*

1. Observe that 71.3–72.1 (as far as ἐπλάττετο) is an obvious insertion into a pre-existing context. The date of the letter of the *catholicus* Fl. Himerius about building a church for Ischyras (85.7) is not altogether clear: Opitz on 164.4 argued for 339 or later, but Athanasius quotes the letter to prove that the Eusebians rewarded Ischyras at once (85.5/6), and the fact that it describes him as a priest, not a bishop, ought to point to a date close to the Council of Tyre, perhaps autumn 335 (*PLRE* 1.437).

2. R. Seiler, *Athanasius, Apologia contra Arianos (Ihre Entstehung und Datierung)* (Diss. Tübingen, 1932), esp. 23–32.

3. Opitz on 87, 167.19ff. The theory of unitary composition, though with a modified date of summer/autumn 356, is restated by V. Twomey, *Apostolikos Thronos: The Primacy of Rome as Reflected in the Church History of Eusebius and the Historico-apologetical Writings of Saint Athanasius the Great* (Münster, 1982), 292–305.

4. R. Seiler, *Athanasius* (1932), 30–32.

5. Opitz on 162.20/21.

6. A. H. M. Jones, 'The Date of the *Apologia contra Arianos* of Athanasius,' *JTS*, N.S. 5 (1954), 224–227, cf. *PLRE* 1.876/7.

7. L. di Salvo, 'Ancora sull'istituzione della dioecesis Aegypti,' *Rivista storica dell'antichità* 9 (1979), 69–74.

8. T. Orlandi, 'Sull'Apologia secunda (contra Arianos) di Atanasio di Alessandria,' *Augustinianum* 15 (1975), 49–79.

9. O. Bardenhewer, *Geschichte der altkirchlichen Literatur* 3 (Freiburg im Breisgau, 1912), 61, cf. C. J. Hefele and H. Leclercq, *Histoire des conciles* 1.2 (Paris, 1907), 912; C. Kannengiesser, 'Athanasius von Alexandrien,' *Gestalten der Kirchengeschichte,* ed. M. Greschat 1 (Stuttgart, 1984), 266–284, at 274/5.

10. Hence Athanasius' reference to exile as something 'which I have suffered in the past and am now suffering' (59.5). Opitz on 140.4 takes this as referring to the exiles of 335 and 356 rather than those of 335 and 339.

11. Chapter XI. Hence the references to 'enemies' (1.1) and to Constantius and Constans as joint emperors (1.2), hence the protests against reopening a case so often decided (1.2–4), and hence too the overall argument.

12. R. Seiler, *Athanasius* (1932), 33.

13. Chapters IV, VI, XI.
14. Chapter XIV.
15. Schwartz, *Ges. Schr.* 3 (1959), 101 n. 1: the *Letter to the Bishops of Egypt and Libya* 'ist, wie die meisten Schriften des Athanasius aus dieser Periode, kein einheitliches Werk.'
16. H.-G. Opitz, *Untersuchungen zur Überlieferung der Schriften des Athanasius* (Berlin/Leipzig, 1935), 158 n. 3. Before Opitz contradicted him, Seiler's analysis had been accepted by K. F. Hagel, *Kirche und Kaisertum in Lehre und Leben des Athanasius* (Diss. Tübingen, 1933), 31.

APPENDIX 3. THE *DEFENSE BEFORE CONSTANTIUS*

1. Gwatkin, *Arianism*[2] (1900), 157; O. Bardenhewer, *Geschichte der altkirchlichen Literatur* 3 (Freiburg im Breisgau, 1912), 62; Opitz on 279.1; M. Tetz, *TRE* 4 (1979), 340; Brennecke, *Hilarius* (1984), 110. Opitz on 210.16 dated the *Defense* to the second half of 357 and put its composition and that of the *Defense of His Flight* between the *Defense against the Arians* and the *History of the Arians*. But the dependence of the *Defense before Constantius* on the *Defense against the Arians,* which he rightly detected (on 279.9ff.), only establishes a *terminus post quem* of 349 (App. 2).
2. Robertson, *Select Writings* (1892), li, 236.
3. J.-M. Szymusiak, *Sources chrétiennes* 56 (1958), 30, 55, 59–63 (unchanged in the second edition of 1987). Szymusiak holds that Athanasius began to compose the *Defense* immediately after the final defeat of Magnentius in the summer of 353.
4. The episode occurred at Easter (14.4–15.5). The year has been variously estimated as 347, 352, or 355: see, respectively, Opitz on 286.34 (347); Seeck, *Geschichte* 4 (Berlin, 1911), 139, 444, followed by Brennecke, *Hilarius* (1984), 118 (352); A. Martin, 'Les premiers siècles du Christianisme à Alexandrie: Essai de topographie religieuse (IIIe–IVe siècles),' *REAug* 30 (1984), 211–235, at 217/8 (between 351 and 353); L. S. Le Nain de Tillemont, *Mémoires pour servir à l'histoire ecclésiastique* 8 (Paris, 1713), 149, followed by Robertson, *Select Writings* (1892), 243 (355). All the dates except 347 are deduced from the *Defense* itself: on the analysis argued here, the year is most likely to be 351.
5. J.-M. Szymusiak, *Sources chrétiennes* 56 (1958), 60/1.
6. For the invitation to visit the speaker's city, cf. *Pan. Lat.* 6(7).22 (an orator from Autun addressing Constantine in 310). A rhetorical handbook of the early fourth century advises a speaker who delivers an imperial panegyric to conclude with a prayer 'beseeching God that the emperor's reign may endure long' (Menander Rhetor, ed. D. A. Russell and N. G. Wilson [Oxford, 1981], 94/5)—a precept to which Eusebius gave a Christian twist when he concluded his panegyric of 336 by looking forward to Constantine's reception into heaven (*Triakontaeterikos* 10.7).
7. Probably on 10 August, cf. Seeck, *Geschichte* 4 (1911), 439.
8. Chapter XIII.
9. *PLRE* 1.119. Unfortunately, there seems to be no evidence for Asterius or his career apart from these two passages and *Hist. Ar.* 51.4, which refers to 'Asterius the *comes* and Palladius the *notarius*' as bringing instructions from Constantius to prevent the arrest of Athanasius in 350.

APPENDIX 4. THE DATE OF *ON THE COUNCIL OF NICAEA*

1. Robertson, *Select Writings* (1892), 149. In his prolegomena to the volume, however, Robertson tentatively accepts J. H. Newman's date of 352 (lxiii, cf. 150 n. 2).
2. Opitz on 2.15/6; J. Quasten, *Patrology* 3 (Utrecht, Antwerp, and Westminster, Md., 1960), 61; B. Altaner and A. Stuiber, *Patrologie*[7] (Freiburg, 1966), 271; M. Tetz, *TRE* 4 (1979), 339; F. Young, *From Nicaea to Chalcedon* (London, 1983), 76. Opitz himself was presumably influenced by 'etwa 350' given as the date by O. Bardenhewer, *Geschichte der altkirchlichen Literatur* 3 (Freiburg im Breisgau, 1912), 71.
3. Schwartz, *Ges. Schr.* 3 (1959), 85.
4. Brennecke, *Hilarius* (1984), 11 n. 41, 306 n. 290. It is not at all clear on what basis Hanson, *Search* (1988), 419, makes the confident pronouncement: '*De Decretis* we can date to 356 or 357.'
5. Chapter XV.
6. Kopecek, *Neo-Arianism* 1 (1979), 116–126.
7. Unfortunately, the complimentary address ἡ σὴ διάθεσις (2.3) does not help to define his status: see L. Dinneen, *Titles of Address in Christian Greek Epistolography to 527 A.D.* (Diss. Washington, 1929), 63/4, 109; H. Zilliacus, *Untersuchungen zu den abstrakten Anredeformen und Höflichkeitstiteln im Griechischen* (Helsinki, 1949), 66: 'ohne Unterschied auf Stand und Rang.'
8. As duly noted by Opitz on 3.10.
9. Also *Orat. c. Ar.* 1.9, 1.17, 2.43, 3.14, cf. Chapter V.
10. See Opitz on 24–28 (*Decr.* 28–32).
11. Kopecek, *Neo-Arianism* 1 (1979), 127–132. He adopts a date of c. 350 with appeal to Schwartz and Opitz (116 n. 4).
12. Chapter XIII.

APPENDIX 5. NARRATIVE AND CHRONOLOGY IN SOCRATES

1. For a similar brief analysis of *HE* 2.3–20, see W. Schneemelcher, 'Die Kirchweihsynode von Antiochien 341,' *Bonner Festgabe Johannes Straub zum 65. Geburtstag am 18. October 1977 dargebracht von Kollegen und Schülern* (Bonn, 1977), 319–346, at 334–336; for an analysis of the whole book by the sources employed, F. Geppert, *Die Quellen des Kirchenhistorikers Socrates Scholasticus* (*Studien zur Geschichte der Theologie und der Kirche* 3.4 [Leipzig, 1898]), 118–121.

One of Socrates' important sources, from which he derived his exact and consular dates for imperial accessions and deaths and other events in the fourth century, was a consular list with historical notices closely related to the relevant section of the text which Theodor Mommsen printed as *Consularia Constantinopolitana* (*Chr. min.* 1.205–247)—which was presumably the source of the extant document. Geppert styled this presumed lost source 'Die Chronik von Constantinopel' (*Quellen* [1898], 32–46), but it began before 330: see O. Seeck, 'Studien zur Geschichte Diocletians und Constantins. II: Idacius und die Chronik von Constantinopel,' *Jahrbücher für classische Philologie* 139 (1889), 601–635, at 619–630. Moreover, R. W. Burgess, 'History vs. Historiography in Late Antiquity,' *Ancient History Bulletin* 4 (1990), 116–124, at 121/2, argues that the *Consularia Constantinopolitana* were originally composed in Gaul in the early 340s, then brought to Constantinople, where a continuation was added in the 360s. Socrates' chronological source was also used before him by Jerome in his continuation of Eusebius' *Chronicle* and after him by Marcellinus and in the *Paschal Chronicle*: see B. Croke, 'City Chronicles of Late Antiquity,' *Reading the Past in Late Antiquity*, ed. G. W. Clarke (Rushcutters Bay, 1990), 165–203, at 182–185.

2.   E. Bihain, 'La source d'un texte de Socrate (H.E.,II.,38,2) relatif à Cyrille de Jérusalem,' *Byzantion* 32 (1962), 81–91, argued that this notice derives from 'the Greek Rufinus' and that its logical place is between 2.27.7 and 2.28.1.

3.   See 'The Date of the Council of Gangra,' *JTS,* N.S. 40 (1989), 121–124.

APPENDIX 6. SOCRATES, SOZOMENUS, AND SABINUS

1.   Alan Cameron, 'The Empress and the Poet: Paganism and Politics at the Court of Theodosius II,' *Yale Classical Studies* 27 (1982), 217–289, at 265–267. His argument proceeds from a striking contrast between Socrates and Sozomenus: the former lavishes praise on Anthemius, who had been in power as praetorian prefect of the East from 405 to 414, and on Theodosius' consort Eudocia (*HE* 7.1, 21.8–10, 47), while the latter is totally silent about Anthemius and Eudocia, but praises Theodosius' sister Pulcheria at length (*HE* 9.1). F. Geppert, *Die Quellen des Kirchenhistorikers Socrates Scholasticus* (*Studien zur Geschichte der Theologie und der Kirche* 3.4 [Leipzig 1898]), 4–9, argued that the second, revised edition of the first two books was produced after 439, though before 444.

2.   Also named at *HE* 2.38.11, 15 (on the violence of Macedonius).

3.   App. 8. On the availability of local written sources, see A. Freund, *Beiträge zur antiochenischen und zur konstantinopolitanischen Stadtchronik* (Diss. Jena, 1882); B. Croke, 'City Chronicles of Late Antiquity,' *Reading the Past in Late Antiquity* (Rushcutters Bay, 1990), 165–203.

4.   F. Geppert, *Quellen* (1898), 19–81, cf. L. Jeep, 'Quellenuntersuchungen zu den griechischen Kirchenhistorikern,' *Jahrbücher für classische Philologie,* Supp. 14 (1885), 53–178, at 105–137; P. Périchon, 'Eutrope ou Paeanius? L'historien Socrate se référait-il à une source latine ou grecque?' *Revue des études grecques* 81 (1968), 378–384, argues that Socrates used both the original Latin and Paeanius' Greek translation of Eutropius.

5.   P. Heseler (with J. Bidez), 'Fragments nouveaux de Philostorge sur la vie de Constantin,' *Byzantion* 10 (1935), 403–442, at 438–440, reprinted photographically in J. Bidez and F. Winkelmann, *Philostorgius Kirchengeschichte²* (Berlin, 1972), 364–393; F. Winkelmann, *Untersuchungen zur Kirchengeschichte des Gelasios von Kaisareia* (*Sitzungsberichte der Deutschen Akademie der Wissenschaften,* Klasse für Sprachen, Literatur and Kunst 1965, Nr. 3 [Berlin, 1966]), 103–105. The point at which Gelasius ended his *Ecclesiastical History* is uncertain, but the death of Julian or thereabouts, where Rufinus ends his tenth book, is a plausible guess.

6.   Schwartz, *Ges. Schr.* 3 (1959), 77–82, cf. G. Schoo, *Die Quellen des Kirchenhistorikers Sozomenos* (*Neue Studien zur Geschichte der Theologie und der Kirche* 11 [Berlin, 1911]), 109–134. For a hypothetical reconstruction of what the *Synodicus* was supposed to contain, see P. Batiffol, 'Le Synodikon de S. Athanase,' *BZ* 10 (1901), 128–143. G. Schoo, *Quellen* (1911), 104–109, argued against Schwartz that there was indeed a *Synodicus* of Athanasius, but that

Geppert and Batiffol had misapplied the term, since the *Synodicus* was (so he held) not an otherwise unknown collection explicitly mentioned only by Socrates, but precisely the 'Vorlage der Sammlung des Theodosius Diaconus,' in other words, the Alexandrian compilation from which the texts preserved in Cod. Ver. LX (58), including the *Historia acephala*, ultimately derive (Chapter I).

7. F. Geppert, *Quellen* (1898), 69–75. On the difficult problem of the sources of Zonaras, see the contrasting treatments by M. DiMaio, 'Smoke in the Wind: Zonaras' Use of Philostorgius, Zosimus, John of Antioch, and John of Rhodes in His Narrative of the Neo-Flavian Emperors,' *Byzantion* 58 (1988), 230–255; B. Bleckmann, 'Die Chronik des Johannes Zonaras und eine pagane Quelle zur Geschichte Konstantins,' *Historia* 40 (1991), 343–363.

8. So, recently, *PLRE* 2.1024; B. Grillet (with G. Sabbah), *Sozomène: Histoire ecclésiastique, livres I–II* (*Sources chrétiennes* 306, 1983), 30 ('le *terminus a quo* est 443, date de la dédicace, le *terminus ad quem* est 448'); G. Chesnut, *The First Christian Histories*[2] (Macon, Ga., 1986), 201.

9. C. Roueché, 'Theodosius II, the Cities, and the Date of the "Church History" of Sozomen,' *JTS*, N.S. 37 (1986), 130–132.

10. Alan Cameron, *Yale Classical Studies* 27 (1982), 265/6. K. G. Holum, *Theodosian Empresses: Women and Imperial Dominion in Late Antiquity* (Berkeley, 1982), 195, similarly deduces a date c. 449 from the encomium of Pulcheria.

11. L. Jeep, *Jahrbücher für classische Philologie*, Supp. 14 (1885), 137–145; G. Schoo, *Quellen* (1911), 11; G. Sabbah, *Sources chrétiennes* 306 (1983), 59–87, cf. P. Allen, 'Some Aspects of Hellenism in the Early Greek Church Historians,' *Traditio* 43 (1987), 368–381, at 373–376. Hence Photius' verdict that Sozomenus is superior in style to Socrates (*Bibliotheca* 30). The corresponding passages of Socrates are conveniently noted in the apparatus to the edition of Sozomenus by J. Bidez and G. C. Hansen (*GCS* 50, 1960).

12. Sozomenus implies that he has seen copies of laws of Constantine in favor of the Christians whose headings named Crispus as Caesar in second place after his father (*HE* 1.5.2). But his chapter on legislation against paganism and Jewish ownership of non-Jewish slaves (*HE* 3.17, cf. *CTh* 16.10.2, 4–6; 9.2) follows the Theodosian Code in wrongly attributing to Constantius a constitution which Constantine addressed to his praetorian prefect Evagrius (*CTh* 16.9.2, cf. *PLRE* 1.284/5; *Constantine* [1981], 392 n. 74). For the importance of law and laws in Sozomenus' conception of ecclesiastical history, see J. Harries, 'Sozomen and Eusebius: The Lawyer as Church Historian in the Fifth Century,' *The Inheritance of Historiography, 350–900*, ed. C. Holdsworth and T. P. Wiseman (Exeter, 1986), 45–52.

13. On the non-documentary sources of Sozomenus, see G. Schoo, *Quellen* (1911), 19–86; G. C. Hansen, in the introduction to the edition prepared by J. Bidez (*GCS* 50, 1960), xliv–lxiv; J. F. Matthews, 'Olympiodorus of Thebes and the History of the West (A.D. 407–425),' *JRS* 60 (1970) 79–97. It ought not to be necessary to discuss the theory that Sozomenus did in fact finish Book IX down to 439, but that the last part was deleted because Theodosius found it too embarrassing (G. Schoo, *Quellen* [1911], 3–8). Although the idea is still sometimes treated as a serious possibility (as by F. M. Young, *From Nicaea to Chalcedon* [London, 1983], 33: 'it is possible that imperial censors were responsible'), Book IX must be pronounced unfinished on purely literary and stylistic grounds: see G. C. Hansen, *GCS* 50 (1960),

lxvi–lxvii; B. Grillet, *Sources chrétiennes* 306 (1983), 27–30.

14. G. Schoo, *Quellen* (1911), 80–83.
15. G. Schoo, *Quellen* (1911), 13/4.
16. For example, the letter of the Council of Ancyra to Constantius in early 358 (*HE* 4.13.4) or the démarche of the party of Eudoxius (*HE* 4.16.20–22).
17. P. Batiffol, 'Sozomène et Sabinos,' *BZ* 7 (1898), 265–284.
18. G. Schoo, *Quellen* (1911), 95–134. Schoo's analysis employs the unfortunate rubric 'Synodikos und Synagoge,' which groups together documents and information taken by Sozomenus both from an Alexandrian collection made by someone close to Athanasius and from the anti-Athanasian compilation by Sabinus of Heraclea.
19. For fuller discussion (and more examples), see G. Schoo, *Quellen* (1911), 117–130.
20. For a brief evaluation of Sozomenus as a source for the council of 341, see W. Schneemelcher, 'Die Kirchweihsynode von Antiochien 341,' *Bonner Festgabe Johannes Straub zum 65. Geburtstag am 18. October 1977 dargebracht von Kollegen und Schülern* (Bonn, 1977), 319–346, at 336/7.
21. Chapter XI; App. 2.
22. For Sozomenus' use of the Greek original of the *Historia acephala*, see P. Batiffol, *BZ* 10 (1901), 130; G. C. Hansen, *GCS* 50 (1960), lxiii; Schwartz, *Ges. Schr.* 3 (1959), 67.
23. On the date and nature of Sabinus' work, see W. D. Hauschild, 'Die antinizänische Synodalensammlung des Sabinus von Heraclea,' *Vig. Chr.* 24 (1970), 105–126; W. A. Löhr, 'Beobachtungen zu Sabinos von Herakleia,' *ZKG* 98 (1987), 386–391. It was written shortly after 367 and seems to have resembled Athanasius' *On the Councils of Ariminum and Seleucia* in purpose, nature of contents, and style of presentation.
24. App. 10, at nn. 13–16.

APPENDIX 7. DOCUMENTS IN THEODORETUS

1. *HE* 5.3.8 seems to be a clear allusion to monophysite ideas and can hardly have been written before c. 447, while 5.36.4 refers to the (plural) sisters of Theodosius as sharing his private devotions (cf. Socrates, *HE* 7.22.5) and hence must have been written before the death of Marina on 3 August 449 (*Chr. min.* 2.83). Despite modern assumptions to the contrary, *Ep.* 113 does not show that the *History* was still unwritten in 448: G. F. Chesnut, 'The Date of Composition of Theodoret's Church History,' *Vig. Chr.* 35 (1981), 245–252. For recent discussion, see B. Croke, 'Dating Theodoret's *Church History* and *Commentary on the Psalms*,' *Byzantion* 54 (1984), 59–73; A. D. Lee, 'Dating a Fifth-Century Persian War in Theodoret,' *Byzantion* 57 (1987), 187–190.
2. For Theodoretus' use of Socrates, see A. Güldenpenning, *Die Kirchengeschichte des Theodoret von Kyrrhos: Eine Untersuchung ihrer Quellen* (Halle, 1889), 39–41. He identified three clear cases of derivation in the first book of Theodoretus: (i) 1.9–10, which not only quotes two documents written from Nicaea in June 325 from Socrates, *HE* 1.9.1–14, 32–46, namely, *Urkunden* 23, 26 (taken by Socrates from Athanasius, *Decr.* 36, and Eusebius, *VC* 3.17–20), but also summarises a document of 333 which Socrates had included between them (9.14 < Socrates, *HE* 1.9.30/31 = *Urkunde* 33); (ii) 15.3 < Socrates, *HE* 1.9.46/7, linking documents taken from Eusebius, *VC* 2.46 and 4.36; and (iii) 31.5, where both the name of

Trier and the note 'this was the thirtieth year of his reign' seem to come from Socrates, *HE* 1.35.4, 37.1. Theodoretus' use of Socrates was in effect denied by L. Parmentier, who declared, in the preface to his edition of the *Ecclesiastical History*, that the similarities between Theodoretus and the other extant continuators of Eusebius are far better explained by his independent use of common sources than by direct borrowing. Among these lost sources, Parmentier gave pride of place to the Greek sources of Rufinus—in other words, the lost *Ecclesiastical History* of Gelasius of Caesarea (*GCS* 19 [1911], lxxxiv). For proof that Theodoret combines Gelasius and Eusebius' *Life of Constantine* in his account of Helena in Jerusalem, see now S. Borgehammar, *How the Holy Cross Was Found: From Event to Medieval Legend* (*Bibliotheca Theologiae Practicae/Kyrkovetenskapliga studier* 47 [Stockholm, 1991]), 17–21.

3. App. 6, at nn. 8–10, cf. n. 1. Hence it is chronologically impossible for Theodoretus to have drawn on Sozomenus, as argued by A. Güldenpenning, *Kirchengeschichte* (1889), 41–49, who dated Theodoretus' *History* to 448/9 (18–25), Sozomenus' to 443/4 (12/3).

4. L. Jeep, 'Quellenuntersuchungen zu den griechischen Kirchenhistorikern,' *Jahrbücher für classische Philologie,* Supp. 14 (1885), 53–178, at 154.

5. L. Parmentier, in his edition (*GCS* 19, 1911), xcviii–cvi; F. Winkelmann, 'Die Kirchengeschichtswerke im oströmischen Reich,' *Byzantinoslavica* 37 (1976), 1–10, 172–190, at 177/8; P. Allen, 'The Use of Heretics and Heresies in the Greek Church Historians: Studies in Socrates and Theodoret,' *Reading the Past in Late Antiquity,* ed. G. W. Clarke, (Rushcutters Bay, 1990), 265–289, at 271–282.

6. For example, the letter of Alexander of Alexandria to Alexander of Byzantium (*HE* 1.4 = *Urkunde* 14) and the full text of the letter of Eusebius of Nicomedia to Paulinus of Tyre, which is also partly preserved in Latin by Marius Victorinus (*HE* 1.6 = *Urkunde* 8). Theodoretus presumably took both of these letters from Sabinus of Heraclea: for discussion, see A. Güldenpenning, *Kirchengeschichte* (1889), 59–61.

7. App. 8.

8. For discussion of the difficult question of Theodoretus' use of Gelasius/Rufinus, see A. Güldenpenning, *Kirchengeschichte* (1889), 26–39 (arguing for Rufinus as the 'Grundquelle'); G. Rauschen, *Jahrbücher der christlichen Kirche unter dem Kaiser Theodosius* (Freiburg, 1897), 559–563; L. Parmentier, *GCS* 19 (1911), lxxxiv–lxxxvi.

9. A. Güldenpenning, *Kirchengeschichte* (1889), 49–56. On the date and scope of the work, see recently G. Zecchini, 'Filostorgio,' *Metodologie della ricerca sulla tarda antichità,* ed. A. Garzya (Naples, 1991), 579–598. Its precise date is uncertain. J. Bidez, in his edition (*GCS* 21 [1913], cxxxii), argued that Philostorgius wrote before 433, but F. M. Clover, 'Olympiodorus of Thebes and the Historia Augusta,' *Bonner Historia-Augusta-Colloquium, 1979/1981* (1983), 136–141, has shown that his arguments are inconclusive. Clover argues for a date in the late 430s, largely based on the account of the period 408–423 in Philostorgius, *HE* 12.7–12, and on Socrates' allusion to Eunomians who quote the letters of Arius (*HE* 1.6.41), but neither argument is decisive—and a date in the 440s might conceivably find advocates.

10. Brennecke, *Homöer* (1988), esp. 134–141. For the fragments, see Philostorgius, ed.

J. Bidez (*GCS* 21, 1911), Anhang VII: 'Fragmente eines arianischen Historiographen,' cf. Gwatkin, *Arianism*² (1900), 219–225; L. Parmentier, *GCS* 19 (1911), lxxxviii–xc.

11. On the interpretation of this obscure fragment, see 'Emperor and Bishops, A.D. 324–344: Some Problems,' *AJAH* 3 (1978), 53–75, at 57–59.

12. L. Parmentier, *GCS* 19 (1911), xci–xcv.

13. The list is based on the analysis by A. Güldenpenning, *Kirchengeschichte* (1889), 67–74.

14. Not in fact an authentic work of Athanasius (Chapter XVII n. 73).

15. E. Bihain, 'Le "Contre Eunome" de Théodore de Mopsueste, source d'un passage de Sozomène et d'un passage de Théodoret concernant Cyrille de Jérusalem,' *Le Muséon* 75 (1962), 331–355, argues that what is said about Cyril of Jerusalem and the feud between him and Acacius of Caesarea in Theodoretus, *HE* 2.26.2, and Sozomenus, *HE* 4.25.2–4, comes from Theodore of Mopsuestia (cf. above n. 12).

16. App. 5.

APPENDIX 8. PAUL OF CONSTANTINOPLE

1. See esp. F. Fischer, 'De patriarcharum Constantinopolitanorum catalogis et de chronologia octo primorum patriarcharum,' *Commentationes philologae Jenenses* 3 (1894), 263–333, at 310–329; Schwartz, *Ges. Schr.* 3 (1959), 273–276 (originally published in 1911); W. Telfer, 'Paul of Constantinople,' *HTR* 43 (1950), 30–92; A. Lippold, 'Paulus 29,' *RE*, Supp. 10 (1965), 510–520; G. Dagron, *Naissance d'une capitale: Constantinople et ses institutions de 330 à 451* (Paris, 1974), 419–435; Klein, *Constantius* (1977), 31, 70–77; Hanson, *Search* (1988), 265, 279–284. The reconstruction offered by Opitz on 178.15ff., 186.11, 13 deserves separate comment. Opitz holds that Alexander died before 330: hence Paul was the first bishop of Constantinople; he was exiled for the first time to Pontus in the winter of 331, but recalled by Constantine before September 335; he was then deposed again and exiled to Thessalonica in 338, whence he traveled via Corinth to Gaul to seek the protection of Maximinus of Trier. Of the five items of evidence which Opitz successively adduces in support (respectively, *Hist. Ar.* 7.1; *CSEL* 65.57; Socrates, *HE* 2.7, 2.16.6; *CSEL* 65.67), only the second is correctly dated. Moreover, the whole reconstruction rests upon the improbable assumption that Athanasius was mistaken in believing that Alexander was still bishop of Constantinople when Arius died (*De Morte Arii* 2.2–3.1; *Letter to the Bishops of Egypt and Libya* 18/9).

2. For example, Klein, *Constantius* (1977), 71–77, and G. Dagron, *Naissance* (1974), 432, hold that Paul spent his first exile in the West, not in Pontus, as Athanasius states, while Girardet, *Kaisergericht* (1975), 142, has Paul exiled to Mesopotamia in 342—which leaves no room for his expulsion by the praetorian prefect Philippus in 344 (Socrates, *HE* 2.16).

3. App. 5.

4. For the argument used here, see 'Emperor and Bishops, A.D. 324–344: Some Problems,' *AJAH* 3 (1976), 53–75, at 64, 66. V. Grumel, *Traité d'études byzantines* 1: *La chronologie* (Paris, 1958), 434, had already dated Alexander's death to August 337—which must be approximately correct.

5. App. 9, cf. *New Empire* (1982), 86.

6. Chapter IV.

7. So Schwartz, *Ges. Schr.* 3 (1959), 274; F. Winkelmann, 'Die Bischöfe Metrophanes und Alexander von Byzanz,' *BZ* 59 (1966), 47–71, at 61. Alan Cameron, 'A Quotation from S. Nilus of Ancyra in an Iconodule Tract?' *JTS*, N.S. 27 (1976), 128–131, appeals to Telfer and Dagron for putting Alexander's death 'as early as August 335,' while Hanson, *Search* (1988), 265, follows Opitz on 186.11 and states boldly that he 'was dead by 330.'

8. *CSEL* 65.57.20–21: 'Paulus vero Athanasi expositioni interfuit manuque propria sententiam scribens cum ceteris eum ipse damnavit.'

9. There was an obvious precedent in 325, when the bishop of old Rome was represented by two priests at the Council of Nicaea: H. Gelzer, H. Hilgenfeld, and O. Cuntz, *Patrum Nicaenorum Nomina* (Leipzig, 1898), xlvii–lii, 2–5, 61, 78/9, 96/7, 118/9, 186/7. The aged bishop of the new city of Constantinople could hardly have been denied the same privilege ten years later. Moreover, the practise of priests representing their bishops at church councils soon became quite common. The ecclesiastical historians imply that by the late 350s there was nothing unusual in deacons and even lectors representing their bishops at distant councils (Socrates, *HE* 2.32.22; Sozomenus, *HE* 4.16.16). At the Council of Seleucia in 359 deacons and even lectors signed on behalf of absent bishops (Socrates, *HE* 2.39.22), and the subscriptions to the synodical letter of the Council of Antioch in 363 include the priest Lamyrion, who signed on behalf of Piso, the bishop of Adana; the two priests Orfitus and Aetius, who signed on behalf of Athanasius of Ancyra; and another priest named Lamyrion, who signed on behalf of Patricius of Paltus (Socrates, *HE* 3.25.18).

10. On the common source of Jerome and the *Consularia Constantinopolitana*, which was also used by Socrates, see App. 5 n. 1.

11. Chapter VII.

12. Chapter VIII.

13. 'Praetorian Prefects, 337–361,' *ZPE* 94 (1992), 249–260, at 254.

14. Chapter X.

15. Edited by P. Franchi de' Cavalieri, 'Una pagina di storia bizantina del secolo IV: Il Martirio dei santi Notari,' *Analecta Bollandiana* 64 (1946), 132–175, at 169–171.

16. W. Telfer, *HTR* 43 (1950), 86–88; A. Lippold, *RE*, Supp. 10 (1965), 519.

17. The confusion of the two names is easy and frequent, not only in ancient writers (for example, Theodoretus, *HE* 3.7.6, 8.1, 21.1), but also in contemporary documents from the reign of Constantius itself (for example, *P. Abinn.* 47, 48, 49, 52) and in modern scholarship ('Structure and Chronology in Ammianus Book 14,' *HSCP* 92 [1989], 413–422, at 415, where the context shows that the restored consular date should read [ὑπάτοις Κωνσταντίῳ Σεβαστῷ τὸ] ζ" καὶ Κωνσταντίῳ Καίσαρι τ[ὸ γ"]).

Opitz's apparatus to 186.16 notes no variant or conjecture for Κωνσταντίνου (which is misprinted as Κωνστατίνου). Schwartz asserted that, while the older editions printed ὑπὸ Κωνσταντίνου, 'die Mauriner haben nach der Pariser Hs. παρὰ Κωνσταντίου eingesetzt, was durch die Fortsetzung widerlegt wird' (*Ges. Schr.* 3 [1959], 274/5 n. 6). The first statement is true: both the *editio princeps* of 1601 (1.630B) and the Paris edition of 1627 (1.813C) print ὑπὸ Κωνσταντίνου. But the second statement is false, and Schwartz has failed to verify what reading actually stands in the Benedictine edition. The facts are simple. Montfaucon printed παρὰ

Κωνσταντίνου (Paris, 1698: 1.348), as did the Padua reprint of his edition in 1777 (1.275). The reading Κωνσταντίου appears for the first time in Migne's reprint of 1857—an edition not noted for its accurate typography. Since the parallel Latin translation has *a Constantino* and the appended footnote is transcribed from Montfaucon (*PG* 25.701), Migne's Κωνσταντίου can hardly be anything other than a sheer misprint. However, it was reproduced by W. Bright, *Historical Works of St. Athanasius* (Oxford, 1881), 188, despite a title-page which proclaims that the text is reprinted from the Benedictine edition (not from Migne), and Schwartz's misstatement about what the manuscripts transmit is repeated by A. Martin, *Sources chrétiennes* 317 (1985), 38 n. 2.

18. For its frequency, see Müller, *Lexicon* (1952), 1084–1089.
19. W. Telfer, *HTR* 43 (1950), 82–assuming a date of late 344.
20. So rightly A. H. M. Jones, 'The Career of Flavius Philippus,' *Historia* 4 (1955), 229–233, at 229.
21. Müller, *Lexicon* (1952), 1091.

APPENDIX 9. IMPERIAL RESIDENCES AND JOURNEYS

1. *New Empire* (1982), 84–87.
2. *Phoenix* 34 (1980), 160–166. On the imperial chronology of the period 337–361, see also D. Kienast, *Römische Kaisertabelle: Grundzüge einer römischen Kaiserchronologie* (Darmstadt, 1989), 305–320 (with helpful bibliographies for each emperor and usurper).
3. The following usurpers proclaimed in 350 are omitted: Magnentius, Augustus in Gaul until 353 (*PLRE* 1.532); his Caesar Decentius (*PLRE* 1.244/5); Nepotianus, who was briefly emperor in Rome from 3 to 30 June 350 (*PLRE* 1.624); and Vetranio, who was Augustus in Illyricum, though loyal to Constantius, from the spring of 350 until he abdicated on 25 December of the same year (*PLRE* 1.954). Also omitted is Silvanus, who was briefly proclaimed Augustus in Cologne in 355 (*PLRE* 1.840/1). As for Poemenius, who rebelled against Magnentius and held Trier against Decentius (Ammianus 15.6.4: not in *PLRE* 1), it seems clear from the coins that he acted in the name of Constantius without assuming the purple himself (*RIC* 8. 164/5, Trier Nos. 328–337, cf. J. P. C. Kent, 'The Revolt of Trier against Magnentius,' *Numismatic Chronicle*[5] 9 (1959), 105–108, P. Bastien, 'Décence, Poemenius: Problèmes de chronologie,' *Quaderni ticinesi: Numismatica e antichità classiche* 12 (1983), 177–189, at 187–189. It should be noted at the outset that Zosimus is used with extreme caution throughout: for a brief catalogue of his errors in 3.1–11, including serious misstatements about the movements of Constantius and Julian in 355–360, see Matthews, *Ammianus* (1989), 493 n. 32; for obvious inventions about Julian, most of which Zosimus may have repeated from Eunapius, D. F. Buck, 'Some Distortions in Eunapius' Account of Julian the Apostate,' *Ancient History Bulletin* 4 (1990), 113–115.
4. For this inscription, see now E. Popescu, *Inscripţiile greceşti şi latine din secolele IV–XIII descoperite în România* (Bucarest, 1976), 251 No. 238 (with photograph). On it, the *dux limitis Scythici* Sappo gives the three imperial brothers the following victory titles:

Constantinus   *Al[aman(icus) ma]x. G[erm(anicus) max.]*
Constantius   *Sarm(aticus) [Per]si[c(us)]*

Constans   *Sarm(aticus)*
The inferences drawn here for their military activities proceed from comparison with the heading of a letter of Constantine to the Senate at Rome in spring 337, where Constantinus is bare *Alaman(icus)*, while the other Caesars lack any victory titles at all (*AE* 1934.158; *New Empire* [1982], 23 No. 8 [heading only]). For discussion, see 'The Victories of Constantine,' *ZPE* 20 (1976), 149–155, at 154; *Phoenix* 34 (1980), 162, 164; J. Arce, 'The Inscription of Troesmis (ILS 724) and the First Victories of Constantius II as Caesar,' *ZPE* 48 (1982), 245–249; T. D. Barnes, 'Two Victory Titles of Constantius,' *ZPE* 52 (1983), 229–235; J. Arce, 'Constantius II Sarmaticus and Persicus: A Reply,' *ZPE* 57 (1984), 225–229 (based on some dubious assumptions).

5. Can Constantinus have addressed a constitution to the proconsul of Africa, which belonged to Constantius? Schwartz, *Ges. Schr.* 3 (1959), 268 n. 1, noted the difficulty and pronounced the year erroneous. But Aurelius Celsinus, the recipient of *CTh* 12.1.27, was certainly proconsul of Africa between 337 and 340 (*CIL* 8.12272, cf. *ILT* 757), and the year is confirmed as 338/9 by *CTh* 10.10.4, issued by Constans at Viminacium on 12 June 338. The constitution, therefore, could be an attempt by Constantinus to assert his fragile theoretical primacy in the imperial college: see Seeck, *Geschichte* 4 (1911), 42; F. Paschoud, *Zosime: Histoire nouvelle* 1 (Paris, 1971), 245; P. Bruun, 'Constans Maximus Augustus,' *Mélanges de numismatique offerts à Pierre Bastien* (Wetteren, 1987), 187 (suggesting that *CTh* 12.1.24–27 show the imperial brothers deliberately issuing contradictory constitutions); J.-P. Callu, 'La dyarchie constantinide (340–350): Les signes d'évolution,' *Institutions, société, et vie politique au IVème siècle ap. J. C. (284–423): Autour de l'œuvre d'A. Chastagnol* (Rome, 1992), 39–63.

6. Schwartz, *Ges. Schr.* 3 (1959), 295 n. 5, pronounced Zonaras' account 'der beste Bericht.' Zosimus 2.41 confuses Constantinus and Constans.

7. For Antioch as the residence of Constantius, see also *Expositio totius mundi et gentium* 23: 'Antiochia . . . ubi et dominus orbis terrarum sedet'; 32: 'ibi imperator sedet.' The Greek original of this work was clearly written between 347 and the death of Constantius (28). J. Rougé, in the introduction to his edition, *Sources chrétiennes* 124 (Paris, 1966), 9–26, reviewed earlier theories and argued for 359/60. But what is said about emperors residing in Sirmium and Trier as well as Antioch points rather to composition before 350.

8. After his interview with the emperor, Athanasius traveled by way of Constantinople to Alexandria, which he entered on 23 November 337 (*Index* 10, cf. Chapter IV).

9. See above, n. 4.

10. J.-P. Callu, 'Un "Miroir des princes": Le "Basilikos" libanien de 348,' *Gerión* 5 (1987), 133–152, at 138 n. 26, dates the meeting of Constantius and Constans to which Libanius refers to 340.

11. On the date, see Chapter IV.

12. P. Peeters, 'L'intervention politique de Constance II dans la Grande Arménie, en 338,' *Bulletin de l'Académie Royale de Belgique*, Classe des Lettres⁵ 17 (1931), 10–47, reprinted in his *Recherches d'histoire et de philologie orientales* 1 (*Subsidia Hagiographica* 27 [Brussels, 1951]), 222–250.

13. On the date, see 'The Career of Abinnaeus,' *Phoenix* 39 (1985), 368–375, at 370.

NOTES TO PAGES 219–220

14. For a critical edition and discussion, see J.-P. Callu, 'La préface à l'*Itinéraire d'Alexandre*,' *De Tertullien aux Mozarabes: Mélanges offerts à J. Fontaine* 1 (Paris, 1992), 429–443.

15. The anecdote in Augustine, *Sermo domini in monte* 1.12.50 (*PL* 34.1254), provides additional indirect testimony for Constantius' presence in Antioch during the consular year 340.

16. Seeck, *Regesten* (1919), 192, emended the date of *CTh* 12.1.35 to 9 June.

17. Theophanes, p. 37.11, 20/1 de Boor = Philostorgius, p. 213.1/2, 11/2 Bidez, registers a victory and triumph of Constantius over 'Assyrians' and a Roman defeat of the Persians in *a.m.* 5834 and 5835, which correspond to the years 341/2 and 342/3: H. Lietzmann and K. Aland, *Zeitrechnung der römischen Kaiserzeit, des Mittelalters und der Neuzeit für die Jahre 1–2000 n. Chr.*⁴ (Berlin and New York, 1984), 20, cf. 11.

18. For the hypothesis that Constantius may have visited Constantinople to celebrate his *vicennalia* there on 8 November 343, see Chapter IX. It is also possible that the transmitted date of *CTh* 12.2.1 + 15.1.6, which was issued in Constantinople and addressed to the *comes Orientis* Marcellinus, should be emended from 3 October 349 to 3 October 343 (below, n. 25).

19. The majority of recent historians have dated this battle, which is distinguished by the sobriquet νυκτομαχία/*bellum nocturnum*, to 348: so Seeck, *Geschichte* 4 (1911), 93; *Regesten* (1919), 196; J. Moreau, 'Constantius II,' *Jahrbuch für Antike und Christentum* 2 (1959), 162–179, at 164; A. H. M. Jones, *Later Roman Empire* (Oxford, 1964), 112; A. Piganiol, *L'empire chrétien*² (Paris, 1972), 85; T. D. Barnes, *Phoenix* 34 (1980), 164; J.-P. Callu, *Gerión* 5 (1987), 135/6. But Jerome and the so-called *Consularia Constantinopolitana,* who give the date of 348, both derive from the same single source and are not necessarily authoritative for the precise year (cf. App. 5 n. 1). Nor does the fact that the first celebration of the victory on the imperial coinage occurs in 348 (J. P. C. Kent, 'Fel. Temp. Reparatio,' *Numismatic Chronicle*⁶ 7 (1967), 83–90, cf. *RIC* 8 [1981], 34–39) confirm that date, given the ambiguous nature of the Roman success (emphasised by Festus, *Brev.* 27).

In favor of 344, see J. B. Bury, 'Date of the Battle of Singara,' *BZ* 5 (1896), 302–305; N. H. Baynes, *Cambridge Medieval History* 1 (Cambridge, 1911), 58; E. Stein, *Geschichte des spätrömischen Reiches* 1 (Vienna, 1928), 213; K. Kraft, 'Die Taten der Kaiser Constans und Constantius II,' *Jahrbuch für Numismatik und Geldgeschichte* 9 (1958), 141–186, reprinted in his *Gesammelte Aufsätze zur antiken Geldgeschichte und Numismatik* 1 (Darmstadt, 1978), 87–132, esp. 104; W. Portmann, 'Die 59. Rede des Libanios und das Datum der Schlacht von Singara,' *BZ* 82 (1989), 1–18. The first four historians named argued principally from Julian's statement that Constans died about five years after the battle (*Orat.* 1, 26b: ἕκτον που μάλιστα μετὰ τὸν πόλεμον ἔτος οὗ μικρῷ πρόσθεν ἐμνήσθην). Portmann has now, in my view, shown that Libanius, *Orat.* 59, which celebrates the battle at length (99–120), was probably delivered in 344/5—though he is mistaken in assuming that Libanius recited the speech in the presence of Constantius (*BZ* 82 [1989], 1, 12/3).

The chronicle of Jacob of Edessa, which puts both Constantius' building of Amida and the nocturnal battle in year 660 of the Seleucid era, which corresponds to 348/9, appears to derive from Jerome's *Chronicle* (ed. and trans. I. Guidi,

312

CSCO, *Scriptores Syri*[3] 4 [1903], Textus 293; Versio 218).

20. Ephraem conspicuously never mentions Constantius' presence at any of the sieges of Nisibis in 337, 346, and 350: consequently, it is mistaken to hold that he relieved the siege of 346, as does J. W. Eadie, *The Breviarium of Festus* (London, 1967), 150/1.

21. The heading to Themistius, *Orat.* 1, which is ancient, reads: οὗτος εἴρηται ἐν Ἀγκύρᾳ τῆς Γαλατίας, ὅτε πρῶτον συνέτυχε τῷ βασιλεῖ, νέος ὢν ἔτι. διόπερ οὐδὲ πάνυ κρατεῖ τῆς ἰδέας. Most scholars who have discussed Themistius' speech have dated it to 350: thus O. Seeck, *Die Briefe des Libanius* (*Texte und Untersuchungen*, N.F. 15.1/2 [Leipzig, 1906]), 293/4; H. Scholze, *De Temporibus librorum Themistii* (Göttingen, 1911), 9–11; W. Stegemann, 'Themistios,' *RE* 5A (1934), 1657; G. Downey, *Themistii Orationes quae supersunt* (Leipzig, 1965), 4; *PLRE* 1.889. And those who have argued for 347 have deduced the date from the erroneous premises that Themistius' speech was known to Libanius when the latter composed his *Orat.* 59 or that it was written before the nocturnal Battle of Singara in 348: thus C. Gladis, *De Themistii Libanii Iuliani in Constantium orationibus* (Diss. Breslau, 1907), 6, 14; R. Foerster, *Libanii Opera* 4 (Leipzig, 1908), 201/2; R. Foerster and K. Münscher, 'Libanios,' *RE* 12 (1925), 2508; T. D. Barnes, 'Himerius and the Fourth Century,' *CP* 82 (1987), 206–225, at 211. The question has perhaps been wrongly posed: since the lack of any perceptible allusion to the death of Constans or the proclamations of Magnentius and Vetranio tells against dating the speech to 350, the choice should lie between the spring of 347, when Constantius' presence is attested in Ancyra, and the autumn of either 343 or 349, in one of which years the emperor appears to have traveled from Antioch to Constantinople and then returned to Syria.

22. *CTh* 5.6.1 is addressed 'ad Bonosum mag(istrum) equitum,' whom *PLRE* 1.164 identifies as Fl. Bonosus, consul in 344. But the latter was a western consul, and he was replaced by Fl. Sallustius c. May—which usually implies dismissal and disgrace (*Consuls* [1987], 222).

23. On this obscure and difficult passage of Festus, see now W. Portmann, *BZ* 82 (1989), 14–18. Since Festus distinguishes between a battle near Singara *praesente Constantio* and the nocturnal battle where Constantius was also present, it is an obvious corollary of dating the latter to 344 (above, n. 19) to date the former to 348, which is the year stated for the latter in Jerome, *Chronicle* 236[l]; *Chr. min.* 1.236.

24. As interpreted in App. 8.

25. For the possibility that the transmitted date should be emended to 343, see above n. 18.

26. On Constantius' movements in 350, see now C. S. Lightfoot, 'Facts and Fiction: The Third Siege of Nisibis (A.D. 350),' *Historia* 37 (1988), 105–125, at 113.

27. Ephraem, *Carmina Nisibena* 2.2, makes it clear that Constantius made no attempt to lift the siege of the city, but it seems unlikely *a priori* that he remained in Antioch, as Theodoretus alleges (cf. Libanius, *Orat.* 18.207).

28. Socrates, *HE* 2.28.17, gives the place as Sirmium: on the confusion of the sources over the date and place, see Seeck, *Geschichte* 4 (1911), 429/30.

29. Julian, *Orat.* 1, 36a, writes as if Constantius took part in the Battle of Mursa: it is hard to construe this as anything other than a deliberate falsehood.

30. T. D. Barnes, *ZPE* 52 (1983), 235; T. D. Barnes and J. Vander Spoel, 'Julian on the Sons of Fausta,' *Phoenix* 38 (1984), 175/6, arguing from (1) Constantius' delay in invading Italy in 352, (2) the fact that Constantius officially took the victory title *Sarmaticus maximus* before 358 (Ammianus 17.13.25, 33) on an otherwise unknown occasion, and (3) Julian's assertion in his first panegyric of Constantius that the emperor 'τὴν πρὸς τοὺς Γέτας ἡμῖν εἰρήνην τοῖς ὅπλοις κρατήσας ἀσφαλῆ παρεσκεύασεν' (*Orat.* 1, 9d).

31. Seeck, *Regesten* (1919), 195, emended the date to 346. However, *CTh* 11.1.6 refers to a 'statutum Constantis (Constantii ms.) fratris mei' relating to Italian landowners: hence its author must be Constantius, not Constans (*PLRE* 1.782).

32. On the addressee of *CTh* 8.7.2, who cannot be the praetorian prefect Philippus if the date of 353 is correct, see below, n. 53. Ammianus records Constantius' completion of thirty years of rule on 10 October 353, even though it is clear that his *dies imperii* was 8 November 324: *CIL* 1², p. 276; *Chr. min.* 1.232, cf. *AE* 1937.119, which has *idibus Nov(embribus)* for *a.d. vi id(us) Nov(embres)*. Perhaps *Octobres* in the text of Ammianus should be emended to *Novembres*.

33. For laws issued by Constantius in Milan between 354 and 357 whose exact year cannot be determined, see Seeck, *Regesten* (1919), 44–47.

34. Both places are otherwise unknown: Mommsen, ad loc., located them in Raetia since he accepted the transmitted dates of both constitutions and regarded them as issued during Constantius' Raetian expedition of 355 (as argued in the prolegomena to his edition [Berlin, 1904], ccxxxi).

35. In favor of Mommsen's emendation of the day to 'id. Ian.,' see 'The Capitulation of Liberius and Hilary of Poitiers,' *Phoenix* 46 (1992), 256–265, at 258. Seeck, *Regesten* (1919), 202, emended the year to 356.

36. The place of issue is transmitted as both *Haerbillo* and *Med(iolani)*: Mommsen, ad loc., identified it as Helvillum on the Via Flaminia between Spoletium and Ariminum.

37. Mommsen, ad loc., declared the subscription to *CTh* 8.5.10 suspect, adducing *CTh* 11.36.14, which, like it, is addressed 'ad Flavianum proc(onsulem) Afric(ae),' but with the transmitted date of 3 August 361. The proconsul Flavianus is also named as the recipient of *CTh* 15.1.1, issued at Milan with the consular date of 2 February 320. Seeck, *Regesten* (1919), 203, corrected the year of both *CTh* 15.1.1 and 11.36.14 to 357—which implies that Flavianus was proconsul of Africa for two years, from spring 356 to spring 358, cf. 'Proconsuls of Africa, 337–392,' *Phoenix* 39 (1985), 144–153, 273/4, at 148.

38. The correct date could also be December 351, cf. *PLRE* 1.456.

39. Seeck, *Regesten* (1919), 207, following Mommsen, also identified as deriving from the same law *CTh* 11.1.1, which the manuscripts present as issued at Constantinople on 17 June 315. In favor of emending its date to 356 or 357 and *dat(a)* to *acc(epta)*, see J. Rougé, 'Le proconsul d'Afrique Proclianus est-il le destinataire de C. Th. XI, 1, 1?' *Revue historique de droit français et étranger* 52 (1974), 285–295; T. D. Barnes, *Phoenix* 39 (1985), 149.

40. Socrates, *HE* 2.44.7, 46.1, appears to imply that Constantius came to Antioch in the spring of 360, but that is probably due to confusion with events of the following winter.

41. In 21.13.8, most editors, including W. Seyfarth (Teubner, 1978), read 'reversus est

Hierapolim': in favor of reading 'Nicopolim urbem,' see G. Pighi, *Studia Ammianea* (Milan, 1935), 134–140 (with a schematic map on p. 136).

42. On *CTh* 8.5.7, see C. E. V. Nixon, 'Aurelius Victor and Julian,' *CP* 86 (1991), 113–125, at 118. This constitution, issued from Antioch, has the transmitted date of 3 August 354, but is addressed to the proconsul of Africa Olybrius, whose proconsular year must be 361/2 (*Phoenix* 39 [1985], 152). Accordingly, Seeck, *Regesten* (1919), 74, 208, emended the year to 361. But the hypothesis that Constantius was in Antioch in early August is incompatible with the narrative of Ammianus Marcellinus, who makes the emperor pass rapidly through the city *en route* from Mesopotamia to confront Julian *autumno iam senescente* (21.15.2). Nor do Constantius' movements in 360 permit the date to be emended to 3 August 360, as Mommsen, ad loc., proposed. Hence the transmitted month must be erroneous as well as the year. Perhaps the constitution was in fact issued on 3 March 361 to form part of Olybrius' initial instructions as the new proconsul of Africa due to take office in April.

43. Matthews, *Ammianus* (1989), 101, retains the date *nonis Octobribus* transmitted at Ammianus 21.15.3: in favor of accepting the evidence of the other sources (and emending the text of the historian), see 'Ammianus Marcellinus and His World,' *CP* 88 (1993), 55–70, at 64/5.

44. Note *Expositio totius mundi et gentium* 58: 'Treviris, ubi et habitare dominus dicitur'; 57: 'Pannonia regio . . . semper habitatio imperatorum est. habet autem et civitates maximas, Sirmium quoque et Noricum.' On the date of the work, see above, n. 7.

45. *PLRE* 1.764, following Gothofredus and Mommsen, ad loc., emends the year to 346.

46. See above, n. 4. The issue of the mint of Siscia which proclaims VICTORIA (D N) CONSTANTIS AUG(USTI) (*RIC* 8.351/2 Siscia 33–38) may be relevant: on the coinage of Constans between 337 and 340, see now P. Bruun, *Mélanges de numismatique offerts à Pierre Bastien* (Wetteren, 1987), 189–199.

47. The *Passio Artemii* states that Constantinus prepared for war against Constans while the latter was in Rome—which implies his presence there in the winter of 339/40. Although the date alleged is impossible, a visit to Rome after the defeat and death of Constantinus is not improbable: see 'Constans and Gratian in Rome,' *HSCP* 79 (1975), 325–333. For a newly published inscription (*AE* 1988.217), which may reinforce the inference drawn there from *ILS* 726 (Rome), see L. Gasperini, 'Dedica ostiense di Aurelio Avianio Simmaco all'imperatore Costante,' *Micellanea greca e romana* 13 (1988), 242–250.

48. The imperial coinage indicates that Constans supervised the settlement of Franci in Toxandria at the mouth of the Rhine: K. Kraft, *Gesammelte Aufsätze* 1 (Darmstadt, 1978), 116–125.

49. On the date of Libanius' speech, see W. Portmann, *BZ* 82 (1989), 1–18. Its occasion is uncertain. J.-P. Callu, *Gerión* 5 (1987), 136, argues that Libanius delivered it as part of a *ludus* in Nicomedia commemorating the anniversary of Constantius' proclamation as emperor; he also suggests that one of the other speakers on the same occasion was the panegyrist Harpocration of Panopolis, who traveled the empire giving speeches in praise of the emperors (*P. Köln inv.* 4533 verso 23–27, published by G. M. Browne, 'Harpocration Panegyrista,' *Illinois Classical Studies* 2

[1975], 184–196). But the fact that Libanius emphasises that he was compelled to compose the speech (4, 6) and praises the emperors for replacing their praetorian prefects regularly (164) suggests that he was forced to speak by the prefect Philippus, whom he disliked (*Orat.* 1.69–70: contrast the warmth of his reference to Montius' 'command' that he compose *hypotheses* to the speeches of Demosthenes). Philippus will have passed through Nicomedia after expelling Paul from Constantinople in the autumn of 344 (App. 8).

50. Also Socrates, *HE* 2.22.5, translated and discussed in Chapter X.

51. For the inferences drawn here from Athanasius' references to his audiences with Constans, see Chapter VII.

52. The constitution is addressed to the praetorian prefect Anatolius: in favor of retaining the transmitted date, see A. F. Norman, 'The Illyrian Prefecture of Anatolius,' *Rheinisches Museum,* N.F. 100 (1957), 253–259; T. D. Barnes, 'Praetorian Prefects, 337–361,' *ZPE* 94 (1992), 249–260, at 258. It was emended to 22 June 357 by Seeck, *Regesten* (1919), 204, and the emended date is adopted in *PLRE* 1.60.

53. These two fragments are addressed 'ad Silvanum com(item) et magistrum militum'—a rank which Silvanus attained only after the Battle of Mursa (*PLRE* 1.840/1). Seeck, *Regesten* (1919), 199, accordingly emended the year to 352. A. H. M. Jones, 'The Career of Flavius Philippus,' *Historia* 4 (1955), 229–233, at 232/3, advanced the adventurous but convincing hypothesis that the compilers of the Theodosian Code have accidentally confused the headings of what are now adjacent extracts in *CTh* 7.1.2, 3 and 8.7.2, 3. He identified their original dates and addresses as follows:

1) *CTh* 7.1.2 + 8.7.3: issued at Sirmium on 27 May 349 and addressed to Constans' praetorian prefect Titianus;

2) *CTh* 8.7.2: issued at Arles on 3 November 353 and addressed to the *magister militum* Silvanus;

(3) *CTh* 7.1.3: issued on 30 May 349 and addressed to Constantius' praetorian prefect Philippus.

54. The date of the appearance of the cross in the sky is given by Cyril of Jerusalem in his letter to Constantius (*BHG*[3] 413 = *CPG* 3587). The *Consularia Constantinopolitana* combine the correct date with that of 30 January, which is preferred in Seeck, *Regesten* (1919), 198.

55. On this revolt, see J. Arce, 'La rebelion de los Judíos durante el gobierno de Constancio Galo Cesar: 353 d.C.,' *Athenaeum* 65 (1987), 109–125 (though his assumed date of 353 is impossible). J. Geiger, 'Ammianus Marcellinus and the Jewish Revolt under Gallus,' *Liverpool Classical Monthly* 4 (1979), 77; 'The Last Jewish Revolt against Rome: A Reconsideration,' *Scripta Classica Israelica* 5 (1979/80), 250–257, argues that the prominence of Ursicinus in the Jerusalem Talmud, combined with the absence of any allusion to Gallus, shows that the Caesar entrusted the suppression of the rebellion to Ursicinus and did not visit the theatre of war himself.

56. For the chronology of Gallus' movements in 353/4, see 'Structure and Chronology in Ammianus, Book 14,' *HSCP* 92 (1989), 413–422.

57. In favor of restoring the consular date as [ὑπάτοις Κωνσταντίῳ Σεβαστῷ τὸ] ζ" καὶ Κωνσταντίῳ Καίσαρι τ[ὸ γ"], see *HSCP* 92 (1989), 414–416—where the emended

date contains the typographical error Κωνσταντίνῳ for the first Κωνσταντίῳ.

58. For Julian's movements from 355 to 361, see G. W. Bowersock, *Julian the Apostate* (Cambridge, Mass., 1978), 33–65; Matthews, *Ammianus* (1989), 81–106, esp. the map 'Julian in Gaul, 356–360' (82) and the chart 'The Rise of Julian, 359–362' (102/3).

59. If the Council of Baeterrae was a provincial council of the bishops of Narbonensis (as suggested in 'Hilary of Poitiers on His Exile,' *Vig. Chr.* 46 [1992], 129–140), then, according to the fifth canon of the Council of Nicaea, it should have met between Easter and Ascension, which in 356 fell on 7 April and 19 May respectively. C. F. A. Borchardt, *Hilary of Poitiers' Role in the Arian Struggle* (The Hague, 1966), 26–29, denies that Julian was on hand for the council.

60. The date is deduced from Julian's remark that the barbarians captured the city ten months before he reoccupied it in combination with Ammianus' report that news of its capture reached Julian at Turin at the very beginning of December 355 (15.8.18/9), cf. G. W. Bowersock, *Julian* (1978), 36. (Julian's 'ten months' could mean nine months on exclusive reckoning.)

61. Matthews, *Ammianus* (1989), 492 n. 16, arguing against the theory that the place named by Ammianus is not Sens, but Senon, which lies between Metz and Verdun, proposed by C. J. Simpson, 'Where Was Senonae? A Problem of Geography in Ammianus Marcellinus XVI, 3, 3,' *Latomus* 34 (1974), 940–942; J. Nicolle, 'Julien apud Senonas (356–357): Un contresens historique,' *Rivista storica dell'antichità* 8 (1978), 133–160.

62. For discussion of the exact site of the battle, see J. J. Hatt and J. Schwartz, 'Le champ de bataille de Oberhausbergen (257–1262),' *Bulletin de la Faculté des Lettres de l'Université de Strasbourg* 42 (1964), 427–430.

63. Ammianus 20.4.2 makes it clear that Julian's proclamation occurred well before the end of the winter of 360/1. Seeck, *Geschichte* 4 (1911), 487, deduced that the month was February from the denunciation of the month Shebat in Ephraem, *Contra Julianum* 1.10, but this interpretation is rejected in the recent translation by K. E. McVey, *Ephrem the Syrian: Hymns* (New York, 1989), 229.

64. On Julian's movements in 361, see now C. E. V. Nixon, *CP* 86 (1991), 113–118. He rightly rejects both the traditional date of October for his arrival in Sirmium (G. W. Bowersock, *Julian* [1978], 58) and the very early date of mid-May advanced by J. Szidat, 'Zur Ankunft Iulians in Sirmium 361 n. Chr. auf seinem Zug gegen Constantius II,' *Historia* 24 (1975), 375–378.

APPENDIX 10. CREEDS AND COUNCILS

1. Kelly, *Creeds*[3] (1972), 263–295.
2. Kelly, *Creeds*[3] (1972), 265.
3. Kelly, *Creeds*[3] (1972), 266–268.
4. On all aspects of this credal statement, and for a critical text of the Latin version, see Chapter VIII, at nn. 35–40 (and the works cited there).
5. The Hahns print Hilary, *Syn.* 34, as their base text. In his edition of the historical fragments deriving from Hilary (*CSEL* 65.69–73), A. L. Feder also prints (1) Hilary, *Syn.* 34; (2) the Latin version of the creed in Cod. Ver. LX (58), fols. 78ᵛ–79ᵛ (*EOMIA* 1.638–640); (3) a Greek retroversion of the Syriac version published by F. Schulthess, *Die syrischen Kanones des Synoden von Nicaea bis Chalcedon*

(*Abhandlungen der königlichen Gesellschaft der Wissenschaften zu Göttingen,* Philologisch-historische Klasse, N.F. 10.2, 1908), 167/8; (4) Athanasius, *Syn.* 25.2–5 + 26.II[b].

6. For a slightly different Greek version of the Latin original, see Athanasius, *Syn.* 30.2–10; Socrates, *HE* 2.31.8–16.

7. For proof that Jerome had access to *acta* of the Council of Ariminum, see P. Battifol, 'Les sources de l'*Altercatio Luciferiani et Orthodoxi* de St. Jérôme,' *Miscellanea Geronimiana* (Rome, 1920), 97–114; Y.-M. Duval, 'Saint Jérôme devant la baptême des hérétiques: D'autres sources de l'*Altercatio Luciferiani et Orthodoxi,*' *REAug* 14 (1968), 145–180.

8. C. J. Hefele and H. Leclercq, *Histoire de conciles* 1.2 (Paris, 1907), 848–852; E. Schwartz, 'Zur Kirchengeschichte des vierten Jahrhunderts,' *ZNW* 34 (1935), 129–213, at 147, reprinted in his *Gesammelte Schriften* 4 (Berlin, 1960), 1–110, at 23/4; H. Lietzmann, *From Constantine to Julian,* trans. B. L. Woolf (London, 1950), 210; Kelly, *Creeds*[3] (1972), 281; L. A. Speller, 'New Light on the Photinians: The Evidence of Ambrosiaster,' *JTS,* N.S. 34 (1983), 88–113, at 101; Brennecke, *Hilarius* (1984), 62. Observe, however, that the article 'Sirmium (formules de)' by E. Amann, *Dictionnaire de théologie catholique* 14 (1941), 2175–2183, locates the council which condemned Photinus in 347 in Milan. Hanson, *Search* (1988), 236, 313, has both a council at Milan in 347 and one in 347/8 in Sirmium, while Simonetti, *Crisi* (1975), 202, registers 'nel 347 un concilio a Milano (e a Sirmio?).'

9. E. Schwartz, *ZNW* 34 (1935), 145 n. 1 = *Gesammelte Schriften* 4 (Berlin, 1960), 22 n. 1, vehemently denied the existence of a lacuna in the text.

10. Chapter X, at nn. 3–10; Chapter XIII, at nn. 1–9.

11. The difficulty was noted but discounted by G. Bardy, *Dictionnaire de théologie catholique* 12 (1934), 1533: 'il est assez difficile à expliquer cette réunion d'Orientaux en une ville qui dépendait alors de Constant et de l'empire d'Occident.' Hanson, *Search* (1988), 313, makes the bizarre statement that 'the Council of Sirmium in 347 or 348 was held in the presence of Constantius, who happened to be passing through the town.'

12. C. J. Hefele and H. Leclercq, *Conciles* 1.2 (1907), 899–902 ('Deuxième grand concile de Sirmium'); Kelly, *Creeds*[3] (1972), 285; Brennecke, *Hilarius* (1984), 312–325. Contrast Simonetti, *Crisi* (1975), 229: 'ben pochi vescovi furono presenti.'

13. Kelly, *Creeds*[3] (1972), 285.

14. A. Hahn and G. L. Hahn, *Bibliothek*[3] (1897), 204 n. 249; C. J. Hefele and H. Leclercq, *Conciles* 1.2 (1907), 908–928; E. Amann, *Dictionnaire de théologie catholique* 14 (1941), 2080/1; Klein, *Constantius* (1977), 89/90; Kopecek, *Neo-Arianism* (1979) 174/5; K. Baus, *History of the Church,* ed. H. Jedin and J. Dolan, trans. A. Biggs 2 (New York, 1980), 46; Brennecke, *Hilarius* (1984), 343–350; Hanson, *Search* (1988), 357–362. Simonetti, *Crisi* (1975), 242, identifies the membership of this alleged council as (1) bishops who were in Sirmium at the time, (2) some eastern bishops, (3) Ursacius, Valens, and Germinius, (4) four African bishops, and (5) Liberius.

15. K. Holl, in annotation on *Epiphanius* 3 (*GCS* 37, 1933), 287.10.

16. Despite L. Duchesne, 'Libère et Fortunatien,' *MEFR* 28 (1908), 31–78, at 64–67; G. Schoo, *Die Quellen des Kirchenhistorikers Sozomenos* (*Neue Studien zur Geschichte der Theologie und der Kirche* 11 [Berlin, 1911]), 125/6.

17. See 'The Capitulation of Liberius and Hilary of Poitiers,' *Phoenix* 46 (1992), 129–140. Long ago Archibald Robertson silently discarded the alleged council of 358, though he still kept a total of four Councils of Sirmium in all, in 347, 351, 357, and 359 respectively (*Select Writings* [1892], lxxxviii–lxxxix).
18. Chapter XIII.

INDEX OF ATHANASIAN TEXTS

INDEX OF COUNCILS OF BISHOPS

INDEX OF MODERN SCHOLARS

This index includes all modern historians, theologians, and scholars (with the exception of the author) whose work is cited or discussed in the text or notes and also, for the convenience of readers, the cooperative volumes *Consuls* (1987), *PLRE* 1, and *PLRE* 2.

GENERAL INDEX